The Unfortunate Duke

Fifth Duke of Newcastle. *Illustrated London News*, 22 December 1860.

The Unfortunate Duke

HENRY PELHAM, FIFTH DUKE OF NEWCASTLE, 1811–1864

F. Darrell Munsell

University of Missouri Press
Columbia, 1985

Copyright © 1985 by
The Curators of the University of Missouri
University of Missouri Press, Columbia, Missouri 65211
Printed and bound in the United States of America

Library of Congress Cataloging in Publication Data

Munsell, F. Darrell.
    The unfortunate Duke.

    Bibliography: p.
    Includes index.
    1. Newcastle, Henry Pelham, Duke of, 1811–1864.
2. Great Britain—Politics and government—1837–1901.
3. Statesmen—Great Britain—Biography. I. Title.
DA565.N53M86   1984   941.081'092'4 [B]
84–20882   ISBN 0–8262–0456–2

To Jane

Acknowledgments

I acknowledge the permission generously given to me by the Duke of Newcastle and the Newcastle Trustees to undertake this biography and to use and quote from the Newcastle papers. I owe special thanks to Mrs. Mary A. Welch, formerly Keeper of the Manuscripts, Alan Cameron, Head of the Department, and to the rest of the staff of the Manuscripts Department, University of Nottingham, where the Newcastle papers are deposited, for their kind assistance, hospitality, and encouragement during my many research visits to Nottingham over the past sixteen years. I am also indebted to Mrs. V. J. Tyler and the other staff members at the Newcastle Estate Office, Warminster, for their kind assistance.

I wish to acknowledge the gracious permission of Her Majesty Queen Elizabeth II to make use of material from the Royal Archives at Windsor. Also, I would like to thank Sir Robin Mackworth-Young, the Librarian, and the other staff members of the Royal Archives for their kind help during my research endeavors at Windsor Castle.

For permission to use and quote from other private manuscript material, I wish to acknowledge my gratitude to Sir William Gladstone and to the Earls of Clarendon, Derby, and Pembroke. I am also grateful to Lord Blake for the right to consult the papers of the fourteenth Earl of Derby in his custody, to the Trevelyan family for their permission to cite and quote from Sir Charles Edward Trevelyan's Letter Book, and to Professor J. Graham Provan for his permission to cite from the Sidney Herbert papers. References to the Henry Goulburn papers appear by permission of Mr. James Hamilton, and those from Lady Frances Waldegrave's letters in the Strachie papers by permission of Lord O'Hagan. I owe thanks to the Trustees of the Broadlands Archives Trust for permission to consult and quote from the Palmerston papers.

For the use of manuscript sources in their care, I am indebted to the Trustees and staffs of the British Library; the Public Record Office, London; the Bodleian Library; the Department of Palaeography and Diplomatic, University of Durham; and the National Register of Archives. To the staff members of the Clwyd, Surrey, and Somerset Record Offices, as well as those of the Wilton Estate Office, the British Library of Political and Economic Science, the British Newspaper Library at Colindale, and the West Texas State University Library, I owe a considerable debt of gratitude.

I am very grateful to Professor Walter L. Arnstein of the University of Illinois for his numerous suggestions for improvement of the manuscript, and I greatly appreciate the information and assistance I received from Professor Colin C. Eldridge of Saint David's University College, Lampeter, Wales, and from Mrs. Virginia Surtees.

Several research and travel grants from Organized Research at West Texas State University and the Shell Companies Foundation made the research and writing of this biography possible. I especially thank Professor James Wood-yard, Coordinator of Research, and the Killgore Executive Committee of West Texas State University for the generous assistance I have received over the past several years.

I am considerably indebted to several other persons. My gratitude is extended to my wife Jane for her encouragement and valuable editorial assistance; to my son Darren for his forbearance; to George and Ann Asquith for their encouragement and support; to Mary Whitten for typing the first manuscript draft; and to Bettie Haimes with special appreciation for typing the final manuscript drafts. I cherish the friendship of Brian and Sally Cleave and of Sam McLaren, and owe a special gratitude for their hospitality during my many sojourns to England.

F.D.M.
Canyon, Texas
October 1984

Contents

Introduction

The fifth duke of Newcastle was one of the bright, capable, and highly motivated political protégés of Sir Robert Peel. He, Sidney Herbert, and William Ewart Gladstone, friends since their Oxford University days, were three of the most distinguished younger Peelites who served Peel in the 1841–1846 ministry. Newcastle's strong sense of public service and capacity for hard work soon earned him recognition, and he was singled out as a possible successor to Peel; but a series of misfortunes, including a tragic marriage, prevented him from fulfilling his political ambitions and left him in shattered health and with a damaged official reputation.

Following Newcastle's death in 1864, Gladstone recorded that no person should ever attempt to write the life of his late "wonderful and valuable friend."[1] He believed that the life of the unfortunate duke was so tragic that it was best forgotten; and as executor and trustee of the estate he removed several boxes of letters and papers from the Newcastle home at Clumber in Nottinghamshire shortly after the death of his life-long friend. Many of those papers pertained to the marital crisis that led to Newcastle's divorce in 1850 (the famous Lincoln divorce case—Newcastle was styled Lord Lincoln until his father's death in early 1851). Perhaps Gladstone wanted to conceal information about his own part in the "painful incident," but more likely his motive was to protect the memory of his late friend and colleague and of Lady Lincoln, whom he had praised and greatly admired many years earlier. Clearly Gladstone did not want these papers and letters to be made public. But in 1968 Sir William Gladstone deposited in St. Deiniol's Library, Hawarden, the materials that his illustrious ancestor had so carefully culled from the Newcastle collection at Clumber in 1864. These papers, along with Lincoln's letters to his father that escaped the executor's match, allow the story of the Lincoln domestic tragedy to be told completely. Probably in no other case has the documentary evidence of marital failure within the Victorian aristocracy been preserved in such detail. The sad tale provides an interesting case study of Victorian morality and attitudes toward sexuality. For this reason alone it is important for the historian to ignore Gladstone's wish to leave the duke's life veiled in obscurity.

Nor did the duke of Newcastle himself want to rest in obscurity. Deeply hurt by the bitter attacks and charges of incapacity that were leveled against

1

him during the Crimean War crisis, and convinced that Alexander W. King-lake's history of the war would be partial and unjust, the duke began in 1856 to arrange carefully every "scrap of paper throwing light upon the momentous events of those months for the use of some future historian."[2] He longed for vindication and believed that the materials were there to prove that he was a victim of military incompetence in the Crimea, of malicious attacks by the press, and of Lord John Russell's political machination. But that vindication did not come in his lifetime, and his bitterness worsened his health and hastened his death.

Newcastle's official reputation and career suffered tremendously from the Crimean War incident. Some of the leading contemporaries were extremely critical in their assessments of him. According to the duke of Argyll, a fellow Peelite and ministerial colleague, "Newcastle was an industrious and conscientious worker, but he had no brilliancy and little initiative."[3] Frederic, Lord Blachford, long-time under-secretary of state for the colonies, described the duke as "an honest and honourable man" who in political administration was "painstaking, clear-headed and just," but whose abilities were far too insufficient "for the management of great affairs—which, however, he was always ambitious of handling." Newcastle also was too standoffish and overcritical of others; and although he respected other people's positions, he was always sensible of his own. "It was said of him," Blachford continues, "that he did not remember his rank unless you forgot it," an expression that described well the duke's relations to subordinates.[4] Chichester Fortescue, Lord Carlingford, another of the duke's subordinate colleagues at the Colonial Office, also believed that Newcastle had overestimated his own abilities. Fortescue obviously was not free from bias. His intimacy with the Russells and his jealousy of the great friendship between the duke and Lady Waldegrave, whom he would marry, prevented him from being completely fair in his attitude toward Newcastle. Goldwin Smith's estimate of the duke's abilities and personality was probably influenced by his great differences of opinion with Newcastle over colonial matters. Arthur Gordon, Lord Stanmore, was subject to filial piety and close personal friendships. Thus in Stanmore's biographies Newcastle's reputation was tarnished somewhat in order to enhance the brilliancy of Lord Aberdeen (Stanmore's father), Sidney Herbert, and William Gladstone, the latter of whom would remain Stanmore's close personal friend long after the duke's death.

Despite these judgments, Newcastle was highly regarded by some of the most prominent of the Victorians; and had it not been for the ill fate of the first Crimean winter, he rather than Palmerston might have succeeded Lord Aberdeen as prime minister. The prince consort, a close friend, seriously considered the duke as a possible governmental leader of the liberal coalition of Whigs and Peelites. In the early 1850s Gladstone and Lord Aberdeen likewise believed that the duke would someday head a government. Gladstone always respected Newcastle and sought his opinions on political and religious matters. Only toward the end of the duke's life did Gladstone see a decline in the abilities that he believed had distinguished the duke more as a statesman than as an administrator.[5] Lord Palmerston regarded Newcastle as an excellent colonial secretary; and in 1864, when failing health forced the duke to retire, Palmerston waited as long as he could before accepting his letter of resignation. A few prominent individuals outside the Court and Parliament also supported and fed the duke's ambitions.

Although his contemporaries did not agree on his abilities and talents, there is no doubt that Newcastle was an extremely important political figure during the period of the 1840s through the early 1860s. A full-length study of his life and official career, therefore, is essential to the understanding of the period. Yet Newcastle has not received the attention from historians he deserves. John Martineau's 1908 biography is incomplete and quite unsatisfactory, as well as out of date.[6] Martineau does not discuss the duke's tragic private life, and his treatment of the duke's administration of the War Office in 1854 and early 1855 is influenced too much by Kinglake's *The Invasion of the Crimea*.[7] Thus Martineau serves as an apologist for Lord Raglan, the commander of the British forces in the Crimea, at Newcastle's expense. Martineau's work also is inadequate on the duke's Colonial Office career. Fortunately, with the discovery of new family letters and with the use of official War and Colonial Office papers, it is now possible to write a comprehensive biography of the fifth duke of Newcastle that puts both his failures and accomplishments into historical perspective.

1. Early Years

The Clintons were a proud family who first came into prominence during the reign of Henry I. Geoffrey de Clinton, chamberlain and treasurer, was one of the men of "ignoble stock" whom Henry I "lifted up from the dust and exalted above earls and burghers."[1] The male line descended from Geoffrey's nephew Osbert, with the barony being created in 1299 when Edward I summoned John de Clinton to Parliament as first Lord de Clinton of Maxtock in Warwickshire.

For centuries the Lords Clinton participated in the affairs of state and the military and naval glories of England. In the sixteenth century Edward, ninth Lord Clinton, lord high admiral, privy councillor, and knight of the Garter, achieved eminence as a naval officer and statesman under four Tudor monarchs. In 1572 Elizabeth advanced him in the peerage as the earl of Lincoln in recognition of his valuable services during the critical period of the Northern Rebellion. In the next century Theophilus, fourth earl of Lincoln, after being imprisoned in the Tower of London in 1626 for refusing to subscribe to the forced loan, nevertheless staunchly supported the crown during the Civil War. In 1692, with the death of the fifth earl of Lincoln, the barony of Clinton fell into abeyance and the earldom passed to Sir Francis Fiennes Clinton of Stourton, a second cousin. His successor, Henry, seventh earl of Lincoln, was a lord of the bedchamber of King George I. As an important Whig politician, he filled successively the offices of paymaster-general, constable of the Tower, and cofferer of the household. In 1717 he married Lucy Pelham, the sister of the soon-to-be eminent Pelham brothers, Henry Pelham and Thomas Pelham-Holles, the duke of Newcastle. Lincoln's two sons, George and Henry, subsequently became the eighth and ninth earls of Lincoln. In 1744 the latter married his cousin Catherine, the eldest daughter of Henry Pelham and favorite niece of the duke of Newcastle.

Through this marriage the ducal title of Newcastle-under-Lyme was eventually entailed upon the Clinton family. By special patent of November 1756, Thomas Pelham-Holles, duke of Newcastle-on-Tyne, was created duke of Newcastle-under-Lyme, with remainder to the earl of Lincoln, his nephew both by blood and marriage. Lincoln's relationship to the powerful and influential Pelhams, which name by royal license he would prefix to that of Clinton, secured for him considerable advancement and wealth. His marriage to Catherine Pelham also garnered him a comfortable annuity provided from portions of the Newcastle estate lying in Nottinghamshire, Yorkshire, and Middlesex.

Over the years, however, the relations between uncle and nephew became increasingly strained. Newcastle harbored several grievances against the "insolent hypochondriac" from whom he received no help; and Lincoln, who preferred to lead an easy life and to mind his own diseases, grew "equally sick of Newcastle's cordiality, jealousy, claims and promptings, and altogether bored with his uncle, for whom he had neither love nor loyalty."[2] Finally, on 17 November 1768, Lincoln succeeded his uncle as second duke of Newcastle-under-Lyme. Though he had great electoral influence, which every section of the Whig party eagerly sought to utilize, the duke kept himself free from political activities and devoted the rest of his life to the pleasures of country and sport. In 1770 he moved the family seat to Clumber House, which the architect Stephen Wright built in the Palladian style in Clumber Park, Nottinghamshire. During the next few years, the duke spent lavishly to transform the park from a boggy waste to a beautiful estate of nearly four thousand acres. At the same time, by crossing the Alpine spaniel with the basset hound, he developed the famous Clumber spaniel, a new breed of sporting spaniels that would long be associated with the dukes of Newcastle and with Clumber Park.

In February 1794 Thomas Pelham-Clinton succeeded his father as third duke of Newcastle, but lived for only another fifteen months. His ten-year-old son, Henry Pelham-Clinton, became the fourth duke of Newcastle and was sent to Eton, where he later claimed that he learned everything that he should not have known. He was in France with his mother when war broke out in 1803 and was detained for nearly four years at Tours. It was a bitter experience for the young man, and in later years he lamented that his "ripening years" were "passed in languishing banishment" away from his country and from wise counselors.[3] Consequently, when he came of age he felt totally unprepared to undertake the great responsibilities of his position in society. Nevertheless, his strong sense of duty prevented him from attempting to escape those responsibilities.

Shortly after his return to England, the duke married a great heiress, Georgiana Elizabeth, the daughter of Edward Miller Mundy of Shipley, Derbyshire. Since Newcastle's own Nottinghamshire estate had been heavily burdened by the extravagances of the first two dukes, Georgiana Elizabeth's landed estate worth £12,000 a year and her fortune of £190,000 were of considerable importance to Newcastle. Greater financial security gave the duke an opportunity to pursue his political interests.

With his vast electoral influence, the fourth duke of Newcastle became one of the most notorious boroughmongers of the early nineteenth century. He did not use his influence, though, to build patronage or increase his income, but instead used it either to maintain the prestige of his family and rank or to support political principles in which he profoundly believed.[4] Being a visionary, he was only sporadically involved in the practical affairs of politics, becoming active only during times of crisis when he apprehended that his cherished principles were endangered. Therefore, he infrequently attended Parliament. But it was for that purpose that he and his family had taken up residence in the spring of 1811 at 39 Charles Street, Berkeley Square, London. In this plain eighteenth-century house on 22 May the duchess gave birth to her third child, the first son. Thus began the life of Henry Pelham Finnes Pelham-Clinton, twelfth earl of Lincoln, the future fifth duke of Newcastle.

II

Lord Lincoln's early years were spent in the shadow of his father's imposing personality. The fourth duke of Newcastle was a proud, fanatical, humorless, and bigoted aristocrat whose political and religious beliefs were inseparable. The British Constitution, he firmly believed, was constructed on the twin pillars of church and state; it was perfection itself. The Church of England held a position of trust with God. As a peer of the realm, he believed that he was one of God's chosen "instruments" to preserve the principles of the church and state as expressed in the British Constitution. In 1837 he wrote, "I assume that England is a favoured land, that her people are Providential Instruments, and that they are Providentially regarded."[5] Those views constituted his political faith; and much of what he did politically and socially was done in the spirit of fulfilling his duty, as he perceived it, to church and state in accordance with those views.

Yet he was always uncertain as to how he should fulfill that duty. He was aware of his own defective knowledge of men and politics and of his inability to speak well in Parliament or to assume a more active leadership role in the country. These weaknesses he constantly bemoaned; though he diligently worked to improve himself by study, he could never overcome them. "How willingly would I make any sacrifice which could benefit . . . my Country," he wrote in his diary in 1823. "Alas! I possess no means of doing so—but the time *may* yet come and if it only pleases God to keep me unspotted from the world, in times of difficulty or danger I may, by the mere influence of character, hope to be of some use."[6] Its pages filled with expressions of hope intermixed with those of despair, the duke's diary records his agonizing wait for God's call to service.

That diary, begun in 1822 shortly before his wife's death and kept almost daily until shortly before his own death in 1851, also served as a confessional. In it the duke recorded his innermost thoughts and emotions on both public and private events. Overwhelmingly, the tone is one of despair, isolation, and anxiety. It is a melancholy, almost pathetic story of a lonely, stricken widower struggling to raise his ten children and to save his country from atheistic revolution.

The first few pages of the diary record the death of his eldest child, Anna Maria, in May 1822, followed four months later by that of his wife in childbirth of stillborn twins. Those deaths devastated Newcastle. Only his devotion to his surviving children eased his loneliness and despondency. He turned with relief from his failures and forebodings of evil in public life to the domestic responsibilities of rearing his children.

The duke never doubted his competency to educate his children and to instill in them the virtues and religious principles that he believed would make them "bright examples" to their contemporaries. Nor did he ever question the methods he used. He asked no advice and deeply resented his mother's "meddling ways," which threatened to unsettle his mode of education for the children. Under his strict supervision, governesses and tutors kept the children isolated from the outside world and made sure that they got plenty of fresh air and exercise and ate only a few plain foods. The duke himself nursed his children when they were sick and wielded the rod occasionally "to conquer an obstinate and undutiful child." The Newcastle homes at Clumber in Nottinghamshire and Portman Square in London were kept secluded from the public and closed to all but the most familiar visitors. The duke only on rare occasions introduced the eldest children to the theater, opera, or some other public function or presented them at court. Otherwise, until one by one the boys left for Eton and afterward either for Oxford, the army, or the navy, there was no opportunity for the children to escape the Spartan system of discipline imposed upon them. The girls were less fortunate. Unable to escape, they remained at home with their ponderous, oppressive father.[7]

The duke had an unbounded pride and trust in his children. "Ten such children—and I thank God for it—I verily believe are not to be found together in one family in the whole world," he wrote in 1838, when most of them were grown.[8] He wanted his children to be ornaments in a country that he hoped would be as glorious in virtue as it was in arms, arts, science, and all worldly achievements. His family was his treasure, but he was crushed when one by one his six sons failed to match his aspirations and expectations. He had loved his children and had devoted his life to them; but this uncompromising man, stately in presence and of unassailable rectitude, had little understanding either of private or public matters.

III

Lord Lincoln, as the eldest son in the family, was the logical recipient of much of his father's ambitious devotion. In the spring of 1824, when Lincoln was nearly thirteen, Newcastle took a house at Chiswick for a few months to escape the memories associated with his wife at Clumber and Portman Square. At this time he attended Parliament regularly and occasionally took his son with him. The duke described the first of these visits in his diary:

> A Debate in the H. of Lords on the Alien Act—I took Lincoln down with me to see and hear what was done there to give him an early notion of such things. He appeared very attentive of what was going on and liked it very much. I afterwards took him to the House of Commons where there was not much going on whilst we were there, but Lincoln saw the nature of the business and how it is conducted. Some [one] of these days, if it should please God that he may live, he will I am sure make a distinguished figure, perhaps in both houses.[9]

On their way to and from Parliament and other appointments, father and son enjoyed their rides together on horseback through the streets and parks of London and Westminster. The duke also took Lincoln and the eldest children on visits to the British Museum, the Tower of London, the zoo, and the botanical garden at Kew. There was even time that spring at Chiswick for cricket, with three of the boys and their tutor playing against the duke and Lincoln on most Sunday afternoons.

The spring had been a delightful one for the duke and his children, but for Lincoln the time had come for formal schooling away from home. On 15 June, Lincoln left his tearful brothers and sisters at Chiswick to travel with his father to Eton. The duke, who remembered his own bad experiences at the school, was apprehensive about Lincoln, but by the end of the first day, Newcastle was satisfied that his son was content in his new environment. But Lincoln's disposition changed overnight, and the next morning the duke left a nervous, dispirited young boy "busily employed in his trials for Dr. Keate's [the Eton headmaster's] inspection" that would decide where he would be placed.[10]

At the end of July, Lincoln returned to Clumber for the summer holidays. Although the boy's health was not good, the duke was delighted to find that his son had returned none the worse in moral character. Some of the credit was given to a family friend and Lincoln's tutor at Eton, Jonathan Thompson, whom the duke described as "a most estimable and invaluable man" and a perfect tutor.[11] The duke expressed deep regret when it came time for Lincoln to return to Eton in mid-September. "It is impossible to know him and not to love, admire and value him," he confided to his diary.[12]

Although he had few friends at Eton during the autumn of 1824, Lincoln did well. Thompson praised his abilities and purity of mind, and Dr. Keate formed a high opinion of him. To the delight of his father, Lincoln in October was honored for a copy of twenty-six Latin verses. Equally to the delight of the duke, Lincoln fought another boy for nearly forty-five minutes until the two were separated by friends. "In a few months," Newcastle remarked upon hearing of the incident, Lincoln "has distinguished himself for ability, remarkable good conduct, and now for unshaken courage, thus showing that he possesses no good quality in an inferior degree."[13]

Three weeks later the effects of the battle were still visible on Lincoln's face when he returned to Clumber for the Christmas holidays. Otherwise, the duke found his son little changed. The family enjoyed a customary holiday. They began the new year by exchanging presents and good wishes, and after dining early, they walked around the estate and concluded the day "as one happy party." The girls, however, were disappointed that the poor people were prevented by an epidemic of smallpox in the surrounding villages from coming to Clumber for the usual distribution of clothing and food.[14]

Lincoln's health was not very good when he returned to Eton in January 1825. He suffered for weeks from a severe cold and bad cough; repeated bleedings, blisters, and doses of calomel failed to end the illness. Late in February, Newcastle took his son away from Eton for awhile to recover. Later in the spring an outbreak of scarlet fever at the school prompted the duke to bring his son home once again. Not until after the summer holidays was Lincoln able to resume his studies in any serious fashion. Nonetheless, he did well, and by the end of the year he had gained six places and was promoted to the fifth form.[15]

Lincoln continued to prosper in his work at Eton during the next two years, although the duke was probably carried away by praise when he noted that his son was regarded as "the most promising and for his standing the cleverest boy in the school."[16] During the summer holiday of 1828, Lincoln and his brothers from Eton joined the rest of the family at Ramsgate, where his father was recuperating from a brief illness. For over a month, the family enjoyed the fine weather and the pleasures of the resort. The duke (in a machine) and the boys bathed in the sea almost daily, and soon Newcastle felt well enough to join his sons in a shooting party. Lincoln delighted in the adventure, which was repeated several times during the next few days. But when it came time for the boys to return to Eton, the duke decided that Lincoln, now nearly seventeen and a half and "so manly in appearance," should not return with them. The duke agreed with Thompson that Lincoln was losing time at school merely learning what he already knew well.[17] Although greatly disappointed, Lincoln accepted the decision and wrote his farewell to the headmaster:

It is with regret that I am obliged to take leave of you and the moreso as circumstances prevent my doing so in person. I did not expect to have had to perform that painful task till Christmas. I beg most sincerely to thank you for the care and kindness you have shewn me during the time I have

been under your charge, and hope that I may always retain and profit by
the good impressions I may have imbibed at Eton. I trust that, although I
have occasionally given you offence and caused you unnecessary trouble,
my conduct has generally been such as to give you satisfaction.[18]

Although Lincoln left Eton without being especially distinguished, perhaps
owing partly to the unusually early age of his departure, he had shown quiet
determination, industry, and aptitude for learning. He had gained confidence
in himself, while the influence of the home was little weakened. The duke had
made certain of that by making frequent trips to Eton when he was in London
and by staying in close touch with the school authorities, with whom he had
very good rapport.[19] He was determined to maintain those domestic ties as
long as he could, and when Lincoln announced his intention to enter Christ
Church College, Oxford University, the duke was not disposed to allow it.
He was not convinced of the value of a university education, and he was
reluctant to risk Lincoln's morals amidst all the vice at Oxford. In the end,
however, he agreed that his son's attendance at Oxford was "a necessary evil,"
and on 10 May 1830 he left Lincoln at Christ Church, convinced that his son
had "too much innate goodness and that the principles of religion, virtue, and
nobleness of nature were too firmly implanted in him to suffer him ever to
deviate from the path of honor and rectitude."[20] After parting from Lincoln,
the duke returned to London to see what he could do to restore unity within
the "Country party."

IV

Newcastle's political interests had grown in intensity during the years Lincoln was at school, and his son's future political involvement seemed certain.
Before 1826, the duke took little interest in political matters. Most of his
political activity had centered on the exercise of his electoral influence for
family reasons in the Yorkshire boroughs of Aldborough and Boroughbridge
and in Nottinghamshire, where he had considerable influence in Newark and
East Retford as well as in the southern division of the county. But with his
growing concern over the Roman Catholic question, the Corn Laws, and
various reform measures, the duke became more actively involved in politics
and more interested in political matters; and shortly after Lord Liverpool's
stroke in February 1827, Lords Falmouth and Mansfield and a few other
friends from among the ultra-Tories prevailed upon him to organize a party
of the "King's Friends" in opposition to Catholic emancipation and parliamentary reform. Only the belief that God had "insensibly called him forth"
induced him to undertake the task.[21]

Newcastle's endeavors as a party leader over the next few years failed mis-
erably. He became despondent following the passage of the Catholic Eman-

Fourth Duke of Newcastle. *Illustrated London News*, 18 January 1851.

cipation Act in 1829, but vowed to continue to use his influence against the reformers to stem the tide of revolution. He remained uncompromisingly opposed to parliamentary reform, a position that brought about his complete political isolation during the early 1830s. In 1831, with the country in an uproar over reform, the duke feared that his own life was endangered. Indeed, in April, after the defeat of Lord Grey's government in committee on the reform bill, an angry mob in the West End of London smashed windows of peers, including the duke's, that were not illuminated in celebration of the dissolution of Parliament; and on 10 October the duke was assaulted in Parliament Street and his windows broken again after the Lords had rejected the bill.[22]

The outcry in the country was far more violent, culminating in riots and disturbances in Bristol, Derby, and Nottingham. Late in the afternoon of 10 October a large crowd of rioters in the latter city stormed Newcastle's seventeenth-century house, which had replaced the old medieval castle, and set fire to it after wrecking the interior. A detachment of hussars arrived too late to stop the fire, and throughout the night the flames consumed the cedarwood paneling and the furniture, leaving a charred shell of exterior stone walls. The following day large crowds of rioters destroyed a silk mill in nearby Beeston and attacked Wollaton Hall and several other residences in the outlying area. The appearance of a reinforced yeomanry prevented further damage.

The violent riots and disturbances in many parts of the country raised the specter of class war, and many landowners took measures to arm and garrison their country houses. Within a few miles of Nottingham, Clumber, Newcastle's seat, was particularly vulnerable to attack. The duke set off for Clumber as soon as he received news of the Nottingham riots. Lincoln was already there, having come from Oxford, and had moved the girls and younger children to the house of William Mansell, the keeper, and had made arrangements for the defense of Clumber. Upon his arrival, the duke was amazed to see the house transformed into a virtual fortress: cannons were positioned in all the windows, and the house was guarded within by two hundred armed men and without by a troop of mounted yeomanry. Although he believed that Lincoln's preparations were too extensive, he was pleased to learn that his son's "ability to perform, his forethought, his kindness of manner, and the pleasant way in which he has given orders and seen to everything" had commanded universal admiration.[23]

The danger passed without incident. The Nottingham rioters dispersed to their homes, and the city and the surrounding countryside were again quiet. On 19 October, Lincoln returned to Oxford, where he continued to keep a close watch on events in Nottinghamshire. "I am extremely sorry to hear such continued bad-news from Notts.," he wrote to his father on 14 November. The riots, he admitted, were making him quite "bloody-minded." "If any thing serious happens," he continued, "I shall trust to your sending for me to be your aid-de-camp. I have sent to Purdey for a brace of pistols in case I should have to go thro' Nottm. when any thing is going on there."[24]

Meanwhile the prisoners captured by the yeomanry during the Nottingham riots were tried by special commission for setting the castle and the Beeston mill on fire. Those found guilty were either sentenced to death or to transportation. In January 1832 some relatives of the condemned men asked Newcastle to sign a petition to the king praying for mercy. The duke refused, even though he thought the real culprits in the whole matter were the ministers rather than the men sentenced to death.[25] In August the duke was awarded £21,000 damages for the castle, but he was not satisfied. The reparation, he complained to Lincoln, would "no more restore the Castle than it would restore the Constitution."[26]

To the duke, the Reform Act of 1832 was the final blow against the British Constitution. He was one of only twenty-two peers who voted against the third reading of the bill. He blamed the duke of Wellington for the failure of the Tory opposition, and throughout the rest of the 1830s he was almost completely isolated from his former political associates. He was a man without a party and without much of his former electoral influence.[27] "I have been robbed of my boroughs, abused, ill treated, and pillaged," he wrote in his diary. Yet his opposition to the Reform Act had brought him national attention, and he sensed a change in public opinion toward him in the country that made his political position far stronger and more certain than it had been before the passage of the Reform Act. "If I balance the whole, I think [I] may own that the advantage is in my favor and that I have not for years occupied so sure a position."[28] He had less electoral influence but a stronger political base from which to operate. He had little standing in Parliament, but he believed he had a growing extraparliamentary power that would enable him to help restore constitutional purity and political virtue in the nation. Thus, encouraged in 1832 by several influential people to support parliamentary candidates for Newark and South Nottinghamshire, where he still retained considerable influence, Newcastle turned to his son Lincoln and to William Ewart Gladstone for help in his effort to enhance his political posture in the country.

V

Lincoln and Gladstone were already close friends. Although Gladstone was Lincoln's senior by eighteen months, they had been together at Eton and then at Christ Church, Oxford, where their friendship ripened into the intimacy that was to last to the end of Lincoln's life. Among Lincoln's other friends at Oxford were Charles Canning, Henry Manning, Lord de Tabley, Sidney Herbert, H. G. Liddell, Roundell Palmer, and Edward Cardwell. Lincoln would have lasting friendships with all these distinguished leaders of Victorian society, but with none was he so closely tied in friendship as with Gladstone. Both Lincoln and Gladstone belonged to the Union Debating Society, where Lincoln spoke frequently and where Gladstone made a brilliant speech against the reform bill in May 1831 that brought him considerable notice even outside the university. Each served as president of the society, and both were charter members of the Essay Club, later called the WEG Club after the initials of

Gladstone, the club's founder. Together the two young men—Gladstone, too intellectual, academic, and detached, and Lincoln, sensible but rather priggish and solemn—were influenced by the broadening experience of a great university. Together they also came under the Tractarian influences just then coming to fruition under the teaching of John Henry Newman, John Keble, and Edward Bouverie Pusey. Oxford, therefore, laid the foundations of High Church beliefs in both Gladstone and Lincoln and widened the experiences of both. Only later would the duke of Newcastle discover the extent to which Lincoln's Oxford experience had severed the paternal ties with which he had so carefully and tightly bound his son.

While Gladstone's path to politics was filled with theological pitfalls, Lincoln's was straight, short, and free from obstacles. It was only a matter of time before Lincoln entered the political arena as a candidate for one of his father's parliamentary constituencies. For Lincoln, who was busily engaged in his academic work for an honors degree, the time had not yet arrived when in June 1832 his father sought a candidate for the borough of Newark. Therefore, Lincoln suggested his friend Gladstone for the nomination. "I have now known him for several years," he wrote his father,

> and feel convinced that his honest unflinching integrity of character combined with talents far above the common stamp even of those who are called clever men will be at once an ornament to, I fear, a most unornamental House, and an honor to the patron who shall introduce him to public life. . . . I believe him to be most perfectly orthodox, and in short think that when you stated in your letter of yesterday what he should be you only drew a picture of what he *is*.[29]

Lincoln wrote to Gladstone a few days later with his father's commission to invite him to come forward as the duke's candidate for Newark at the next election.

Gladstone was traveling on the Continent when he received Lincoln's letter. He had gone there to complete his education by a grand tour after taking his bachelor's degree with the honor of a double-first in classics and mathematics and to resolve his future career between church and state. He had probably abandoned the thought of taking holy orders when he received Lincoln's "stunning and overpowering proposal," which left him "the whole of the evening . . . in a flutter of confusion." Considerable introspection raised serious doubts in his mind, but ultimately he accepted the duke's "flattering proffer" after receiving assurance from his father and brother that Newcastle was not in the habit of asking for pledges or inquiring minutely into the views and opinions of his candidates.[30]

Lincoln, of course, was delighted with Gladstone's decision. From Cuddesdon, he wrote:

I cannot say how glad I am that your highly honourable objections have been overruled, and that you are now the declared candidate for Newark. I trust that you will be successful, and I must say that I have little doubt of it, though which Member you will turn out seems to be doubtful.

I have a request to make to you, which will no doubt make you laugh— it is that you will send me your first *frank*, if it is not already bespoken by some of your own family; it is for the collection of a friend who will prize it much if, as I have no doubt, your Parliamentary career is as satisfactory to your friends and creditable to yourself as your Academic has been.[31]

The friend of whom Lincoln wrote was Lady Susan Harriet Catherine Douglas-Hamilton, only daughter of the tenth duke and duchess of Hamilton and Brandon, who was increasingly in Lincoln's thoughts. Indeed, Lady Susan had already accepted Lincoln's marriage proposal by proxy.[32]

The courtship between Lincoln and Lady Susan had been planned by correspondence late the previous year. On 21 November 1831, the duke of Newcastle had written to the duke of Hamilton to propose a marriage between Lady Georgiana, Newcastle's eldest daughter, and Lord Douglas, the duke of Hamilton's only son. The marquess of Douglas and Clydesdale was one of Lincoln's friends from Eton and Oxford. The two young men had little in common except a fondness for shooting, and occasionally Lincoln had accepted invitations to shoot on the Hamilton preserves in Scotland. Therefore, he was known to the Hamilton family; and by a strange coincidence, Hamilton noted in reply to Newcastle, when the letter from Clumber arrived he had almost resolved to address the duke in a similar strain, but to propose instead a marriage arrangement between his daughter Lady Susan and Lord Lincoln.[33]

Newcastle was elated by the letter from Hamilton Palace. Of the two Hamilton children, the duke concluded that for his own family situation Lady Susan was by far the best catch. Therefore, he immediately responded favorably to Hamilton's counterproposal. At the first opportunity, he informed Hamilton, he would instruct Lincoln to turn his attention to Lady Susan to see whether she met his view of what he wanted in a wife.[34]

The duke of Hamilton counseled moderation, stressing the need for an independent choice for the participants in the proposed courtship. "I entirely concur in all your Grace's opinions," the duke of Newcastle answered. "I have seen so much misery resulting from forced marriages & so much mischief done by officious interference on the part of the Parents, that I would not for any consideration place myself in that situation." But he added, "It is however perfectly legitimate to lead without appearing to do so, & to manage the matter in such a measure as to let it seem to be one of individual choice."[35]

Within a short time, Newcastle had additional reason to press the matter forward. During the Christmas vacation, the duke queried his son, and the result, as he had anticipated, was most satisfactory. "He has the strongest inclination towards Lady Susan & would be most happy to cultivate the acquaintance, which I learn from him is already formed between them," Newcastle hurriedly penned to Hamilton Palace. Lincoln, he added, was captivated by Susan's "perfect, gay & cheerful" manner and was pleased that she engaged in "that sort of conversation which is agreeable to his notions." He was most eager to rest his "hopes of comfort & happiness upon an alliance with Lady Susan." "The consummation of our wishes," the duke concluded, "therefore rests with the Lady, if she does not object on a farther acquaintance, 'c' est une affaire finie.'"[36]

Lady Susan did not object to a cultivation of the acquaintance, and the courtship began in the spring of 1832. Lincoln stole what time he could from his studies at Oxford to see Susan and her parents. Newcastle kept an anxious eye on the developments, frequently pressing his son to reach a marriage agreement with Susan. On 20 June, after one of these attempts, Lincoln admonished his father that these were matters of "delicacy" that "should begin with the parties themselves on both sides" and in which there should be "no parti-making . . . if there is to be happiness."[37]

Lincoln was determined to take a first-class degree before he married, and in July he went to Cuddesdon to prepare for his examinations. But certain that the attachment between himself and Susan was mutual, he wrote on the morning of his arrival at Cuddesdon to authorize his father to speak to the duchess on his behalf. "Say any thing," he wrote, "for whatever you say will fall short of my thoughts and my affection."[38] The duke immediately called on the duchess and Susan at the Hamilton residence in Portman Square. To his great delight, he found Susan fully prepared to give her consent and whole heart to Lincoln. It was settled that they would be married as soon as Lincoln took his degree.

The duke of Newcastle was ecstatic. He lavished praise on Susan: "She is not a common person, & possesses a mind & devotion capable of any thing— full of talent, spirit, & energy, but yet tempered by the most winning feminine graces—beautiful in face & figure, without affectation, the picture of good humour & happiness." The duke also noted that the duchess was a most extraordinary and superior person: "The handsomest & most perfect woman in appearance that I ever saw, with a dignity & pervading grace & elegance which must be seen to be understood." Her singing and execution of music, the duke believed, was superior to that of a professional. Her conversation came from a "soul & elevation of mind that excites reflection." She was a devoted mother and her devotion was repaid by "unbounden affection—it is an edifying sight to see her & the watchful attention of the other, waiting as it were upon every turn of her mother's countenance."[39]

It is surprising that Newcastle, a rigid, intolerant man, an ultra-Tory, had been captivated by the Hamiltons. Their way of life and most of their views were antithetical to his own. But the Hamiltons were fascinating, and the duke had not perceived, as many others had, the streak of insincerity in their characters or the exaggeration in their manners. The duke of Hamilton was a Whig, an avowed Bonapartist, a rake, although highly cultivated and consummate in his taste. He was worldly and intensely proud of his ancient lineage. The duchess, nearly twenty years younger than her husband, was the daughter of William Beckford of Fonthill Abbey, the author of *Vathek*, an eccentric dilettante noted for his extravagance and dissipated, perverse life. Her girlhood and her marriage had taught the duchess to be exceedingly indulgent and somewhat dissimulating.[40]

It was in this extremely free atmosphere of the Hamilton family circle that Susan grew up. She inherited much of her mother's charm and beauty, but it was her lovable and vivacious nature as much as her beauty that made her so attractive. To Gladstone, with his keen eye for beauty in women, she was "a creature of ethereal grace, and of a thousand gifts, . . . so bright, so gentle, so refined, bearing so few outward marks of the curse that is the race of Adam."[41] However, there was another side of Susan of which Gladstone was not yet aware. Spoiled from infancy by lovingly indulgent parents who had constantly praised her, Susan developed an unbounded need for adulation. Beneath the veneer of social elegance and refinement, the outward signs of her extensive formal education and trips abroad, there were within her volatile affections and emotions. She was lovely, prepossessing, and vivacious, as her grandfather observed, but perhaps her greatest inheritance from William Beckford was her total sense of irresponsibility.[42]

Late in August the Hamiltons accepted Newcastle's invitation to come to Clumber to discuss details of the marriage settlement. At the insistence of the duchess and Susan, Lincoln interrupted his studies at Cuddesdon to join them. But only the most preliminary terms for the financial settlement of the marriage were discussed, for Newcastle, with his own estates heavily encumbered by debts, was unable to determine the exact sum for Lincoln's allowance. The two dukes agreed to set final terms after they had a chance to consult their agents.

At the moment there was another matter of almost equal importance on Newcastle's mind. Earlier in the month several of the duke's friends had urged him to bring Lincoln forward as a candidate for South Nottinghamshire during the next general election. At first the duke was not particularly interested in the invitation, for he believed that it might be a maneuver to bribe him away from Retford. Nevertheless, he mentioned the proposal to Lincoln, and they discussed the matter at length when Lincoln was at Clumber for the Hamiltons' visit. The decision was a difficult one to reach. Still not wanting to give up his studies for an honors degree and fearful that a parliamentary career at that time would mean an early and prolonged separation from his intended wife, Lincoln was at first reluctant to pursue the matter. On 2 September, however, after weighing the considerations fully, Lincoln agreed to come forward as a candidate. "I fought shy of starting for a long time," he wrote Gladstone, "for it so happens that a Parliamentary life is far from what is suitable to my inclinations at the present time; but I was so importuned and entreated by a great many both of the gentry and the yeomanry that I was obliged to make the personal sacrifice and come forward."[43] Newcastle himself could not say that he was pleased with the idea, "but," he wrote in his diary, "I believe that we have done politically well by aiding the well disposed."[44]

Shortly after the Clumber party had dispersed, with Susan and the duchess going to Leamington Spa where the latter could partake of the waters, Lincoln made a canvass of South Nottinghamshire, where he met with unexpected success. "I went to the markets at Newark, Bingham, and Southwell last week and addressed the electors at each place," he noted to Gladstone. "They received me with marked demonstrations of kindness everywhere; indeed my friends consider my success as certain."[45] On 11 September he returned to Cuddesdon to resume his studies, but with all hope of gaining honors at an end. Unable to be at once a candidate for the honors both of the "Schools and of the Senate," he was now prepared to content himself with an ordinary degree.

The duke of Hamilton took a keen interest in the progress of Lincoln's canvass. "*Vile Whig as I am*," he exclaimed to Newcastle, "you must be sure I feel an anxious interest, where your interests are concerned." He wrote again later to rejoice in Lincoln's success. "I hear Lincoln distinguished himself every way upon this occasion," he wrote, "and I congratulate myself, as well as you, for I feel a party concerned, and believe me not an indifferent one."[46]

But Hamilton's main reason for writing these letters was to hurry Newcastle on to a financial settlement for the marriage. Newcastle seemed most unwilling to engage in any negotiations that would reveal the sad plight of his finances. Nevertheless, with considerable tact and kindness, and only a touch of sarcasm, Hamilton continued to raise these matters with him; and finally Newcastle agreed to terms on the subjects of pin money for Susan, jointure, and provision for younger children. The marriage settlement was reached in time to set the wedding for late November in Scotland.

VI

The autumn of 1832 was a hectic time for Lincoln. Between reading for his degree and canvassing South Nottinghamshire, he was kept in a constant state of agitation. There was barely time to finish both before the wedding. After completing his canvass on 16 October, he returned immediately to Oxford to finish his work for an ordinary degree, which he took on 9 November. It was a great mortification to the duke of Newcastle to have his son forgo the attempt for an honors degree, for he believed that Lincoln, with his "purity of mind & soundness of principle, great ability and extraordinary judgement," was destined for great things.[47] Lincoln had proved himself to be a tireless and conscientious worker, and, though he lacked the brilliance of some of his contemporaries at Oxford, there is no doubt that he would have come out fairly well in the class list had he attempted an honors degree.

Lincoln and Newcastle traveled separately to Scotland for the wedding, with Lincoln arriving at Hamilton Palace on 24 November and the duke on the following day. Newcastle found everything about the house on the grandest scale and in the most perfect taste. After a day's delay caused by the news of Lord Douglas's illness from smallpox at Oxford, the marriage between Lincoln and Lady Susan took place on 27 November. The ceremony was celebrated first according to the forms of the Established Church and then by a clergyman of the Scots Church. The broose, an ancient marriage custom, was enacted as the young couple left for their honeymoon at Lord Belhaven's house in nearby Wishaw. That evening the duke of Hamilton gave dinners to all of his tenants in the stables and outhouses, the arrangements for which, according to Newcastle, were excellent and the supply most bountiful. The gentlemen and superior tenants, nearly two thousand in all, were treated to a dinner in town. "Nothing was wanting to do honor to the occasion or credit to the exalted owners of this magnificent place," Newcastle noted enviously in his diary.[48]

Lincoln wrote to his father on the following morning to tell him that he was supremely happy. On 7 December the two dukes visited the young couple at Wishaw to observe this happiness for themselves. Newcastle was pleased with the young couple's behavior toward one another—"respectful, affectionate, & confiding, but no fondling which is so unpleasant to see." He was sure that the "delicacy of feeling" between the two would ensure their happiness.[49] A few days later Lincoln journeyed southward to attend to his election business. On 17 December he and J. Evelyn Denison, a Whig, were elected to Parliament for South Nottinghamshire without a contest. Gladstone, who had been elected at the head of the poll at Newark a few days earlier, witnessed Lincoln's procession and heard him speak well after the dinner.[50] The two friends were now set to enter Parliament together at the opening of the new session.

In January, Lincoln brought his bride to Clumber, where great preparations had been made for their reception. On the first evening there was a display of fireworks. On the following evening, 12 January, twelve hundred tenants and friends dined with the duke and the newly married couple. A few evenings later there was a servants' ball for four hundred people; and on the following day, 17 January, about three thousand people from the neighboring borough of Worksop were feasted at Clumber until the provisions ran out at last, and the marriage celebration was finally brought to an end.[51]

The new year seemed full of promise for the young couple. Lincoln had matured into a fine-looking man, tall, with a well-proportioned figure and dark expressive eyes. "His person, manner, and address," Newcastle noted with pride, "are . . . so prepossessing that they never fail to engage a person in his favour at the first view."[52] Although greatly prejudiced, there was nonetheless considerable truth in the duke's observation. As a young man, Lincoln presented an open, warm, and affectionate nature that later, perhaps as a result of personal tragedy, disappeared behind a mask of reserve. He was an effective, convincing speaker who by his sincerity gained the respect of many. In 1832 he had won not only the heart of a impressionable girl, but also the enthusiastic support of a large number of electors in a constituency that had returned two Whigs to Parliament in the previous election. All the elements were converging to augur well for Lincoln's future.

2. *Apprenticeship to Peel*

The Lincolns set off for London late in February 1833 after a month's stay at Clumber. Lincoln was eager to begin his parliamentary duties and to present his new bride to London society. The young couple soon attracted considerable attention in London, and Lincoln was quickly accepted into the inner circle of the Conservative party. At the traditional fish dinner at Greenwich in June, attended by about forty leading members of the opposition, Lincoln's name appeared in the list of "new fish" who joined Sir Robert Peel and the other "old fish" who led the Conservative party.[1] Already the process of uniting the Conservative opposition under Peel had commenced. To the bitter disappointment of Newcastle, Lincoln would play a part in that process of unification.

Badly disunited since the days of the Catholic Emancipation Act and the agitation over the reform bill, and severely reduced in number by the general election of 1832, the Conservatives in the 1833 session awaited the onslaught of Whig measures with great anxiety, for most of them thought that the Reform Act marked the beginning rather than the end of a radical era. The worst was avoided, however, and such controversial measures as the Irish coercion bill and the Irish Church bill passed into law with some of the sting removed from them by Peel's constructive and temporizing opposition. Thus in 1833 the Conservatives successfully defended the great interests upon which conservatism stood by turning back proposals made by the Radicals to allow the admission of Dissenters to the universities, to adopt a secret ballot at elections, to rescind the Corn Laws, and to substitute a property and income tax for the house and window tax. By doing this, the Conservatives helped to drive a wedge between the Whigs and the Radicals; and by the end of the parliamentary session the Whigs were nearly as divided as were the Conservatives.

But neither Lincoln nor Gladstone expected the same situation to prevail during the 1834 session. They expected the Whigs to resume their work of demolition in the form of bills to abolish church rates and to establish a system of open election for corporate offices. Both believed that these two "pernicious changes," as Gladstone called them, were likely to be the first concessions to the democratic element in the next session, and both were filled with apprehension about the Conservatives' ability to prevent the Whigs from destroying the great pillars of society. "Your lamentations upon the disorganization of our party are indeed too just," Lincoln wrote to Gladstone on the eve of the new session; "there is a bickering and evil spirit amongst us which will be the ruin of ourselves and the Country, and looks quite like fatality. I do hope something may be done soon to remedy this most crying evil."[2]

But despite these grave matters, the bliss of domestic life kept Lincoln away from Parliament when the new session opened in 1834. The Lincolns had returned to the country shortly after the birth of their son, Henry Pelham Alexander Clinton, on 25 January. For a time Susan's health was good and she was in fine spirits. Enjoying his new role as a family man, Lincoln stretched his vacation as long as he could. But on 9 April, with the business of the House picking up, Gladstone wrote to urge his friend to give up the agreeable and salubrious country for London in time to take part in the important divisions of tithe commutation, church rates, and admission of Dissenters to the universities.[3] Lincoln could no longer resist the call to duty, and a few days later he set off with Susan and Henry for the Hamiltons' residence in London. Later in the year they settled in their new house on Park Lane, which Newcastle had purchased completely fitted up and furnished for them for the sum of £13,000.

The expense of the house was one that Newcastle then could ill afford, but he was determined to get the Lincolns out from under the Hamilton roof in Portman Square. Since late in 1833, the relationship between the duke and the young couple had become increasingly strained, a situation the duke ascribed in part to Hamilton influence and in part to his son's political and social ambitions. A year of marriage had increased Lincoln's desire to cut the parental ties that Newcastle had refused to relinquish willingly. The duke was convinced that the Lincolns were deviating from the path of righteousness.

The situation greatly deteriorated over the next few months. Late in September 1834, the duke severely condemned the Lincolns' behavior:

> I see that you have both been engaged in attending what *I* call a Tom
> foolery meeting . . . where grown up ladies, as well as grown up gentlemen
> shoot with a bow & arrow & exhibit themselves according to my notion to
> any thing but advantage. . . . Such affairs may seem as a clap trap for a
> certain kind of popularity and may precisely suit the Duke of Sussex and
> the Duchess of St. Albans, but it really angers and hurts me to see you and
> Susan give importance to such nonsense, mischievous besides, as I conceive
> in its affects, encouraging a most objectionable display, vanity, freedom
> and boldness in the women, and absurd folly and contemptible puerility in
> the men. Such meetings are what is called gay, but in fact are only intended
> to do away with distinctions of the sexes, & bring them together in license

& freedom to the great injury of morality & good conduct. Once you thought as I do upon these matters, but of late years, my dear Lincoln, you have been much loosened in your notions, and I have seen and observed it with frequent pain and grief.[4]

Thus Newcastle, in his endeavor to maintain his control over Lincoln's life and to extend it over Susan's, greatly increased the tensions within the family.

Unexpected political events late in the year intruded upon these familial matters and thrust Lincoln into a new role. On 14 November, William IV, believing that the ministry was firmly committed to Irish Church reform, seized the opportunity presented by the elevation of Lord Althorp to the Lords as the earl of Spencer to dismiss Lord Melbourne and the ministry and to send for Sir Robert Peel, then traveling in Italy, to form a new government. Lord Melbourne, who had succeeded Lord Grey as prime minister only four months earlier, did not protest the king's arbitrary course of action, and the duke of Wellington filled in as first lord until Peel returned from his Italian holiday. The king's action made a general election necessary, and many candidates took to the field even before Peel arrived in London early in the morning of 9 December. Expecting an early dissolution, Lincoln wrote to Gladstone at Fasque to invite him to Clumber to be nearer the scene of action. But on the same day that he received Lincoln's letter, Gladstone received one from Peel summoning him to London and offering him a junior lordship at the Treasury. Lincoln received a similar letter with the same offer from Peel the same day.[5]

In constructing his ministry in 1834, Peel insisted upon providing several youthful politicians with their first experience of office. It was his practice to seek out young men from the universities who were distinguished by rank and social position or by academic success and to assist them early in their political careers. Lincoln, Gladstone, Sidney Herbert, and Winthrop Mackworth Praed, a brilliant young Cambridge barrister, were all thus favored by Peel in 1834. Gladstone was delighted to learn that Lincoln would be one of his colleagues at the Treasury. Characteristically, however, he noted, "People call Lord Lincoln my friend and he acts as such. But it is well for me to remind myself of the difference of rank between us. . . . Oh God, that I were better worth having."[6]

In the general election of January 1835, Lincoln and Gladstone were re-elected without contests. Using Peel's *Tamworth Manifesto*, a statement outlining the new government's attitude toward the main political issues of the day, many of the other Conservative candidates were also successful at the polls. During the election, the Conservatives, following Peel's lead, generally made it clear that they were reconciled to the Reform Act and were ready to review all institutions, correct all proved abuses, and redress all real grievances. With this moderate approach, the Conservatives picked up about one hundred seats; however, they still remained a minority.[7] Peel himself had not expected an absolute majority. His hopes for the survival of the government rested elsewhere, as he explained to Lincoln:

> I think the returns are on the whole very favourable, all circumstances considered, but my confidence in our success, which is very great, does not rest so much upon returns, as upon my conviction that we shall do whatever is reasonable and just, and that reason and justice must ultimately prevail.[8]

With a reasonable and practical program, he believed, they would attract far more support than they presently could calculate upon from the election returns. Even Gladstone, who had lamented the early dissolution, was hopeful that, notwithstanding the ten-pound clause, a moderate Parliament had been returned; and he urged Lincoln, who had lingered on at Clumber after the election, to hasten his appearance at the Treasury so that they could "drill a little antecedently to the commencement of the Session."[9]

As much as he wanted to assume his duties in London, Lincoln felt that he could not leave his wife while she was confined to her bed with illness. Never well since August of the previous year, Susan suddenly became worse late in January. The situation, according to Newcastle, was acerbated by the Hamiltons "doing what would be better not done, fretting and worrying their dear child by over kindness and anxiety." Newcastle deeply lamented this "parental meddling & fidgetting interference," which he believed did a great deal of harm to Susan and plagued poor Lincoln to death. Susan was still unable to travel on 3 February when Lincoln, who no longer could resist the call to duty, left to take up his new post in London. "I have seen him leave her with very great regret," Newcastle confided to his diary,

> & have done all in my power to prevent his absence—but in vain—his itch for politics & to commence business in office overpower every other feeling. . . . In his situation I could not have done such a thing—home is the first care[;] when all is right there, then other matters may receive due attention.[10]

On the following day, Susan became worse. "Lincoln's self-gratification has, I fear, caused this," the duke wrote. "How much, I lament that he should have gone when his presence is so much required here."[11] The duke continued to be anxious as Susan remained confined to her bed very much weakened by the return of severe pains and spasms. Lincoln's return from London, Newcastle thought, "would be the greatest relief for then, poor soul, she would at least have the benefit of his society & attentions, the absence of which I am certain she inwardly feels." But on the next day, when she was better, the duke was surprised to discover that on no account would she have Lincoln return to "fidget her to death" and that she would prefer to travel to London without him. "This is Hamilton fashion, not Clinton fashion," the duke wrote indignantly in his diary.[12]

On 11 February, Lincoln arrived at Clumber with a bed carriage to convey Susan to London. The duke thought the move was a rash, unwise, and desperate step, but there seemed nothing he could do to prevent it. A few days later, he heard with relief that the Lincolns had arrived safely and that Susan had stood the journey quite well and was much the better for the trip.[13]

Once again in London, Lincoln settled down to his parliamentary and official duties. Parliament opened on 19 February 1835 in buildings that had been damaged in the Westminster fire of the previous October. From the beginning it was evident that the government would not attract the independent support that it needed to stay in power. The Stanleyites remained aloof, and the Whigs, Radicals, and Irish O'Connellites united in opposition to the ministry. The king's dismissal of the previous government and the dissolution had hardened party divisions. Peel's government would not be given a fair trial. Early in April, Lord John Russell carried opposition motions for applying the surplus revenues of the Church of Ireland to secular use and for refusing any Irish tithe settlement that did not embody the principle of the first resolution. Beaten on these two motions, the ministers resigned on 18 April.

Although short-lived, the Hundred Days' Ministry was extremely important. From it Peel emerged as the acknowledged leader of the Conservative party. A truly Conservative party, as distinguished from the scattered Tory forces of old, had been created; and with the general adoption of the *Tamworth Manifesto*, the Peelite formula for conservatism had been endorsed by both the party's leaders and the rank and file. Conservatives had doubled their numbers in the Commons, and a sense of optimism and confidence had been gained.[14] At a dinner in his own house a few days after the ministry's resignation, Peel expressed his confidence in the future to some of his outgoing colleagues in reply to Lincoln's toast proposing his health. He told them that in undertaking the government he had never expected to succeed; his conviction had been that good might be done, and he trusted that good had been achieved. Continuing, he noted that even if a Conservative government had not been strong enough to carry on the country's affairs, at least the Conservatives were now strong enough to prevent any other government from doing serious mischief to the country's institutions. He also touched on the close bond of friendship that had been established between himself and his colleagues in the struggle that had just come to a close. "I really can hardly call you gentlemen alone," he observed. "I would rather address you as my warm and attached friends in whom I have the fullest confidence."[15] That bond of friendship was particularly strong between Peel and the young subordinate colleagues whom he had introduced to official life in 1834. Their friendship would last to the end of Peel's life. Peelism had been born, and Lincoln had become a Peelite.

II

The duke of Newcastle was aghast at the resignation of Peel's government. Although he despised Peel as a man of expediency, he still preferred him to the reformers. It was a mere choice between evils, and he believed that the "scoundrels" once again in power would do incalculable mischief to the nation.[16]

Since the beginning of 1835, the duke had been in one of his despondent moods. He felt helpless in the wake of the "Jesuit and republican" tide. On the first day of the year, he wrote:

> I toil, but in vain, I devote myself, but without avail. I seek to be useful but
> my efforts are abortive. I am expected to be the laborer & the contributor
> on all occasions, but never do I find others disposed to render the slightest
> return. All this is heart breaking, humiliating & painful of endurance. It
> chills the generous feelings, damps all noble aspirations & paralises every
> animating inducements [sic]. . . . I submit because it is God's will but it is
> pain & grief to me.[17]

Throughout the year he remained separated from his former political associates. The major point of difference was over the role of the Tory opposition in the House of Lords. Newcastle found Wellington's political course abhorrent, particularly with regard to the corporation bill. At deliberative meetings held at Wellington's house, he continued to speak out vehemently against the policy of allowing the major Whig measures to pass first and second readings without opposition, with the view of altering them in committee. But he spoke in vain, for Wellington's ascendancy over the Tory peers was too great for him to overcome. So extreme was Newcastle that Wellington and his political associates stopped inviting him to their political meetings later in the year. And in January 1836, for the first time in many years, he was not invited to Wellington's political dinner at the beginning of the parliamentary session. It was a compliment and not a slight, Newcastle told himself; nonetheless, by this time he was bitterly disheartened with politics and politicians. He became increasingly visionary. As God's instrument, he vowed to carry on the struggle against delusion outside Parliament. He was supremely confident that he and his family—the Clintons—would be the "Providential Instruments" destined to lead the chosen people of England out of the wilderness and into the "blessed state of peace and tranquility."[18]

Newcastle and Lincoln, however, disagreed on the means to achieve this political influence and position of leadership in the country, and the duke's relationship with his eldest son troubled him greatly and added to his despondency. The duke continued to crave his son's dependence, while deluding himself into thinking that he acted in Lincoln's best interest; and his heart was filled with bitter disappointment and loneliness when Lincoln rejected this parental control. With a promising career before him, Lincoln continued to stray from the domestic and political fold; he turned his back on his father's constricting conventions and tried to escape his admonitions by avoiding him in face-to-face confrontations. By the summer of 1835 the duke felt compelled by his son's conduct to complain to his diary. On 21 June, after spending a pleasant day at home with his children—"a practice which I cherish and anxiously wish that I could hope to see perpetuated by Lincoln"—he recorded that Lincoln's

> wife is giddy and he suffers himself to look complacently upon a vital evil—the seeking happiness elsewhere than at home in the domestic circle. It is a vicious poison which affects & influences every relation of life. The prospect of what I see resulting from it & what will assuredly follow grieves me to the soul and eternally embitters my thoughts.[19]

A few days later the duke complained directly to Lincoln. "In thought, word or deed," he wrote, "you have departed from all the principles of your earlier youth, you have separated yourself wholly from me and indeed from your family, and have adopted the miserable exchange of a citizen of the world."[20]

Angered by his father's condemnation of his activities and attitudes, Lincoln retorted:

> You call me a "citizen of the world"—in what do I show it? do I join in the dissipations of a London life? do I frequent places of amusement? do I associate with any but persons of the highest and most unimpeachable respectability? No, you know I do none of these; you know that I am to be found at home, unless when public business calls me away earlier, until 3 or 4 every day, and that from home I go down to the House, unless I stop for 10 minutes at the Carlton to revel in the dissipation of the Whig papers, which I do not take in at home, or to learn what business is to come on.[21]

Newcastle still believed that Lincoln was "on the road to ruin" and that his son's worldly ambition and Susan's craving for adulation and social entertainment were the main causes of it. He regarded his son's announcement in the summer of 1835 that he and Susan would reside either on the Continent or at Hamilton Palace in Scotland during the parliamentary break to avoid another miserable scene at Clumber as a complete "abandonment of filial ties and filial affection."[22] For the next few months, the duke closed his doors to the Lincolns and refused to enter theirs.

Newcastle and the Lincolns were reconciled early in 1836 through the efforts of the duke of Hamilton, but the reconciliation was extremely precarious. Newcastle remained dissatisfied with the Lincolns' mode of life, although there was an abatement in their social activities during the year. Lincoln conscientiously attended his parliamentary duties, while Susan bore her second child, another boy, whom they named Edward. Lincoln's involvement with

Lord Lincoln, by John Hayter, 1836. Courtesy of the Ninth Duke of Newcastle.

Peel and the Conservative party continued to irritate the duke, who disliked Peel as much as Lincoln liked and admired him. In particular, Newcastle resented Peel's growing political ascendancy over the Conservative party in the House of Lords, which greatly diminished the influence of the ultra-Tory peers in general and Newcastle specifically. In January 1836 Lincoln attended the Conservative party's inner council hosted by Peel at Drayton Manor. The meeting went well, and the participants left with a feeling of unity and sociability. "Our chief is in excellent health and spirits," Lincoln reported to Francis Bonham, Conservative party agent, "and if he knocks over Whigs as cleverly and as surely as he does pheasants, woe be to them." [23]

But during the parliamentary session the main work of defeating the two major Whig measures—the Irish corporation bill and the Irish Church revenue bill—was done in the Lords rather than in the Commons. Newcastle took heart in this and rejoiced in the belief that he had had a great deal to do with inducing the Lords, irrespective of Peel's opinion and position in the Commons, to reject the dangerous bills. "The country rejoices at the course which has been taken," the duke confided to his diary; "it is what I long preached & I am not disinclined to think that my speech at the Marylebone dinner which was so well received was the initiative, & gave the final impulse to these proceedings of the H. of Lords." [24] At last, he believed, the political pendulum was swinging in his favor.

Lincoln was also enjoying political favor. Early in 1837 he attended a dinner in Newark given in his honor by the Conservative electors of South Nottinghamshire. Nearly 330 members of the nobility, clergy, and yeomanry filled the spacious Town Hall to express their approval of Lincoln's conduct and political principles and to register their support of conservatism. In his speech, Lincoln observed that although the meeting manifested the growing fervor and strength of conservatism in the country, there was much to be done to rescue the church from the infidel, the constitution from the democrat, the peerage from its republican assailants, and the nation from the incubus that was paralyzing all its efforts and neutralizing all its energies in the House of Commons. He denounced the major Whig measures of the last session and defended the action of the agricultural committee, of which he had been a member, in rejecting the proposal of a reduction or even abolition of the malt tax as the compensation for the reduction of the scale of duties on imported corn. He pledged his continued support of the agricultural interest. [25] The speech was well received. Gladstone, who followed with a lengthy discourse of his own in accepting the toast to Sir Robert Peel and the Conservative members of Parliament, recorded that Lincoln spoke very well. It was a most successful meeting, he added. [26]

Gladstone returned with Lincoln to Clumber following the meeting. He found Lady Lincoln with "much of her usual buoyancy," but feared that she still suffered much, "bravely & in secret."[27] Susan had been ill since the birth of Edward the previous year, and late in January she was badly attacked by influenza. Nonetheless, Lincoln made plans to leave Clumber on 28 January in time for the opening of Parliament and a party meeting at Peel's house two days later. But his plans had to be deferred when the day arrived, for Susan was still too ill to travel. Newcastle thought that she was in very precarious health. Lincoln became restive. On 29 January the duke scornfully remarked, "Lincoln is anxious to worship his juggernaut the H. of C." But the duke was determined to keep him at Clumber as long as Susan was unwell. Susan was no better the next day. "It snowed all day," the duke recorded in his diary, "& we are all in an uncertain & uncomfortable mood."[28] Lincoln wrote to Bonham to explain his absence from the party meeting at Peel's house. "What would I not rather have done than be thus absent when every thing is at stake!" he exclaimed.[29]

Yet more was at stake than Lincoln was aware of. On 31 January tensions were elevated to a frenzied state when Susan's maid, Miss Pratchett, handed a love letter to Lincoln that she had discovered in her mistress's room. Lady Lincoln had been caught in a serious indiscretion, the first of many that she would commit over the next few years.

III

The letter was addressed to "My Own Angel," contained the words "I fear you never will be mine—what a cold set we are surrounded by," and referred to Lincoln's inconsiderate nature.[30] Lincoln quickly ascertained that Lord William, one of his younger brothers, had written the letter to Susan. From its contents, Susan was clearly carrying on some kind of love affair with Lord William and had obviously imparted matters of the most personal kind to him in order to gain his sympathy; and from the ensuing family correspondence, it is evident that the relationship between Lord William and Susan was far from innocent.[31]

Stunned by the revelation, Lincoln confronted his wife with the letter. Susan, refusing to divulge anything, immediately took refuge in fainting spells and spasms. She was soon too weak to rise from her bed. Lincoln then consulted his father and with him worked out a plan to meet the crisis. It was decided that Susan should live in seclusion for a time and that Lincoln should neither see her nor correspond with her until the parliamentary recess at Easter. At that time Lincoln would approach her for a complete explanation of her past conduct and discuss with her the prospects for their future happiness together. A successful termination of these discussions, Lincoln and Newcastle thought, would pave the way for a reconciliation during the summer. In the meantime, Lincoln would return to London to resume his parliamentary duties, using the excuse of his wife's illness as the cause of their separation. As for Lord William, the duke decided to send him off immediately to East Sheen with Thompson, the duke's trusted friend and Lincoln's former tutor, to study religious works and to reflect upon his sins.

There followed nearly a full year of torment for Lincoln caused by the most unusual circumstances. The duke and duchess of Hamilton took Susan to Paris to consult foreign physicians who were practitioners of the latest medical arts, among whom were Dr. Samuel Hahnemann, the celebrated founder of homeopathy, and Doctors Koreff and Wolowski, advocates of hypnotism. In Paris, Lady Lincoln became seriously ill from a nervous and hysterical condition that deprived her temporarily of speech, sight, and hearing. On Good Friday, 24 March, she suffered a violent attack at the moment of her husband's arrival in Paris. Everyone thought that she was dying. But the crisis passed after an apparent death-bed reconciliation with Lincoln. Still Susan remained seriously ill for several months. Throughout the spring and summer she suffered from violent attacks that left her in a state of near insanity. There were periods of somnambulism induced by the doctors' use of hypnosis, and the use of laudanum greatly acerbated her condition.

The symptoms of Lady Lincoln's illness were those of hysteria; the cause was probably a combination of physical impairment and psychological distress. Susan had habitually used illness to avoid responsibility, particularly moral responsibility, and Lincoln's insistence upon seriously discussing her past and future conduct caused "heart-rending scenes." Lincoln remained in Paris with his wife for over a month; but finally the doctors and the duke of Hamilton, arguing that Susan needed moral as well as physical tranquillity, forced Lincoln from the patient's bedside late in April. "I look upon my departure . . . with great pain and uneasiness," Lincoln wrote to his father on the eve of his return to England, "but I believe it will be for the best. . . . I am really torn to pieces with conflicting sentiments and inclinations and wishes."[32]

Lincoln's health had been greatly affected by the extreme anxiety of mind and depression of spirits that he had suffered over the past three months. Upon his return to London he found that he had neither the physical strength nor the mental energies to resume his parliamentary duties. By late May he was confined to his room for several days by what he described as "a sharp attack of nervous fever." Shortly after his recovery he decided to join Thompson and his family on a tour of the Continent. The decision was a painful one for him. With his wife still confined by illness in Paris and himself forbidden by the doctors to visit her, he found domestic happiness and relief from his disconsolate condition only in the presence of his two young sons. He hated to part from them, even for a short time, but he believed that it was his duty to them to seek restoration of his physical and mental well-being.

On 16 June, leaving his two boys in the care of their nurse, Lincoln set off for Dover with the Thompson family. After a rough crossing, they traveled by carriage from Calais to Brussels. From Brussels they passed over the field of Waterloo and through Luxembourg to Trèves and from there by way of Basel to Switzerland. Lincoln kept a journal during the first few days of the trip in which he recorded his extreme melancholy and loneliness, as constantly his thoughts turned to his wife.[33] Later he had to concede to his father that the object of the tour had failed entirely.

Early in July, Lincoln gave up the tour and proceeded to Paris with the Thompson family. His hopes of finding an altered situation there were quickly shattered; the doctors still refused to allow him to see Susan. Although her health was greatly improved, she apparently did not want to see her husband. The effect of "magnetism," Thompson believed, had deadened all the best feelings of her heart. On 10 July, Lincoln, bitterly distressed, decided to return to England to attend to his election business in South Nottinghamshire. As a last desperate measure, he informed the Hamiltons that during the course of the next two or three weeks he must either be restored to domestic peace or "placed in that situation where I can only look forward to a short life of misery and unhappiness, and a state of things which I shudder and tremble to contemplate."[34]

Quite unexpectedly, everything was set right for Lincoln late the same day. Susan defied the advice and injunctions of her doctors and begged Lincoln to come to her. He went immediately, and after a dreadful scene during which she suffered another attack, the two were again reconciled. Susan fervently promised to behave. Lincoln accepted her promises and forgave her for her past conduct.[35]

Lincoln's joy was unbounded. He was convinced that his wife had broken the spell cast by her doctors and their "vile magnetism," the horrors of which he could not describe. Over his father's objections, Lincoln sent for the two boys in order that they could be with their mother while she continued to recover. Shortly after their arrival in Paris, Lincoln returned to Nottinghamshire for the election, in which he was returned to Parliament for the Southern Division without a contest.

Upon his return to Paris, Lincoln found his wife somewhat improved in health, although she continued to suffer from a nervous disorder. The duchess of Hamilton arranged a holiday for Susan, Lincoln, and the two boys in Switzerland, but the holiday failed to produce the desired improvement in Susan. Although the physical cause of her hysteria was gone, the mental anguish remained. Lincoln constantly lectured her, and soon the very sight of him precipitated fits of hysteria and distressing scenes. Susan longed to escape from her intolerant, humorless, and moralizing husband, who insistently bound her to a marital situation she now loathed.[36]

As if there were not trouble enough, a serious controversy with Doctors Koreff and Wolowski awaited Lincoln and the duchess on their return to Paris. On 26 October the doctors demanded that the duchess and Lincoln pay 400,000 francs as remuneration for their professional attendance of Lady Susan earlier in the year. On the following morning Lincoln was arrested in his quarters in the presence of his family at the Hotel Bristol in the Place Vendôme. The news of Lincoln's arrest and the doctors' exorbitant claims created a great sensation both in France and in England. The doctors, perhaps uneasy about their own reputations in light of the rash of calumnious reports published about them, stirred up the controversy even more by circulating throughout Paris a lithographed letter in which they denounced Lincoln and the Hamiltons. They also threatened to publish some of the sordid details contained in a journal that they had prepared from their observations of Susan's statements and actions during the periods of her somnambulism.[37]

Lincoln refused to be intimidated into accepting an excessive compromise of the affair. Instead, he entered a counterdemand against the doctors for damages for false arrest. Hearings on the case were held on 1 and 14 December before the Tribunal De Premiere Instance. On both occasions, large crowds were attracted to the chambers by the prospect of scandal. Lincoln, accompanied by the counsel of the British Embassy and Lord Douglas, his brother-in-law, attended the first day's session but returned to England with Susan and the children before the hearings resumed on 14 December. The doctors had already desisted from the original proceedings, and only Doctor Wolowski appeared at the hearings to answer Lincoln's counterdemand for the restitution of the journal and for damages. The court announced in Lincoln's favor, denying damages to him but ordering the doctors to surrender the complete journal with notes to Lincoln.[38] Although he was not totally vindicated, it was for Lincoln a satisfactory conclusion to a most unsatisfactory matter.

IV

The reconciliation between Lord and Lady Lincoln continued on a tenuous basis. Susan remained in poor health for a considerable time. In March 1838 she went to Leamington for her health while Lincoln remained in London to attend Parliament. Her "warm and affectionate letters," Lincoln told the duchess of Hamilton, were a great comfort to him. "She is the best & kindest of wives & her conduct towards our dear Children is admirable," he added. The duchess was incredulous. She told her husband that "warm and affectional letters" from Susan to Lincoln were "*inconceivable* when contrasted with those she writes to us on the subject of her husband!"[39] Earlier Susan had noted in one of her letters to the duchess:

You must know that when once the flame of love is *extinguished* it is rarely
to be kindled once more. I *did* love tenderly, & would have done all, &
did do every thing in my power to please, tho' *God knows* I respect, I *cannot*
love. There are words, looks, & impressions which *none* but me can have
seen, which I never would, & which I never shall name.[40]

After her return, Lincoln took a house at Kew for his family, perhaps for
the purpose of providing isolation for his wife. The move, however, greatly
worsened Susan's state of mind, and by July 1838 Lincoln was driven to despair. He spoke to his father of another separation. Newcastle advised his son
to exercise patience and forbearance, and wrote to Susan to urge her to allow
her will to be regulated by the spirit of religion. It grieved him "to the soul"
to see his son's happiness "disturbed & possibly destroyed," but he refused to
abandon hope for an accommodation to save the marriage.[41]

In August 1838 the Lincolns journeyed to the Continent once again. They
traveled extensively with their children through Belgium, Germany, and
northern Italy before going to Rome for the winter. Susan and the children
withstood the rigors of the journey quite well, and for Lincoln the trip was
delightful, especially the works of art and the major historic sights. His journal
account of his impressions, although brief, clearly indicates how deeply sensitive he was.[42] In Rome early in December they enjoyed Gladstone's company. Gladstone frequently dined with them and on one occasion went with
Lincoln to visit the future Cardinal Wiseman and to see the Vatican and St.
Peters.[43] The following March, Lincoln and his family returned to England.
A month later, Susan was confined for the birth of a girl, whom they named
Susan Charlotte Catherine Pelham Clinton.

V

Despite the apparent restoration of his marriage, domestic contentment
continued to elude Lincoln. Late in 1839 Newcastle observed that his son's
inward suffering caused his heart to bleed.[44] But the duke himself contributed
considerably to Lincoln's anxiety by reckless spending that threatened to im-
poverish the Newcastle estate. The duke was driven by an obsession for
power, and during the late 1830s he turned almost entirely from orthodox
political activities to more unusual means to increase his influence in the country. His landed estates, his art collection, his library, and his electioneering
influence were to him the means and symbols of his power.[45] His desire to
own more and more became a mania; and his purchases, especially of landed
estates, brought him to the verge of bankruptcy. "My purchases," he proudly
proclaimed in his diary in 1838, "have amounted in Nottinghamshire within
the last two years to no less than £450,000 . . . which is pretty well for one
who has no capital at command."[46]

These excessive purchases by a man who had so incessantly sought moderation in the actions of his son can only be explained by Newcastle's own reasoning. They were made to increase his territorial prestige and family influence, which he believed were absolutely necessary for the execution of his plans to launch a political movement that would save the country from ruin. "I trust that I and mine will not abuse the encreased [*sic*] opportunities" brought about by family aggrandizement, he wrote in his diary at the end of 1838, "& that we shall use them for good & not for evil." [47]

By 1841, Newcastle's expenditures had become so extravagant and his debts so great that Lincoln felt compelled to intervene. The crisis was close at hand, he told his father, and the only satisfactory way to avert it was to put the duke's affairs in trust. He implored the duke not to allow his grandchildren, whose only provision came from the family estate, to suffer the fate that generally befell "a race of titled paupers." [48] But Newcastle paid no attention to his son's advice. He continued to borrow money to pay interest on his mortgages. From time to time, he also sold large amounts of oak and beech timber from his Clumber estate to stave off his creditors. Thus year after year the duke's financial situation became more desperate, until finally in 1845 he was forced to sell Haford in Wales and put his estate business under the direction of a trust.

Father and son also remained at odds over politics, but for a brief time during the late 1830s the duke was less pessimistic about the political climate of the nation and less hostile toward Peel. Although the dismemberment of the old constitution continued in Parliament, the duke sensed that the nation had been roused to a better sense of its duty and that the public mind was imbued with feelings that portended well for the future. [49] In January 1839 Newcastle visited Peel at Drayton Manor. The visit was most agreeable to the duke, and he left with the satisfaction that he had helped to strengthen Peel's ideas on the Corn Laws and popery. And with his profound contempt for the Melbourne ministry, caused to a large extent by his dismissal as lord lieutenant of Nottinghamshire, Newcastle looked forward to Peel and the Conservatives coming to power. [50]

Newcastle was correct in observing that the relentless attacks of the Dissenters and Irish Catholics against the Establishment, the incessant Radical demands, the ominous threat of Chartism, and the continued failure of the Whigs to provide resolute leadership all were certain to produce a reaction in the country. But the move toward conservatism during the late 1830s was not what the duke thought it to be; it was not his rigid toryism but rather Peel's progressive conservatism that was gaining favor in the country. Peel had both consolidated and enlarged the forces of conservatism, transforming the party of landed toryism into a party of national conservatism. It had become a formidable party both in Parliament and in the country at large, and with a weak Whig ministry the Conservative opposition actually had assumed some of the functions of government. The Whig legislative measures, such as the trio of Irish bills—Irish corporations, Irish tithe, and Irish Poor Law—were passed only after the Conservative opposition in both houses had amended them substantially. Power rested with the opposition rather than with the government. In the spring of 1841, the opposition seized an opportunity to translate power into office and its concomitants of place and patronage, for which Peel's supporters impatiently longed.[51]

Faced with a deficit for the fourth year in a row, Francis Baring, chancellor of the Exchequer, adopted the 1840 report of Joseph Hume's committee on import duties as the basis for his new budget. The report concluded that a decrease in the rate of duties on sugar, coffee, and timber would produce a higher revenue as a result of a greater volume of imports. Lord John Russell also gave notice as leader of the Lords that he would move for a committee of the whole House to consider the Corn Laws. His intention was to propose a fixed duty of 8s a quarter on wheat in lieu of the sliding scale of the 1828 Corn Law. Thus in the course of one day, 30 April 1841, the Whigs launched the great debate both in Parliament and in the country over the most controversial issue of the political era. Writing to his father on the morning after, Lincoln expressed his utter contempt for the government's action:

> The whole town is astounded and disgusted at what took place last night. We went to the House expecting resignation or at all events dissolution, and instead we had a budget with repeal of the Corn Laws and other less obnoxious crudities.
>
> It is impossible to say what will be the end of it. Our party is so completely *up* at what has taken place and Peel and Co. are so thoroughly indignant that I think we shall go at them but what will come of it nobody can yet tell. . . . They have now indeed filled up the measure of their wickedness and tho' it is an atrocious scheme for the purpose of maintaining power I do not despair of seeing it become the final grave of the whole accursed crew.[52]

The opposition leaders decided to counter the government's new proposals by a specific motion against the reduction of sugar duties, to be followed if successful by a general motion of no confidence. On 18 May the ministers were beaten by a majority of 36 on the sugar duties, and on 5 June, Peel's no-confidence motion was carried 312 to 311. The government's defeat was followed by the dissolution of Parliament.

In the general election that followed, Lord Lincoln was again returned for South Nottinghamshire unopposed. The Conservatives did extremely well, scoring a net gain of twenty-two seats in the English counties, a net gain of fifteen in urban constituencies throughout the whole of the United Kingdom, and a net gain of eight in Ireland. The total was more than enough for a working majority for the Conservatives in the new Parliament. Although it was clear that the end of the Melbourne ministry had come, the Whigs by custom met the new Parliament when it convened on 24 August 1841. The Conservatives, however, immediately moved in for the kill, and on 28 August Peel's amendment to the address was carried by a majority of ninety-one. Two days later the ministers resigned, and the queen asked Peel to form a new government.

The ministerial appointments were made quickly and with ease. With the exception of four positions, the old cabinet of 1834–1835 was restored. The four vacancies were filled with the Whig seceders of 1834—Lord Stanley, Sir James Graham, and Lord Ripon—and the duke of Buckingham, the titular head of the Agriculturalists. The posts below cabinet rank were filled with equal ease. All the young men of 1834 returned to office. Gladstone, although disappointed that he was not offered a cabinet post, accepted the vice-presidency of the Board of Trade; Sidney Herbert that of secretary to the Admiralty; Lord Canning became under-secretary at the Foreign Office; and Lincoln, after Lord Sandon declined the offer, took the office of commissioner for woods and forests.

Lord Melbourne privately expressed his strong reservations to Queen Victoria concerning the latter appointment on the grounds that Lincoln was ignorant of the work, inexperienced in business, and reputedly of quarrelsome nature. George Anson, secretary to the prince consort, took the matter up with Peel, who quickly and decisively defended the appointment. Peel assured Anson that the appointment for the Office of Woods and Forests was a political one, even though its superintendence of royal estates and buildings involved it in a considerable amount of direct business with the crown. He therefore would not have the appointment challenged. Besides, he assured Anson, Lincoln was "one of the best men we have."[53] The matter was allowed to drop. Perhaps knowing Peel's particular affection for Lincoln, Charles Greville noted in his diary after the appointment that "Lincoln has turned out worth a dozen Sidney Herberts and is the most rising man we have."[54] Yet the Alastor, the evil spirit, had already fallen on this young man of promise who in 1841 entered a government from which there were great expectations.

3. *Office under Peel*

As superintendent of royal and public lands, parks, and buildings, Lincoln frequently communicated with the queen and the prince consort, who both took a keen interest in the business of his office. The steadily increasing expenditure for the administration of his office was a constant worry to Lincoln and a source of difficulty with the court. Between 1838 and 1842, for example, the amount expended on royal palaces and parks alone had increased from £89,000 to £151,000.[1] Such increases in public expenditures evoked the cry of economy in the House of Commons, and Lincoln was faced with the task of making expenditure for the crown's claims palatable to the public. Even with the popularity of the queen, the task was not always an easy one, and frequently Lincoln felt compelled to oppose certain royal requests.

Lincoln justified such increases on the basis that it was necessary to provide more public accessibility to royal buildings and parks. Early in his administration he received the queen's permission to allow the British Association for the Advancement of Science to use the observatory at Kew to conduct important experiments.[2] He also laid a plan before the queen for adding forty acres of the Kew pleasure grounds to the Botanic Gardens for an arboretum and conservatory. The queen quickly accepted the plan, although Prince Albert later registered his concern over the original estimated cost of the conservatory. Lincoln, however, assured Peel that he had reduced the expense from £30,000 to £23,000 by altering the design of the building. "If the Prince would look at these things fairly," he added, "he would find that objects of *mere personal enjoyment* of the Sovereign cost the Office of Woods more *annually* than this object of scientific and national importance will cost altogether."[3]

In 1842 Lincoln suggested to the queen that Richmond Park be opened to the public. The queen consented to the admission of private carriages and horsemen, the same arrangement that prevailed at Windsor and Bushy Parks.[4] Upon the death of Sturges Bourne, the lord warden of New Forest, Lincoln advocated the abolition of the vacant wardenship, although he knew Peel, sensitive to the views of the court, was reluctant to make such a proposal to the queen. "I dare say," he wrote with acidity to Peel, "Her Majesty will propose to give it to Prince Albert, and we shall have an attempt to carry out

Mr. Grantly Berkeley's principles and enforce the rigor of old Forest Laws in order to get up Red Deer and Black Game for the Prince's sport."[5]

The disagreements between Prince Albert and Lincoln extended into other areas. One major point of contention concerned the reorganization of the duchy estates. With persistence and with the complete support of Peel, Lincoln finally prevailed over the prince in this matter. The result was the Duchy of Cornwall Assessionable Act of 1844, which established a commission to determine the boundaries of the duchy and to set the rents, fees, and fines for the manors therein.[6] Lincoln sat on the duchy council chaired by Prince Albert from February 1842 until his appointment early in 1846 as Irish chief secretary, and again from January 1847 to late March 1849.

In another matter, the purchase of the estate at Osborne, Lincoln's advice was unheeded. In October 1843 Peel asked Lincoln to employ an agent for the queen and prince to open private negotiations for the purchase of Osborne. A year later Lincoln concluded from the agent's report that the deal was not a good one. "I never saw a place less likely to suit the queen or more calculated to lead to endless follies in brick and mortar," he told Peel.[7] Nonetheless, the prince and the queen leased Osborne for a year with the option to purchase.

These occasional differences of opinion between Prince Albert and Lord Lincoln, both known for their strong-willed natures, did not prevent the two men from becoming close friends. By 1843, they were already developing a friendship that would deepen into mutual admiration as the years passed.

II

At the time of his appointment as commissioner for woods and forests in 1841, Lord Lincoln's domestic life was again deeply troubled. Susan had continued to vex him by engaging in conduct that he could "only characterize as a complete plan of moral assassination."[8] Again and again, however, she had charmed him into forgiving her past "indiscretions." Matters steadily worsened, and on 14 December, Lincoln told his father that Susan had a new lover and that he was resolved upon immediate separation. Newcastle was astounded and grieved by the news. Nevertheless, he counseled his son to delay the separation until the duke could talk with Susan. Lincoln agreed, and on 21 December the duke in a desperate effort to save the marriage rode to Ranby Hall, where Susan remained with the children, now numbering four after the birth of Arthur the previous summer. She confessed that she regarded Lincoln with horror and that she neither loved nor could love him. She also expressed her desire to escape from her husband at all risks, even if it meant leaving home and children and being socially degraded. Susan's avowals stunned the duke, who concluded that an accommodation between two people with such different dispositions was utterly impossible. He wrote in his diary:

> It pained me to the soul to think that such a creature as was there before me, so beautiful, so fascinating, so intellectual—could deliberately make such confessions as she announced to me. Besides how such a person who is really a good & attentive mother could almost unmoved contemplate an eternal separation from 4 of the most lovely and loveable children I ever beheld—or that such a one who values position & is ambitious of moving in the very first place should forgo & sacrifice all the advantages which her present situation gives her, and sink into a degraded outcast of society . . . merely to indulge in a sinful propensity.[9]

Following Newcastle's failure to reconcile them, Lincoln retained two lawyers and threatened to take legal action to gain absolute custody of the children and to make public all that he knew about his wife's extramarital activities unless the duke or duchess of Hamilton wrote a letter exonerating him from all blame for the miserable situation. Lincoln's threat finally had its effect. In January 1842 Susan appealed to Lincoln for forgiveness; and after consulting Sir Robert Peel on the matter, Lincoln granted it. Peel observed to his wife that Susan's letter to Lincoln was

> so becoming in every respect, so submissive, so fully acquitting Lincoln of misconduct, expressing such proper feelings with respect to her own future conduct . . . that I said at once that if I were in this situation I should write to Lady Lincoln by this post and say at once that the feelings she expressed in her letter and the mode of expressing them revived all feelings of tenderness towards her, that I would give her credit for the assurances in her letter with regard to her future conduct, that I would not expose her to the risk of obloquy but would overlook and forget all that had passed.[10]

A few days later Peel informed his wife that Susan, with some hesitation and delay, and with her parents' wishes, had accepted Lincoln's offer of forgiveness. But, he added, there was room for grave concern. Susan, he had heard, had been in a very excited state and had recently taken large quantities of laudanum. "Their prospects of happiness are very small, I fear," he concluded.[11]

Events soon justified Peel's skepticism. Lincoln was greatly angered when he arrived at Clumber to learn that Susan, professing that agitation might destroy her, wanted a little more time before they met and resumed living together. "A Hamilton seems to be differently constituted from other people," Newcastle commented in his diary. "Her parents are her curse."[12] For the next few weeks Susan remained at Ranby, where she complained of constant headaches and a sharp pain at the heart that made her short of breath. Slowly she regained her strength. In mid-February she went to Clumber with the chil-

Lord Lincoln, by F. R. Say, 1848. Courtesy of the National Portrait Gallery, London.

dren, and early in April she rejoined Lincoln in London at 14 Carlton House Terrace (next door to the Gladstones), as the house in Park Lane was under lease. Lincoln maintained a moody silence, leaving Susan alone for long periods of time to brood over her misconduct while he attended his parliamentary and official duties.

All too soon Susan relapsed into frivolous behavior. She committed an "indiscretion" at a ball shortly after her return to London, and Lincoln apparently intercepted a love letter addressed to her.[13] Evidently she was under the spell of a new infatuation. Lincoln demanded an explanation and confined her to the house until one was forthcoming. Susan refused to talk about the matter. By late May she no longer dined downstairs with her husband and children, and her isolation from her own family increased as she was overcome by illness. Until mid-August, Lord and Lady Lincoln lived apart under the same roof. They never met and corresponded only through notes delivered by servants.

The Hamiltons were furious with Lincoln over such harsh treatment of their daughter. They had realized that Susan could never live in harmony with her husband. Late in May the "Incarnation of Satan from Hamilton," as Lincoln referred to the duke, came to town for the purpose of freeing his daughter and arranging an amicable separation. He urged Newcastle to join him in devising a family arrangement that would mitigate the wounded sensibilities of all parties and save their respective families from "publick animadversion."[14]

Although he did not expect to accomplish much, Newcastle finally agreed to visit Susan. When he called on her at Carlton House Terrace on 14 June, the duke found Susan in a pitiable condition, attacked by spasms and fainting spells. He was forced to return the next day to have his serious conversation with her. But the answer from her was still the same. "She says," he recorded in his diary,

> she cannot live with Lincoln. I say that is her own fault & not his. In short I
> see so dogged a determination to persist in error & evil that there is no
> hope whatsoever of reform & consequent reconciliation. I now give up the
> case with deep sorrow that Lincoln should have ever had the misfortune
> to be united to such a woman.[15]

He left the interview convinced that legal separation would benefit Lincoln privately and publicly, and he advised his son to pursue that course. But, the duke wrote disgustedly in his diary, Lincoln was so engrossed in "the office & politics of the party . . . that he hardly allows himself to think upon any other subject."[16]

Lincoln remained obstinately opposed to separation. For the next few weeks he neither saw his wife nor allowed her out of the house. The situation

Lady Lincoln, by Sir Francis Grant, 1842. Brodick Castle, Isle of Arran; used by permission of the National Trust for Scotland.

became intolerable for Susan, who finally wrote to Lincoln in a condemnatory tone: "Here have I been for more than a month stretched on the bed of sickness suffering torture in body and mind without the alleviation of one single token of compassion or interest on yr. part. What am I to understand of this?" The only way that she could recover her health and strength, she added, was by a temporary change of air and scene. She appealed to both Lincoln and Newcastle to sanction such a move. Lincoln refused and Newcastle remained silent. Temporary changes of this sort in the past, Lincoln reminded his wife, had failed to provide mental remedy. What she needed instead, he stressed, was a permanent change of a very different nature.[17]

This acrimonious exchange of notes continued for over a month, with Susan becoming more desperate and Lincoln more obstinate. Susan appealed to her parents for help, but in vain, for even they seemed to have abandoned her. Finally, on 29 July, defying Lincoln's strict injunction, Susan announced that she would soon depart for Anglesea Ville, Gosport, on the south coast, where she could benefit from sea bathing and good medical advice. Immediately, Lincoln issued an explicit warning :

> I shall enter into no discussion of the misrepresentations contained in your letter further than to say that I know from your Doctors that what you propose to do is *not necessary* for your health. I have forbidden it— "contumaciously" you resolve to do it—you must then abide the certain consequences of your wicked obstinacy and disobedience. You talk of "returning!" Understand me—if once you go, you *never shall* return, or ever see the children you now wilfully desert in order to indulge your own perverse will and evil passions.
>
> You know *all* the consequences of your act—you have heard all. You have found me for eight long years *merciful and generous*—you will now find me *firm* and *inexorable*.[18]

Lincoln's stern warning had no effect, however, and on 19 August, trembling at the idea of being stopped but with greater courage than she had ever felt before, Susan left Carlton Terrace in a private carriage for Anglesea Ville, where her cousin, Madge Orde, had procured a house for her. That same day Lincoln wrote to his father-in-law that Susan had gone to the seaside to be near a lover, presumably an officer of the Guards. The duke of Hamilton later vehemently denied the charge.[19]

Although the affair became a subject of conversation in London and in the press, Lincoln, now that his wife had left him against his will, was determined to continue the separation until he had received a full explanation from Susan of her past conduct and a promise of good behavior in the future. He denied her any communication with or access to the children, and he closed his mind to her oft-repeated promises that she would return to him and her children as a dutiful wife and mother as soon as her health permitted. He was distressed to learn from Dr. Gairdner, the Hamilton family physician, of Susan's exaggerated illness, repeated blindness (brought on by frequent attacks of hysteria), and renewed use of laudanum. Nonetheless, he refused to give way to her, maintaining that illness was not a valid reason for her leaving him in the first place.

Lincoln was also furious with Susan, her family, and her friends for repeating "base insinuations" against his character as a husband. Even at court, Archdeacon Samuel Wilberforce, recently appointed chaplain to Prince Albert, spread rumors gleaned from the Hamilton camp concerning Lincoln's nature. He confided to the queen that Susan was the "*victim* of an uncontrollable temper & a character totally unsuited to hers" and that she was "an *injured* person & fully justified by circumstances in having endeavoured to find restored health."[20]

Lincoln, however, was busy on his own behalf. He counseled with Sir Robert Peel and Sir James Graham, both of whom extended their full support and sympathy. No man, Graham told Lincoln, "ought to be cast down by the heartless caprice of an unworthy woman, when his conscience tells him, that he has acted towards her with fidelity, with generosity, and in the spirit of Christian forgiveness."[21] Although the duke of Newcastle found the conduct of the Hamiltons "odious, vile & abominable beyond all description,"[22] he washed his hands of the whole business. His daughters, however, did not. They defended their brother by saying publicly that Susan was living with an officer at Anglesea Ville and that Lincoln could divorce her if he chose. Even the duke of Hamilton, despite his devotion to his daughter, became embarrassed by Susan's equivocal position. Fearful that any scandal associated with his family might dim the luster of his son Lord Douglas's betrothal to Princess Marie of Baden, he advised Susan to return to her husband and children.[23]

By this time, Susan, with her latest love affair dying, was ready to return to Lincoln, but only on her own terms. If she returned, she told her father, she would attempt only what in her opinion duty required.[24] On this basis she proposed to Lincoln on 30 November to join him and the children "at such time & place as your convenience & my weak state may suggest." It would be her fixed determination, she continued, "as I expect it to be yours to avoid entirely entering upon any conditions, faithfully abstaining from all reproaches, all recriminations, all references to the past and forgiving even as we hope to be forgiven."[25]

Lincoln was astonished and angered by her letter, his first from her in well over a month. He sent a draft of his reply to Peel, enclosing Susan's letter, which the prime minister found most unbecoming in tone and spirit. "I have not seen the decisive proofs of Lady Lincoln's actual criminality," Peel responded, "and therefore I write under the assumption that you unfortunately have these proofs, and that they are unequivocal and unquestionable. I think nothing short of this would justify the decided accusations of extreme criminality which your letter contains." Assuming that Lincoln had proof of Susan's sexual criminality, Peel advised his young friend and colleague to declare his "fixed resolution in most positive terms," but to avoid "the use of phrases of superfluous harshness" that would weaken the intrinsic form of his statement.[26]

Lincoln took Peel's advice and struck out such phrases as "course of falsehood" and "brazen hardihood" in his reply to Susan's overture. However, probably having no absolute proof of her adultery, Lincoln did not charge her explicitly with criminality; but he did condemn the "mean schemes and efforts of malignity" with which she had endeavored to destroy his character as a husband and excuse hers as a wife. He specifically denounced her for writing letters "which no married woman can pen without sin" and for making religion "a convenient cloak for a vicious course of life" that concealed its deformities even from herself. For the sake of the children, he stressed, he would never consent to the return of a mother who had habitually disregarded her duties as a wife.[27]

According to Madge Orde, Susan's first words after reading Lincoln's letter were "Thank God it is a refusal." Susan later confessed that she was terrified by the thought of returning to Lincoln.[28] Nonetheless, with her love affair at an end and the financial support from her parents withdrawn, Susan was ready to leave Anglesea Ville. She returned to her parents early in 1843 following Lord Douglas's marriage in Mannheim late in February. The Hamiltons continued to proclaim their daughter's innocence and Lincoln's responsibility for the failure of the marriage. In the company of the duchess during the season of 1843, Susan attended receptions, concerts, balls, and the opera in an effort to reinstate herself in society. In July, Lincoln received a letter from the Hamiltons' lawyer giving him notice of their intention to go to the Court of Chancery to obtain custody of the two youngest children and free access to the two eldest. Lincoln was sure that it was mere bluff. A few days later he observed to his father that Susan and her parents had attended a ball at Buckingham Palace and had also been to a party hosted by the duchess of Somerset in Susan's honor. "All of this however is doing them no good," he wrote,

> and I am sure I could not mistake the manner of some of our mutual female friends towards me at Buckingham Palace on Monday [at a second ball which Lincoln attended but to which Susan and the Hamiltons were not invited]. Everybody blessed with common sense must interpret rightly her separation from her Children and her going into Society under such circumstances strikes home to the heart of every Mother. I have heard no more about Law.[29]

Lincoln continued to pour out his feelings on his domestic situation to Gladstone, who was stunned by the view he received. Late in 1842 Lincoln dined with Gladstone and talked of his children and of his father's impending financial ruin. Later that evening Gladstone observed in his diary that Lincoln met these sad affairs "with a truly English heart." What "a speaking lesson" they were, however, "when the contrast with what once was or seemed to be is considered."[30]

III

In July 1843 Lincoln accompanied Prince Albert to Bristol for the launching of the *Great Britain*, an event witnessed by nearly two hundred thousand persons. This was only one of the many activities that kept him busy during the year, and the fact that he was both father and mother to his children added to his cares. Lincoln's sad domestic affairs seriously affected his work. Nonetheless, throughout the last part of 1843 he spent long hours on the Report of the Metropolitan Improvements Commission, over which he served as chairman.

With the opening of Parliament on 1 February 1844, Lincoln's official responsibilities increased. He was prepared to proceed with two major pieces of legislation, both of which reflected the growing concern over public health matters and the living conditions of the poor, particularly in London, and Lincoln's involvement in such matters as commissioner of woods and forests. The first was the metropolitan improvements bill, which provided for limited embarkment along the Thames in accordance with the recommendations of the Metropolitan Improvements Commission. The bill allowed the commissioners of woods and forests to borrow up to £250,000 from the Bank of England for embankment, street paving and widening, and related projects. The measure sailed through Parliament with little debate.

The second and far more controversial measure was the metropolitan buildings bill, on which Lincoln had labored for two years. This important measure established a standard width for streets, courts, and alleys; prescribed stringent regulations for new buildings, including houses; and required the construction of adequate drains for new houses and proper ventilation in crowded areas. District surveyors appointed by the home secretary were to supervise implementation of the new regulations. Opposition to the bill was quickly mustered by various nobles who owned urban land and by Edwin Chadwick, the author of the 1842 *Sanitary Report*, who believed the measure would deal inadequately with the terrible problems of overcrowding, poor drainage and sewerage facilities, and impure water supplies.[31] Nonetheless, debate on the bill moved rapidly and Lincoln received comfortable majorities at the divisions. The bill received royal assent on 9 August. Its passage marked the end of an exhausting but very successful session for Lincoln.

IV

Tired, ill, and embroiled in fresh difficulties with his father, Lincoln left London as soon as the parliamentary session was over early in September. But shortly before his departure, he received an unexpected letter from Susan concerning her son Arthur's recent illness. Susan implored her husband to let her come immediately to her child's bedside to watch over him.[32] Unable to write because of a severe attack of rheumatic gout, Lincoln had Dr. Gairdner inform Susan that Arthur had recovered and was quite well again. The next day Lincoln traveled to Ryde on the Isle of Wight. Susan addressed her next letter to him there: "I really believe I should have been on my road to the Isle of Wight if illness had not confined me to my room. Lincoln could I be of any use or comfort to you during yr. sufferings? If so bid me come and I shall be ready."[33] Lincoln was astounded by this startling overture. He still felt deeply the bitterness of being left solitary for more than two years. Although he doubted her sincerity, he felt compelled to write to her fully and explicitly. "I could not," he wrote,

> except in case of a *last* illness, consent to receive you under my roof without
> a frank atonement for the past, an ample guarantee for the future, and an
> unreserved willingness on your part to subscribe to all such conditions for
> the regulation of your future conduct as my often deceived forgiveness
> (without conditions) has proved to be indispensably necessary.[34]

Lincoln's strict conditions were acceptable to Susan, for, wasting no time, she arrived at Ryde the next day, throwing herself upon her husband's forgiveness and indulgence. Doubtlessly, Lincoln told his father, his wife's changed sentiment was attributable to the good advice of Douglas and his wife and to her parents' anxiousness to get rid of her. Still, he resolved to take her back. "I *hope* for the best. That is all I dare say. At any rate (even at the cost of fresh misery) I can never regret an act of generosity to my wife."[35]

Newcastle was stunned and revolted by his son's action. To accept back now "this bad woman of bad blood" whom Lincoln had "taken especial pains to proclaim infamous" among his relations, friends, and even acquaintances, he told Lincoln, must stamp him with being "the weakest and most inconsistent of human beings." Her character was gone, he continued, "or has been so publicly canvassed, and so unsparingly blamed that you must not hope, and you ought not to try to force her upon society and expect that others can blow hot and cold, and at once to permit her to regain her lost footing in society." He could never receive Susan again as Lincoln's wife, and he would not allow his daughters to have any communion with her.[36]

The thought that he might endanger his own character and standing in society by accepting Susan back had already crossed Lincoln's mind. Perhaps some of his friends would find him guilty of weakness, he told Peel, but "it is an infirmity of which I can never be ashamed though I may suffer from it."[37] Far from finding him weak, Lincoln's closest friends praised his decision as one that manifested strength and justice. Peel believed that he had acted wisely. Gladstone dined with the Lincolns in late October and was delighted to find them together and happy again. Lady Peel and Catherine Gladstone graciously welcomed Lady Lincoln back into their circle of friends. Sidney Herbert praised Lincoln for his action, but cautioned him to show great tenderness toward a person whose character was so unlike his own. Jonathan Thompson, Lincoln's former tutor, put the advice even more candidly. "Knowing your heart better than you do yourself," he wrote, "I depreciate your acting the stern philosopher, and the moralist, and my warmest prayer is that you will let Lady Lincoln feel that she is forgiven and that your happiness is still in her keeping."[38]

For a time it appeared that the reconciliation would last. There were no outward signs of marital trouble during the next two years. Susan was pleased to be accepted back into society and at court. Lincoln again turned assiduously to his parliamentary and official duties, which were greatly increased by his promotion to the cabinet in 1845. In December of the same year, Susan gave birth to her fifth child, Albert, for whom Prince Albert stood as godfather.

But Lincoln's reconciliation with his wife aggravated his already acerbic relationship with his father. At the time of this unexpected development in Lincoln's marital status in 1844, father and son were in bitter dispute over estate matters, with Lincoln accusing Newcastle of trying to disinherit him and his children to the extent that the law would allow. Greatly shocked by Lincoln's "insolent, abusive, and undutiful" manner,[39] Newcastle broke off all communication with his son. The great political and religious issues of 1845 completed their alienation.

V

The political and religious issues of 1845 also strained the relations between Sir Robert Peel and the rank and file of his party. Since 1841 the Conservative backbenchers in the Commons had grown increasingly dissatisfied with Peel's policies and methods of leadership, and those feelings were strengthened in 1844 by the government's factory and sugar bills. With the support of numerous Conservatives, Lord Ashley and Philip Miles carried amendments to those bills that Peel found unacceptable. Although the Commons, under Peel's threat of resignation, reversed those decisions and accepted the government's sugar tariff schedule and the twelve-hour day, many Conservative backbenchers found both the principles of the measures and Peel's uncompromising attitude on them distasteful. But their protest was largely lost on Peel, for rather than trim his measures to fit the mood of the dissidents in his party,

Sir Robert Peel, by John Linnell, 1838. Courtesy
of the National Portrait Gallery, London.

Peel decided in 1845 to introduce an Irish religious measure and a budget that
were sure to cut across the protectionist and anti–Catholic principles of the
Tory country gentlemen.[40]

    An explanation for this apparent political rashness is not difficult to find.
Peel and his ministerial colleagues were eager to take advantage of the vastly

improved social, economic, and political conditions on both sides of the Irish Sea to introduce extensive reform measures. Peel argued convincingly in cabinet that the improved conditions in England provided an excellent opportunity for an extension of the free-trade principles and practices that had been adopted with the 1842 budget. Consequently, early in 1845 he committed his government to a bold budget that included the renewal of the income tax for two years and a massive program of tariff reform. In Ireland, with the abatement of repeal agitation and agrarian disorders, Peel argued that the conditions were favorable for the introduction of a new program of reforms and liberal concessions, including measures to increase the state grant to Maynooth College, the Roman Catholic seminary, and to establish provincial colleges at Cork and Belfast. Once these decisions were made on the ministerial level, Peel saw no need to consult his followers in the Commons. Indeed, Peel held an authoritarian concept on the functions of party. He insisted upon the right of leaders to propose measures in the national interest and demanded party loyalty even when the measures conflicted with the social and political interests of many party followers.[41]

Not everyone in the cabinet agreed with the decision to introduce a bill to increase the Maynooth grant. Gladstone, because of past pledges, resigned from the cabinet he had entered in May 1843 as president of the Board of Trade. Faced with this and other vacancies early in 1845, Peel was forced to reshuffle offices. Lincoln and Sidney Herbert were promoted to the cabinet, with the former remaining at the Office of Woods and Forests and the latter succeeding Sir Thomas Fremantle as secretary at war. Fremantle took Lord Eliot's place as Irish secretary. Newcastle, who was adamantly opposed to the Maynooth grant, was vexed "to the soul" by Lincoln's acceptance of a seat in the cabinet. Lincoln, he ruefully wrote in his diary, "was too much like an office clerk," with "all the pedantry of a mere office drudge." The cabinet would consist of "submissive boys, pupils, & parasites of wiley Peel."[42]

Lincoln entered the cabinet at a politically perilous time. He was asked to stand with and to defend ministerial colleagues who had become weary from the drudgery of office and who resented, if not despised, the "blockheads" in the party who showed energy only when differing from their leaders. Moreover, his advocacy of the increased Maynooth grant meant complete political alienation from his father. Yet he took all these political dangers in stride and looked upon his new responsibilities as a matter of duty, undertaking them with a sense of pride and with the assurance that what he did was right. Far from retreating from a confrontation with his father, he was eager to carry the political fight to him. "I have so much to do and so much to prepare for our hard warfare after the recess that I cannot afford even two days of idleness," he wrote to his friend Thompson late in March. "Amongst other things I must look into the subjects of Maynooth and the Jews—upon both of which

I shall be inclined to speak after reading His Grace's [Newcastle's] idiotic letter in the Standard of this evening."[43]

The letter in the *Standard* was the first shot of Newcastle's new campaign to redeem the nation from political, social, and religious damnation. For years, he noted, he had watched helplessly as the political leaders had brought down the wrath of God upon the nation by destroying the Protestant pillars of society. He had long awaited the final plunge to revolutionary destruction, from which state he was destined to reclaim the nation. He regarded the crisis over the Maynooth proposal as a providential call to launch his national movement of redemption. In two addresses to the people of England, the first published in most of the major papers on 13 April and the second on 19 May, he implored his countrymen to organize opposition to the Maynooth bill and to join him in forming a new movement of political virtue against "the base and vile" practice of political expediency and parliamentary intrigue.[44] In this way the duke hoped to unite a broad group of people behind him in his endeavor to drive "'Bobby Peel & Co' out of business" and to restore Parliament to the principles he cherished. "This is almost an Utopian idea," he wrote with elation in his diary,

> but if we are fit for it, by God's help it may be accomplished. Weak &
> feeble in intellectual strength & wholly unversed as I am in matters of this
> kind, & extraordinary as it may be in every point of view, I cannot conceal
> from myself that if any one can be instrumental in accomplishing this end, I
> am probably the only man in the country in a position to bring it
> about. . . . Oh, that I had my Son with me & not against me in the fulfill-
> ment of all that maybe [sic] good, great, glorious, generous, elevated &
> christianlike.[45]

But Newcastle did not have his son with him. On 15 April, Lincoln, although suffering severely from rheumatic gout, delivered his speech on Maynooth to an attentive House, saying that he was firmly convinced of the propriety, excellence, and justice of the measure. It was a measure of high national policy that would contribute to the prosperity of Ireland and help secure the civil and ecclesiastical institutions of both countries. There was in Ireland, he continued, a priesthood placed in the midst of a poor and ignorant population. It was necessary for the government to educate the Irish Catholic priests in order to strike at the general conditions of ignorance and poverty. He did not despair of seeing the influence of the priesthood enlisted in the common cause of the United Empire. With tranquillity in Ireland, the time was right to confer the measure with grace. "And I pray to God it may be accepted by the people of Ireland in the spirit in which it is given," he stated. "But let me remind the House that if this measure is now rejected you will not be in the same position as if it never was proposed. We have held up this cup to the lips of the Roman Catholics in Ireland. I sincerely trust the House will not dash it from them."

Lincoln noted that although he had never given a more unhesitating vote in his twelve-year parliamentary career, it was, nonetheless, a painful one. He knew that the vast majority of his constituents were opposed to the proposal and that his father, whose first address to the people of England Lincoln had read only a few minutes before he rose to speak, would exploit this sentiment against him.[46] In a letter a few days later he told Thompson, "I have no doubt my speech completely seals the fate of my future prospects. Worksop and Newark were no doubt willed away on Thursday last if the document were not previously signed." Nevertheless, so strong were his convictions that the measure was just and wise that he would not have failed "to speak for the gain of the whole County of Nottingham."[47]

Indeed Lincoln's speech and vote on the Maynooth bill were for his father unforgivable transgressions. With unspeakable regret, the duke noted that Lincoln had thrown over every principle in which he had been educated.[48] Lincoln now was just as much the duke's bitter enemy as was Peel, and Newcastle was determined to do everything in his power to ruin them both.

Newcastle's position, however, was a difficult one. Although his addresses to the nation received considerable attention, his agitation failed to achieve the desired results, and the bill passed the Commons with comfortable majorities supplied by the official opposition. Newcastle was thus forced to play his last card in the House of Lords, where, though he gallantly fought the measure at every stage, he was unable to prevent its passage. Nevertheless, the House by his own admission had been unusually attentive to him; and, although he admitted that his speech on the third reading was a bad one, he believed that he had "rattled the ministers" with some "unpleasant blows."[49]

Although the duke's cause on this occasion was lost and the Maynooth grant was increased and made permanent, the controversy severely damaged Peel's government and badly split the Conservative party. The duke's "unpleasant blows," struck singularly and in a highly romantic, utopian fashion, contributed significantly to the damage. Newcastle helped to strengthen the ultra-Tory faction and to prepare them for the next great onslaught upon their fundamental principles. When that time came, as they knew it would, they were determined to make their opposition to Peel and his ministerial colleagues decidedly more fatal.

VI

Although he remained at the Office of Woods and Forests, Lincoln's appointment to the cabinet early in 1845 was a mark of Peel's confidence in him. Peel regarded highly Lincoln's abilities, and over the years the two men had

developed a warm friendship. Peel, a sensitive, reserved man with few inti-
mates, conversed easily with Lincoln, advising and consulting him frequently
on political as well as private matters. After Lincoln's estrangement from his
father, Peel almost took the place of a parent. He took great interest in his
young friend's political career and cared deeply about his personal problems.
By 1845, Lincoln occupied a prominent position among the leaders of the
party and was regarded as a strong candidate to succeed Peel as its leader.[50]

Lincoln's administrative skills were put to a severe test by the myriad tasks
and controversies he encountered in his department in 1845 and early 1846. A
frequent adversary he had to face in the House of Commons was Joseph
Hume, Radical member for Montrose. In March 1845, Hume charged that
Lincoln had used his position as first commissioner of woods and forests to
secure a highly favorable settlement for his father concerning the crown's
claims to part of Newcastle's Haford estate in Cardiganshire. In a candid and
thorough statement, Lincoln denied the imputation of official corruption and
influence. In fact, he professed to have treated his father more harshly than
would have been the usual case by forcing him to pay a higher rate of interest
on the amount he owed the crown from the 1832 settlement.[51] The next day
Hume told the House that as "long as his experience had been in Parliament,
he had never heard an explanation more satisfactory, or more exculpatory than
that of the noble Lord." Hume was satisfied that Lincoln had exonerated himself from any suspicion with "his candid and manly explanation."[52]

Hume was also disturbed by the proposal to extend and improve Buckingham Palace. Lincoln had concluded that the rapidly increasing royal family
made the expansion of the palace necessary. Consequently, he had approved a
plan at an estimated cost of £99,500 for alterations and additions to the palace
that included the removal of the Marble Arch, which then stood in front of
the palace. The government agreed to the sale of Brighton Pavilion for
£60,000 to pay part of the cost; and despite Hume's opposition, the balance
was obtained from Parliament during the 1846 session.[53]

In 1845 the duke of Wellington figured significantly in a matter that confronted Lincoln in his capacity as commissioner of woods and forests. In this
instance the duke blocked a major proposal of the Metropolitan Improvements Commission. The publication of the commission's second report,
which Lincoln drafted, was delayed by the opposition of the duke and Sir
Edward Paget, governor of Chelsea Hospital, to the commission's recommendations to open some of the hospital grounds to the public and to build
a road through the grounds to the Thames. These recommendations formed
part of a larger proposal for the embankment of the Thames between Vauxhall
and Battersea bridges and the construction of Battersea Park. The duke found
the proposal most objectionable; and in the interests of the comfort, convenience, and happiness of the pensioners, he urged Lincoln to drop it. Lincoln

and the commissioners bowed to the duke's will. The rest of the commission's recommendations, however, were adopted.[54]

The embankment projects formed only one part of the government's growing concern over public welfare. In 1845 Lincoln introduced two other measures related to this area of legislation. The first, the coal trade (Port of London) bill, which passed the Commons in July, increased the tax on coal to improve poor, densely populated districts in the metropolis. The other measure, the health of towns bill, was founded on the evidence taken by the 1843 Commission on the Health of Towns. This measure, which Lincoln had drafted, provided for the improvement of the sewerage, drainage, and water supplies of large towns through the employment of surveyors, inspectors, and medical officers working with local boards under the jurisdiction of the home secretary.[55] Even though the bill was substantially more far-reaching than earlier proposals, Edwin Chadwick, the most advanced and dedicated sanitary reformer of the day, was greatly dissatisfied with it. He became even more unhappy when he discovered that Lincoln had introduced the bill with the intention of postponing it until the next session to allow time during the recess for members of Parliament to deliberate on the matter among themselves.[56]

Lincoln's bill was reintroduced in 1846 unchanged, but it was soon brushed aside by the Corn Law crisis, withdrawn in April, and bequeathed to the new Whig government later in the year. Chadwick found the Whigs and Lord Morpeth, Lincoln's successor at the Office of Woods and Forests, more amenable; yet his struggle continued until 1848, when Parliament finally passed the Public Health Act. Although far from perfect in Chadwick's eyes, the act was more to his liking than Lincoln's measure had been. Nonetheless, there were still traces of Lincoln's handiwork in the act.

The zeal with which Lincoln pursued departmental business was clearly evident in the legislation he introduced in 1845. The administrative characteristics that would distinguish his official career were already well established by this time. He was a vigorous and demanding administrator who frequently became involved in the smallest details of official business. He refused to delegate authority or to be a mere "head" or "cipher" under whom strong subordinates conducted the business of the office. He was often intolerant of those who disagreed with him over policy or who seemingly challenged his authority. As a result, at times he was unable to work well with subordinates or other officials. A good example of this occurred in 1845 when Lincoln clashed with his subordinates over the British Geological Survey and the Northern Receivership of Crown Rents.

Lincoln became embroiled in controversy with the junior commissioners of woods, Alexander Milne and Charles Gore, and with the Treasury over both matters. The dispute centered on the organization of the Commission of Woods and Forests, particularly with regard to the authority of the first commissioner. In a letter to Peel of 9 June 1845, Lincoln complained of the junior commissioners' systematic attack upon his authority. The long-standing struggle was, he explained to Peel, a move on the part of his colleagues to gain paramount power within the commission. To resolve the dispute and to prevent the recurrence of similar problems, he stressed, it was absolutely necessary to change the constitution of the commission so as to give supreme authority to the chief commissioner over all financial and administrative affairs of the office.[57]

While the Treasury pondered the questions raised in the dispute between Lincoln and the junior commissioners over authority in the Office of Woods and Forests, much of the business related to these two matters was brought to a standstill. Lincoln loaned money from private funds to authorities to conduct some of the business of the Geological Survey, but the business of the crown tenants in the north remained untended during the additional three months it took the Treasury to reach a decision. On 28 August Lincoln wrote a scathing letter to Henry Goulburn, chancellor of the Exchequer, in which he angrily complained of the Treasury's unwillingness to take quick, decisive action. The Treasury, he believed, wanted to find an easy way out of the dilemma without directly addressing the issue of ultimate authority in the office. "If the matter is to be settled at all," he warned, "the two junior commissioners must knock under. I consent to nothing else. If they hold out, then either they or I must go. The Government must decide which."[58]

The tone of Lincoln's letter angered Goulburn, who complained to Peel of being "bullied" by a colleague. Peel shared Goulburn's feelings concerning the letter and regretted that Lincoln had failed to resolve the dispute through unofficial correspondence with the junior commissioners.[59] As the dispute continued, however, Peel became increasingly exasperated with the legalistic attitude of Milne and Gore, who refused to take responsibility for the conduct of business over which they had no direct control. "I cannot conceive public servants quarrelling about such matters as who is to sign official papers about the necessity for which there is no manner of doubt," Peel wrote with considerable disgust to Goulburn. The affair had gotten completely out of hand, and Peel agreed with Goulburn that the matters in dispute between Lincoln and the junior commissioners would have to be brought officially before the Treasury.[60]

In a minute dated 16 September 1846, the Treasury announced a decision on the two matters. The lords of the Treasury agreed with Lincoln's plan for the union of the Yorkshire and Northern receiverships and endorsed his right to appoint the receiver to the newly formed district. Lincoln's choice for the position was his old friend and former tutor, Jonathan Thompson, whom he had appointed to the Yorkshire district in 1844. With regard to the Geological Survey, although they found no legal obligation for the junior commissioners to sign the drafts of money to be applied to that service, the lords urged Milne and Gore to reconsider their position for the good of the public service.[61]

The junior commissioners accepted the Treasury's decision on the Northern Receivership but persisted in their opposition to the survey arrangement. Consequently, in November the Treasury authorized Lincoln as chief commissioner to conduct all official business related to the survey in Great Britain and Ireland and the geological museums in London and Dublin, and transferred all credits for the business to a separate account in his name at the Bank of England.[62]

Although the Treasury decisions essentially upheld Lincoln's authority, they failed to reorganize thoroughly the Commission of Woods and Forests as Lincoln had strongly recommended. Lincoln was furious with the Treasury's timidity. He argued that even though his authority had been upheld, the fundamental reasons for the disputes remained.[63] By the time of the Treasury decisions, however, there were weightier problems for Lincoln and the Treasury officials than the organization of the Office of Woods. In November the very life of the government hung in the balance.

4. Corn Laws and Ireland

The ministers faced a grave crisis in the autumn of 1845 as a result of the potato failure in Ireland. They received the news of the disaster from Peel during a meeting of the cabinet at his house at Whitehall Gardens on 31 October. The following day they reassembled to hear Peel read a long memorandum in which he reviewed the evidence of pending food deficiency in Ireland and parts of England and Scotland and stressed the need to provide substantial public assistance to the people of those areas. But he noted that the provision of public funds would raise the wider question of the Corn Laws. Could they, he asked, vote public money for the sustenance of needy people and still maintain the existing restrictions on the free importation of grain? He thought not; therefore he advised the suspension of the duties on corn either by order in council or by legislative action.[1]

The discussion that followed in the cabinet brought no agreement among the ministers either on the course of action to be pursued or even on whether it was necessary to undertake extraordinary measures. Only Sir James Graham agreed with Peel on the necessity of proposing a repeal of the Corn Laws. Lord Stanley, on the other hand, argued strongly that such a course was both disastrous and unjustifiable. Upon this note of discord, the ministers postponed further discussion until the next scheduled cabinet meeting on 6 November.[2]

On the eve of the November cabinet meeting, Lincoln, conscious of his own increasingly difficult electoral problems, wrote a long and frank letter to Peel. He proposed an alternative to Peel's plan for immediate suspension, which, he noted, the cabinet regarded as tantamount to repeal. To avoid the politically intolerable consequences that would accompany the immediate and total repeal of the Corn Laws, Lincoln advised Peel to leave the laws intact during the 1846 session, except for the admittance of American Indian corn and possibly Australian wheat, and to announce immediately before dissolution in 1847 his intention of carrying in the new Parliament either a modification of the Corn Laws with a view toward gradual abolition or a total repeal coupled with any measure of relief that might be necessary to lighten the burden upon those who would be most affected. "I think this would be a manly and honorable course," he added. "I cannot see that it would be otherwise than statesmanlike." To fight the general election on that issue would cost some of them their seats, particularly those representing counties, and would probably result in the defeat of the government. Nonetheless, the price would be worth it, for, Lincoln noted,

> we would have done our duty to the Queen; we should have given the
> country the fullest and fairest opportunity of weighing well our measures
> and reasons for them . . .; we should be under no just imputation of betray-
> ing party attachments; we should preserve our honor as public men; and
> we should not have the reproach cast upon us by posterity that in our hands
> the cause of Constitutional Government had received a heavy—perhaps
> even a deadly—blow.[3]

Thus Lincoln, with the greatest diffidence, laid his views on the issue before Peel. Peel responded cordially, saying that he knew the letter conveyed the frank opinions of "a very intelligent and honourable mind" and that the letter expressed independently the sentiments shared by some of his own cabinet and many more in the party.[4] For these reasons, he carefully considered the main suggestions proffered by his young colleague.

Peel agreed with Lincoln that it was the ministers' duty to take full respon-sibility for proposing measures to the queen that exigencies required. But he disagreed with him on all the other points in the letter. Lincoln's plan, he argued, offered no solution to the immediate problem of pending scarcity. Furthermore, the ministers could not defend the Corn Laws in public after condemning them in private merely for the sake of preserving personal con-sistency. He was strongly convinced that true party interests would not be promoted, nor the honor of public men maintained, nor the cause of consti-tutional government served, if ministers shrank from their duty to the nation in order to avoid the personal sacrifices and the party strife entailed by the fulfillment of that duty. In the matter of public interests, he added, only time could repair "the temporary evil of unjust suspicion and unjust reproach cast upon the motives and conduct of public men."[5]

Peel's idealistic notion of a minister's duty to the crown and nation and his political perspective were of little comfort to a man who faced the realistic problems of the contemporary political arena, and at the cabinet meeting of 6 November, Lincoln expressed his dissent from Peel's plan for an immediate opening of the ports and a modification of the Corn Laws. Only Aberdeen, Graham, and Sidney Herbert supported the prime minister. A final decision was postponed until the end of the month. On 26 November, Peel again stressed the absolute need to suspend the Corn Laws as early as possible, either by order in council or by parliamentary action. But the cabinet remained divided. Neither Lord John Russell's *Edinburgh Letter*, published on 22 Novem-ber, in which he scored the ministers for inaction and chartered his own course in favor of total repeal of the Corn Laws, nor the Playfair Commission's final report, which apprised the ministry that at least one-half the potato crop in Ireland was either destroyed or unfit for human consumption, brought the ministers into agreement on the matter. Therefore, the debate in cabinet continued into early December.

By this time, Lincoln had modified his views to the extent that he now agreed with Peel as to the obligation imposed upon them by public duty to suspend the laws immediately. On 3 December he informed the prime minister that he would not "row in the same boat with those of the cabinet" who opposed Peel.[6] Lincoln explained his change of mind while dining at his house with Gladstone a few evenings later. He told Gladstone that the 1842 law was not working well. Even though a great deficiency was anticipated, little or no foreign corn was entering for consumption as a result of the artificially high price produced by the law. Those who defended the Corn Law were put in a false position, and the interests of the aristocracy were seriously compromised by it. The great question now was how best to get rid of the law.[7]

As it became clear during the next few days that the crisis in Ireland was catastrophic, Lincoln's support of Peel became complete. From no other colleague throughout the contest over the Corn Laws, Peel noted, did he receive "a more decided and unvarying support, or more signal proofs of his willingness to incur any obloquy, and submit to any sacrifice to which the giving of that support might expose him."[8] The crisis over the Corn Laws strengthened Lincoln's devotion to Peel and separated him irrevocably from many of his earlier political positions.

But Peel's hopes of receiving the support of a united cabinet on a proposal to repeal the Corn Laws ultimately were dashed when Lord Stanley and the duke of Buccleuch chose to retire from office rather than accept the prime minister's plan. Peel promptly resigned, and on 10 December the cabinet went to Osborne for a final council. The queen asked Lord John Russell to form a government; but after ten days of negotiation and intense suspense, Russell declined the commission. Later the same day Peel withdrew his resignation and accepted office once again. That evening he told the reassembled cabinet that he was determined to meet Parliament with proposals necessary to resolve the crisis in Ireland.

II

On the afternoon preceding the cabinet meeting of 20 December, Lincoln advised Gladstone that Stanley would resign and that Peel would ask Gladstone to rejoin the cabinet from which he had resigned the previous year over the Maynooth bill. In advising him of the matter, Lincoln hoped to pave the way for Gladstone's acceptance of the repeal measure. Gladstone was still convinced that the Conservatives could not repeal the Corn Laws unless conditions in Ireland justified it. Lincoln generally agreed, but begged Gladstone to keep an open mind and to trust that Peel could justify repeal on the basis of the facts relating to the potato disease. He detailed to Gladstone all the circumstances connected with the cabinet crisis and stressed that Peel would seek parliamentary approval of a comprehensive plan for the repeal of the Corn Laws rather than suspend them by order in council. Lincoln called on Gladstone again the following afternoon to make an appointment with him for Peel. At Lincoln's house two hours later, Peel offered Stanley's old post at the Colonial Office to Gladstone and showed him the correspondence on the Irish famine. Another interview between the two men the next afternoon settled the matter; Gladstone accepted office and a seat in the cabinet.[9]

By accepting office in Peel's reconstituted administration, Gladstone brought down the duke of Newcastle's wrath upon himself, and now both he and Lincoln faced the duke's hostility in the field. Newcastle immediately brought forth a candidate against him at Newark, the seat he vacated by accepting office, and Gladstone declined to seek reelection even though the majority of the Conservative Committee favored his return. Lincoln later suggested to Gladstone that he stand for the northern division of Nottinghamshire; but Gladstone, after consulting both Peel and Graham, concluded that it would not be wise. Except for Newark, Gladstone explained to Lincoln, he was a total stranger in the county. What little connection he had there he owed to the duke of Newcastle, although he would never forget that he owed exclusively to Lincoln whatever countenances he had had from the duke. Furthermore, he said, "it is not for one of my political opinions, without an extreme necessity, to stand upon the basis of democratic or popular feeling against the local proprietary: for you who are planted in the soil the case is very different."[10]

It was indeed by virtue of "being planted in the soil" that Lincoln hoped to stand successfully on popular sentiment against his father's interest in South Nottinghamshire, the seat Lincoln had vacated when he accepted the office of chief secretary for Ireland early in 1846. Lincoln knew that by accepting the office he would rekindle the flames of the Maynooth controversy and make himself the major spokesman for measures in Parliament that were repugnant to his father and to many of his constituents. For these reasons he had been reluctant to accept the post, but his sense of duty and his conviction that it was the right course induced him to take on the new responsibilities in spite of his private considerations.[11] Furthermore, there seemed to be little chance for him to salvage anything from his family situation, for by the autumn of 1845 his estrangement from his father had become bitter. Public evidence of the estrangement occurred when the two met without recognizing one another during the quarter sessions and the annual meeting of the county magistracy, over both of which Lincoln presided in October. The news of this incident reached Thompson, the trusted friend to both father and son, who immediately rebuked the duke sharply:

> I feel a sorrow which I cannot express. The world thinks of you, My Lord Duke, as a kind parent, a good Christian, and a high minded patriot; it knows nothing of Lord Lincoln inconsistent with the same high character; it is a scandal therefore to see you at variance, and it greatly derogates from the influence of your high example, that this variance should continue and be the subject of conversation. There are differences I own in Lord Lincoln's political views and your own, but there are still a thousand points in which you may act together for the general good, and knowing Lord Lincoln's motives as I do, I cannot conceive a course of action more highly to your honor and credit than his. I appeal to your Grace's sympathies in his favour. Is he not the second Mr. Pelham of your family? Is it possible to produce an instance in which his honor, his high mindedness, or his morality has been found wanting?[12]

But Thompson's words fell on a closed mind. There was no chance for reconciliation, for Lincoln's support of the repeal of the Corn Laws was the final straw for the duke, who was more determined than ever to drive his son from the South Nottinghamshire seat. Lincoln was just as determined to retain it.

Encouraged by Peel, Lincoln decided to make the 1846 by-election in the southern division a trial of strength between protectionists and Peelites in Nottinghamshire. Although the risks were great, Peel calculated that a victory for Lincoln would vindicate the popularity of the ministers' free-trade policy and would be "a most useful lesson to certain peers" who long had been an obstacle to the constitutional freedom of elections.[13] But the prime minister overestimated Lincoln's influence and popularity in South Nottinghamshire, and neither he nor Lincoln was prepared for Newcastle's extreme efforts to defeat his son and deal Peelism a severe blow in the county. Outraged by Lincoln's temerity in forcing the contest, the duke outdid himself in the electioneering tactics he adopted. He wrote a letter to the electors of South Nottinghamshire appealing to them to maintain their protectionist phalanx against the Peelite emissary who was attempting to seduce them into accepting a "vicious and revolutionary system."[14] He spent money lavishly in support of Thomas B. T. Hildyard, a young local gentleman who had come forward as the protectionist candidate, and played a significant part in the activities of the Nottinghamshire Agricultural Protection Association. There was no doubt that the duke would go to almost any length to throw Lincoln out of his county seat.[15]

In this election, personal and national considerations were neatly blended in a contest that gained considerable attention around the country. Newcastle was determined not only to punish Lincoln for his political and filial transgres-

sion, but also to inflict another wound on Peel and to strengthen the protectionist cause, especially in Nottinghamshire. On the other hand, Lincoln was
determined to break his father's influence in the county and to lead the free-
trade vanguard, gaining in the process greater recognition for himself as a
national leader. The bitter contest revealed to the nation how rigidly both
father and son held to political principles and to a sense of public duty, each
convinced of the necessity of putting public duty above private concern and
neither capable of seeing the matter from any point of view other than his
own. Only extreme rancor could result from such a collision of inflexible
wills.

Lincoln stole a march on his father by beginning his canvass of the constituency first and by retaining all the solicitors in the county, tactics that further
enraged Newcastle.[16] Lincoln's electoral address, which he had carefully considered with Peel, came to be regarded as a ministerial manifesto. "In 1841,"
he began the address, "honestly, and not from any party motives, I advocated
measures for what is now called 'Protection of Native Industry.'" But, he said,
the experience of the past few years had convinced him not only that the Corn
Laws should be abolished, but also that the whole commercial system should
be subjected to a bold and comprehensive revision. Although he had hoped
that the repeal of the Corn Laws could be postponed until after the next
dissolution of Parliament, the famine in Ireland compelled the government to
bring forward at once a final settlement of the question. An act of Providence,
he continued, had frustrated the desires of politicians and thwarted the calcu-
lations of statesmen. "What would have been praiseworthy caution and deference to existing circumstances in times of abundance and prosperity," he
stressed, "would now be culpable neglect, or a slavish submission to the fear
of reproach and personal odium."[17]

Many of Lincoln's constituents found this address and his answer to the
Nottinghamshire Protection Association's petition requesting his resignation
to be unnecessarily offensive in tone. But Lincoln's honor was at stake. "Oh
how amply revenged will I and my 'honor' be if I can return to the House
M.P. for South Notts," he told Thompson.[18] The contempt with which Lincoln regarded the protectionists for years to come originated in part with the
emotions of this election. A man of less strict principle and more pragmatic
political vision would have fled the scene; but Lincoln was too honor bound,
too firmly convinced of his public duty, and too proud to accept defeat before
the battle was joined. By far the strongest trait in his personality, one that
matched his father's, was his unswerving determination to strive for his version of truth and righteousness, regardless of the consequences. "Consistency," he told the crowd in Newark on nomination day, "is only of value
when we are consistent in what we believe to be right, and consistency in
what we believe to be wrong is nothing more than moral cowardice."[19]

But it was with hope rather than despair that he entered the contest. "He still writes in good heart, which is a great thing," the queen told Peel after reading one of Lincoln's letters on his canvass.[20] Lincoln informed Peel daily on the progress of his canvass, which seemed to improve as the days passed. On 11 February 1846 he wrote, "I find my exertions gradually telling, and my long popularity is to some extent returning and shaking the determination of those who had resolved to oppose me. . . . Nothing can be said at present, but I think my prospects improve." And a week later he observed, "My personal exertions have done more than I could have ventured to hope, but time is wanting, and it has been the most desperate and uphill contest that you can conceive."[21] He found the farmers and many of his oldest and staunchest friends among the yeomanry keenly against him. The duke of Rutland and Lords Brownlow and Manvers also opposed him; of the peers, only Lord Howe was a strong supporter. The Conservative opposition was offset somewhat, however, by the Whigs and Radicals who worked actively but discreetly for him.[22]

Lincoln's electioneering agents redoubled their efforts to reduce the protectionist majority after Newcastle's appeal to the electorate was published in the *Nottingham Journal*, but it became a last-minute effort to persuade the farmers not to vote at all rather than to convert them into supporters. By nomination day, the strain of the canvass and the anxieties of prolonging the contest after his father's public appeal had taken their toll on Lincoln. He looked pale and unwell as he addressed the crowd at Newark.[23] Physically and mentally exhausted from the ordeal, he waited with mortification for polling day.

Lincoln's personal mortification deepened on election day as the majority against him steadily increased. The news of Hildyard's victory excited a crowd of farmers at Newark, who vented their enthusiasm in uproarious cheering. They were delighted to have defeated the most powerful free-trade candidate that could have been brought into the field against them and to have delivered a well-aimed blow against Peel and his measures.[24] Lincoln had relied too heavily upon personal support from his old constituents in the division and had sadly miscalculated his father's strength, particularly with regard to the duke's tenants. At the close of the election Lincoln had polled 1,049 to Hildyard's 1,736. It was an important setback for Peel, showing how Newcastle and a few other members of the protectionist minority could prevent the prime minister from translating widespread national support for his policies into parliamentary power.[25]

Newcastle regarded the matter in a different light. To him the victory in the South Nottinghamshire election precipitated the rebirth of the "Country party." As early as the opening of Parliament in January 1846, the duke, no longer the knight errant fighting Peel alone, had supported the party. But until after the South Nottinghamshire by-election, little progress had been

South Nottinghamshire Election, 1846. *Illustrated London News*, 28 February 1846.

made in regrouping the old Tory dissidents. "My labours to form a party," the duke complained on 22 February, "are not succeeding." A few days later, however, he rejoiced that the party at last was formed. He predicted that it would become the strongest party since the time of Pitt and would defeat Peel's attempt to repeal the Corn Laws.[26]

III

Lincoln parted from his former constituents with mixed feelings of remorse and bitterness. Before setting out for London to confer with Peel and Graham on Irish matters, he addressed the family tenants. In his speech he noted that he had been defeated but not disgraced in the election. "I know," he stated, "the time is approaching when your feelings will be changed, irritation of moment over, and then you will look back upon the days of our friendly connection with regret and upon this . . . separation with remorse. You will then think me your *true* friend."[27] Once in London he immediately began to look for a new seat. "Here I am, returned to town, seatless," he wrote to Francis Bonham. "Can you find me—even a three-legged stool—to rest my wearied limbs upon for a month or two?"[28] But no opening was then available, and late in March Lincoln left for Ireland as Irish secretary without a seat in Parliament.

Nevertheless Bonham remained busy trying to find constituencies for the defeated Peelite ministers, for it was a great inconvenience to Peel to have Lincoln and Gladstone absent from the Commons while the government proceeded with legislation for the repeal of the Corn Laws. In April he made arrangements with James Baird, the sitting member for the Falkirk Burghs, to vacate the seat in Lincoln's favor. The arrangement, achieved with the help of the duke of Hamilton, Lincoln's father-in-law, contradicted an earlier one whereby John Wilson of Dundyvan, a local gentleman, would stand for the Burghs as a free-trade candidate upon Baird's retirement. Many of the voters in the constituency were greatly nettled over the private bargain struck between Baird and Lincoln at the expense of Wilson; and on 23 April the free-trade electors of the Burghs passed a resolution drafted by the duke of Hamilton requesting Lincoln to sign a written pledge that in return for their present support he would agree not to stand as a candidate for that constituency at the next general election. The terms of the resolution were made by the duke of Hamilton without Lincoln's knowledge, and Lincoln quickly refused to sign the pledge on the ground that it was unconstitutional to bind a constituency in any way. Wilson came forward as a candidate as soon as Lincoln repudiated the resolution, and the free-trade voters vowed to work diligently for him. The protectionists, on the other hand, who were without a candidate, agreed to support Lincoln, whom they discerned to be far less radical than Wilson. Under these unusual circumstances, the contest created more excitement and anxiety in the constituency than any had for many years.[29]

Lincoln arrived at Falkirk on 25 April 1846 to begin his canvass. He was received on the hustings for the nomination with considerable coldness. The Liberal interest was clearly divided, but with an energetic canvass and a conciliatory demeanor on the hustings he was able to win over enough of them to make the difference. He scraped through with a majority of eleven. There was no doubt that his position as an important minister in a government engaged in commercial reform was the major factor that induced many free traders to vote for him when their general political sentiments accorded more closely with Wilson's. There also was no doubt that the duke of Hamilton's influence at Hamilton and Lanark produced comfortable margins for Lincoln in the only two burghs he won in the district.[30] Commenting on Lincoln's victory in guarded terms, the *Glasgow Citizen* noted:

> The Ministerial defeat of South Nottinghamshire has thus been repaired by
> the spontaneous act of an independent Scottish constituency. . . . Let us
> . . . hope that the present election will prove instrumental in strengthening
> the liberal bias of a nobleman of high rank, talent, and influence, and thus

securing his future services and his future example on the side of truth and the people.[31]

Partially vindicated, Lincoln returned to Parliament just in time to take part in the resolution of the greatest commercial question of the time.

IV

The office of chief secretary for Ireland had long been considered a difficult and laborious office that could make or break the careers of young politicians. The chief secretary was the principal administrator under the lord lieutenant, who controlled the armed forces and administered the offices and boards that made up the civil services of that country. The chief secretary wielded the authority that the lord lieutenant delegated to him and served as the sole channel for the flow of executive power and patronage. But these were only part of the responsibilities of the chief secretary, for which he was expected to reside in Dublin at least half the time. The rest of the time, he was expected to attend Parliament in Westminster as the representative of the Irish government and as the expounder and defender in the House of Commons of the cabinet's Irish policy.

With these parliamentary duties, the Falkirk election had become even more critical to the government as the Irish crisis deepened, and Lincoln's return to Parliament was a great boon to the ministry. The ministers needed the expert knowledge of the conditions in Ireland that he had obtained during his trip there in March and early April. Immediately upon his return to the House of Commons, he was asked to refute protectionist charges that the government had exaggerated the distress in Ireland. Lincoln was quick to confirm the government's position. Not only did he describe the deplorable famine conditions, especially in the south and west, but he also defended the government's relief measures.[32] Those measures had already embroiled him in controversy with the doctrinaire opponents of large-scale state assistance to the Irish people.

The main aspects of Peelite famine relief had been established even before the December 1845 ministerial crisis. Once the early reports of pending disaster in Ireland were confirmed, Peel and Sir James Graham concluded that relief to meet this new crisis would have to be conducted on a larger scale than had ever before been attempted. Both men realized that the task before them would "require all the united energies of the Government and the well regulated use of all the means and appliances at their disposal." Peel immediately ordered the purchase of £100,000 worth of Indian corn from the United States and set an enormous program of public works in motion.[33]

From the beginning of the government's intervention in the crisis, critics believed that Peel's plans were too costly and too large. They wanted the government to use the existing Irish Poor Law, but Peel decided to erect a temporary system of relief parallel with, but distinct from, the Poor Law. In November he appointed the Relief Commission to work with Lord Heytesbury, the lord lieutenant, as a central authority to coordinate the work of this auxiliary scheme. The duties of the commission fell under two main headings: to ascertain the extent of the approaching famine and to assist in devising and executing measures for the employment and relief of the people. Graham's initial instructions to the commission were broad and flexible, giving the commissioners ample latitude to solve the problems at hand. He believed, however, that the commissioners must endeavor to obtain the cooperation and financial assistance of local landowners, to demand adequate security for the repayment of all state loans advanced to individuals or companies for improvements of a private nature, and to sell food from the government depots only to those who had received wages from the public works projects and only when prices rose unreasonably. "Yet," Graham told the lord lieutenant, "in the last extremity of want, especially where it arises from a dispensation of Providence, these rules must necessarily be relaxed."[34]

Although based on precedent and fortified by strict Treasury rules, Graham's instructions largely ignored the experience of 1838, which proved that local Irish landowners or their agents had been unable or unwilling to make contributions and to offer any sufficient security for the repayment of proposed loans. Reminded of these past difficulties, Graham still insisted that the commission obtain local contributions, if possible, as securities for grants and loans from the public purse. He added, however, that "if the distress became general and severe, public money must be advanced by the Treasury with little or no hope of repayment."[35] It was the commission's inability to obtain private subscriptions and securities to the extent deemed necessary by the Treasury, the steadily worsening famine conditions in Ireland, and the innumerable other difficulties that arose in the administration of relief that later forced Graham to redeem his statement; and it was Lord Lincoln who was sent to Ireland as the redeemer of that pledge.

While Lincoln was seeking reelection in February after his appointment as chief secretary, Graham carried four Irish bills through the Commons that extended the public employment schemes. These measures enabled presentment sessions of five or more persons of respectability in any barony to send proposals for local works to the lord lieutenant; provided the means for private contractors to execute specified works of road repairing, leveling, and sewerage; and facilitated the development of harbors, the erection of piers, and the extension of drainage projects. The Presentment Sessions Act, the most important of the four measures, was financed by a combination of one-half grant and one-half loan, which was repayable by the local landowners over a number of years. The lord lieutenant, the Relief Commission, and the Board of Works in Ireland had to approve the proposals for these works before they were forwarded to the Treasury for final approval. Graham also appointed Sir Randolph Routh, commissary general in Ireland, as head of an executive committee to expedite the business of the Relief Commission.

The passage of the new legislation and the appointment of Routh brought the administration of Irish famine relief more directly under the control of the British Treasury, for both the Irish Board of Works and the Commissariat were subordinate to that department. The Treasury was therefore put in a commanding position not only to control expenditure, its ordinary function, but also to supervise Irish relief. This dual role gave Charles Edward Trevelyan, assistant secretary and permanent head of the Treasury, an excellent opportunity to promote his own fiscal and administrative principles and policies rather than those of the ministers. The result was a conflict between the Treasury and the executive government that prevented the smooth and complete execution of the ministers' measures for the relief of Ireland during the last months of Peel's administration.[36]

Trevelyan, an energetic though officious civil servant, a man with a powerful intellect but rigid opinions, was the most forceful assistant secretary to serve the Treasury during the nineteenth century. He derived his principles from Adam Smith's *Wealth of Nations* and, more specifically in regard to the Irish famine itself, from Edmund Burke's *Thoughts and Details on Scarcity*. He believed that the intervention of the state to avert starvation in Ireland would discourage commercial enterprise, demoralize the Irish people, and spread the "moral disease" of dependency upon the government. The famine, he believed, was God's way of teaching an "indolent and unselfreliant people" a lesson. The death of thousands from starvation was a smaller evil than bankruptcy and would serve as "a discipline" to bring about a social regeneration in Ireland.[37] Such a regeneration, he believed, could not be achieved by the state through a system of grants and loans, an opinion he expressed to Henry Labouchere in September 1846: "For the government to undertake by its own direct agency the detailed drainage and improvement of the whole country, is a task for which the nature and functions of government are totally unsuited."[38]

Trevelyan's opposition to the use of the state to help reconstruct Irish society brought him into sharp conflict with the Peelite administration. Although Peel's Irish program of reconciliation used the state only sparingly for ultimate improvements in such areas as agriculture, education, and tenant-landlord relations, Trevelyan was convinced that much of this program interfered with private commercial matters. He therefore believed that the government's general plan for the relief of the Irish people contained a flaw that would stymie the efforts of private enterprise and damage chronically the true interests of Ireland. The Public Works Acts, he observed, were designed to encourage rather than discourage dependency upon the government. In the guise of providing work for the suffering poor, the landed proprietors were invited, at half the cost to the government, to begin works that would benefit them personally and also relieve them of their moral responsibility to bear the burden of the distress.[39]

Although Trevelyan recognized the lord lieutenant as the chief authority in Ireland, he was not deterred from issuing orders, usually in semiofficial or private letters, to Routh and to Colonel Harry Jones, chairman of the Irish Board of Works, that were frequently contrary to the intentions of the Peelite administration. Indeed, from early March, when the Presentment Sessions and Public Works Acts of 1846 became law, until they were replaced by the Labour Rate Act in August, Trevelyan did his best to circumscribe those acts.[40] He argued against adopting public employment schemes that encouraged the execution of productive works. Although he admitted to Routh and Jones that his views were overruled, he still insisted that they maintain "effectual securities" that would enable them to distinguish between projects that were absolutely required to relieve the people suffering because of the poor potato crop and those that were designed "principally or entirely for the benefit of the proprietors." To effect the test, he issued orders to Routh and Jones to require landed proprietors and others interested in or benefited by proposed improvements made under the Public Works Acts to contribute a sum equivalent to one-quarter of the total cost of the projects as a prerequisite for Treasury sanction.[41]

The responsibility for determining the degree to which particular proprietors were benefited by proposed works fell to the Board of Works, whose meager staff of engineers was not equal to the new duties imposed upon it. Applications for assistance flooded the board, and the new rule meant further delay in processing those applications. Thus Trevelyan's rule seriously obstructed the Peelite program of famine relief. It was not surprising, therefore, that very little had been done in the way of public works by late March when Lincoln took up the duties of his new office in Ireland.

Lincoln found little cooperation and confidence among the administrators of the government's relief measures. The source of this unsatisfactory state, he told Graham, was the "secret and underhand instructions to individuals in this country from subordinate authorities in London."[42] The ministers were aware of the "double correspondence" from London and were convinced that the Treasury rule pertaining to contributions must either be modified or revoked before there could be a smooth and rapid execution of their relief plans. With this in mind, Peel and Graham assigned Lincoln the arduous task of negotiating a new arrangement in Ireland that would enable the Board of Works to comply with an expanded scheme of public employment. "You will observe," Graham wrote to Lincoln, "that there is a hitch in the movements of the Board of Works; and with great caution, in concert with the Lord Lieutenant, you must endeavour to remove it, and to render the operations of the Board more smooth and expeditious." Three days later Graham wrote again: "I am very glad that you are on the spot. I am confident that you will infuse some vigor and order into the system, by which we must endeavour to grapple with the difficulties of this great crisis."[43]

After consulting with Colonel Jones, Lincoln ordered the staffs of the Ordnance Survey Department, the County Surveyors, and the Royal Engineers to assist the staff of the Board of Works in the task of investigating proposals for public works. In effect, Lincoln shifted most of the responsibility for recommending proposals from the Board of Works to Richard Griffith and Thomas Larcom of the Ordnance Survey.[44] With the additional staff and with the slow routine of the Board of Works by-passed, Lincoln assured Peel that all preparatory surveys and measures would be completed in time to commence works as soon as the pressing needs of the population required them. But, he added,

> This should have been done a month ago, and I do hope that no consideration will be allowed to weigh in the scale against the necessity of making every effort to make up for lost time and at the eleventh hour endeavouring to outstrip the impending danger of being taken unawares.

Since the new arrangement had been agreed to by all parties in Ireland, Lincoln told Peel that he had "every confidence that all will now act harmoniously as well as efficiently—neither of which has hitherto been the case." But he warned Graham that it would be vain to attempt any arrangement if the authorities in London continued secretly to instruct officials in Ireland.[45]

Peel and Graham were pleased with Lincoln's new arrangement. "I congratulate you sincerely on the success of your measures," Graham wrote to Lincoln. "All your arrangements appear to me to have been judicious; and the good effects I anticipated from your visit to Ireland, will be realized." He added that he had impressed upon Henry Goulburn, the chancellor of the Exchequer, the absolute necessity of preventing Trevelyan from counteracting their policy through his private correspondence to Routh and Jones. "I have traced all our difficulties and delays to this source," he concluded, "and when you return, they will arise again, if all attention to these unauthorized communications be not strictly prohibited."[46] Peel urged Goulburn to give Lincoln full authority to amend the Treasury regulations in order to increase the discretionary power of the Irish officials and to dispense with the Treasury rule requiring private contributions equal to the state grant. Goulburn reluctantly complied with the prime minister's request.[47]

With his characteristic vigor and industry, Lincoln struggled to implement the details of the new arrangement and to coordinate the other activities of famine relief. He disagreed sharply with Trevelyan's optimistic evaluation of the crisis in Ireland. Whereas Trevelyan wrote of the declining threat of famine and the possibility of bringing relief to an early end, Lincoln cautioned Peel that the famine was nearing a critical stage and that the government would have to take more action in the months ahead. Even assuming that the potato blight did not reappear in the new crop, Lincoln warned, the people still would face worse circumstances in the year to come. He asked for more staff members from the Ordnance and for more steam transports to convey flour or meal to depots in Clare, Limerick, and other places where food was needed. He worked with Griffith and Larcom to insure that all the pending applications for works, some 150 of them, were immediately investigated.[48]

Lincoln soon discovered, however, that he had stirred up a hornets' nest in his effort to cut through red tape by circumventing the usual administrative and official channels. Part of the problem was in the Ordnance Department, where dissension among the staff threatened to upset the new arrangements even before they were implemented. Colonel Colby and Sir John Burgoyne, intensely jealous of Captain Larcom, refused to comply with Lincoln's request for more sappers and miners from England. "Wretched personal feelings and not the public service" were at the bottom of the difficulties at the Ordnance, Lincoln disgustedly told Peel. Without the additional personnel, he stressed, it was impossible to meet the exigencies of the spreading calamity.[49] Peel was firm in his support of Lincoln. "I will support you to the utmost in resisting the presumptuous interference of Col. Colby with yr. arrangements," he wrote.[50] Nevertheless, the trouble at the Ordnance was never completely resolved during Lincoln's tenure at the Irish Office. In June both Lincoln and Peel were furious with Sir John Burgoyne for superceding Captain Larcom, "apparently," Peel commented, "for no other reason than that at a time of great public difficulty he [Larcom] had zealously cooperated with the Irish Government and had acceded to their appeal for his assistance."[51]

But the resentment of the Treasury and the Public Works Commission toward the Irish government's interference with the administration of relief and the pressure of increasing famine were far more responsible for the breakdown of Lincoln's new arrangements than was the friction within the Ordnance Department. The commissioners of public works became more and more discontented as the applications were forwarded to the Board of Works, where the majority of them piled up unanswered. Riots and demonstrations in the west of Ireland at places where work was delayed or proposed projects were not inspected increased the pressure on the Relief Commission, and the lord lieutenant advanced small sums of money to enable the board to commence work in a few cases before the projects were completely assessed. Colonel Jones complained of the pressure put on him by the lord lieutenant to forward proposals for work projects that he thought unnecessary; and the commissioners of public works, with a strong sense of grievance, complained to Trevelyan that they were "compelled, from the urgent representations sent to us by the Irish Government and Relief Commissioners, to do that which we feel ought not to be done."[52]

Alarmed over the rush of applications for works, Trevelyan on 4 April issued new orders to the commissioners of public works. He now required the board to state to the Treasury at the time the applications were forwarded whether destitution in the immediate neighborhood of the places where works were proposed was severe enough, or likely to become severe enough, to require employment of the people on public works; whether the proposed works were designed to provide employment for the laboring class in general and not merely for artisans; whether any particular proprietors would be benefited by the proposed works to a greater degree than the other taxpayers; and whether the proprietors in question were willing to contribute toward meeting the cost of the works. This information was essential, Trevelyan told Richard Pennefather, under-secretary to the lord lieutenant, to prevent the misapplication of funds for private projects of a reproductive nature.[53] To back up his argument, the Treasury suspended sanction of proposed works amounting to several thousand pounds in counties Kerry and Clare until the Board of Works supplied the Treasury with the information requested in the new instructions.

Lincoln was furious with this new Treasury interference and, in his opinion, this breach of the new arrangement. "Mr. Trevelyan," he wrote to Peel,

> appears to go upon the principle that *because* somebody will be benefited by these works *therefore* they ought not to be undertaken at the joint expense of the State and the District although not that benefit but feeding a starving people is the object in view.

He could not see what more the Irish officials or the relief commissioners could do to prevent imposition, nor could he see what other object Trevelyan had in mind than to prevent the government from feeding the starving poor in Ireland. "Really the task undertaken is no light one," he continued, "and if you wish your intentions to be really carried out, and the promises made in the House of Commons to be fulfilled, *some* confidence must be placed in those upon whom you have developed these arduous and responsible duties." In his closing paragraph Lincoln reveals profound compassion:

> Do let us endeavour to elicit some good out of this great calamity. To do this, we must be able to act promptly, and to give—not grudgingly and when all grace has departed from the gift—but generously and the moment when it is wanted—though of course not wantonly or without full enquiry. I hope and think such a mode of proceeding will meet with *some* gratitude in Ireland and *but little* disapprobation in England.[54]

Another incident of Treasury interference came to Lincoln's attention the very next day. Trevelyan, apparently not satisfied with the reports of Richard Griffith, one of the men Lincoln selected to investigate proposed work projects, instructed Routh to send Edward Pine Coffin on a tour of inspection in the west of Ireland. Lincoln countermanded the order, but complained to Peel once again of Trevelyan's violation of the recent arrangement and his infringement upon the authority of the Irish government. The officials in Ireland under Treasury control, he commented, felt the real measure of disunion between the Irish Office and the Treasury:

> They feel that I am sent over here to make arrangements which have the approbation of the *Heads* of the Govt. and that these arrangements are thwarted by a *subordinate*, and then they reflect that I must soon leave Dublin and however ready I may be to incur any responsibility by disobeying Mr. Trevelyan they dare not do so.

He asked for discretionary power, since a man of ordinary ability on the spot could do far more than a clever man sitting in London to check deception and save public money.[55]

Peel shared Lincoln's vexation over Treasury interference with the administration of famine relief and agreed with him that the Irish government should have discretionary powers. Although he was reluctant to destroy all restraint, Peel nonetheless complained to Goulburn of the present mode of conducting business at the Treasury and requested that he direct Trevelyan not to issue instructions on important matters in his private letters. "We are not good judges at the Treasury of the extent of the immediate pressure there may be in some particular locality," he wrote, "and before we can have collected those proofs of it (which in ordinary times it may be quite right and absolutely necessary to collect) scarcity may have turned into absolute famine, and we may have on our hands not merely a suffering, but an outrageous multitude having broken the bounds of law." He assured Goulburn that it was absolutely necessary to give a wide discretionary authority to the lord lieutenant and the chief secretary. "Everything I have seen of Lincoln," he added, "inclines me to believe that there is no one more desirous than he is to check abuse and prevent imposition."[56]

Goulburn defended Trevelyan and suggested that Lincoln and Heytesbury had misunderstood the instruction of 4 April, which, he pointed out, already allowed the lord lieutenant the right to authorize works that he judged to be imperative. This explanation satisfied Peel, but Lincoln insisted that the instruction and Trevelyan's letters were meant to fetter the government's relief operations in Ireland. The Treasury, he complained, still refused to sanction most of the works recommended by the lord lieutenant, "and unless the existence of actual starvation is to be the guide it is difficult to know how he is intended to exercise this discretion."[57]

While this matter was still pending, difficulty between the Irish Office and the Treasury arose over the role of the government as a supplier of food in Ireland. The ministers and the Treasury officials expected private traders to supply most of the food to those drawing wages from public works. Only enough Indian meal from the government depots was to be thrown upon the market from time to time to prevent speculators from cornering the market and charging exorbitant prices for native produce. By mid-April, however, it was evident to the Irish officials, particularly to the chief Commissariat officers, that the private food suppliers would not be able to feed the estimated four million people who would have to be fed during May, June, and July before the harvest of the new potato crop.[58] Demand for the release of more meal from the depots was already quite pressing in many parts of Ireland; but Trevelyan, holding to his original plans, ordered the Commissariat not to open the depots for the sale of meal until 15 May. Until that time, he continued to insist, the landowners, Poor Law officials, and the local relief committees were to exert themselves to meet the existing distress. Routh, despairing of his continued failures to raise private subscriptions, repeatedly warned Trevelyan of the hopelessly inadequate food supplies and petitioned the Treasury to sanction the purchase of additional meal, and Pine Coffin urged the government to buy and store the grain that was sent to Limerick for export.[59] Trevelyan refused both men. He told Routh that the government must defer as long as possible from interfering with private enterprise.[60] To Pine Coffin's request he answered:

> The extent to which a govt can assist in feeding a whole people is so limited,
> and even to the extent to wh. it is in its power to assist, its interference is
> open to so many objections, that our first efforts shd. be directed to support
> the exertions of private benevolence, and to give the utmost possible scope
> to the importation of food on private account.[61]

Food riots and attacks upon mills and bakeries prompted Lincoln to disregard Trevelyan's order against the purchase of additional meal on government account. He instructed Routh to purchase four hundred tons of oatmeal at Clonmel, where severe riots had occurred from want of food and employment. "I must tell you," Lincoln wrote to Goulburn, "the danger is frightful if Trevelyan is allowed to be the judge of what is to be done." Although expecting a "good rap on the knuckles for buying oatmeal," he told Graham that he was prepared to ignore "a Philippic from Trevelyan" since the purchase of additional meal was necessary to prevent the failure of the government's relief plans.[62]

Peel again supported Lincoln. He told Goulburn that ordinary considerations must be overruled because of the conditions in Ireland. "I think something worse is at hand than we have yet calculated upon and that no time should be lost in providing [for] these extraordinary and unexpected difficulties. Increase of Government supplies is the first and essential step."[63] Thus prompted by Peel, Goulburn sanctioned the purchase of several cargoes of Indian corn at Liverpool for conveyance to Ireland, but he informed Lincoln that further purchases in Irish markets were to be avoided, especially in areas where distress had caused riots and attacks upon mills, for such purchases only enhanced the price of food and the incentive to violence.[64]

Neither Heytesbury nor Lincoln, however, was yet successful in convincing Goulburn that he should take action on the Treasury's instruction of 4 April, which remained the major official barrier to the complete execution of the government's relief plans. Heytesbury bombarded Graham with letters filled with complaints of Treasury interference and forewarnings of violent disorder if employment were not found for the Irish people.[65] Lincoln reminded Peel that before he left London they had agreed to relax Trevelyan's rule requiring private subscriptions since it was inconsistent with the government's primary objective of supplying food to a starving people: "It is really as if Mr. Trevelyan wished to bring down ridicule as well as disgrace upon the Government and all concerned in these affairs! . . . Believe me, these are not times for *strict* Treasury rules—still less for Trevelyan quirks and pedantries."[66]

Late in April, when the crisis in Ireland grew more desperate, the continued refusal of the Treasury to sanction the large and expensive public works recommended by the Relief Commission and the lord lieutenant finally forced the ministers to take more positive action to remove "the undercurrent" from the Treasury. After meeting with Peel and Goulburn following the Easter recess, Graham instructed the lord lieutenant to authorize public works that he deemed necessary, even if they conflicted with the strict rules of the Board of Works and the Treasury. He promised Heytesbury unlimited credit and the authority to grant assistance even in doubtful cases. "And tho' the saving of needless expenditure is a duty," Graham wrote, "yet the rescue of a starving multitude from the last extremity of want is a paramount consideration; and you may rely on our unhesitating sanction of any measures which you may adopt as necessary in your judgment."[67]

The lord lieutenant's hands were now freed somewhat, and in the following weeks, while Lincoln was back in London, Lord Heytesbury acted on his own responsibility to meet cases of extreme need. But the Irish government and the Board of Works still disagreed about which works were to be undertaken and when. Heytesbury advanced money to aid local subscriptions and urged the board to commence works that he considered absolutely necessary for the employment of the people; but the commissioners of public works, acting under the Treasury's instruction of 15 May, refused to begin any works until they were satisfied that distress arising from the failure of the potato crop was urgent enough to require them.[68] The commissioners, jealous of their own prerogatives yet constantly complaining of their excessive responsibilities, refused the services of everyone except members of their own staff to make the impossible distinction required by Trevelyan between distress caused solely by the recent potato failure and distress caused by the natural backwardness of Irish society. They assumed that all of the urgent demands were exaggerated, and they disregarded the information supplied to their office by the agents of the Irish government and checked by the Relief Commission. Furthermore, another Treasury instruction prohibited the Board of Works from undertaking extensive projects that might not be completed before the official end of the famine.[69]

These new instructions further delayed the commencement of public works projects, and the discretionary power granted to the lord lieutenant proved to be of limited value. But the ministers were too embroiled in parliamentary battles at Westminster over repeal of the Corn Laws and passage of the Irish crimes bill to correct the situation. Therefore, nothing more was done by Peel's ministry to expedite public works in Ireland.

By this time the situation in Ireland had reached critical proportions. The supplies in the government depots were almost exhausted. Applications for public assistance under the Public Works Acts continued to pour in, even though the business of the Board of Works was hopelessly in arrears. Reports on the early crop all indicated that the potato would fail again. The probability of a greatly increased number of people needing relief became reality. But these ominous developments only strengthened Trevelyan's determination to end the state's part in providing relief for the Irish people, and the new Whig ministers eventually helped him achieve his goal.

Although Peel and his colleagues had tried to keep state intervention at a minimum, their measures for the relief of Ireland were contrary to extreme laissez-faire principles, and a few civil servants, led by the doctrinaire Trevelyan, had attempted to impose on the country their own views by refusing to execute ministerial policy properly. As Lincoln indicated, Trevelyan's interference was much more than just a sincere desire to save public money and to maintain fiscal and administrative principles; it was a systematic attack upon ministerial policy. Such attacks were frequent until modern rules and conventions for ministerial responsibility reduced the civil servant to a neutral subordinate of the political minister. Thus it was possible for Trevelyan to enter the arena of politics and to ignore the dim line that separated purely administrative measures from policy measures. His political role in early 1846 only complicated the administration of Peel's relief scheme; it did not prevent the Peelites from achieving their immediate aims of averting Irish starvation.

Through Lincoln's and Heytesbury's persistence, the Irish government was able to broaden the Treasury's administration of Irish famine relief, at least to the extent necessary to prevent exceptional suffering during the first half of 1846. Lincoln believed that the poor in Ireland must be regarded with as much care and solicitude as were the poor in England; and with the help of Lord Heytesbury he saw to it that enough food was distributed and enough work was provided to get the Irish through the spring and early summer. Nobody died of famine in Ireland during that time.[70]

Although Trevelyan's interference did not prevent Peel's administration from successfully dealing with the immediate problem of Irish famine, his resistance to the government's relief policy delayed and in some cases prevented the execution of productive works that were necessary to prepare Ireland for the greater calamity that was yet to come when the potato crops failed again. Instead of approving applications for productive works that would add to the future wealth and result in the permanent improvement of Ireland, the Treasury sanctioned only temporary and unproductive works of a public nature. Thus drainage works and land reclamation projects that would have improved private estates and subsequently increased agricultural output were rejected, primarily because of Trevelyan's opposition to the use of state money for those improvements. Consequently, little progress was made toward improving the productive capacities of the country. The evidence from Lincoln's short tenure at the Irish Office clearly proves that Treasury parsimony rather than the narrow vision of the Peelite ministers was the principal cause of this failure of social and economic regeneration.

Much of the credit for the short-term success of Peelite famine relief was due to Lincoln.[71] He had fought the doctrinaire civil officials tenaciously. Still, he left Ireland with a sense of frustration and failure, for he was forced to leave office before he could correct a system that he found amiss. He had done his best for Ireland, and in Ireland he was not soon forgotten.

V

Lord Heytesbury had warned Lincoln at the time of his appointment as Irish secretary that it was "impossible to conceive a more ungrateful task than that of administering the affairs of Ireland."[72] True as the observation was during normal times, it was even truer during times of scarcity. Lincoln had spent most of his time during March and April in the administration of famine relief. In May and June he turned his attention to the introduction of measures in the Commons that had grown out of the Devon Commission's report. The most important of these measures was the landlord and tenant (Ireland) bill. In this measure Lincoln proposed the appointment of special commissioners to determine whether proposed improvements on the land were justified.

Landlords would be forced to consent to improvements that were sanctioned by the commissioners and to pay compensation to dispossessed tenants for them. Lincoln argued that the limited interference with the rights of property that was proposed in the bill was absolutely necessary for the general prosperity of the empire.[73] The measure, however, did not provide security for tenants, the real crux of the whole problem. But it mattered very little, for the bill died with the government a few days after it was introduced.

Lincoln introduced several other bills relating to Ireland before his short tenure at the Irish office was terminated.[74] But his main concern in the closing days of the administration was the protection of life (Ireland) bill. Peel had insisted that this measure be introduced along with the other measures based on the report of the Devon Commission, and consequently Sir James Graham had introduced the bill in the Commons in March after it had been passed in the Lords. The measure was not particularly harsh by the standards of the day; nonetheless, opposition soon mounted. The opposition caused delay, and the bill became entangled with the corn importation bill. It soon became apparent that no further progress could be made on the measure until the fate of the Corn Laws was settled. On that issue the debate had become increasingly bitter, with Benjamin Disraeli leading the attack against Peel. Disraeli's invective, however, could not stop the passage of the bill. By a majority of 98, the corn importation bill gained the approval of the House on 15 May and was sent up to the Lords.[75]

With the corn importation bill safely through the Commons, the government revived the debate on the Irish crimes bill (Irish protection of life bill), which would give the lord lieutenant power to proclaim disturbed districts, employ additional constabulary at the expense of the districts concerned, and enforce a curfew at night. Anyone convicted under the law could be transported for up to seven years. On 8 June, Lincoln, in a very thin and apathetic House, moved the second reading of the bill. He argued that as distasteful and "unconstitutional" as the measure was, it was clearly required in order to produce the peace and tranquility that was necessary to achieve the government's objectives of employment and education in Ireland. In a long, detailed speech Lincoln cited case after case of disorder and criminal outrage in parts of Ireland. He reviewed the positive measures that the government had passed and previewed other proposals that they planned to introduce. He ended his speech by noting that the bill was not introduced as a panacea for Ireland but as a corrective for the country's disorganized society.[76]

The verdict on the bill had already been decided, for a few days earlier, Irish, Liberal, and protectionist members of the Commons had separately agreed to oppose the second reading. On the night Lincoln moved the reading, Lord George Bentinck invited the Whigs to join with the protectionists to throw out both ministers and bill. In a vicious attack upon the prime minister, Bentinck declared that Peel had lost the confidence of every honest man in the House and charged that Peel had "chased and hunted" Canning to death in 1827 over Catholic emancipation, only to admit later that he had secretly changed his mind on the question before attacking Canning. Thus Bentinck accused Peel of "base and dishonest conduct," of treachery and treason in the past as well as in the present.[77]

Peel was too deeply wounded by Bentinck's savage attack to reply that evening. In fact Peel was so angered and hurt by the aspersion on his honor that he decided to send Bentinck a challenge. He chose Lincoln to act as his second. After the close of the debate, Lincoln and Peel walked up and down Whitehall discussing the matter until the early hours of the morning. Lincoln refused to act for Peel and remonstrated vehemently with him when he stubbornly persisted and indicated that he would find someone else to deliver the challenge to Bentinck. Lincoln threatened to go to the police. Finally, when early-morning workmen were beginning to appear on the street, Lincoln talked Peel into going to bed on the matter. Later in the day, Lincoln called on Peel and found him as determined as ever to challenge Bentinck. Again the two men argued at length before Lincoln was finally able to persuade Peel to abandon his intention.[78]

Peel contented himself with a moderate reply in the Commons a few days later. But Disraeli would not let the matter rest; and on 19 April, aided by evidence collected by Lincoln and other friends, Peel refuted each point of the charge leveled against him. Peel's speech, Lincoln reported to Heytesbury, was "a smasher." He was enthusiastically cheered, and Bentinck and Disraeli were widely scorned. Yet, as Heytesbury noted, even Peel's great speech would not subdue the venom of such men as Disraeli who were out for revenge for the repeal of the Corn Laws.[79] Peel's approach was too temperate, too far removed from the arena of personal conflict. Lincoln was partially responsible for this, for he had continued to counsel caution and moderation to Peel. On this occasion he dissuaded Peel from reading a letter in the House in which Disraeli had written to Peel in 1841 asking for office.[80] This evidence would have caught Disraeli in an earlier lie in which he had denied ever soliciting office or favors from the prime minister. Both Lincoln and Peel were hypersensitive on points of honor, and perhaps it was this appeal by Lincoln to gentlemanly fair play that restrained Peel from reading out a personal communication in the House.

Although the debate in the Commons on 19 June resulted in a decided vindication of Peel, the protectionist leaders were not deterred from their pursuit of revenge. On 25 June, a few hours after the corn bill received final approval in the House of Lords, the government was defeated on the second reading of the protection of life bill. An assortment of protectionists, Liberals, Irish, and Radicals voted against the measure. On the following day the ministers met for their final cabinet. It was the shortest cabinet meeting Gladstone had ever known. Peel argued for the resignation of the government as opposed to the dissolution of Parliament. Not one voice was raised in dissent when he asked whether the vote was unanimous.[81] On the following Monday, 29 June, the resignation of the government was announced in both houses.

The end had come to an administration that would in retrospect gain the reputation of being one of the best of the nineteenth century. The legacy of that administration was great, with the repeal of the Corn Laws perhaps being its greatest achievement. This controversial issue had destroyed Peel's Conservative party, but the resolution of it had ended the serious prospect of class conflict over the matter. The repeal of the Corn Laws connected the Peelite programs of economic and social enhancement. When the Peelites left office in June 1846, there was more economic prosperity and less social tension in the country than there had been when they took office in 1841. The ministers also had launched a new Irish policy of reforms and concessions. With the failure of the potato crop in 1845 they had faced a crisis in Ireland of enormous magnitude and had reacted with a successful relief program to meet the distress. Lord Lincoln played a very significant part in these affairs during the last year of the ministry. He had established himself as an efficient, industrious, and judicious administrator. He had gained the complete confidence and friendship of Peel. In 1846 he was one of the principal leaders of the small group of "young" men whom Sir James Graham noted with great satisfaction had become fit to govern the country.[82]

5. The Early Peelite Years

Like all his fellow Peelites, Lincoln in the autumn and winter of 1846 faced an uncertain political future. Separated from the main body of the old Conservative party, shortly to be organized as the Protectionists under the leadership of Lord George Bentinck in the Commons and Lord Stanley in the Lords, Lincoln and his closest personal and political friends, many of whom he had known since his Oxford days, entered the political limbo between two loosely organized political parties. This close circle of friends—Lincoln, William Gladstone, Sidney Herbert, Lord Dalhousie, Lord Canning, Edward Cardwell, and Sir John Young—represented the best young administrative talent in Parliament. The bitter struggle over the repeal of the Corn Laws bound them together firmly and deepened their loyalty to Peel.

More than mere friendship and loyalty to Peel, however, bound these young Peelites to one another. All were motivated by a strong sense of duty, and all were guided by high ideals. They shared a political philosophy that allowed them to combine a deep conservatism with an equally basic desire for improvement through constant but cautious reform. And foremost, they were united by the compelling duty to complete the commercial revolution that they had helped launch during Peel's administration and to instill a greater degree of administrative expertise in government. They shared Peel's low opinion of the Whigs as administrators; and, notwithstanding Peel's professions that he would neither seek office nor lead the party again, they believed it possible that a country gripped by crisis might sweep Peel and themselves back into office. For the moment, then, the only acceptable alternative for the younger Peelites was to join Peel in political isolation, the duration of which Lincoln believed would be brief.

Necessity did not dictate this decision, for Lord John Russell, the new prime minister, sent, with Peel's approval but not his encouragement, identical invitations to Lincoln, Herbert, and Dalhousie to join the new Whig administration. All three declined on the double ground of public duty and private honor. Lincoln was particularly offended by the offer. Writing to Peel, he exclaimed that this was "a new mode of beating up for a cabinet—by circular!"[1] Later in the year Lincoln, along with Sir James Graham, agreed to become a member of the newly formed Council for the Duchy of Lancaster

William Ewart Gladstone, by G. F. Watts, 1858.
Courtesy of the National Portrait Gallery, London.

after Russell assured him that the position would not be political. Lincoln consulted Peel about the offer, and Peel advised him to accept since the queen strongly supported it. Lord George Bentinck, always ready to vent his spleen against the Peelites, was not surprised to find Lincoln putting money before principle in taking a paid office under the crown. Only later did he discover that the position was unpaid, which led him to presume that Lincoln was

Sidney Herbert, painter anonymous, c. 1847.
Courtesy of the National Portrait Gallery, London.

overcoming "the false delicacy which prevented his acceptance of office under the Whigs in July."[2]

Personal animosities over the repeal of the Corn Laws, especially in the Commons, precluded any chance for reconciliation between Peelites and Protectionists during the remainder of the 1846 season. Soon after Peel's resignation, Lords Brougham and Lyndhurst had attempted to reunite the Conservatives, but neither the leaders of the Peelites nor those of the Protectionists desired that end. Lyndhurst had hoped that the two wings of the Conservative party would unite against Russell's sugar bill, but Peel and Graham would have no part of the "intrigue." Peel, in fact, asked Lyndhurst to make public his letter repudiating any party combination for the purpose of returning to office.[3] Although opposed to Lyndhurst's activities, Lincoln regretted the public disclosure of Peel's "repudiation of office in *prospectu*."[4] The incident nonetheless strengthened the younger Peelites in their desire to give a fair trial to the government. By a margin of 47 to 14, the Peelites opposed Lord George Bentinck's amendment against the government's sugar bill. With this vote the Peelites both helped the Whigs out of a very tight spot and also widened the gulf between themselves and the Protectionists over the question of free trade. Bentinck, who had rejected Lyndhurst's scheme for Conservative reunion, even though it had excluded Peel, Graham, Lincoln, and Herbert, was determined to rouse the country during the next election to drive the Peelites "from the face of the Earth."[5]

Lincoln found it most unnatural to help prop up the weak Whig ministry. Although convinced that the Peelites should stay outside either major party, he believed that they must organize as an opposition body in the Commons. But Peel and Sir James Graham thought differently. As independent arbiters between the major parties, they were determined to keep the Whigs in and the Protectionists out of office as long as there was any threat to free trade. Peel emphatically told Lord Hardinge that he intended to keep aloof from party combinations and to remain out of office so far as he could.[6] Late in the year, Peel's leading followers, with the exception of Graham, vainly endeavored to change his mind on these matters.

Lincoln was one of the main participants in these activities. Following a short holiday with his wife in the Highlands after the close of the parliamentary session and an extensive tour of Ireland during the fall, Lincoln returned to London early in December to meet with Henry Goulburn, Edward Cardwell, Sir John Young, and Francis Bonham to discuss organizing the Peelites as a party. The political activity of the Protectionists, which concerned them greatly, convinced them that they should demonstrate pointedly the independence of the Peelite section during the upcoming session. It was decided that Young, on the authority of the Peelites who had conferred, should write the usual letter of summons of attendance for the opening of Parliament to the friends of the late government. "A Republican opposition is a novelty," Goulburn observed to Lord Aberdeen, "but I see no other alternative and we all agree so well that when the House is once at work I have no fear of our party gaining strength daily if men do not previously commit themselves."[7]

This small group of Peelite leaders viewed the state of the country with apprehension and feared the worst from Whigs and Protectionists alike. They concluded that there was ample reason for members and supporters of the late government to form a party of observation, constantly keeping themselves alive to the country's real interests. Although Peel refused involvement, judging that a party of observation without the traditional competition for power would not succeed, he did not object to the letters if his name was not used. Peel's attitude led Goulburn to ask:

> What are we to do who cannot approve of the acts of the Government on
> the one hand nor of the acts and opinions of Lord G. Bentinck or D' Israeli
> on the other? We must either enlist ourselves dishonourably under one
> banner or the other or acting individually and without concert make our-
> selves the ridicule of both and lose all power of public usefulness.[8]

The Peelite activists hoped to avoid these pitfalls. Those who had discussed the organization of the Peelites decided to go ahead with their plan to send the letters, notwithstanding Peel's lack of enthusiasm and refusal to lead them. Young sent out about 240 letters over his signature, and by 1 January ninety answers, "all of them in a friendly tone and many of them cordial," Lincoln told Peel, had been returned. "Whenever there is even an assumption that the letter was written by your direction," Lincoln continued, "Young will write to say that such has not been the case. I hope you will not think the course we have taken either wrong in itself or disagreeable to you. I am sure it has made Ld. G. Bentinck's game a much more difficult one."[9]

Although greatly disappointed by Peel's refusal to support them, the Peelite activists were in a combative mood when the 1847 parliamentary session began in January. Their spirits were raised by the favorable response to their circular and by signs of rebellion within the Protectionist camp. Sir John Young reported to Peel that several of his friends believed that Lord Stanley's course of action would drive some of his followers over to the Peelite camp.[10] Writing to Peel the same day, Lincoln confirmed Young's observations. The "truce" between the "Noble Friends"—the suspected secret understanding between Bentinck and Russell—and Disraeli's "propinquity to the red box and ostentatious familiarity with Lord Stanley" would alienate the more respectable Conservatives from the Protectionists. Lincoln explained that the alleged truce extended even to seating arrangements in the Commons. At the beginning of the session, Bentinck and Russell agreed that the Protectionist leaders would cross over to take seats below the red box on the opposition front bench. The move, however, did not threaten Peelite territory on the other side of the red box, as Lincoln, with a rare display of humor, reported to the temporarily absent Peel:

> The Protectionist leaders have attempted no further encroachments, neither Lord G. Bentinck nor Mr. D' Israeli having come above the red box though they are generally flanked on that wing by Mr. Bankes and Mr. Christopher or both. We have continued to occupy the places we took the first night, and the *buffers* of the two parties have been the not very thickly wadded forms of Mr. Goulburn and Mr. Bankes. Young, Cardwell, and G. Hope have however occasionally thrown out pickets into the enemy's camp and upon the whole I think our left wing is generally better defended than it was on Tuesday. Graham continues to sit under the post, vis a vis to Plumridge and Barnard, and upon the whole tho' there is an obvious absurdity in it I should be sorry to see him *now* change it. He evidently had made up his mind to go there from the first and he is much too long-headed not to have had a reason for the decision. I confess however I should be very sorry to see *you* anywhere but on the front bench and I do not think you will find your seat there at all inconvenient. You can always have 3 or 4 friends to your left and the benches immediately behind are never occupied by the hostile forces.[11]

So arranged, the two opposing forces of the old Conservative party were prepared to battle one another, while the weak Whig ministry was left to govern the best it could.

II

The confused state of politics in 1846 extended beyond the walls of Parliament into many constituencies where prominent citizens were already lining up candidates for the political battles ahead. As a leading Peelite and close friend of Peel, Lincoln was courted by several important constituencies, and in the autumn of 1846 he became "half engaged" to the City of London. He had just broken off that agreement when a delegation from Manchester began to woo him as a possible candidate at the next general election to stand against John Bright, the chief partner with Richard Cobden in the leadership of the Anti-Corn Law League. John Peel conveyed the invitation to Lincoln through his relative, Sir Robert Peel. "I know," John wrote,

> that the whole of the Conservative party, as well as a large portion of the Whigs and Liberals, are very much averse to the idea of having Mr. Bright as their representative, and they are now looking out for a man of talent and influence, Free Trade opinions, and moderate political principles.
>
> Several persons have been named, but the one most generally approved by a majority of the electors appears to be Lord Lincoln, and I have been requested to write to you and ask if you think, if he could receive a well-

founded assurance of being returned free of expense, he would consent
to offer himself as a candidate for the representation of Manchester.[12]

Although the requisition asking him to stand was signed by a large and
influential group from Manchester, Lincoln approached the offer cautiously.
He met with a deputation from that city late in November but refused to
commit himself. "I must be very coy," he wrote to Thompson, "for my
Representative Virtue cannot afford another false step or I shall become a
confirmed political W[hore]."[13] He did not believe that the Conservative party
was strong enough in Manchester to ensure his election, and he did not trust
the Whigs to unite with them against Bright. "On the contrary," he told Peel,
"I believe at the last moment they would throw all their weight into his scale
and leave me in a very ridiculous position." Peel agreed, and late in the year
he advised Lincoln to reject the offer. Lincoln, however, was not ready to close
the door on the matter. Although he realized it was a dangerous political
venture, the honor paid to him as well as the thrill of a prospective political
challenge prompted him to postpone his decision until after the start of the
new year.[14]

In a state of utter uncertainty as to what he should do—whether to accept,
decline, or postpone a decision—Lincoln agreed to address the interested electorate in Manchester from the Corn Exchange on 13 January. "I confess," he
told Peel, "I do not much like appearances and the prospect of speechifying
whether I stand or not is any thing but agreeable. I did not see however how
I could refuse under the peculiar circumstances. I shall be glad to know that
you think my decision right."[15] In his speech Lincoln defended the recent
commercial changes and pledged himself to support the extension of free trade
when the considerations of revenue allowed it. He was decidedly against the
repeal of the malt tax and uncertain about the tea duty. On other matters, he
was convinced that the state must intervene to extend the system of education;
that means must be found to pay Roman Catholic clergy in Ireland; that it
was unwise to regulate the labor of adults as opposed to children; that "the
most anxious and careful attention" should be given to any measure designed
to promote the health and enhance "the happiness and habits of order and
comfort among the labouring population"; that equality of civil rights between Ireland and England was desirable; and that church rates should be
abolished.[16]

Being aware of his newly elevated position before the public, Lincoln took
great pains with this speech. He realized the pitfalls it contained for his can-
didacy. Nevertheless, he chose to be candid and plainspoken. Maynooth beat
him in South Nottinghamshire, he noted to Thompson. "Payment of Priests
may beat me in Manchester. Still I shall not regret that I have been the first to
speak out on this question. I feel it strongly and I could not smother it."[17]

The prospect of a Peelite, indeed of a Peelite as close to Peel as was Lincoln,

standing against the league-sponsored John Bright attracted considerable attention. Bright himself considered Lincoln "an opponent worth powder and
shot."[18] The *Times* billed Lincoln's speech as the first salvo in a Peelite political
campaign. The *Chronicle, Globe, Herald,* and *Standard,* Lincoln complained,
wrote him down while writing Bright up.[19] Indeed, Tory, Radical, and Whig
presses seemed to join forces against Lincoln at the first indication that he
might become a candidate. In approving the Tory presses' endorsement of
John Bright against Lincoln, Lord George Bentinck told Stanley that Lincoln's
return at Manchester "would be an immense moral triumph for Peel," and he
would far rather see Bright "or any other bold Radical in for Manchester than
any Renegade Janissary from Drayton Manor." Lord Stanley, however, was
appalled by such political action. He asked Beresford, the Protectionist whip,
to stop the Tory press from running Lincoln down and building up "a Black-
guard and a Democrat." But Beresford sided with Bentinck; Lincoln, he told
Stanley, was "Peel's double or representative, and his return for Manchester
would do more to reestablish a Peelite Party than ten ordinary Borough seats
gained would." He added that Lincoln was far more dangerous than Bright,
for being a gentleman he could cover the iniquity better.[20]

The publicity gave Lincoln considerable national exposure. His most ardent
supporters, despite realizing that Manchester would be a severe test of his
political convictions, believed that he had a good chance of success, a view
shared early by Lord George Bentinck. Nonetheless, as Lincoln could not
predict with any certainty the outcome of an election that was still quite distant, late in February he declined to be a candidate.[21]

Perhaps it was the interest generated by the Manchester contest that
prompted Lord Ellenborough prior to the opening of the parliamentary session in 1847 to regard Lincoln as a possible leader of a reunited Conservative
party in the Commons. "Lincoln's position in society, and his talents as a man
of business," Ellenborough told Lord Lyndhurst, "together with his real lib-
erality of his views, not extreme upon any point, but rational and suited to
the times gave him advantages possessed by no other man who could be
considered as a possible Leader in the House of Commons." He also believed
that by virtue of resigning his seat and facing his constituents on the issue of
the Corn Laws, something the other leading Peelites had not done, Lincoln
would be well received by the Protectionists. Ellenborough recounted those
ideas to Lincoln and urged him to lead the supporters of the late government
back into the ranks of the Conservative party, not as penitents but as men
willing to cooperate on new ground with those from whom they had differed
during the previous year.[22]

Ellenborough's remarks were hyperbole, as Lincoln was quick to point out
to him: "I have never been presumptuous enough to *dream* of taking the lead
of men in the House of Commons, many of whom are not only old enough

to be my father, but are both in experience and ability greatly my superiors."
He told Ellenborough that high station, wealth, and speaking ability were
insufficient qualifications for leadership. Personal acceptability to one's followers was also required. This he did not have from the Protectionists; for, he
noted, with the exception of Sir Robert Peel, no other person in the late
government was hated more by the Protectionists than he was. "If you had
been in the House of Commons, or even if you had lately read the leading
articles in their Organs of the Press, you would have been satisfied of this. I
am one of the four who have all along been placed by them out of the pale of
forgiveness." Concurring with Ellenborough that the Peelites must not "be
thrown adrift and left to find their way individually into the ranks of the
Protectionists," Lincoln offered his services in conjunction with others to prevent that from happening.[23] But as far as he was concerned, the Protectionists
would have to come to the Peelites if the old Conservative party were to be
reunified.

III

Lincoln's defiance toward the Protectionists typified the mood of the Peelites as the 1847 parliamentary session began. Even without Peel's endorsement, they were determined to act, in Goulburn's words, as the conscience of
the nation. They would oppose all measures that they considered dangerous
to the country, while awaiting the time when the force of circumstances would
impel them and Peel back into office.

On the other hand, Peel and Graham were determined to keep the Whigs
in office as long as the Protectionists constituted a threat to the recent commercial changes. Although there were few important divisions during the
1847 session, Lincoln voted with Peel and Graham and the majority of the
Peelites in support of the government on the most important matters. One of
the most crucial issues was Bentinck's measure for a government-sponsored
program of railway construction in Ireland. The bill had considerable support
on both sides of the Commons, for it was doubly attractive in that it provided
relief both through capital for the growth of Irish industry and employment
for an estimated 110,000 Irish laborers. The Peelites vigorously opposed the
measure on economic as well as political grounds. A victory for Bentinck on
this matter, they stressed, would hand the government over to the Protectionists. Stiffened by Peelite opposition, Russell threatened to resign if the bill
carried. Together the Whigs and the majority of Peelites defeated the measure
easily.[24]

The Whig ministry was not seriously threatened again during the remainder of the session, and when Parliament was dissolved in July for the general

election, the Whig administration was still alive. The Irish crisis had not over-whelmed the government and driven the Peelites back to power, as Lincoln earlier had predicted; nor had the Protectionists, who were increasingly dis-satisfied with Bentinck's leadership, been able to mount a serious threat to the recent commercial changes. Lincoln and some of the other prominent Peelites were greatly troubled by Peel's attitude; they were convinced that he was being trapped by Whig policy because he feared a Protectionist succession to power. Thus the political situation at the time of the 1847 election was as confused as it had been a year earlier.

Peel's disinterest in the Peelite section placed its members at a disadvantage during the 1847 general election, and several of the leading Peelites were hard pressed. Among them was Gladstone, who had been without a seat since he quit Newark in 1845 when he was appointed colonial secretary in the Peel administration. Early in April he informed Lincoln of his predicament and said that he would come to town with his father to confer with Lincoln on the matter later in the month. "My father is very desirous to meet you in London when he comes there," Gladstone added, "but I must give you notice that he may probably administer a dose of Protection doctrine. He has a high opinion of your sagacity and being a genuine lover of truth he thinks either you could convince him or he you."[25]

Lincoln's problem was somewhat different from Gladstone's. He already had a seat, but keeping it was very much in doubt. Nonetheless, he decided to set up his "Popery Standard" in Puritan Scotland once again rather than accept one of the eighteen English seats that had been offered to him since his venture in Manchester earlier in the year.[26] Protection was not a serious issue in Falkirk, but the ultra-Protestants were ready to cast stones at Lincoln for his Maynooth vote and for his advocacy of payment of Roman Catholic priests in Ireland. In turn, Lincoln was ready to meet his religious opponents head on and to defend Peelite policy as a whole. "Whatever Liverpool Orange-men or University Bigots may say of it," he wrote to Peel in reference to the latter's *Tamworth Letter*, "I am quite prepared to make Scotch Puritans swallow it. I shall not evade any of the points in deference to their love of Papist-burning." He thanked Peel for sending a copy and told him that his friends would thank him for this "admirable Handbook to the Hustings." He contin-ued, "The House of Coms. this evening presents a curious appearance, every other Member on the benches having a copy in his hand."[27]

With the aid of his father-in-law, the duke of Hamilton, Lincoln again pre-vailed in Falkirk. He noted to Peel:

> I have had a most tremendous contest. The opium money has been poured
> out freely and bribery, treating and every other electioneering trick the
> order of the day. The Free Kirk and all the Dissenting Ministers have been

most active against me and denounced the pains of Hell on Sunday last in
their Chapels against those who voted for a Friend of the Papists.

What was even more disturbing to Lincoln was that sixteen of the twenty
Roman Catholic voters were bribed to vote for his opponent.[28] Gladstone
marveled at Lincoln's victory. "You certainly bearded the lion in his den," he
wrote in congratulating Lincoln. "For a man of conservative politics, charged
with Maynooth in the rear, and with possible Romish endowment in the
front, to carry a set of Scottish Boroughs, is no small achievement."[29]

The Peelites did well in the election. Coupled with the severe losses of the
Protectionists, the Peelite-Liberal success at the polls indicated an endorsement
of Peel's free-trade policy. Lincoln was not alone among the Peelites in having
more trouble with religious views than with economic policy. "Maynooth,"
Francis Bonham told Peel, "has destroyed several of our friends. 'Free Trade'
hardly any."[30] The frank language Peel had used in the *Tamworth Letter* to
defend the Maynooth grant hurt several of his followers, even though Peel
explicitly explained that the views therein were his exclusively and that any
person was "at full liberty to disclaim participation in them."[31] Notwithstanding this disclaimer, there was scant chance for many of the Peelites to escape
the "No Popery" cry, the one issue that aroused the electorate in 1847. The
Peelites, therefore, had good reason to be satisfied with the election results.
All the leading Peelites were returned, and the record of the rank-and-file was
almost as good. Including the newly elected recruits, the Peelite section stood
at 113, just one short of their original number. Even Lord George Bentinck
had to concede that for the moment the Protectionist party was "smashed"
and that the Peelites remained a compact and formidable body in the Commons.[32]

Although the Peelites contested the election as individuals rather than as
members of an organized political party, they formed a group still very loyal
to Peel. Many of them, including Lincoln, had been returned, as Bentinck
observed to Stanley, "by the grace of an entente cordiale with the Whigs."[33]
Therefore, it was natural for the Protectionist leaders to assume that the Peelites would support the Whig government. Certainly there was every reason
to believe that the Whigs would be dependent upon the Peelites in the new
Parliament. The election had changed very little.

Nor did the election change the attitude of either Peel or Graham toward
party leadership. Although he had no intention of abandoning leadership in
Parliament, Peel expressed his disinterest in the fortunes of the Peelites. And
Graham was content for the moment to remain a spectator. He believed that
the prospects both at home and abroad were dismal and that Russell's skill
was probably insufficient to meet the storm. Still, he told Lincoln, "I had
rather . . . be a passenger than one of the crew; and in present circumstances
a berth below under hatches, altho' inglorious is most comfortable."[34]

Thus there was little else for Lincoln to do when Parliament reopened but to resume the role of independent critic, attacking the ministers as bad workmen when they proposed poorly prepared bills. On 18 November he sent his observations on the opening of the session to Peel, who would not arrive in London for another few days. "There appeared to me in the House today the same coquetting between Ministers and Ld. G. Bentinck and Mr. D' Israeli etc. as went on last year," he wrote, "and the thousand and one rumours which as usual are afloat on the first day of a Session all run in that direction." He was convinced, therefore, that there was a complete understanding between Russell and the Protectionists that was designed to keep the Peelites from coming back to power. The House seemed very much the same, he added. "We all took up our places. The only alteration on our bench was that Feargus O'Connor sat between me and Thesiger!" That the Chartist leader sat on the opposition bench in Peel's place next to Lincoln did not escape the observant eye of George Cornewall Lewis from the Whig side of the House.[35]

It appeared briefly late in 1847 that the political uncertainty might force Peel to change his mind about political organization. Early in December he told Young that some attempt should be made to organize the Peelites. Shortly thereafter, Young and Lincoln dined at Gladstone's house to discuss the suggestion. The three young Peelites discussed at length the difficulty the members of the party would have with Peel if he continued to refuse to lead the party or to consider resuming office. "We all felt," Gladstone wrote in a memorandum, "that an organization if formed ought to be led by him, that this could not be, and that the only remaining alternative of an admissible kind would be that it should be in constant communication with him." Finally it was agreed that the party would have no head, but that the members of the late government would discuss with Peel subjects in the different departments with which they had been officially connected. Young reported the substance of their conversation to Peel, but the matter was quietly dropped. "It is singular," Gladstone observed a year later, "that Peel should have started such a subject without knowing his own mind upon it, as it seemed that he placed the necessity of some kind on rather high grounds, e.g. that without it we could not give effective support to the Govt."[36]

However, the political situation had changed by the time Young reported the results of the deliberations to Peel. Bentinck had been deposed as leader of the Protectionists in the Commons late in December for his support of the Jewish claims. Apparently Peel no longer believed it necessary to organize the Peelites since Bentinck's repudiation made a Protectionist-Whig combination impossible, or at least much less likely. With this development, the Protectionists, now reduced more than ever to a "No Popery" and "No Jew" party, gave up any chance they might have had to gain concessions from the Whigs. They surrendered flexibility for intransigence, refusing anything less than the complete reversal of free trade. Peel now realized that the political differences between the Whigs and the Protectionists were so great that it would be impossible for them to join together to modify the act of 1846.

IV

The interval between the election and the opening of the autumn session of Parliament was filled with both pain and pleasure for Lincoln. After disposing of some personal business in London following the election, he visited the Peels briefly at Drayton in mid-August. He always enjoyed his Drayton visits, looking forward to them as most school boys did to their holidays. Later in the month he settled the four youngest children at Brighton for a few weeks and set off for Scotland shortly after Henry returned to Eton. Lady Lincoln had already "run away," as the duke of Newcastle put it in his diary; but despite rumors that were reaching a few newspapers of another separation between them, Lincoln met her and the Hamiltons and their guest Prince Louis Napoleon, a cousin of Lady Douglas, in Arran in mid-October.[37] Susan, however, suffering from an "inflammatory attack," remained at Leamington Spa in the company of her mother and a medical specialist when Lincoln returned to London early in November. There she would remain for the rest of the year, ill and unwilling to return to her husband.

Other family problems also pressed upon Lincoln. He was still estranged from his father and, except for Robert, the youngest, from his brothers as well. Newcastle devoted heart and soul and some money to Protectionist politics, all of which activities Lincoln regarded as personal attacks. In the general election of 1847 the duke exercised his influence in Newark and Nottinghamshire while also putting up his sons Charles for Sandwich and Thomas for Canterbury. Both lost, to the duke's great dismay. But it was Gladstone's and Lincoln's return that most upset him. Referring to Gladstone's victory at Oxford, the duke noted in his diary, "No return has given me more pain." As for Lincoln, Newcastle grieved to think that so unworthy a son should be returned for the Falkirk Burghs; yet to represent them, he added, "is no very exalted honour."[38]

The success of the Peelites in the general election added greatly to Newcastle's despondency. Although he continued for a time to be active in the politics of the Protectionist party, he slipped back gradually into a fatalistic acceptance of political events as the fulfillment of biblical prophecy. He became more broody and disillusioned as one after another of his sons became alienated from him. But his estrangement from Lincoln was the most bitter; for over four years they did not meet or correspond, nor did the duke see his grandchildren.

Father and son would remain estranged from one another until shortly before the duke's death early in 1851. Rarely in two such closely related individuals has there ever been more contrast between political romanticism and political realism. Each idealistic in his own way, neither man could comprehend the political attitude of the other. But more than just bitter political differences caused the estrangement. Lincoln's marital situation greatly concerned the duke, while the duke's extreme recklessness in estate matters equally concerned Lincoln, who looked on helplessly as his father brought financial ruin to the Newcastle property. Lincoln realized that he would soon inherit a bankrupt estate.

V

With his domestic troubles steadily mounting, the autumn session of 1847 accented Lincoln's growing despondency. Despair replaced hope in his letters to his friend Thompson, and he became increasingly critical of Lord John Russell and anxious about the Whig measures. Russell took the opportunity of the special session, called because of the worsening financial crisis, to introduce the Jewish relief bill in December, an action Lincoln deemed most inopportune. The election of Baron Lionel de Rothschild, a Jew, for the City of London prompted the prime minister's introduction of the measure. Lincoln, although he had hoped Russell would postpone the measure until after the holidays, realized that Lord John, with the "City Election hanging about his neck," could not resist Rothschild's demands that the matter suffer no further delays; and even though he felt there was "great indecency in the Prime Minister making himself a party to the Jews forcing the doors of Parliament by the City Election," Lincoln was committed to the principle of Jewish emancipation. Thus he joined seventeen other Peelites to vote for first reading of the bill, "careless," as he told Gladstone, "of the anger of Constituents or other parties."[39]

The introduction of the Jewish relief bill under the existing circumstances convinced Lincoln that Russell was incapable of providing the leadership that was lacking in the House, and Irish matters strengthened his conviction. From the moment he left office, Lincoln had doubted the Whigs' ability to meet the crisis of famine in Ireland. In August 1846 he told Peel, "Ireland will be 'the chief difficulty' of the Whigs." There was much cause for concern:

> Every reader of the debates must see that there is the want of a master mind in the Government, and that none of the Cabinet are able to take an effective line, even in the business of their own departments. Anything, however crude, that is brought forward or suggested by an independent member is instantly adopted in that *paulo post futurum*, and "taken into mature consideration."[40]

The Whig government's response to the famine in Ireland during the remnant of the 1846 session further convinced Lincoln that the ministers were incapable of meeting the crisis successfully. The majority in the cabinet, he told Peel, were "rigid adherents to the ordinary rules of political economy," although Russell himself was ready to relax them.[41] Neither the first lord of the Treasury nor the chancellor of the Exchequer, he feared, could stand up to Charles Trevelyan at home; and in Ireland Lord Bessborough, the lord lieutenant, was indolent and Henry Labouchere, the chief secretary, was pitiably incompetent and too timid to attempt anything.[42] On the day following the enactment of the Labour Rate Act, which transferred the entire cost of public works to the Irish ratepayers, Lincoln noted that the measure would become unpopular with all classes and would prove to be both insufficient and inefficient.[43] Lord John, he smugly told Peel, was not in an enviable position. Ireland, he was sure, would cause him often to regret the vote that put him there. After observing Russell at Windsor, Peel agreed: "He looked miserable enough. Every Irish murder must give him a twinge—a shooting pain under the left ribs."[44]

Other Peelites joined Lincoln in the chorus of opposition to the Whig Irish relief measures in 1846. Lord Jocelyn believed that the government's decision to end the policy of importing cheap food to fill depots would cause many thousands in the south and west of Ireland to perish from starvation. Sir James Graham condemned the withdrawal of government grants to the Irish landowners: "The real extent and magnitude of the Irish difficulty are underestimated by the Government, and cannot be met by measures within the strict rules of economical science." Peel also criticized the new legislation, noting to Goulburn that before the end of winter many parts of Ireland would need more "than the doctrine of Adam Smith on the New Principles of demand and supply and the danger of government interference."[45]

Yet none among the Peelites was as concerned with the fate of Ireland as was Lincoln, who, as ex-secretary, continued to receive much mail from people in Ireland; and in mid-October 1846, after an enjoyable month's visit with friends in Scotland, he undertook a five-week tour of Ireland to check for himself the condition of that troubled country. On 17 November, after traveling over nearly all the country, he forwarded his observations to Peel. He noted the almost universal feeling of contempt for the government, "whilst in every direction one hears the declaration that they 'must have Sir Robert Peel back.'" This desire, he conceded, "is accompanied with extravagant notions of what you could and would have done, but the result of it all is that not only are you most popular but in some of the western parts where Young Ireland is strong your popularity is far greater than O'Connell's." Continuing, he noted that the political situation was becoming alarming. The Young Ireland party was acquiring strength that would raise it to a dangerous position, and the demand for guns and pistols among farmers' boys was so great that weapons could not be imported quickly enough from Birmingham. In many parts of the country he saw that the distress was far worse than the daily newspaper accounts had reported. The Labour Rate Act, he believed, increased the moral and financial mischiefs, which, if continued for a few months longer, would be felt for years. He noted that all cultivation of the soil for the new crops had ceased, since landlords could no longer afford to employ workers for ordinary cultivation, and that improvements on estates, such as the construction of new buildings and the drainage of lands, also had stopped. To his great consternation, all this was occurring while Lord Bessborough was at home "enjoying himself with his Queen," coolly leaving matters in Ireland in the hands of "a timid Secretary!"[46]

Some of Lincoln's criticism of the Whigs' relief measures was justified. Public works proved impossible to control under the Labour Rate Act. Rather than repressing the demands for public works by placing the entire charge of them on the landowners, the deferment for ten years of the repayment of the debt incurred for the projects stimulated the demand. The number of persons employed on works by the end of the year had increased to three hundred thousand, as landowners, having no money for wages, had turned their laborers from the cultivation of the soil to public works, exactly contrary to the government's wishes.[47] The ministers soon recognized the failure of their relief scheme in the context of their plans for Ireland, and early in 1847 they proposed to end the system of public works completely.

Without much enthusiasm, Lincoln and the majority of the Peelites supported the Whig Irish relief measures in 1847, all of which were designed to transfer the financial burdens of relief from the national treasury to the landed proprietors in Ireland. The laboring poor, the landed property, the destitute persons, and the poor relief bills increased the rates of the landed proprietors in the areas of Ireland where poverty was the greatest. These measures were mainly the work of the doctrinaire laissez-faire group in the cabinet, consisting of Lord Grey, Sir Charles Wood, and Sir George Grey—the "family cabinet" within the cabinet—and their formidable ally, Charles Trevelyan, at the Treasury. The latter measure, the Irish Poor Relief Act, enabled guardians at their discretion to grant outdoor relief to able-bodied paupers. Thus the destitute in Ireland were transferred to the Poor Law, and relief from the Treasury virtually ended.[48]

Although the Peelites believed that the magnitude of the crisis in Ireland necessitated moderate use of the public purse, they felt compelled by the temper of Parliament and the country to support the Whig measures. For the moment, at least, they realized that it was impossible to defend the Irish landowners or to assist them in raising the much-needed capital for improvements on the land. As undesirable as the Whig relief legislation was, particularly to

Irish landowners, most of the Peelites, including Lincoln, concluded that the
crisis in Ireland left them no choice but to vote for the government's measures.[49]

Nevertheless, Lincoln was quite concerned about the government's failure
to introduce means for more immediate relief of the starving Irish people and
for more lasting reconstruction of Irish society. In June 1847 he was particularly interested in promoting emigration as a measure auxiliary with others to
effect the social amelioration of the Irish people. His notion for the creation
of a commission on emigration, however, was vigorously opposed by Lords
Russell and Grey in the cabinet. Both Whig magnates believed that it was first
necessary to improve the condition of the Irish "before we people our colonies
with them."[50] Even Peel and Graham were rather skeptical of Lincoln's emigration scheme, and the motion was lost. Lincoln also advocated amending
the Irish Poor Law in such a way as to allow immense sums of money to be
spent for public works and the development of waste lands. As in the case of
the emigration scheme, Peel showed very little enthusiasm for the proposal,
and he even urged Russell to postpone action on the government's waste lands
bill, which was later dropped altogether.[51]

The introduction of the crime and outrage bill during the special session of
1847 further convinced Lincoln that the government was incapable of solving
the problems of Ireland. Lincoln, who had long anticipated the introduction
of such a measure, expressed his contempt for it and the Whigs in a letter to
Sidney Herbert:

> It is the most wretched piece of imbecility that can be conceived, utterly
> ineffectual for its object, and really appears as if it had been designed to
> show that they were quite prepared to abandon the principle upon which
> they came into office—governing Ireland without extra Constitutional
> powers—but that they were not prepared to take any powers which could
> enable them to govern it at all. How men could think it worth while to lose
> their character for the sake of a measure which *must* fail surpasses compre-
> hension, but nobody who knows Ireland dreams of the Bill stopping a
> single murder.[52]

Bad as the bill was in their eyes, the Peelites, defeated on a coercion measure
the previous year, were forced to support it. The crimes bill was a compromise
plan between the positions of Russell and Lord Clarendon, the lord lieutenant
of Ireland. Public opinion had forced Russell to assent to a moderate measure
of coercion, although he was not ready to bring in a restrictive law without
restraining the power of the landlords at the same time. Clarendon had wanted
a stronger coercive measure.[53] Lincoln was particularly sympathetic to Clarendon's point of view. During the previous year, he had traced the number of
firearms sent from Birmingham to Ireland by the W. Thompson firm; and

he, like Clarendon, was alarmed at the number of firearms, even with "bad Birmingham barrels," that were in the hands of a starving, ferocious people.[54] He was confident that an insurrection would break out in Ireland sometime in 1848. Along with the other leading Peelites, Lincoln believed that the real evils of Ireland could be overcome only by increasing the productivity of the land through improvements made by the Irish landed proprietors on their own property. This could be achieved, Peel stated in the Commons, only when the loyal subjects in Ireland were protected from conspiracy and assassination.[55] Lincoln had no quarrel with this view, but he was at the same time convinced that remedial legislation was needed along with the means of protection.

Although the Whig coercion measure passed with little opposition, the Peelites pressed their arguments again when Parliament resumed in 1848. Throughout the spring, the *Morning Chronicle*, purchased in February by Lincoln and Sidney Herbert, supported Lord Clarendon's position. The paper stressed that the suppression of sedition required a double-edged sword: "Those who stimulate the people to obtain by force and arms what they want, should be treated as rebels; of the materials on which they work with so much success, they should be deprived by remedial legislation."[56] Later in the year the paper returned to the same theme. There was need for coercive machinery, indeed even the suspension of the Habeas Corpus Act, but once the rebellion was suppressed there was compelling need to consider how to remove the grievances that produced rebels in Ireland. "Then should come a reform in the startling and anomalous condition of the Church in Ireland—the holding of land, the management of their poor, the many real and profound miseries which are at the root of this rebellion."[57]

Whether or not Lincoln had anything to do with penning these lines, the views expressed in them were his own. By 1848 he had become one of the strongest advocates of remedial legislation for Ireland. He warmly supported the tenant rights bill, a measure designed to grant compensation to tenants for bona fide improvements without abolishing the power of the landlord to fix the rent and transfer or use his property as he wished. Lincoln emphasized that the bill would protect the property and interest of both landlord and tenant.[58] The measure, however, was soon caught in the crosscurrents of the Commons and was swept away into a select committee, where at least, Russell stated, it got an airing.[59] Lincoln also supported the encumbered estates (Ireland) bill. Although in his estimation the measure did not go far enough, he believed it was a good beginning in the emancipation of the land from debt.[60] The bill passed with considerable Peelite support.

Lincoln continued to oppose strongly the government's Irish policy, and in 1849 he wanted to make Irish affairs the centerpiece of an attack against the ministers. The crisis in Ireland had worsened, and a larger number of the

Peelites were now more inclined to join Lincoln in condemning the government's policies. Peel and Graham, however, even though they were more critical of ministerial policy, were as determined as ever to keep the Whigs in office. Their attitude on this matter greatly irritated Lincoln and the other Peelite leaders.

To meet the growing distress in Ireland, the government decided in 1849 to ask Parliament for a grant of £50,000 and for a rate increase of one shilling per pound on Irish landed property to aid relief and emigration. The main purpose of this legislation and grant was to make the Poor Law in Ireland more efficient as the instrument for forcing the Irish landowners to pay for Irish distress. It was an approach very much to the liking of Charles Trevelyan and the doctrinaires in the cabinet.[61]

The Peelites took an active role in the debates on the rate in aid bill. Peel used the occasion to outline his comprehensive proposals for the reconstruction of Ireland. He advocated the appointment of commissions to manage the distressed areas; to take over the Poor Law Unions; to advance loans for drainage, fisheries, public works, and emigration; and to supplant the Court of Chancery in administering the transfer and sale of encumbered, insolvent estates.[62] The ministers opposed Peel's suggestions, but they agreed to introduce another Irish encumbered estates measure later in the session to supplant the failed act of the previous year.

Lincoln and other Peelites supported Peel's Irish proposals, yet many of the Peelites disagreed with Peel's qualified support of the rate in aid bill. Lincoln, who was recognized as the leading Peelite authority on Ireland in the House of Commons, was outspoken in opposing the measure. He continued to press for the introduction of far-reaching remedial programs. "The maxim has been laid down," he told the House in a speech on the rate in aid bill, "and it is a very proper one, that the property of Ireland should support the poverty of Ireland. That is an aphorism which must be generally admitted if properly interpreted." However, instead of increasing the rates on real property to meet the needs of Irish distress, Lincoln advocated the introduction of an income tax, equal in degree on all property of all classes in Ireland and equal between England and Ireland.[63] This same argument was developed in the *Morning Chronicle*, which asked, "Why must the additional charge be made on land in the extension of the area called upon to feed the paupers? Why should a Belfast merchant or a Dublin barrister be free from a rate or tax on property?"[64] Lincoln, along with Gladstone, Goulburn, and Herbert, opposed the bill, which became law on 24 May, while Peel and Graham supported it on the ground that to refuse all extrinsic aid to the distressed Poor Law Unions would further expose the people of Ireland to death by famine and disease.[65]

Lincoln remained consistent in his advocacy of large-scale measures of reconstruction for Ireland. Like Peel, he hoped that the abolition of the old system of land tenure would produce a new capitalist class in Ireland.[66] But his ideas were far more advanced than the Whigs could accept. Rather than a program of governmental assistance and interference to solve the problems of Ireland, the ministers instead chose, according to the *Morning Chronicle*, to "feed Irish poverty with the squeezings of Irish property . . . [and to let] nature do its work."[67]

Although the prime minister now realized that the parliamentary action of the past few years had been more significant in producing the present difficulties in Ireland than were natural causes, he could not persuade his economy-minded cabinet to adopt expensive remedial legislation for the troubled country.[68] Therefore, nature was allowed to take its course, with nothing really significant undertaken for Ireland during the remainder of the government's tenure. The financial crisis in England and the abortive insurrection of 1848 in Ireland hardened the government's attitude. By 1849, the "family circle" of ministers who controlled the cabinet had abandoned Ireland completely to Trevelyan and "the operation of natural causes."[69] The famine finally abated in 1850, but the failure over the years to enact measures of reconstruction and agricultural improvement left Ireland no better and perhaps even worse off than before the famine. The Whig government's relief measures had destroyed nearly as many lives as they had saved,[70] without solving or even addressing the root problems of the country. In his criticism of the Whig measures, Lincoln showed keen insight into the problems of Ireland; yet his position ran counter to public opinion in England, which overwhelmingly supported the government's parsimony and disinterest in long-term measures of reconstruction and improvement. Some of the measures advocated by Lincoln in the late 1840s would be adopted much later, but far too late to accomplish what he had envisaged or to save Ireland for England.

VI

But it was financial matters rather than Irish difficulties that threatened to destroy Russell's government in 1848. The government was never weaker than it was during that session, and the ministers desperately needed the support of the Peelites to stay in office. Their problem began in February when Russell introduced a budget that called for an increase in the income tax from seven pence to one shilling in the pound for a period of five years. The proposal met with considerable indignation in the Commons, with Protectionists and Radicals joined in opposition. A few days later Sir Charles Wood, chancellor of the Exchequer, introduced a revised budget that left the rate at seven pence for three years. Still the income tax opponents geared for action, and Joseph Hume offered an amendment to limit the continuance of the tax to one year. Several of the prominent Peelites spoke against the amendment and defended

Peelite financial policy, and sixty-seven Free Trade Conservatives helped to defeat the amendment. Peelite free-trade support also helped to save the government's bill for the repeal of the Navigation Laws.

Lincoln enthusiastically joined Peel and Russell in the same lobby on these divisions. These were clear-cut free-trade issues. But some of the Peelites were eager to join the Protectionists in opposing the government's sugar bill. Increased pressure for a relief program to deal with the distress in the West Indies prompted Russell to propose a loan of half a million pounds to encourage immigration of labor and to seek a reduced duty on colonial sugar and an increased one on certain kinds of foreign sugar. The principle of equal duties between foreign and colonial sugar, as set in the 1846 act, thus was to be temporarily postponed until 1855. The proposition pleased no one. The extreme Free Traders were not happy with the abandonment of parity between colonial and foreign sugar, and the Protectionists wanted a ten shilling discriminating duty for six years. The majority of the Peelites held opinions midway between the two extremes. Even Peel and Graham were reluctant to support the government's plan, but the latter told Greville that they would not do anything to turn Russell out of office.[71]

The future of the bill and of Russell's government remained very much in doubt. Lincoln, Goulburn, Gladstone, Cardwell, Herbert, and Lord Jocelyn pressed their attack on the weak Whig administration in tandem with the Protectionists. Encouraged by what seemed to him to be a revolt of some of the eminent Peelites from Peel, Lord Londonderry suggested to Disraeli that Goulburn was a man around whom all might rally in an attempt to reconstruct the old Conservative party. Even Sir James Graham suspected that the Peelites who were determined to vote for Sir John Pakington's amendment against the government's bill were ready to take office under Stanley, for, he believed, "they were impatient, could no longer be restrained and were resolved to join the Protectionists." Beresford, however, would not tolerate "the Lincoln and Co set" as leaders of a reunified Conservative party. But the impatient Peelites were not playing that game; they had no intention whatever of joining Stanley or of helping to bring the Protectionists to power. Instead, they joined the attack against the Whigs in order to pave the way for Peel's return to office and to facilitate the reconstruction of parties in the House of Commons. Once in office, they believed, Peel would gain the support of all House moderates.[72]

The Peelite impatients, however, were motivated by more than mere party considerations. They believed that the new sugar proposals were contrary to the true principles of Peelite financial philosophy. They opposed simple protection and advocated maintaining the 1846 settlement. Although they agreed that relief to the planters in the West Indies should be extended through loans and grants for improvements, they opposed the extension of relief through increased duties on foreign sugar.

Yet the Peelite impatients failed completely in their stratagem. Peel and Graham, with a few other Peelites, voted against Pakington's amendment, and the government prevailed by the close vote of 260 to 245. Lincoln, Gladstone, Goulburn, Herbert, and Cardwell all voted with the Protectionists in the minority. Summing up the situation, Gladstone wrote:

> Lincoln said he thought Peel would vote with the Government. I said I felt convinced he never would countenance it on account of the financial principles involved in it. Lincoln was right, and I was wrong; but I now think Peel would have voted with us had he not seen that we were so strong and that with his aid we should be a majority and probably put out the Government. . . . I am now enabled to perceive the intensity of his anxiety to keep them in, since it has led him to give a vote so outrageous to sound financial administration by which he had been very particularly distinguished.[73]

Like Gladstone, Lincoln worried whether the immense power Peel possessed to aid the ineffectual Whig government against any parliamentary movement might not be a serious threat to the political and social security of the country. Certainly it was difficult for these young, confident, ambitious, and idealistic Peelites to tolerate for long Peel's support of an inefficient ministry. They became increasingly critical of Peel's lack of concern for them and his disregard for principle, and they were determined to develop an independent attitude. They opposed the government on the Canadian rebellion losses bill, which, however, was easily passed with the support of Peel and the majority of the Peelites. Both Peel and Graham were particularly provoked in 1848 by the "impatient" and "injudicious" support Gladstone and Lincoln gave to Bankes's motion of censure of Palmerston's dispatch to Sir Henry Bulwer; but, Graham confided to Greville, neither he nor Peel would interfere with such independent action. "If Peel was like other men," Greville remarked, "he would keep Lincoln straight, and it behooves him especially to do so, as Lincoln is supposed to be his favourite adherent."[74]

Russell and the Whig leaders were also perplexed over the opposition of the Peelite impatients. "I don't understand the Peelites," Lord Clarendon wrote to George Cornewall Lewis after seeing the division list on Pakington's amendment,

> for they seem ill disposed to the Protectionists, and Lincoln and Co. are writing articles in the *Chronicle* that will never be forgiven; yet they are throwing off the man who alone gives them importance in the country. I know they are angry with Peel and complain of his selfish determination

neither to act as they wish nor to advise them what they should do; but they are acting as if they meant to isolate themselves. Their course is not one that can lead to fusion with the Whigs, if that is what they are aiming at.[75]

Lewis had already correctly guessed the Peelite plan of action. Realizing that there was no chance for a reconciliation between the Peelite and Protectionist leaders in the Commons, particularly between Lincoln and Beresford, he presumed that Lincoln's and Herbert's game was to "go merely upon the system of weakening the government" to pave the way for the return of Peel and the Peelites to office. The purchase of the *Morning Chronicle* indicated to Lewis that Lincoln himself believed that he was capable of forming a party and turning the government out.[76]

Although the tattered Whig administration was safe for the rest of the year after the vote on Pakington's sugar amendment, the budgetary problems, the postponement of the repeal of the Navigation Laws, and the failure to introduce substantial remedial legislation for Ireland made the younger Peelite leaders more determined than ever to oppose the ministers. Whig blunders in administration fed the Peelite superiority complex, and 1848 was the most miserable session Russell could remember.[77] Lincoln in particular desired to strike at the very heart of the old system of "Whig Cliquery." He, Sidney Herbert, and Gladstone resolved to be a center group bent on capturing a party. They continued to challenge the Whigs' claim of being the enlightened exponents of a popular policy.

The strongest expressions of enmity against the Whigs were saved for the columns of the *Morning Chronicle*, which under Lincoln's and Herbert's close supervision continued to expound the viewpoints of the younger Peelite politicians. On 18 July 1848, a leader summed up the paper's attitude toward the ministers: "The whole tenor of Ministerial endeavours at legislation, during this singularly unfortunate session, has been characterized by an irresolution, a self-contradiction, and an aptitude for bungling, which would suffice to explain any imaginable amount of failure."[78] Throughout the rest of the year and on into the next, the paper continued to focus attention on the points of disagreement between the Peelites and the Whigs. The campaign of the *Morning Chronicle* against the Whigs, it was noted in the *Times*, was an animated one, for "they who carried it on felt that it must be decisive." The *Times* editorial writer accused the young Peelites of attempting to force Russell to decapitate his ministry and party by demanding the sacrifice of Lords Palmerston and Grey, but he was quite optimistic that Russell would eventually succeed in his effort to bring individual Peelites into his cabinet without destroying the Whig party. "The accession of the Peelites to the ranks of the Whigs," the writer concluded, "by constituting a great party in which all persons who wish to satisfy the exigencies of their *amour propre* by refinements, subtleties, and distinctions, will be lost, will stifle these *tiers-parti* attempts, and these culpable endeavours to substitute class rivalries for contests of opinion."[79]

Statements such as this further aroused Peelite antipathies toward the Whigs, and Lincoln in particular was geared for another attack upon them in 1849. Russell's campaign to recruit leading Peelites for his cabinet in January rankled Lincoln, who expressed his astonishment to Peel that Graham had entertained Russell's offer of the Admiralty seriously and had hesitated so long in declining it. Furthermore, Lincoln understood that Russell had intended, after recruiting Graham, to invite him and either Cardwell or Herbert to join the cabinet. To preclude any break in the Peelite ranks, Lincoln immediately upon hearing the rumor informed Cardwell that he would at once refuse the offer. As if to underscore this attitude, the *Morning Chronicle* bitterly attacked the government in its comments on the affair.[80] Thus the gap between the Whigs and the younger Peelites was wider than ever when Parliament resumed.

VII

The parliamentary session of 1849 was filled with important business on Ireland, colonial matters, and commercial policy, but Lincoln's personal life prevented him from concentrating on these matters. His chronic depression, caused by his alienation from his father and the failure of his marriage, extended to his parliamentary life. "The time for returning to the dreary work of this most melancholy and I fear mischievous Session draws much too near," he told Peel at the Easter recess.[81] It was to be one of the most miserable years of his life.

Yet he could never shut himself off completely from politics, and despite his depression and physical debility, his spirits at the beginning of the new year were revived to the point that he became interested in political news and gossip once again. Political rumors were particularly rife at the time, and Lincoln let his mind and pen dwell on some of them in letters to Thompson and to Gladstone. He did not know who Lord Auckland's successor at the Admiralty would be, he wrote, but he knew that Lord Minto was "hungry" and that Lady Russell was "so anxious for her Father that if he is not appointed she will probably miscarry, whilst if he is, Ld. John Russell will certainly miscarry." Almost anything was possible, he believed, for he did not entirely discount the rumor that Lord John Russell's mind was beginning to fail, "not in the way of madness but rather of idiotry," and that he was in a state of utter indifference. Lincoln also pondered the future of the Protectionists and the Peelites. He believed that Bentinck's death the previous autumn would make the policy of the Protectionists more than ever a visionary dream. As for the

Peelites, he was afraid that until someone capable of leading them appeared, they were destined to remain in a wretched state of "time-killing do-nothing-ness."[82]

To do nothing was abhorrent to Lincoln, who urged his friends to press the attack upon the government, particularly with regard to Irish, colonial, and foreign-policy matters. Gladstone and Herbert agreed with Lincoln, and in 1849 the trio of young Peelites once again singled out Lords Grey and Palmerston for attack. They applied the "virtuous theory" of opposition, which Lord Aberdeen explained to Peel in 1850 in an effort to get him to condemn Palmerston's policy in the Commons. The attack, Aberdeen noted, had nothing to do with party interests, nor was it concerned with overthrowing the government. It was designed instead to correct or make less mischievous any "faulty portion of their conduct."[83]

In 1849 Lincoln, Gladstone, and Sidney Herbert applied the "virtuous theory" of opposition to Lord Grey's colonial policy. Although a colonial reformer, Grey was determined in his extension of colonial self-government to the Australian colonies to maintain constitutional checks in the form of provisions for indirect election to colonial assemblies, single chambers with a composition partly nominated, and reserved powers for the crown. Lincoln and his Peelite friends opposed both Grey's political conservatism in colonial matters and Edward Gibbon Wakefield's theory of "systematic" colonization, in which an imperial policy would be emphasized that would produce a hierarchical social organization as a check to democracy in the colonies. Thus the young Peelites' views on colonial matters were closer to the views of the Manchester Radicals than to those of the Benthamite colonial reformers. Lincoln, Gladstone, and Herbert wrote leading articles for the *Morning Chronicle* on colonial policy in which they argued that Parliament must extend unfettered self-government to the Australian colonies.

The Peelite critics, however, failed to gain enough support from the Radicals and Protectionists in the Commons to defeat or amend the colonial measures in 1849; and again in 1850, when the real battle was fought over Lord Grey's colonial policy, the opponents failed to carry the day against the Australian colonies government bill. Although the Peelite impatients had failed to defeat or to modify Lord Grey's Australian bills, they had charted an important course in colonial matters. Lincoln had gone through a formative period, and his views on colonial policy were now quite fixed. He would help implement the policy of colonial self-government during his tenure as colonial secretary in the 1850s and 1860s.

In 1849 Lord Aberdeen and the younger Peelite leaders had little success in convincing Peel to join them in criticizing either Lord Grey's colonial policy or Lord Palmerston's foreign policy. Nor did they succeed in winning him over to their view on the repeal of the Navigation Laws. All except Peel were inclined to press on the administration the policy of conditional legislation based on reciprocity with respect to the repeal of the Navigation Laws. Gladstone angrily noted after a meeting with Peel on the matter that it was another example of Peel's intention of keeping in complete agreement with the government and of not voting against them on any point of importance.[84] But when Peel remained adamant, the younger Peelites gave way and voted for the repeal of the Navigation Laws. Thus the ministers were assured of a solid majority in the Commons and a narrow one in the Lords.

The political frustration that the younger Peelites felt on these matters is clearly revealed in a letter that Edward Cardwell sent Lincoln in the autumn of 1849 shortly after the latter had left England on a Mediterranean cruise. After congratulating Lincoln on breaking away from the distressing ties of politics, Cardwell noted:

> In the feelings of disappointment you so truly express it is impossible not to
> join. The wishes we cherished and the hopes we formed are scattered to
> the winds, and the party we thought so worthy of power and preeminence
> has fallen into forgetfulness of itself and is actually forgotten by the world.
> These things are, of course, most painful, and I have shared in this feeling
> as keenly as others. . . . That Sir Robert Peel's party saved England from
> confusion and has been rewarded by its own annihilation is the simple fact;
> and with this we must reconcile ourselves as best we can.[85]

Despair had taken the place of hope in politics; and for Lincoln, who had fled England, political despair was more than matched by the hopelessness of his marriage.

6. The Lincoln Divorce

"What novel comes up to realities of life?," Catherine Gladstone asked her husband in 1849 after learning the scandalous details of Lady Lincoln's latest amorous escapade.[1] Perhaps in this case the answer to Catherine's question was none, for the Lady Lincoln affair was one of the most notorious scandals of the Victorian period. It was extensively discussed in the press, in the private circles of London society, and in the correspondence of prominent people. The story of the Lincolns' wretched, protracted domestic struggle also caught the attention of Anthony Trollope, who used details of it fictionally in his parliamentary novels and who, knowledgeable contemporaries believed, used Lord Lincoln as his model for Plantagenet Palliser.[2] But Trollope did not have access to the private papers and letters that document this tragicomic tale of marital breakdown. The affair involved not only the two principal characters, but also some of the most prominent members of Victorian society. Thus it provides a penetrating view of early Victorian aristocratic values, standards of morality, and attitudes toward sexuality.

It appeared for a time following their reconciliation in 1844 that the Lincolns had resolved their marital problems. They enjoyed two years of family tranquillity. When they were apart, Susan wrote affectionate letters to Lincoln that were filled with promises of good behavior. By the summer of 1847, however, it was clear that, as before, her promises were not to be fulfilled. Susan had not changed her ways. In September she fled from her husband and children, not to return until early the next year. But she was soon off again. Late in May, Lincoln ordered her home. She returned, albeit defiantly; but an addiction to laudanum and an infatuation with a new lover prompted her to prepare to seize the first opportunity to escape from the tedious, self-righteous admonitions of her husband.

That opportunity was not long in coming. On the afternoon of 2 August 1848, Susan, without notice, drove with her two eldest sons to her father's London house in Portman Square, where she sent them on to meet their governess.[3] She then set off alone in a hackney cab, never to return to her husband and children.

Upon his return home that evening, Lincoln found a note from her informing him that she was on her way to Germany to consult Dr. Chilius in Heidelberg. On 16 August Lincoln received a three-line letter from her, the last he would ever receive, announcing in the coolest terms her safe arrival in Baden, "as if," he told Thompson, "she had done nothing wrong or even extraordinary." It was evident, he noted, that Susan's plans were "contrived with secrecy and cunning" well in advance. He vowed never to allow her to return home.[4]

Lord Douglas, who with his wife was visiting the grand duchess in Baden, expressed to Lincoln his "great grief and his utter astonishment" at his sister's "extraordinary and criminal conduct." Embarrassed by her presence in Baden, he packed her off to the fashionable spa at Ems as fast as he could. Taking everything into account, Lincoln thought Douglas had acted correctly, "though for a person with her views and rules of conduct," Lincoln told Catherine Gladstone, "it is difficult to conceive a much worse place than Ems." Catherine suggested that Lincoln urge Susan to place herself under the care of a lady traveling companion, but Lincoln thought this course hopeless, although he had no objection to her suggesting it to Susan.[5]

Over the next few months, many of Lincoln's close friends consoled him and offered to help him in various ways. Gladstone expressed his encouragement:

> I trust indeed that the future has many brighter blessings in store for you
> than you can at this moment anticipate, since never has there been affliction
> well borne that has not had its fruit in far greater good. . . . It has pleased
> God to endow you with great strength both of mind and body, or you
> could not have gone through what has been laid upon you.[6]

A few days earlier Gladstone had used his own sister Helen's case as a parable to point out to Lincoln how laudanum destroyed responsibility and made its users unfit for punishment or for abandonment to themselves.[7] Catherine Gladstone offered to assist Lincoln in bringing up the children, but Lincoln declined the offer. Although he was tempted to flee England for Spain or Greece, he lingered on at Ryde with his children until mid-September. Then he pocketed his pride and left his three youngest children at Wilton, where the Herberts had graciously offered them a home for the winter; and, after taking Henry and Edward back to Eton, he left for Drayton for a visit with the Peels.

The Peels took him in affectionately, and for days, before Lord Lyndhurst and other friends arrived, Lincoln lived at Drayton *en famille*, the only guest. His visit stretched into early October, forcing him to abandon a Scottish holiday. He was deeply affected by the warm kindness of his hosts and friends. Although he lamented that he had been born with an iron bit rather than a silver spoon in his mouth, his friends, he told Thompson, prevented him from being unlucky in everything. "I possess as warm and sincere friends as any man," he wrote, "and they are friendships which atone for much misery. If friendships could reconcile a man to the loss of all domestic enjoyments I must yet indeed be happy, but that cannot be, and happy I neither am nor am likely to be."[8]

Among the guests at Drayton were Lady Frances Waldegrave and her elderly and pompous third husband, George Granville Harcourt. Lady Frances was a witty, intelligent, impulsive, and very pretty young woman who, after marrying the two sons of Lord Waldegrave in quick succession, had been left doubly widowed and a dowager countess at the age of twenty-five. She married Harcourt in 1847 and was quickly drawn into the Peelite social and political circle. She would eventually become one of the great hostesses of the Victorian age.

Lady Frances was outraged by the way many people at the Drayton party took sly pleasure at Lincoln's misfortune, for, although Lincoln was yet unaware of them, rumors were circulating that the real reason Lady Susan had gone to Germany was to meet Lord Horatio Walpole, a notorious philanderer and a man of vicious temper. Although there was considerable sympathy for Lord Walpole's wife, many felt that Lincoln's absolute probity and uncompromising integrity partly excused Lady Lincoln's behavior. Such a sentiment disgusted Lady Frances, who became Lincoln's zealous champion, and for the rest of her stay with the Peels she bravely attempted to distract him from his unhappiness.[9]

By late October Lincoln's information about his wife was almost depleted. Previously he had heard from Lord Douglas and from Lady Shaw Stewart, who had been staying at Ems and had written on her own accord to him and to Catherine Gladstone. The news from Lady Shaw Stewart was far from pleasant. Her letters only proved, Lincoln lamented to Gladstone, that Susan had not lost her "natural tact and talent" in the art of deluding herself and others. He was disappointed by Lord Douglas's failure to produce some effect upon Susan, who he now believed was on her way to Rome to convert to Catholicism. "It makes me sick at heart," he told Gladstone, "to look forward to the future and to contemplate my name paraded in trials and the filthy ribaldry of the worst portion of the Press!"[10]

Lady Lincoln was in fact on her way to Rome. After spending six weeks at Ems in the company of Lord Walpole, Susan traveled by public stagecoach to Wiesbaden, where Walpole had arrived a few hours earlier. Sometimes traveling together in Walpole's private carriage and sometimes separately with Susan riding with her servants in a hired carriage, the two lovers traveled leisurely from Wiesbaden to Genoa. At Genoa they boarded a steamer for Rome, arriving there in mid-November. From Turin early in November, Susan addressed a letter to Catherine Gladstone couched in terms of innocence and purity:

God bless you for doing me justice and contradicting the falsehoods spread about me. I may have acted rashly & imprudently (in a worldly point of view) in coming abroad for my health as I did, but my notion was *pure* and after all the years of suffering I had endured can you wonder that I (finding my health getting worse and worse) would wish to try any new treatment in order to gain health.[11]

Earlier, in announcing her intention of wintering in Rome, Susan had informed her father that she was trying to forget the last fourteen years and to avoid thinking of what was destroying her health and breaking her heart. "The deed is done," she wrote. "I have chosen exile, solitude, seclusion, slander, in preference to living with him."[12]

As hopeless as the situation appeared, the Gladstones, particularly Catherine, still endeavored to save the marriage. Early in November, Catherine begged "Suzy" to accept a lady companion to protect her from scandal. "When I think of you abroad & alone it makes me shudder," she wrote.[13] Catherine also appealed to Lord de Tabley, an old friend of the Lincolns and Hamiltons, who with his wife was staying with the Douglasses at Brodick Castle on the Isle of Arran, to press this course of action on Lord Douglas. De Tabley's reply was not encouraging. He reported that Douglas was not prepared to adopt the suggestion and that the duke and duchess of Hamilton were content with things as they stood. He believed that any effort undertaken by friends would be useless—"perhaps worse than useless."[14]

Nevertheless, Catherine sent her letter to an address in Rome given her by the duchess of Hamilton. She urged Susan either to return home or to accept a lady companion. Catherine still trusted and loved Susan; and with her strongly Christian, innocent, and compassionate character, it probably never entered her mind that Susan could be guilty of adultery. But there was enough in Susan's answer to raise some suspicion; she refused to have a "lady appendage," preferring instead to be alone with her books and "different occupations." Catherine wrote again, stressing that the children were an increasing responsibility to Lincoln and that he needed her desperately. Catherine was now convinced that Susan was not justified in leaving and told her that she must repent and return and not "walk along the edge of a precipice blindfold."[15]

Late in November, Lady de Tabley candidly revealed the true nature of the situation to Catherine and cautioned her against endeavoring to overcome "so poisonous an influence" as Lord Walpole had on Susan. "I have no words to say how sorry I am for Lord L.," she added. "Do you know," she continued,

I really think he is dying. I never saw a man so altered in so short a time. . . . I have written very unguardedly what I think—and nothing but my firm belief that Lord Lincoln's character will be gone, in the eyes of the world, if he ever sees Lady L. again, makes me tell you this. I think he

claims just now all the support that true friends can give—for *he* is *really* to
be pitied—and do what one may, he never can be again the man he was—
she has blighted his existence and I fear is totally without feeling for her
children.[16]

There now could be little doubt about the future of the Lincoln marriage.
Still, the Gladstones refused to give up hope, and Lincoln, greviously missing
his wife and still loving her, prayed that their mission to save his marriage and
Susan from utter destruction would be successful. "I mourn for her even more
than for myself," Lincoln told his old friend Henry Manning, archdeacon of
Chichester. "I know I am indifferent to the scoffs of men and the rebukes of
friends when they see that I care for her still—and in one sense at least, that
in which I believe forgiveness is enjoined, I have forgiven her already."[17]

Lincoln's despair contributed greatly to the decline of his health, and he
became seriously ill in November. He complained of suppressed gout that
caused him severe pains and headaches, "mind and matter," he told Peel, "acting and reacting one upon the other in no very pleasant or cheering mode."[18]
By early December he was corporally well enough to return to London for a
few days to await the arrival of his boys from Eton for the Christmas holidays.
But he remained weak and dispirited. He confessed to Peel that between som-
ber politics and melancholy private matters he was tempted to shut himself
up, and he told Thompson that if Parliament did not rouse him he would
close up shop.[19] Later in the month he declined several invitations, including
one from Peel for a Christmas visit, choosing instead to remain with his
children at Wilton House with the Herberts until mid-January.

II

The new year, 1849, brought added misery. Early in the summer disquiet-
ing rumors of Susan's misconduct reached England. On 20 June, Gladstone
learned of "new & very painful evidence" that raised for the first time in his
mind the serious fear that Susan might have committed "the last act of infi-
delity."[20] He immediately saw Lincoln and Peel on the matter, and during the
next few days the three men settled the preliminaries for sending a friend to
Italy on a mission either to confirm the rumors and thus substantiate a case
of criminality against Lady Lincoln, or to induce her to come home or join
friends abroad for the sake of protection and security. Lincoln first asked
Archdeacon Henry Manning to undertake the task, but later asked Gladstone
to go when Manning declined on grounds of poor health and previous commitments. Gladstone, with the earnest support of his wife but not that of his
father, Sir John Gladstone, agreed to accept the mission. On 14 July he crossed
the Channel, taking with him a letter from his wife addressed to "My Dearest

Suzie," entreating her to listen to Gladstone and to return to her ill and sorrowful husband and lonely children.[21]

Gladstone's willingness to undertake such a mission was somewhat unconventional by Victorian standards, yet he was determined to do what he could to rescue Lady Lincoln and avert further tragedy. He traveled three thousand miles in twenty-seven days during his quixotic journey.[22] After missing Lady Lincoln in Naples, he traveled to Milan, where her mail was being forwarded and where he believed she had gone. After unsuccessfully searching the police registry and those of several of the better inns for a reference to Lady Lincoln, he discovered from the landlord at the Gran Bretagna that she had probably assumed the name of Mrs. Laurence and that she was residing at Lake Como.

Reaching Como on the morning of 31 July, Gladstone after breakfast "set about the sad purpose" of his visit.[23] He presented himself at the iron gate of the Villa Mancini, where the police had informed him Mrs. Laurence lived, and sent in his card. When Saccomani Santi, Lady Lincoln's courier, appeared at the gate, Gladstone asked to see Mrs. Laurence. He was told that Mrs. Laurence was too ill to see anyone. Gladstone then asked "in a rather marked manner" for the countess of Lincoln. He was assured that no person of that name lived there. He then gave the courier a brief note requesting an interview with Mrs. Laurence and enclosed Catherine's letter on the chance that Lady Lincoln's desire to know something about her children might induce her to open the letter. He also hoped to receive a written response in Lady Lincoln's hand, which he immediately would recognize. However, after about ten minutes Santi returned with Catherine's letter unopened and with a verbal message that Lady Lincoln was unknown and that Mrs. Laurence could not see him.[24]

That evening Gladstone, having learned from his guide that the occupants of the villa were preparing to leave, returned to play out the farce. He saw a female figure entering a carriage; although it was too dark for positive recognition, he believed that the woman was Lady Lincoln. He raised himself up on his tiptoes in an attempt to see inside the carriage as it drove past him through the gates, but the blinds were down. Later that night he revealed in a letter to his wife what had long been suspected. Mrs. Laurence, he observed, "is far advanced in pregnancy!" It was, he added, "the triumph of hellish wickedness over a woman of the rarest gifts, and the utter devastation of heart & home & profanation of the holy mystery of marriage."[25]

The next day Gladstone followed Lady Lincoln (or Mrs. Laurence, for he was still not certain that Mrs. Laurence was Lady Lincoln) as far as Lecco by way of Varenna. At Varenna he tried unsuccessfully to ascertain information about Lord Walpole, who was staying in that town at the Hotel de la Poste. During the evening of 30 July, on the eve of Gladstone's arrival at Como, Walpole and Susan had learned of the arrival of an Englishman who was making inquiries in Milan at the Gran Bretagna. Believing the Englishman to be Lincoln, Walpole had hastily fled the Villa Mancini at three o'clock the following morning, just a few hours before Gladstone's arrival at Como. He had crossed the lake, catching a violent cold, and was confined for several weeks at the hotel in Varenna.[26]

Finding that Susan had driven on to Bergamo the previous night, Gladstone gave up the chase and returned to Como. Disheartened and worried about Catherine, he started for home on 2 August. Unbeknown to him, on that very day, one year to the day since she had left London, Lady Susan gave birth to a baby boy at the Hotel Torre de Londra, Verona. At Lausanne on 5 August, Gladstone, after taking Holy Communion, wrote in his diary:

> Oh that poor miserable Lady L.—once the dream of dreams, the image that to my young eye combined everything that earth could offer of beauty and joy. What is she now! But may that Spotless Sacrifice whereof I partook, unworthy as I am, today avail for her, to the washing away of sin, & to the renewal of the image of God.[27]

From Paris three days later he again wrote to Catherine of the details of his unsuccessful mission. "The same post which carries this," he lamented, "carries also the dagger to Lincoln."[28]

Although Gladstone's journey failed to bring about the desired results, his efforts helped to reassure Lincoln's circle of friends that every effort had been made to secure a reconciliation. Sir Robert Peel, who had become virtually a second father to Lincoln and who was aware of all the circumstances of the affair, praised Gladstone for his "unparalleled kindness and generosity" in undertaking the thankless task. "Your errand," Peel consoled Gladstone,

> has not been a fruitless one, for it affords the conclusive proof that everything that the forbearance and tender consideration of a husband and the devotion of a friend could suggest as the means of averting the necessity for appealing to the Law for such protection as it can afford, has been essayed and essayed with the utmost delicacy. The proof is valuable so far as the world and the world's opinion is concerned—much more valuable as it respects the heart and conscience of those who have been the active agents in a work of charity.[29]

With this proof, Peel intimated that the public would be more sympathetic to Lincoln and would regard him with greater esteem, in part mitigating the pain of his divorce.

But the pain Lincoln felt was hardly diminished. The sadness and bitterness that Gladstone's letter produced in Lincoln's heart were never to be extinguished. Although he was now resolved to initiate divorce proceedings, Lincoln embarked upon this course of action "like a man on his way to the scaffold."[30] But even as he undertook these proceedings, Lincoln informed

Manning and Gladstone that he still hoped for Susan's repentance. Just before leaving England in late September, he visited Manning in Sussex and wrote to Gladstone to solicit their opinions on both the general effect of divorce on repentance and his duty in the future. Lincoln's letter made Gladstone "stagger with admiration." Writing to Manning, Gladstone noted that he now held Lincoln in higher esteem than ever: "He has a very high creation, written by the hand of God, in the lineaments of his own character, its splendid integrity, its bravery, its manful will, and its deep affection."[31]

Gladstone took advantage of Lincoln's "piece of true Christian heroism" to express his views on divorce. Although he recognized God's permission for the aggrieved party in a marriage to be liberated from the contract in the event of adultery, Gladstone strongly believed that God never made that right an obligation. The highest path, he continued in his letter to Lincoln, was the one that sought conversion of the fallen without the dissolution of the contract. He realized that it was a path very few have strength and grace to follow, "a path so difficult and so much beyond the range of common application, that much of the sounder part of public opinion, which generally is an aid to acts of virtue, here changes sides and discountenances the highest virtue." Therefore, Gladstone believed that Lincoln, having already demonstrated the requisite strength and grace, should wait to see if it pleased God to recall the heart of the wanderer. He agreed with Manning that repentance "so deep and solid, so given into the habit and frame of mind, as well as so vivid and sharp in its emotions," would correct the past, and he did not think that the interests of the children constituted an absolute bar to the restoration of the marriage.[32]

Catherine Gladstone also gained new hope from Lincoln's letter. Perhaps, she thought, Susan could enter a type of "penitentiary," with Archdeacon Manning at the head, from which she might come out a new woman after a year.[33] Catherine felt compelled to write another letter to Susan to urge her to turn to God while there was still time. It was, of course, a most forlorn attempt to rescue a friend. Susan instructed Charles Rankin, the duke of Hamilton's solicitor, to return the letter to Catherine; she told Rankin that she had not read it and never would have opened it had she known from whom it came. Later Susan asked a mutual friend to give Catherine a terrible message. "She is likely to see a great deal of my children," she stated. "For most things they could not be better than with her, but tell her that if ever she speaks against their mother my ghost will haunt her. When she is happy with her children let her think of me."[34] Thus ended the communication between the two women. Even the Gladstones had to accept the inevitable.

Despite his reluctance, Lincoln allowed the divorce proceedings to continue. Sir Robert Peel was convinced that his young friend had no other safe or honorable alternative.[35] Lincoln retained John Parkinson to prepare to present the case before the ecclesiastical and civil authorities. Parkinson employed another solicitor, Lewis Raphael, to collect evidence on the Continent against Lady Lincoln and sent with him Joseph Asman, formerly Lincoln's butler, to identify her indisputably. This much done, Lincoln, still greatly distraught and suffering from a heart complaint, prepared to set sail for the Mediterranean. He planned to remain on the cruise for eight or nine months, or at least for the duration of the divorce ordeal. The sea agreed with him, he told Bonham, and he hoped that it would help him bear up against his cares and anxieties. Were it not for his five pledges—"hostages for my return"—he would remain abroad until old age dulled his memory to all that once gave interest, energy, and meaning to his life, but that now he found hateful. Yet, almost as a postscript, he added:

> Write to me often. Politics are odious to me—yet the squirrel hunter picks
> up his ears at the voice of the hounds; society's gossip and scandal have
> no charm for me—yet those who may be its food like to know how they
> are to be cooked. Write to me *frankly* and *freely* and you will prove your
> friendship as you have always done.[36]

Originally set for late August, Lincoln's departure was delayed until 19 September, the eve of his two eldest boys' return to Eton. He had found a small house for the younger children and their nurse in the Cloisters at Windsor, where all the children would be near one another. He asked the Thompsons to take the children in at Christmas and to visit them at Eton and Windsor. With this last detail arranged, he sailed from Portsmouth, not with a sense of bitterness toward Susan, he told Thompson, but with "mourning yearning affectionate compassion as the memory of the days when I hoped to find in her a Wife not only in name but in heart and the yet lingering sparks of a sincere and manly love must engender." The wind was fair and the autumn sun was bright. "Where is the one conducting me—where will the other shine on me before long?," he asked himself.[37]

III

Lord Lincoln's yacht, the *Gitana*, carried him to Athens, Constantinople, Asia Minor, Palestine, and Egypt. Although the cruise was filled with misfortunes and mishaps, the sights of the East refreshed him and his health improved; but after ten months he longed to see his children. In mid-July 1850 he arrived at Gibraltar after enduring nineteen days of rough sea from Malta. The shocking news of the death of Sir Robert Peel awaited him from the pen of Sidney Herbert, who observed that the very last time he had been with Peel they had talked about Lincoln's affairs, with Peel giving the "attention and the anxious advice which a Father would have given for a son."[38] The loss of Peel was one more sorrow "*deeply* graven" on Lincoln's heart. "I should indeed be most ungrateful if his memory were not ever dear to me," he wrote to Gladstone,

> for the sorrows of my domestic life have been so associated with his ready
> and friendly counsels, and I have ever found in him so delicate a sympathy
> and so sagacious advice, that the termination of my married life and the
> simultaneous death of Friend and Counsellor seem to leave me in a void
> which yet appears bewildering.[39]

Lincoln's bewilderment was understandable, for there could not have been a more rapid succession of crucial events so calculated to affect his private and public life than he witnessed in 1850. In addition to the painful dissolution of his marriage and the death of Peel, he learned upon his return that his friend Archdeacon Henry Manning was on the edge of the precipice poised for the leap to Rome. Lincoln's homecoming was made even more unpleasant by his father's illness that autumn. Lincoln and his five children were left virtually homeless; the duke would have none of his grandchildren in the house at Clumber. "You know not the misery I have to undergo here," Lincoln lamented to Francis Bonham, whom he asked to find an inexpensive cottage for his family in London. "My Father," he continued,

> has no other care or thought than to order every sort of extravagance both
> in the shape of purchases and works and to raise money to pay for them
> in every possible and impossible objectionable way, and this with his affairs
> on the verge of bankruptcy! If I could tell you half what has occurred in
> the last fortnight you would hardly believe me.[40]

Lincoln's marital crisis had not induced much sympathy in Newcastle for his son, even though over the past year the duke had become profoundly interested in the divorce proceedings. Late in August 1849, Newcastle wrote at length to William Henderson, his solicitor, with particulars of how he should advise Parkinson to proceed in the matter "so that Ly Lincoln's infamy shall be completely proved & exposed, & that this little bastard shall not be palmed upon my family as a legitimate child & a Clinton."[41] He also wanted to make sure that action was taken to force Susan into forfeiting her jointure from the Newcastle estates and to assure Lincoln's right to marry again. Henderson promised the duke that there would be an action at law and a divorce in the Ecclesiastical Court before a special act of Parliament was sought to dissolve the marriage. With the passage of the divorce bill, Lincoln would be enabled to marry again. Henderson also thought that the parliamentary decree would be drafted in such a way as to declare Lady Susan's baby illegitimate. He anticipated little difficulty in the matter. "I should think the case is safe for a Divorce," he wrote to Newcastle,

> if the evidence is properly collected, as I have no doubt it will be. As your
> Grace observes a year has elapsed, with the channel between them (Lord

and Lady Lincoln)—one of the parties has been "extra quattuor maria" as in
olden times they used to say, at the time when the child was begotten. In
the present instance the absence of the parties from each other exceeds a
year.[42]

Since the Divorce Acts did not interfere with marriage settlements, Newcastle was forced to arrange the forfeit of Susan's jointure from the Newcastle
estates privately with the duke of Hamilton. The Hamiltons and the Douglasses were eager to cooperate and complete the divorce. The duke of Hamilton instructed his solicitor, Charles Rankin, to appear for Susan for any
process that was issued and to offer no defense against the proceedings.[43] He
also agreed that Susan should forfeit her jointure and receive income from her
own property only. Nonetheless, the duke and duchess were quick to point
out to Newcastle that the breakdown in the marriage was just as much the
fault of Lincoln as it was of their own daughter. "This melancholy affair in
which we are all involved," Hamilton wrote to Newcastle, perhaps to assuage
his own pride, "is advancing &—I grieve to say—is gradually making its way
into the mouths of the Publick. We are miserable. The Duchess in despair &
you will sympathize with us as we sympathize with you, in the common
calamity of the whole family—for you like myself come within the sphere of
this distressing scene."[44]

The divorce proceedings moved slowly, dragging on well into the next year.
Eventually the charge of adultery against Lady Lincoln was proved in the
Ecclesiastical Court as well as in the House of Lords. The story of Susan's
elopement at Ems with Lord Walpole and their cohabitation during their subsequent sojourn through Germany, Switzerland, and Italy was revealed in the
testimony before the Lords. Lord Walpole's valet furnished details of the
couple's adultery. Parkinson presented a certificate of baptism of a male child
born to Lady Lincoln and named Horace; his parents were listed as Horace
Walpole Laurance and Harriet. Raphael and Asman presented the detailed
evidence they had collected on the Continent, and Gladstone recounted the
details of his unsuccessful mission to Italy.[45] Early in May 1850, while Lincoln
was still on his cruise, the Ecclesiastical Court pronounced in favor of the
divorce, and Lincoln's divorce bill was read a second time at the end of the
month. The marriage was officially dissolved on 14 August 1850.

Although he was relieved to have his prolonged and agonizing marital situation resolved at last, Lincoln was by no means free from its devastating
events. The dissolution of his marriage was a traumatic experience from
which he would never recover. The anxiety it caused greatly affected his health
and certainly contributed to his early death. He would never again have the
strength to withstand for long the pressures of office, and the difficulties he
would face in 1854 as secretary of state for war further impaired his health.

The unfortunate affair was a personal tragedy that cut short a productive career.

Since he was seen by most as the innocent party, the costs of the divorce for Lincoln were personal rather than political or social. The divorce did not affect his standing at court, where he remained a favorite. Indeed, the queen and Prince Albert continued to extend their sympathy for him in his unending misfortunes. Nor did the divorce affect his political career, except in the more restricted sense of undermining his health. In fact, the divorce freed Lincoln from domestic restraints and allowed him to pursue his political ambitions. His subsequent failure to fulfill his goals was due far more to poor health, political misfortunes, and serious miscalculations than to personal difficulties caused by the dissolution of his marriage.

Another factor that contributed to Lincoln's failure, both in marriage and in politics, was his inability to overcome problems of temperament. Although the extent to which his humorless, rigid nature contributed to Lady Lincoln's unhappiness can only be a matter of conjecture, it undoubtedly played a significant role. Likewise, his dogged determination, uncompromising nature, and intense political prejudices often impeded his career. In this respect, he was much like his father, from whom he remained alienated until shortly before the duke's death on 12 January 1851. On that day, with shattered hopes but at peace with all his family,[46] the old duke left a world that he had long since ceased to understand or appreciate. Upon his father's death, Lincoln inherited enormous debts and a ruined fortune; he also assumed the title and honors of the fifth duke of Newcastle.

7. In Search of a Party

Newcastle's translation to the House of Lords brought him mixed political blessings. He was now separated from his closest friends in the Commons and removed from an arena in which he had shown considerable skill. Still, as Edward Cardwell pointed out to him, he at least had the advantage of being called away from the "disagreeable circumstances" to which there seemed no end in the Commons. "In the House of Lords," Cardwell continued, "your high rank, your powers and antecedents, will all contribute to ensure to you your proper place; and I sincerely hope you may derive satisfaction from the change, and see reason to believe that the time of its occurrence is not impropitious."[1]

Sir George Cornewall Lewis believed that Newcastle's move to the House of Lords was a greater event in politics than most people realized. He told Lord Clarendon that it was a blessing to the Whigs to have Newcastle separated from Gladstone. Had the two remained together in the House of Commons, freed from all restraints by Peel's death, they would have carried on a most active opposition to the government, particularly concerning colonial matters. Gladstone by himself, Lewis continued, would be a different man, for, in terms of opposition at least, "a man by himself is not equal to half two men." Yet, Lewis conceded, Newcastle's move "to a quieter & better place" might propel him as an individual leader. He had no domestic ties and no literary amusements, and "He considers himself a first rate man of business & a speaker good enough to lead a party. He has unbounded confidence in himself—he has much pluck & spirit, & is fully impressed with the advantages of his social position."[2]

As Lewis shrewdly noted, the deaths of Peel and the fourth duke of Newcastle had substantially altered the position of the Peelite party. With the reluctance or refusal of Lord Aberdeen and Sir James Graham to lead the Peelites, the fifth duke of Newcastle, partly by action of his own and partly by circumstances, was cast in a leadership role. From this position he would attempt for about the next eighteen months to keep the Peelites together, to strengthen them as a party, and to bring them to power at the head of a coalition of moderates in the House of Commons. Clearly, these were the political aspirations of an ambitious politician, perhaps carried to an extreme.

120

But it was the bitterness of his feelings rather than the excess of his ambitions that was Newcastle's major fault in politics. He was not, as often has been argued, an impractical dreamer whose colossal ambition far exceeded his limited ability; he was instead an able organizer who had a great depth of political perception. His abilities were readily recognized by his friends as well as by his political opponents, and his ambitions were encouraged by the court. Intimate friends of the royal couple knew that Prince Albert's estimation of Newcastle was so great that any government in which the duke had a prominent part would meet with little opposition from Windsor. In April 1854 Prince Albert and Aberdeen even discussed the possibility of Newcastle forming a new government with Gladstone as leader of the Commons if Russell carried out his threat to resign over the postponement of the reform bill. Gladstone agreed with Aberdeen that Newcastle was "the description of man who would discharge well all the duties of that office," and urged the prime minister to bring the duke forward as his successor.[3]

Newcastle's equal hatred of the Whigs and Protectionists and his impassioned obstinacy, however, made him a difficult choice as leader of the Peelites. Even his close friendship with Gladstone was severely strained early in 1852 over party matters and party leadership. Nonetheless, Newcastle played a significant role in keeping the Peelites together during these politically confused years of the early 1850s, and his part in forming the coalition government under Lord Aberdeen was crucial.

II

The political paralysis of which Cardwell complained grew worse during the opening weeks of the 1851 session. Although slight in content, the Whig government's legislative program was highly controversial. Russell's ecclesiastical titles bill won overwhelming support in both Houses after lengthy, heated debate but united the Peelite leaders against it and the government. Sir Charles Wood's budget disappointed everyone but was reluctantly supported by the Peelites. Newcastle was greatly upset by both matters. He considered "insidious" Russell's response to the papal brief restoring the Roman Catholic episcopacy in England, the event that prompted the introduction of the ecclesiastical titles bill. He told Gladstone that it exposed Englishmen to Europe "as a set of fanatics panting for fire and faggots." They had no right, he believed, to interfere with the introduction of Roman Catholic prelates in Great Britain or to deny them territorial jurisdiction.[4] As for the budget, Newcastle disliked Wood's "peddling" commercial reform and his "hand-to-mouth tinkering of taxation"; though he was no longer in the Commons to "bear the brunt of obnoxious proposals," he was anxious to express his views to Herbert when the "small Family Party of Peelites" met to discuss the budget. He urged his Peelite colleagues to accept the income tax as a permanent tax and to press for a reduction of the rates on trades and the professions as a way to make it more equitable.[5]

These parliamentary matters were interrupted by a prolonged ministerial crisis. The lengthy sequence of events began when Russell resigned on 21 February after the government was defeated on Locke King's motion for the extension of the franchise. Newcastle spent the next few days trying to prevent Gladstone and Lord Canning from joining Stanley, and Lord Aberdeen and Sir James Graham from joining Russell. "Those who take office under Stanley at this moment," he told Graham, "must, and will, be considered renegades to our commercial policy."[6] He was considerably more circumspect to Gladstone:

> I am sure our rule of conduct at this juncture must be prudent waiting on events and a perfect readiness for any self-sacrifice which those events may prove to be a *duty*. I think a coalition at this moment would be fatal to character and most mischievous to the Queen and the country.[7]

That same day he told Herbert, "The pride of Protectionists is not yet humbled enough or the love of Cliquery of the Whigs dissipated enough for us to appear on the scene of action."[8] Three days later he called at Carlton Gardens on Gladstone, who had just returned from Italy, and urged him not to accept office under Stanley. If the Peelites held off now, Newcastle told his friend, "the crisis must end shortly in placing the *summa rerum* in our hands."[9]

Throughout these negotiations, as Charles Greville noted in his diary, "nobody was in earnest."[10] No new political junctures were effected, and the situation in Parliament remained much the same. "There *never* was *such* a *complicated & difficult* state of affairs," the queen exclaimed to her uncle.[11] Stanley's intention to place a five or six shilling duty on corn and Russell's determination to carry the ecclesiastical titles bill provided the Peelite leaders with reasons to refuse coalition with either. Without Peelite help, the Protectionists could not form a government; and the Whigs, even though they returned to power under Russell, could not hope to remain long in office. To Newcastle's great satisfaction, the Peelites for the moment withstood the endeavors of both Lords Russell and Stanley to extirpate them as an independent group in Parliament.

Although the ministerial crisis of February 1851 demonstrated the strength of the Peelites as individuals, it also marked their weaknesses as a group. Without a recognized leader and without party organization, they could come to power only individually as appendages to either of the major parties. But some of the prominent younger Peelites believed that with a leader they could retain their independent position, from which perhaps eventually they could form either the nucleus of a new party or an independent Peelite administration. Therefore, with an independent third-party government in mind, New-castle, Gladstone, and Sidney Herbert intensified their search for a leader and redoubled their efforts to organize the Peelites following the ministerial crisis. In'April, Gladstone urged Graham to lead an independent party, and early in July, Lord Londonderry, an advocate of Conservative reunion, appealed to Aberdeen "to weld the scattered fragments into some consolidated shape."[12] Aberdeen remained uninterested in such an endeavor, and Graham, believing that a third party was fatal to the country, thought in terms of an eventual fusion with the Whigs.

Notwithstanding his personal problems, Newcastle became deeply in-volved in these party matters. He told Bonham in April:

> If I were to consult my own inclinations and my own interests—to say nothing of my much-impaired health and energies—I should confine my remaining activities and powers of usefulness to the attempt to retrieve the fortunes of my Family and estates and leave public affairs to others to whom office is an object of desire and who have more sanguine hopes of being able to do good service in their Country than any I now entertain. I have not however so learned the duties of my position, and I at once answer your question by the reply, I am willing to take a part in the proceedings which must soon succeed to this state of transition and I entirely agree in the necessity for some more decisive and explicit line than hitherto we have been enabled to take.[13]

In June he drafted a memorandum on party matters in which he stressed the need for the Peelites, as the legitimate heirs of Peel's policies, to retain a position apart from both Protectionists and Whigs.[14] During the summer and autumn he corresponded extensively with Gladstone on party matters. Both agreed that Russell would be hard-pressed to carry on, and both believed that he would introduce a reform measure as a last desperate effort to rally support. But Newcastle did not view reform with quite the apprehension that Glad-stone did. He believed that the people could be trusted with a broadly based franchise. "My fears," he confided to Gladstone, "such as they are, arise more from distrust of the hands which are to give rather than of those which are to receive the boon." Probably, he added, the government would not stand long enough to press the reform matter.[15] He thought that Lord Derby (formerly Lord Stanley) was too weak to attempt an administration. "What then?," he asked Bonham:

> Where is our Leader? If we had one, I should not despair of success even tho' the hope looks a little forlorn, but a leader in our case is an *essential*. Of this truth however I am deeply sensible—if Ld. J. R. resigns and Ld. D refuses, the game of Feby. last *must not* for the honor of the Country and the dignity of the Queen be played again. In such a case we *must* (and so far

as I am concerned we *will*) try, though we destroy all our political prospects
for ever.[16]

With the prospect of the Peelites being called upon to form a government,
Newcastle was anxious to meet with Gladstone, Herbert, Sir John Young, and
a few other leading Peelites to chart their course before the start of another
parliamentary session.

The idea of an independent Peelite government had been planted in Newcastle's mind in June when Prince Albert informed him, through Baron Stockmar, that the queen would summon him to form an administration if Russell
resigned. The duke apparently discussed this matter with Gladstone during a
visit at Carlton Gardens soon after the prince's intimation reached him. But
Gladstone still believed that Aberdeen, because of his advanced age, should
lead the Peelite party and that Newcastle should succeed him when the former
could no longer act in that capacity. Late in October, Gladstone again told
Newcastle that the leadership of the Peelites properly belonged to Aberdeen;
but, he added, if Aberdeen persisted in refusing to assume it publicly, the
party should elect the duke as its leader.[17]

Newcastle sent Gladstone's letter to Herbert, noting that the election of a
party leader was "an inversion of the proper constitutional view of party
mechanism." He continued:

> A leader should become such, either because he is generally recognized as
> *facile princeps* in position, popularity, talent, discretion, debating power,
> or other qualifications necessary to balance the differences of opinion to be
> found in all parties, or by being selected by the Sovereign as her adviser
> when her Ministers have resigned. . . . You will at once see that the drift of
> all this is that Lord Aberdeen may *take* the leadership by consent of all, if
> he will leave his easy-chair and summon his friends; but as for Gladstone's
> alternative, it is *impossible*. I hope I am not a man to shrink from anything
> that can be proved to be a duty, and, as you know, I would, if my friends
> were willing to assist, have even placed myself in a position for which I am
> so little qualified, when my friend Baron [Stockmar] intimated to me that
> I might be called upon in the manner indicated in my second case, but this
> was only if forced by circumstances which, however improbable success
> might be, would fully acquit the individual of arrogance and presumption,
> and could endanger no great principle of Government, and prejudice no
> national interest. Unless, therefore, Lord A. will seize the reins, I think,
> notwithstanding G's strong opinion, we must still go on without a leader.
> Still, I think a meeting of the few who will talk freely to one another
> may be very useful.[18]

Herbert fully concurred in Newcastle's views, adding that whatever the duke's
personal fitness as a leader, it would be absurd to expect Aberdeen and Gra-

ham to place themselves as followers of a man some twenty-five years their junior.

Still hoping for a Peelite administration, Newcastle early in December made plans for a small "friendly reunion" at Clumber during the middle of January. He told Gladstone that the Herberts and Cannings were coming and that he had asked Aberdeen, Young, Goulburn, and Bonham. He stressed the importance of organizing to prevent Russell from absorbing their little band. "So long as the present anomalous state of Government exists," he continued, "I confess I look upon it as almost a national duty imposed upon us to endeavour to keep together." As for whom they should adopt as leader, a question upon which Gladstone still laid great stress, Newcastle admitted that he was unfitted for the position. "I do not dream of it, and if I did, I am sure few would concur in such an hallucination," he wrote. However, he would, "at the risk of derision, or any other personal detriment," place himself in any position that he deemed necessary to help ward off mischief and "stand in the gap till the Queen could make some arrangement better for herself and the Country." He had some reservations about Aberdeen as leader, particularly his age and "his want of manner or knowledge of how to deal with mankind, his leaning to despotism on the Continent, his utter ignorance of Finance, and . . . his lack of courage." Nevertheless, he admitted, Aberdeen was the only man under whom he would serve willingly; even though he feared the consequences of his leadership in opposition, he was willing, if the others concurred, and if Aberdeen himself agreed, to recognize him as their leader.[19]

The events of late December and the part Newcastle played in them made his "innocent Cabal" at Clumber in January 1852 most inauspicious. Had these circumstances been anticipated, Newcastle told Bonham on the eve of the meeting, "I should not at this moment have invited a party of political friends, but having invited them I was quite content to bear the brunt of any illnatured remarks."[20] In fact, Newcastle intended to take advantage of the occasion to explain his part in the events.

The sequence of events began on 30 December when Russell, anxious to strengthen his ministry with an addition of Peelites following Palmerston's forced resignation earlier in the month, held an hour-and-a-half interview at Pembroke Lodge with Newcastle, whom upon the recommendation of Graham he recognized as the leader of the Peelites. Russell wanted Newcastle to take the office of lord lieutenant of Ireland upon the resignation of Lord Clarendon at Easter and to ascertain the views of his friends regarding merging with the Whigs. Newcastle immediately raised three difficulties to his acceptance of office under Russell. As lord lieutenant he could not enforce the Ecclesiastical Titles Act, which he had spoken and voted against in the Lords. He was critical of Russell's ecclesiastical appointments, fearing that they would cause a further secession of High Church men from the Church. He also opposed Lord Grey's colonial policy, especially with regard to New Zealand. He was, therefore, most disinclined to take office, adding in his comments to Russell that he could not anticipate any benefit to the government or to the public by his doing so and "that, generally speaking, junctions of this kind did not strengthen the existing Government, and injured *or even tainted* those who joined it."[21]

As requested, however, Newcastle informed the leading Peelites of what had been discussed and passed on Russell's offer of office to Cardwell and Herbert, both of whom promptly declined. On 7 January, Newcastle went to Windsor to explain his position to the queen and Prince Albert. A few days later the queen informed Russell that she thought he probably could not absorb the leading Peelites into the Whig party, a point the duke had made to Prince Albert.[22] On 17 and 19 January, Newcastle exchanged argumentative, almost rancorous letters with Russell to close the negotiations.[23] The ground between the two men was wider than ever.

Most of the ministers had pressed Russell to make the overture to Newcastle. Although they knew how difficult and pretentious the duke was and how drastically his Church views differed from their own, they realized the importance of bringing him and one or two (besides Gladstone) of his Peelite friends into the cabinet.[24] With the exception of Lord Minto, they were sorry to see the negotiations with the duke fail, and the two Greys and Sir Charles Wood criticized the way Russell had managed the whole affair. They believed that Russell had not been forthright in the talks with Newcastle, leaving the impression of insincerity and Whig exclusiveness. Therefore, they urged Russell to see Graham in an effort to rectify the situation and reopen negotiations with the Peelites.[25] Russell reluctantly invited Graham to see him, but the latter, doubting Lord John's good faith in these discussions, dashed any hope of success. Thereupon, Russell promptly closed the negotiations.[26]

The abortive negotiations led Greville to comment that "personal predilections and antipathies" between the Peelites and Whigs would continue to create enormous difficulties. He also noted that the Peelites were badly divided, with mutual dislike existing between Graham on the one side and Newcastle, Gladstone, and Herbert, the High Church Peelites, on the other.[27] Some of the Whigs also discussed "the nuances of Peelism" and the rivalry and jealousies among the Peelite leaders. Sir Charles Wood told General Charles Grey that Graham and Newcastle disliked each other cordially.[28] Graham, Sir George Grey observed to Clarendon, was jealous of the duke and was offended by the communication Russell had made to him concerning Peelite help in strengthening the government. By talking with Newcastle, Graham believed that Russell had made him "dangerous & intractable, & raised him 100 per cent in his own estimation."[29] Graham refused to attend the Clumber meeting, which he thought might be interpreted as a "high church intrigue" against the government, and he was delighted that Cardwell also declined Newcastle's invitation.

Aberdeen decided to attend, but he promised Graham that he would try to put the meeting to good use.[30]

Under these circumstances, it was not surprising that the Peelite leaders did not find complete unanimity of purpose at the Clumber conference in mid-January 1852. For the next few months, Newcastle continued to be the strongest advocate of Peelite independence. He sensed that the government was on its last legs, and he still believed that a purely Peelite administration was possible. Therefore, he argued that it was more important than ever for the Peelites to resist piecemeal absorption by either of the major parties. On this last point, if on little else, the small band of Peelites who had assembled at Clumber essentially agreed when the new session began.[31]

Newcastle had judged the weakness of the government correctly. On 20 February, after Lord Palmerston carried an amendment to their militia bill, the ministers resigned. But if the duke had hopes for a Peelite administration over which he would preside, they were soon dashed; for the queen, acting upon Russell's advice, summoned Lord Derby, who formed a government entirely from the ranks of the Protectionists.

III

The formation of Derby's government increased the divisions among the Peelite leaders. Gladstone took the initiative of sounding out the opinions of his friends. Aberdeen, he found, favored closer cooperation with Russell, although he was not at all inclined to exert leadership over the Peelites. Graham even more strongly favored fusion with the Whigs, speaking of his contemplated return to the "Liberal" party. Herbert agreed with Gladstone that the Peelites should hold themselves free from Russell and Derby alike for the time being in order to give the new government a fair trial. Gladstone in particular believed that the most natural position of the Peelites was to work out a liberal policy through the medium of the Conservative party. It would be far better to wait and see what Derby would do about protection, he argued, than to alienate the moderate members of his party by immediate, general opposition to the government.[32]

Newcastle disagreed with all the Peelite leaders concerning the course to pursue; his conversation with Gladstone, held on a sofa at the Carlton, became rather heated. The duke, Gladstone recorded, clung to the "high-flown idea that we are to create and lead a great, virtuous, powerful, intelligent party . . . containing all the good elements of both parties." Newcastle spoke "with great asperity against Lord Derby and his party," being particularly angry with William Beresford, the Conservative whip, who had instructed Tory newspapers to condemn the Peelites and who, it was alleged, had said, "The Peelites, let them go to hell." The duke, Gladstone continued, did not believe that the Protectionists were men of honor. He "inveighed against the baseness of which he had no doubt the new Government were about to be guilty" by clinging to office simply as a Conservative government, refusing either to propose protection or dissolve unless compelled to do so. Therefore, the duke was thoroughly convinced that the Peelites must take every fair opportunity to oppose the ministers, for "those who led the charge against them would reap the reward." He insisted that Gladstone would separate himself from the rest of the Peelites if he acted on his negative policy of virtually supporting the ministers.

Gladstone, on the other hand, thought the whole idea of a separate party completely impracticable and the duke intemperate for advancing it. "So all was well as [*sic*] possible between us individually," he concluded his account of their conversation, "but upon the whole recent experience has heightened the fears I more or less entertained before that his mind is too combative and his temper too little conciliatory not to cause uneasy anticipation if he were actively engaged in leading a party."[33]

Newcastle's political disagreement with Gladstone, which temporarily strained the relations between them, and the pressure of domestic difficulties put the duke in a very nervous state. Depression soon followed. "What a singular life mine is and seemingly *must* be to its close!," the duke told Gladstone:

> Always deluded by some phantom hope—always pursuing—when seemingly nearest really farthest—a deep plunge—mire below, vacancy around!
> I cannot write on other topics today. How gladly would I change any little political station I may possess for a small share of domestic happiness.[34]

But politics was in his blood, and he could no more escape the exasperation of the current political situation than he could his depressing personal life. In another letter to Gladstone four days later, he expressed his grave concern over the fate of the Peelite section. Unless they took action, he wrote, they would lose both the English Peelites and the Irish Brigade to the Derbyites. "The rot is in the Party, and no wonder," he said:

> If Easter finds us as we are, we had better shut up shop altogether, for Derby and Russell are agreed in this, if in nothing else, "extirpate the Peelites."
> I hope you are doing something about a general meeting. Such a reassurance would do much just now. You know it is no idleness or indifference on my part if I am not there.[35]

Gladstone had no intention of letting the Peelite rank and file dissipate in the Commons. When the session resumed, he joined the main body of about forty Peelites on the opposition side of the House, where they had been for the past six years. Together with Sidney Herbert, he intended to use this small band of men to prevent a Whig-Peelite junction and to force Derby to settle the question of protection.[36]

Newcastle returned to town for the resumption of Parliament in mid-March 1852 and took an active part in the meetings of the Peelite leaders at Aberdeen's house. Despite their previous differences, the Peelites agreed upon terms regarding parliamentary business. They informed Derby that in return for their restraint in opposition they would demand an early dissolution of Parliament immediately following the conclusion of all necessary business, the settlement of protection by the new Parliament after its opening in November, and the continuation of the income tax for a year. On 19 March, Newcastle, speaking on behalf of the Manchester Commercial Association, announced those terms in the Lords in a moderate speech in which he promised to refrain from any factious opposition. Although Derby was not prepared to give any public assurance in the Lords on free trade, he notified Gladstone the same day of his acquiescence to the "private understanding."[37]

The Peelites thus were prepared to follow Gladstone's line of giving the ministers a fair trial as long as they abided by the terms of the understanding. Newcastle, while taking a leading part in the debates preceding the dissolution, honored his pledge to avoid factious opposition. Nonetheless, he continued to press Derby to state more definitely the government's commercial policy. At Lord Grey's urging, he took the lead for the Free Traders on the second reading of the property tax continuance bill.[38] His speech was a brilliant eulogy of free trade, summarizing lucidly Peelite financial ideas and strongly warning Derby not to attempt a reversal of free-trade policies. Any such attempt, he strongly warned, would be resisted by the majority of the people by means that would endanger the foundations of the nation. He promised his support in defending British institutions against the rising tide of democracy, but he emphatically informed Derby that he would not support a program of reaction. "I repeat, my Lords," he concluded in strong Peelite fashion, "the policy of a Conservative Government is that of steady progress; to stand still, again I say, is dangerous; and in my conscience I believe that at the present day a Government of reaction, however slow, is a Government of revolution."[39]

Parliament was dissolved early in July 1852. The leading Peelites were greatly angered by Derby's electoral tactics (particularly his refusal to allow the electorate to decide the issue between free trade and protection) during the general election that followed. "Protection and religious liberty," Gladstone wrote to Aberdeen, "are subjects on which my main complaints would turn; shuffling as to the former, trading on bigotry as to the latter." Newcastle was thoroughly disgusted at the conduct of the whole ministerial body in their political war against the Peelites. "Truth is a word unknown to them," he wrote to Gladstone, "and honour no more regarded than if it were only a garment intended for special use. I have seldom read speeches less creditable than Pakington's, Walpole's and Henley's." Like Aberdeen, whose hostility toward the Derbyites was roused by their campaign of religious bigotry, Newcastle put all thought of Conservative reunion behind him. He told Aberdeen that he could not join Derby without a sense of moral and political degradation.[40]

Newcastle's contemptuous view of the ministers provoked several responses from the Conservative camp. Sir William Heathcote complained to Gladstone about the duke's attitude:

> I cannot imagine what made the Duke of Newcastle take the very bitter
> tone of hostility which marked his speeches. I know how very intimate he
> is with you and Sidney Herbert, whose line has been very different, and I
> know too . . . how estimable he is—and yet he seemed to be doing all
> he could to prevent reconciliation, on which depends our only chance of
> avoiding such a radical Govt. as we have never seen.[41]

Heathcote was not the only one to speculate about Newcastle's statements and ambitions. Leading Protectionists in Newark spread the rumor among the duke's friends that if the ministers were driven from office, he intended to form an administration in which the Radicals Cobden and Bright would hold important offices. Angered by the falsehood, Newcastle instructed Godfrey Tallents, an old friend and former election agent, to tell his Conservative friends that he opposed Derby's government for more unselfish reasons. The government, he observed, was reactionary, and their policies would soon lead to renewed efforts on the part of the democratic party to undermine the institutions of the country through agitation. "I have no personal object to gain," he wrote concerning the displacement of the government,

> and have no wish to see a Radical Government in office. On the other hand,
> however, let not people be deluded by the interested misrepresentations of
> the Protectionist Press. A Radical Govt. is *not* the only alternative to Lord
> Derby's Ministry. If he fails to obtain a majority at the elections, the Queen
> will have no difficulty in forming another Govt. which will be *quite* as
> conservative in its opinions, and much more conservative in its results. But
> it will be neither Tory nor Whig![42]

But the election results forced Newcastle to abandon his plans for a third party. Although the ministers failed to win a majority in the Commons, they cut into the opposition ranks. The Peelites suffered heavy losses. The exact number of their survivors was uncertain, as was the case with all the parties during this period of political confusion in the Commons, but they probably numbered between forty and fifty.[43] The defeat of such prominent Peelites as Edward Cardwell at Liverpool, Roundell Palmer at Plymouth, and Sir George Clerk at Dover especially distressed Gladstone and Newcastle, who exchanged post-election correspondence with Sir John Young and Bonham concerning the Peelite status. Gladstone was inclined to carry on as before the election, noting that the government was more dependent than ever on the Peelites, but Newcastle bowed to the reality of the situation and advocated the opposite alternative. Writing to Aberdeen on 2 August, the duke succinctly drew his conclusions: "Union with Lord Derby is impossible. Isolation is pleasant but not patriotic. Co-operation with other Liberals is requisite."[44]

Aberdeen agreed with this assessment. He had already been in contact with Graham and Russell and had concluded that the government, which he held in deep contempt, must be made to show its hand. He favored Russell's proposal of a free-trade amendment to the address. On 25 July he began the process of sounding out Newcastle, Herbert, and Gladstone by corresponding with the duke and enclosing Russell's letter of 21 July, which Newcastle was to send on to Gladstone and Herbert. Although the election had thinned the Peelite ranks, Aberdeen noted that they still must be regarded "as the representatives of Peel's policy, and as the party of Conservative progress." He believed the time had come for a cordial concert with Lord John and the Whigs.[45]

In his response Newcastle generally agreed with Aberdeen but argued that the question of leadership must be resolved before there could be a cordial concert. Lord John, he stressed, could not be the head of a Liberal government. Many of Russell's friends no longer would serve under him; the Radicals disliked his Whiggishness; the Irish would "pursue to the death" any government of which he was head; and many Peelites would desert to Derby if any of their friends took office under him. "My own opinion is and has been for some time," the duke continued,

> that, if Lord John Russell approved of and consented to such a plan, *you* could best unite and consolidate the various elements which ought to be collected together in a Liberal Government. I know you plead your ignorance of finance, and I am aware that your name has not been so much associated with our Domestic Administration and Legislation as the antecedents of Prime Ministers have been wont to be; but the times are peculiar, the state of parties unprecedented, and I believe that, if *all* will lay aside selfish and personal views and wishes, you can better serve the Queen and the Country than any other person.

He agreed with Aberdeen that on the important questions of free trade, civil and religious liberty, colonial and law reform, "a careful and Popular (but not Democratic) Revision of our Representative System," and a foreign policy "at once respecting the rights of other Countries and firmly maintaining our own," there were no differences of opinion between them. However, he differed slightly from Aberdeen and the other Peelites on the subject of direct

Lord John Russell, by G. F. Watts, c. 1851.
Courtesy of the National Portrait Gallery, London.

Fourth Earl of Aberdeen. *Illustrated London News*, 29 December 1860.

taxation, which he believed must be retained as an important part of the revenue with the ulterior objective of effecting important social and financial changes.[46]

On the following day he wrote again to clarify his views. He was not only in favor of another reform bill as a remedy for corruption, but was also anxious to make that measure so complete as to render another operation unnecessary for a long time. He also believed that it was necessary, "with a view to real fusion of all Liberals," to abandon the names "Whig" and "Peelite." They must construct a new Liberal party on a new basis, "not by one party joining another. With this view all old names as well as old jealousies must be abandoned." He continued:

> Though I fear there is much in both my letters which will annoy and displease Ld. J. R. yet as I have said nothing but what I know to be true and somebody must say to him what is disagreable [sic] I have no objection whatever to your sending him my letters if you think fit.[47]

Aberdeen forwarded the responses he received from the younger Peelites to Russell, who responded immediately. He was far more provoked by Gladstone's remarks about the immorality of the Whigs with respect to previous political action than he was by Newcastle's insistence upon fusion rather than Whig absorption of the Peelites.[48] Yet his comments on the letters brought out the worst in the duke. "I have read Lord John Russell's letter to you," Newcastle wrote to Aberdeen, "with all my impressions of his absolute unfitness for the post of Prime Minister or even Party Leader greatly strengthened and confirmed." The duke complained of "a petulance, a spirit of prejudice and injustice, a tone of soreness betraying a mind ill at ease, a want of real nobility of thought and purpose—in short a *littleness* of mind." A few days later, after reading another letter from Russell, Newcastle attacked again with an even greater display of hauteur. Whiggery was a fossil, he wrote. "The Whigs are buried with Mr. Fox and 'Mr. Pitt' (save the mark!) but alas the spirit of Whig Oligarchical Cliquery, it is too clear, still lives."[49]

Aberdeen assumed the role of mediator, soothing Russell's pride and tempering Newcastle's resentment against the Whig leader. He told Russell that it was presumptuous of Newcastle to suggest "the propriety and expediency of sinking the title of Whig." However, he added, the Peelites in any connection with Russell and the Whigs would not be prepared to abandon a conservative policy.[50] At the same time, he urged Newcastle to be more charitable, for to act with Russell required mutual confidence and respect. "He may have many failings, as we all have," he counseled, "but if I did not think him essentially honourable, and true, there could be no cordiality between us, and therefore no common actions." As for party labels, it was best to let things rest as they were. "Lord John," he observed,

> may do what he pleases; but he will be called a Whig to the end of his life. This is a title of which some persons are proud; but which in the present day, really means nothing at all. At all events, whatever it may mean, we do not become Whigs by acting with Lord John; nor does he become a Tory by acting with us.[51]

During the rest of the summer and autumn, Newcastle softened his tone toward Russell, but he never concurred that Russell was fit to head a Liberal government. "I certainly would not willingly be unjust to Lord John Russell or anybody else," the duke wrote to Aberdeen early in September,

> and am very sensible how great need *every* public man has of charitable construction of his motives by those who are or have been his opponents or his rivals. My interpretation of some of the passages of his letters to you *may* have been a little *twisted* by the recollection of what I certainly felt was very unfair in his latter letters to me in January last. I am *sure* however that my opinion of his unfitness to serve the Crown as Prime Minister is not warped by any of these considerations.[52]

Newcastle continued to suspect Russell of playing the same old Whig game of trying to absorb as many of the Peelites as possible. His strong liberal tendencies convinced him that the Peelites must cooperate with Russell, but not under his lead.

There were also rumblings in the Whig camp against Russell's leadership, and Newcastle was well aware of them. Lord Grey was among the Whigs most critical of Russell's leadership, and he implied to Newcastle that Lord John would have great difficulty in gaining the support of a majority in the House of Commons again. Joseph Parkes learned from Edward Ellice that some of the Old Whigs who were alarmed at a further reform bill saw "almost insuperable difficulties" to Russell's formation of the next cabinet. Increasingly, they looked to Lord Lansdowne as the best solution. Clarendon noted to Sir Charles Wood that Russell's name "is always mentioned with a snarl," but he believed that Russell could overcome the prejudices against his leadership by a good showing in opposition. Both he and Wood advised Russell not to make a hasty attack against Derby that might drive the Conservatives from office before there was a chance to consolidate the Liberals and form a strong government. Wood also urged Russell to court the Peelites, especially Graham and Newcastle, for without them a Liberal government would not be able to gain the support of the Irish members who constituted, Wood believed, the rank and file of the Newcastle party and who were a very important element in the calculation of forces.[53]

All this led Lord Minto, Russell's father-in-law, to conclude that there was an intrigue against Lord John that was fed by the ambitions of Newcastle and Palmerston.[54] Clarendon assured Russell that this was not the case, but also lamented to George Cornewall Lewis that Russell, led by his wife and Lord Minto, "wilfully shuts his eyes to the truth" about the widespread opposition to his leadership. But Lewis severely criticized Newcastle for fomenting negative feelings against Russell. Indeed, Lewis told Wood, Newcastle did not understand that the favorable opinion he entertained of his own pretensions to the office of prime minister was not shared by many others. The duke, Lord Grey told Wood, was "such an arch humbug" that whenever he was tried in high office the public would discover "on what a small foundation he has built a kind of reputation by newspaper jobbing & puffing." But, Grey added, "as to Newcastle's taking my place (if I have a place left) in the House of Lords he is very welcome." Lord Panmure, as he had earlier in the year, urged Russell to have no association with Newcastle, whom he described as a rock that would "prevent the streams from uniting in one smooth liberal concert."[55] Along with Minto, Grey and Panmure remained hostile toward Newcastle for years.

But there was too much evidence of Liberal dissatisfaction with his leadership for Russell to ignore, and early in October he hinted to Lord Minto that he might be willing to serve under Lord Lansdowne. In response, Minto agreed that there might be circumstances in which Russell could take office under a peer; but he strongly urged his son-in-law to confine any decision on the matter to his own house and not "let it go forth that you may be induced to renounce any of your pretensions, till the moment for decision has arrived." Minto also urged Lord John to continue to act as head of the Whig party.[56]

To this advice was added that of several of Russell's other Whig colleagues. They counseled patience, believing that with time all would be well. Lansdowne, they believed, would not be able to form an administration; Palmerston would not join Derby; and Newcastle and the Peelites would not persist in opposing Russell's leadership, particularly if free trade were threatened. Even Lord Grey argued that Russell was the only person who could attempt to lead a Liberal government. But, Grey told Wood, Russell must do penance in the "cold shade of opposition" for some time for his past faults, especially for his Durham letter and his conduct on the militia bills.[57] Thus the Whig leaders on the eve of a new Parliament were content to wait upon circumstances, leaving the question of Liberal leadership in abeyance.

The Peelite leaders were likewise ready to leave the question of Liberal leadership open for the moment. A more immediate task for them during the late summer and early autumn was to keep their own party from falling into greater disunion. Aberdeen corresponded at length with Graham to discourage him from separating himself further from Peel's friends by sealing an alliance with the Whigs before "the force of events" brought about such a fusion in a more gradual and natural way.[58] At the same time, Newcastle succeeded in drawing Gladstone, who had persisted in believing that the Peelites should remain on the liberal side of the Conservative party, closer to his own position. The duke stressed to his friend the necessity of a substantial measure of parliamentary reform and the impossibility of their acting with Derby and Disraeli on financial matters. Like Aberdeen, Newcastle sensed that Gladstone would be drawn into coalition with Russell through a financial conduit. The duke was, however, quite content, as was Gladstone, to wait until Disraeli had "smashed the bottle and cut his own fingers" before they agreed to a concert against the government.[59]

IV

The duke of Wellington's death in September 1852 broke the spell of politics briefly and forced Newcastle to abandon his plans for a Highland holiday and a visit to Lord Aberdeen at Haddo. The great duke's death left vacant the chancellorship of Oxford. Greatly to Newcastle's satisfaction, a party of university reformers and High Church men brought his name forward as a candidate to fill the position. Lords Derby and Shaftesbury were also suggested, and there was considerable fear that a contest between Derby and Newcastle might bring in Shaftesbury, a Low Church man. Newcastle urged his Oxford supporters not to enter into a contest if there was any danger of a "Lydian" party triumph; but, he told Bonham, "If . . . the battle is a stand-up fight between the 'chivalrous' Premier and myself, I am ready for the fray."[60] A few days later, however, the duke, failing to get the support of the Hebdomadal Board, withdrew from the contest and allowed Derby to "walk the course."

Newcastle's respite from politics lasted through October, at the end of which he returned to town to confer with his friends. The Peelite leaders were still not settled on a course of action when Parliament met on 4 November. The three Oxford friends were clearly divided. Gladstone was eager to carry a free-trade motion in order to remove the barrier that separated him from the Derbyites. Newcastle, Graham told Russell, was a reformer with "strong Liberal tendencies" and "no affinity to Lord Derby." Sidney Herbert was torn between his two friends and "much perplexed."[61] With the exception of Graham, the Peelite leaders met twice at Aberdeen's house during the first week of the session, and several of them dined together on 9 November at the house of Abraham Hayward, who told his sister that his dinner had gone off capitally and had done much to consolidate the Peelite party.[62]

During these and subsequent meetings the Peelite leaders charted a course of action relative to the queen's speech, which they found evasive and unsatisfactory. They were far more inclined to support an independent free-trade resolution than an amendment to the queen's speech, but circumstances forced them to approve the latter course. Nonetheless, they hoped to avoid unnecessary antagonism in settling the issue of free trade, and for that reason they found the Villiers amendment, which described the act of 1846 as "wise, just and beneficial," too extreme for the ministers to accept. Gladstone expressed their common fear that the ministers, backed into the corner by the amendment, would resign before there was a chance to bring in the financial measures. Consequently, the Peelites decided to support a compromise amendment that Gladstone and Herbert helped Palmerston draft. On 25 November, Palmerston moved the amendment, which the ministers were willing to accept, and on the following night the Villiers amendment was soundly defeated and the Palmerston version overwhelmingly approved.[63] At long last the question of protection was put to rest.

The sequel in the Lords to this great debate in the Commons was a mild affair. Lord Clanricarde gave notice of a free-trade motion, but the mood on both sides was against the introduction of a strongly worded resolution. Newcastle agreed with Aberdeen that it was not wise to impose on Derby and his supporters "a formal recantation of the principles they believed they had been right in advocating." Nevertheless, although he believed that the free-trade principles were safe in the Lords, he seconded a brief, innocuous motion moved by the Peelite Lord Harrowby, which passed without opposition.[64]

The debates over a free-trade motion drew the Whigs and Peelites closer together. All the principals involved had been able to find common ground on Palmerston's resolution. In supporting the resolution, the Peelites, contrary to Derby's indictment later in the session, had been particularly anxious to prevent the fall of the government before Disraeli had a chance to produce his budget. Indeed, rather than assuming the responsibility themselves, they had maneuvered the chancellor of the Exchequer into the position of being the one to destroy the government; and from late summer until Disraeli introduced his budget on 3 December, the Peelites braced themselves for a struggle over direct taxation. It was not likely, the *Morning Chronicle* stated early in August, that a popularity-seeking government, which a minority government had to be, would have the courage to uphold, much less extend, the income tax.[65] Newcastle continually urged his friends to be ready to defend the income tax and to assume power if Disraeli wrecked the government over the issue.

As expected, there was little in Disraeli's budget that the Peelites liked; after a series of meetings early in December, they decided to oppose it. To Gladstone, who along with Goulburn and Graham led the attack in the Commons, the budget was "the most subversive in its tendencies and ultimate effects" that he had ever seen submitted to the House. The changes in the income tax, he believed, would mean the disruption of that tax, "with confusion in finance, as an immediate sequitur." The gravity of the financial question convinced him that the day had come to replace the Derby ministry with a "mixed government" that would defend the income tax and secure the financial foundations of the country;[66] and on 16 December he delivered a devastating attack in the Commons upon the budget. In the early hours of the following day, thirty-four Peelites joined with the Whigs and Liberals to defeat the budget resolutions by a vote of 305 to 286. The ministers resigned later that day.

Lord Derby announced the government's resignation in the Lords on the following Monday, 20 December 1852, in a most intemperate speech that bitterly attacked Aberdeen and the Peelites and blamed the fall of the government on a factious coalition. Newcastle rose in the absence of Aberdeen to defend the Peelites against Derby's charge of unfair combination. Contrary to Derby's statement, he noted, the Peelites had helped to prepare a resolution for the purpose of uniting the friends of free trade in a spirit that was free from hostility or even the appearance of opposition to the government.[67] Although ably stated, Newcastle's answer did little to abate the Derbyites' bitterness.

Final preparations for a coalition had been made on the eve of Derby's resignation. From 15 to 17 December, the duke of Bedford, acting as a secret link between the court and the opposition leaders, had hosted a meeting at Woburn for the purpose of uniting Whigs and Peelites and selecting a leader. Attending the meeting were Russell, Lansdowne, Clarendon, Aberdeen, and Newcastle; and on the final day Colonel Phipps, Prince Albert's private secretary, joined them. Bedford informed Baron Stockmar that his "little meeting of politicians" had been "of infinite use, by putting the parties in good humour with each other and by smoothing jealousies and asperities, for a common object." Nonetheless, he saw the difficulties ahead in the formation of a new government, especially with regard to the Peelites' relationship with Lord John, his younger brother. He found that Aberdeen was "very friendly both personally and politically" with Russell and that Newcastle was "friendly, and quite prepared to do his best to facilitate the formation of a good government by a fusion of Whigs and Peelites, even if it should not be quite what he likes, as to some of its details." Colonel Phipps's report to Prince Albert was very similar to Bedford's. Newcastle, he noted, strongly favored a coalition, as long as it was a real coalition and not merely an attempt to join Peelites to Whigs. There was "no sacrifice of feelings or opinion" that the duke was not prepared to make for a real coalition, he added.[68]

The question of leadership of the coalition was finally resolved at the Woburn meeting. Without Russell's knowledge, the duke of Bedford advised the queen to send jointly for Lansdowne and Aberdeen for consultation in the event Derby resigned. The queen followed this advice when the ministry fell, although on 19 December she selected Aberdeen alone to form a new government. In accepting the commission, Aberdeen stressed that the new government would not be a revival of the old Whig cabinet with an addition of some Peelites, but rather would be "a liberal Conservative Government in the sense of that of Sir Robert Peel."[69] Thus he insisted that Peelites fill at least two secretaries of state and make up at least half the cabinet, a number considerably out of proportion to their numerical strength in the House of Commons. The final cabinet consisted of six Peelites, six Whigs, and the Radical Sir William Molesworth. The cake had not been large enough, but the Peelites took the largest slice, at least in terms of important offices. They controlled four of the six great departments of state: Newcastle went to the Colonial Office, Graham to the Admiralty, Gladstone to the Treasury as chancellor of the Exchequer, and Herbert to the War Office as secretary at war.

The Whigs did not conceal their discontent with their places in the coalition government. Russell, Brougham, and Clarendon complained that the tiny

Peelite party was attempting to swallow the great Whig party and that the Peelites were trying to "kick down the Whig ladder by which *alone* they have climbed to power."[70] Indeed, Russell had second thoughts about joining the ministry at all. When the queen and several Whigs pleaded with him to join, he responded by proposing that he take the lead in the Commons and sit in the cabinet without office. Aberdeen and the Peelite leaders refused to accept this. Finally, on 22 December, Lord John agreed to join the cabinet and take the seals of the Foreign Office, but only after Aberdeen hinted to him that he would retire from the premiership in Russell's favor as soon as circumstances permitted. Even so, Russell intended to surrender the Foreign Office to Clarendon within a few weeks.[71]

Misunderstandings and difficulties between Russell and Aberdeen continued even after the former consented to join the ministry. Under tremendous Whig pressure to obtain more places for his supporters, Russell tenaciously attempted to get Aberdeen to recast the administration; Aberdeen just as tenaciously refused to make major concessions. "The same wrangle continues for places," Graham wrote, "and the same unabated jealousy of Whigs against Peelites."[72] Sir Charles Wood complained to Lord Grey, who was happy not to have any part in the arrangement, that had Russell managed matters better the Whigs would have been in a better position. "Aberdeen," he wrote, "was very fair in his offers & proposals, but he always had Newcastle in the next room, who kept him up to the most favorable view for their side, & Johnny had neither the sense or disposition to struggle for himself or his friends as he ought to have done."[73] Nonetheless, on the evening of 26 December, Russell, Aberdeen, Graham, Newcastle, Herbert, and Haytor, the Whig whip, resolved most of the remaining appointments. The next day Aberdeen announced in the Lords the formation of the government.

Although the patronage difficulties were over, the tensions and animosities evident between the Whigs and Peelites during these negotiations were never far below the surface throughout the duration of the government. Some of the Whig leaders had accepted the necessity of the coalition reluctantly, and they remained uncomfortable in their relationship with the High Church Peelites. Furthermore, lingering political traditions continued to keep the Whigs of the older generation apart from the younger men of liberal views. Newcastle pointed out this generation gap to Lord Granville in the spring of 1855:

> I never heard you called a "Peelite" but I have always perceived that if bygone nicknames are abandoned, there is no more difference of opinion between you and me than there must always be for any two men who think for themselves. . . . The fact is that among men of Liberal opinions the difference is not Whig and Peelite, but the men of forty years of age (more or less) and those of the former generation. *Peelism*—if I must still use the word—is really the more advanced form of Liberal opinion, cleared of that demagogic Liberalism which characterised the Liberalism of twenty years

ago, and on the other hand, of that oligarchic tendency of the old Whigs, who, wishing to extend freedom, sought to do *it* by *making use* of the people, instead of identifying themselves and their own interests *with* the people.[74]

With this observation, Newcastle underscored the main difference between the old Whigs and the new Liberals, a difference not of opinion, but of policy. Traditional Whig leadership, which Newcastle continually scorned, was based narrowly on social prestige and parliamentary support. In the changed nature of politics, this narrow base of support was not enough for a major, national party. What the country wanted, the duke argued, was the constitution of a new party upon a new basis—a national party with broad popular support rather than an oligarchical party, one with its parliamentary interests identified with those of the national constituencies. Although he did not live to see it, what Newcastle envisaged in the early 1850s came to pass under Gladstone's leadership of the Liberal party after 1867.[75]

When the coalition government began, there was no stronger advocate of a new Liberal party composed of former Whigs and Peelites, with the latter becoming the natural leaders, than Newcastle. In 1855 Gladstone noted to Sidney Herbert:

I . . . had now for two years been holding my mind in suspense upon the question I used to debate with Newcastle who used to argue that we should grow into the natural leaders of the Liberal Party. I said it is now plain this will not be; we get on very well with the independent Liberals, but the Whigs stand as an opaque body between us and others & moreover thus they will stand & ought to stand.[76]

Because of his views on party, Newcastle remained seriously at odds with Russell, who could not then submit willingly to the extinction of the old Whig party; and the events of early 1855 seemed to prove Newcastle wrong and Gladstone and Russell right. From the day he reluctantly agreed to join the coalition ministry, Russell set out to regain the premiership and to transform the government into a Whig administration. These ambitions led to an attack upon Newcastle in late 1854 that was designed to accomplish both in one bold move, but Russell failed. He helped to destroy the Aberdeen coalition and to inflict a damaging blow to Newcastle's administrative reputation and political career, but he failed to reap the benefits from this wrecking policy that he expected. The Whig party could not be revived. Russell would not become prime minister again for another decade, and only after he finally had realized that Whiggery was not enough. By then, Aberdeen, Newcastle, and Palmerston were dead, but the Liberal party that Newcastle had helped to found was very much alive.

8. Preparations for War

The storm clouds of war began to form in eastern Europe shortly after the coalition government came to power. In May 1853 Emperor Nicholas I demanded a protectorate for Russia over the Greek Christians in the Ottoman Empire; the Porte, acting upon the advice of Lord Stratford de Redcliffe, British ambassador to the Ottoman Empire, refused to accept the Russian demands. Early in July the Russian emperor dispatched troops to occupy the Danubian Principalities of Wallachia and Moldavia. Although Russia had certain treaty rights in the Principalities, they were nominally the property of Turkey, and the Russian occupation of them on the condition that the Porte fulfill its treaty obligations to Russia forced the Four Powers of England, France, Austria, and Prussia to react.

The British government, in consequence of Russia's ultimatum to the Porte, had already ordered the Mediterranean fleet eastward to join the French fleet at the entrance to the Dardanelles and had empowered Lord Stratford to call it to Turkey's assistance if Russia declared war. The cabinet, however, was clearly divided between the views of Palmerston and Aberdeen on the need for further naval demonstration to deter Russian moves against Turkey. Palmerston wanted to make the Russian entrance into the Principalities a *casus belli* and to send the English and French fleets through the straits into the Black Sea in support of Turkey; Aberdeen, complaining that they were "drifting hopelessly towards war," strongly resisted Palmerston's proposals and urged instead negotiations between the Four Powers and Russia.[1] Newcastle supported Palmerston's view, but the majority of the cabinet endorsed Aberdeen's plan. Thus when the news of Russia's occupation of the Principalities reached London in July, Britain was committed to a diplomatic approach to the Eastern Crisis.[2]

The Turkish rejection of the Vienna Note proposals for peace, which were supported by the Four Powers and Russia, brought war a step closer. Aberdeen, although greatly disheartened, still clung to the hope that negotiations would eventually succeed if hostilities could be prevented between Turkey and Russia. But the task was made more difficult by the mounting war fever in Constantinople and by "the violence and scurrility of the Press" in England against Aberdeen and the emperor of Russia. As the illusions of peace were shattered by the failure of diplomacy, newspaper after newspaper joined the attack against the government's pacific policy. By early September even the Peelite *Morning Chronicle* had deserted the government and denounced those who would join Aberdeen in an attempt to force Turkey to accept the Vienna Note.[3]

The Turkish declaration of war on Russia early in October increased the difficulties of diplomacy. With the opening of actual hostilities, Lord Clarendon, the British foreign secretary, supported by Russell, his immediate predecessor, discarded the latest Russian overtures, which in historical perspective seem to have been sincerely offered as a peaceful solution to the Eastern difficulties. At a cabinet meeting on 7 October, the first in six weeks, Palmerston and Russell advocated sending the fleet into the Black Sea in support of Turkey and signing a convention with the Porte that would allow the enlistment of British nationals in the Turkish forces. Aberdeen, desiring to maintain unanimity in the cabinet, supported, and the cabinet approved, Clarendon's more moderate proposal of instructing Stratford to summon the fleet into the Black Sea for strictly defensive purposes in the event of a Russian attack upon Turkish territory. "The aspect of the Cabinet was on the whole good," Aberdeen wrote the next day to Graham, who had missed the meeting. "Gladstone active and energetic for peace. Argyll, Herbert, Ch. Wood and Granville all in the same sense. Newcastle not quite so much so, but good. Lansdowne not so warlike as formerly. Lord John warlike enough, but subdued in tone. Palmerston urged his views perseveringly, but not disagreeably."[4] Thus in virtual agreement, the ministers present at the cabinet of 7 October turned their backs on the Russian Olmutz proposals. "With reference to public feeling in England," Clarendon explained to Cornewall Lewis, "we could not well do less."[5]

Aberdeen's concessions did not end there, nor did the cabinet remain harmonious. With the support of Newcastle, Gladstone, and Graham, Aberdeen wanted to inform the Porte that the British government would not permit themselves to be dragged into a war by Turkish folly. The statement, he believed, "can only be objected to by those who want to make peace impossible." But the prime minister did not press the clause when he found that both Palmerston and Russell were determined to resist it "to the utmost extremity." Aberdeen was convinced that the breakup of the government would mean the formation of a war ministry and the collapse of the new negotiations that had commenced in Vienna.[6]

Thus another opportunity was lost for the peace party in the cabinet to thwart Palmerston and Russell, now joined by Clarendon. Soon Turkish folly drove England over the precipice. As long feared by the peaceful members of the cabinet, the presence of the Turkish fleet in the Black Sea provoked a Russian naval attack. On 30 November a superior Russian force from Sebas-

The Coalition Ministry of 1854, by John Gilbert, 1855.
From left: Wood, Graham, Molesworth, Gladstone, Argyll, Clarendon, Lansdowne, Russell, Granville, Aberdeen, Cranworth, Palmerston, Grey, Herbert, Newcastle. Courtesy of the National Portrait Gallery, London.

topol entered the harbor of Sinope and sank about a dozen anchored Turkish ships with great loss of life. Although a justifiable act of war, the incident, angrily described as a massacre, aroused the war spirit in England to fever pitch. The newspapers almost unanimously cried for war against Russia. Russell and Palmerston expressed their deep humiliation as Englishmen at the affair of Sinope and demanded that something be done to wipe away the stain. In the face of these demands and strong public opinion, Aberdeen gave way. On 22 December the cabinet agreed to a French proposal for the Allied occupation of the Black Sea to prevent the passage of Russian ships and munitions. In justifying the cabinet's action to the queen, Aberdeen noted that he would have hesitated to agree to the proposal had it not been evident that the continuance of the French alliance depended upon its adoption.[7] Curiously, this decision was taken during Palmerston's absence from the cabinet.

The determination of the Allies to sweep the Black Sea clear of Russian ships and to resist further attacks upon Turkish territory forced the Tsar's hand. After protesting the Allied activity in the Black Sea, Count Nesselrode, the Russian chancellor, recalled the Russian ambassadors from Paris and London early in February 1854. The English public remained fervent for war. Succumbing to this fever, the cabinet on 27 February sent a joint ultimatum with the French to the Russian government demanding the evacuation of the Principalities by the end of April. Receiving no answer, Great Britain declared war on 27 March, and France followed. The decision for war was reached unanimously by the British ministers.

II

As secretary for war and colonies, Newcastle commenced military preparations long before the ultimatum was sent to the Tsar on 27 February 1854. Shortly after the Allied fleets entered the Black Sea, Newcastle began preparing an expeditionary force for embarkation to Malta. On 9 February he instructed the commander-in-chief, Lord Hardinge, to hold a force of ten thousand infantry and two regiments of cavalry in readiness for embarkation and to bring the regiments up to full strength. He ordered Lord Raglan, still master-general of the Ordnance, to appoint four batteries of field guns with two companies each of artillery, miners, and sappers. Also, he requested Sir Charles Trevelyan of the Treasury to appoint an adequate staff of Commissariat officers to join the army at Malta. On 28 February, the day following the British ultimatum to the Tsar, the first brigade of the Guards departed England for the East.[8]

In late February and early March, additional regiments of infantry and cavalry and companies of artillery prepared for embarkation. A second brigade of three regiments of infantry was held in reserve, and another ten regiments were recalled from the colonies. On 29 March, immediately following the declaration of war, the military contingent already at Malta was ordered on to Gallipoli in Turkey to join the advance party of sappers and miners under the command of Lt.-Gen. Sir George Brown. The rest of what the *Times* called "the finest army that has ever left these shores" arrived in Turkey during the next few weeks.

This expeditionary force of twenty-five thousand men was placed under the command of Fitzroy Somerset, Lord Raglan, born in 1788, who had been the duke of Wellington's aide-de-camp in Spain and subsequently had served many years as military secretary at the Horse Guards until his appointment as master-general of the Ordnance in 1852. He was a gentleman of the highest qualities, and, notwithstanding his age and the long years of routine in Whitehall, he was the logical, if not inevitable, choice as commander of the expeditionary force. He had an intense pride and a profound sense of duty and honor. His tact and even temper were greatly admired and were instrumental in enabling him to establish ascendancy over Marshal St. Arnaud, the French commander, and the French officers. At times, however, he was too generous, and his greatest fault was his uncritical nature. He was unwilling to see the shortcomings of his own staff, and he intervened far too infrequently to assure the satisfactory resolution of critical problems.

Lord Raglan left England on 10 April under orders from the duke of Newcastle to proceed to Gallipoli via Paris. Newcastle's instructions in his first official dispatch to the commander were ambiguous and allowed Raglan considerable discretion. In a private letter that followed, however, the duke assured Raglan that he would not disclaim responsibility for what the commander did in the East. "I know you will show yourself worthy of that Great Man at whose side you learnt the art of war and if like him you are occasionally assailed by the impatience or complaint of a too exacting Public you will find me prepared to stand between you and their ill humor."[9] Little did Newcastle realize how quickly and how severely his pledge to Raglan would be tested.

Soon after his arrival in Turkey on 2 May, Raglan moved the bulk of his army to Constantinople and Scutari to prepare lines of defense along the Bosphorus between the Black Sea and the Sea of Marmara. The defensive site had been recommended by Sir John Burgoyne, a senior engineer officer, whom the ministers had sent to Turkey in February to inspect Turkish defenses. There the main body of troops remained throughout May.

The encampment of the army in Turkey concluded the early military preparations for the war; for the most part, they had gone well. The rapidity with which Great Britain sent forth supplies and troops during the spring of 1854 was quite impressive. Nonetheless, Newcastle encountered difficulties. The battering train, consisting of 250 artillery pieces, which he promised late in March, was not shipped until mid-May and did not reach Constantinople until 10 June. Lack of steam conveyance was the main reason for the delay, and the same problem existed for the transport of cavalry and artillery horses to the East. There also was difficulty at Gallipoli in receiving and quartering the British troops as they arrived, and reports published in the *Times* charging the Commissariat and other departments with inadequate preparations were debated in Parliament. The Commissariat was still under the authority of the Treasury, but on 27 April, in anticipation of the debate in the Lords, Newcastle asked Sir Charles Trevelyan to send him the letters and reports of Commissary-General William Filder and Assistant Commissary-General John W. Smith concerning the arrangements made at Gallipoli before the arrival of the first troop contingency. Armed with these sources, Newcastle denied the validity of the newspaper accounts. Yet on the following day, the duke apprised Raglan of the controversy and asked him to inquire into the truth of the complaints against the Commissariat and medical service.[10]

The trouble was not one of supplies, but of means to move and distribute them. The Commissariat, relying upon the traditional practice of procuring animals and wagons locally, had failed to provide a sufficient land transport service. Early in May, Trevelyan assured Newcastle that these difficulties would be resolved by whatever mode the circumstances required;[11] and for the next month, Commissary-General Filder turned his full attention to obtaining sufficient transport for the troops in the East. But Filder adhered to the contract system of hired transport, a system that had already failed. "With the uncertainty that hangs over us," he informed Trevelyan, "I am not disposed to buy animals for this service, if I can avoid it."[12] Not until he again failed to hire the requisite number of animals and wagons in Turkey and Bulgaria did he urge the Treasury to purchase animals in Spain and the Levant. Reluctantly, for it was a maxim with him that hired transport was better than government transport, Trevelyan partially complied with Filder's request. Thus the civilian authorities in London failed to heed this early warning of the inadequacies of the land transport service for the army. Newcastle accepted Trevelyan's assurances that Lord Raglan and General Brown were satisfied with the exertions of the Commissariat at Gallipoli.[13]

III

The criticism of the arrangements made for the reception of the British troops at Gallipoli stimulated the campaign launched by the *Times* earlier in the year for a reform of the antiquated system of military administration. In March the question of consolidation and centralization of the military departments was debated in the Commons, and early in April, Earl Grey brought the subject to the floor of the Lords in a long and minutely detailed speech on his motion for papers relating to the military departments. With each report of administrative confusion, the demand for a reform of the military system increased. Thus the attention of the ministers was inescapably drawn to a subject upon which they disagreed considerably.

The cabinet was divided on the subject between the consolidators, mainly Whigs, and the Peelites. The major difference between them was over the nature and degree of change necessary within the military departments. Although not a minister, Lord Grey made the case for the consolidators in his speech on 7 April, in which he described the cumbrous military system, with its incredible division of responsibility. As the system then existed, the commander-in-chief at the Horse Guards commanded the troops, except for the artillery and engineers, and was responsible for such matters as discipline, appointments, and promotions. The master-general of the Ordnance commanded the artillery and the engineers, and through the Board of Ordnance was responsible for supplying the army with arms, ammunition, and clothing. The Treasury, which was completely independent, administered the Commissariat, which provided provisions and land transport for the army in the field. The home secretary controlled the militia and the use of troops in support of civil authority in Great Britain. A separate Medical Department existed, as well as a Paymaster-General's Department. The financial work of the War Office was done by the secretary at war, who submitted the estimates for the army to Parliament and checked to see that the money approved was appropriately applied.

Lord Grey noted that in theory all the offices and authorities that played a role in the administration of the army except the Treasury were controlled by the secretary of state for war and colonies, who was responsible for their coordination and for deciding important questions of military policy. In practice, however, Grey observed, this was impossible, particularly since the office was also responsible for the detailed administration of the colonies. Therefore, Grey urged the creation of a separate authority for colonial administration and the consolidation of all the functions of the military under a board supervised by a minister responsible to Parliament.[14]

Although they agreed that some reorganization was necessary, the Peelites opposed consolidation of the departments under either a powerful secretary of state or a military board. They favored instead the maintenance of most of the independent departments subject to a supervising authority. The Peelite case was made by Sidney Herbert, secretary at war, in the Commons and by Newcastle in the Lords. It was human capacity and not systems that mattered, Herbert informed the Commons, while Newcastle asserted that he had found no want of promptitude or harmony among the various authorities responsible for the army during the recent preparations for war. Thus he denied that the system was as radically vicious as Lord Grey represented, although he admitted that improvements could be made. In words that would later return to haunt him, Newcastle praised the military departments for their efficiency and careful preparations. He strongly urged the Lords not to change extensively the existing system while the nation was at war.[15]

The consolidators were far from convinced by Newcastle's and Herbert's arguments. In winding up the debate in the Lords, Grey reminded the duke in reference to his claim of harmony and efficiency within the present system "that the time for boasting was not when the harness was put on, but when it was taken off."[16] Grey had substantial support in Parliament and in the press for his position of centralization. The pressure of public opinion throughout April and May and the intervention of Russell, a veteran army reformer, forced Aberdeen and the cabinet to accept a measure of reform.

On 24 April, Russell submitted a plan to Aberdeen for separating the Colonial Office from the War Office by the creation of a fourth secretary of state and for devolving upon the secretary of state for war authority over the commander-in-chief, the Board of Ordnance, the secretary at war, and the Commissariat.[17] Russell's plan was a compromise between the views of the consolidators and those of the Peelites, for in a later memorandum he stressed that "this is not the moment for consolidating and rearranging departments which have at least practice and experience in the conduct of military affairs."

Under the plan, therefore, the new secretary of state would merely "survey and examine" the working of the four departments with a view to consolidation at a later date.[18]

The members of the cabinet accepted the plan for various reasons. Lords Clarendon and Palmerston regarded the division of the War and Colonial Offices as a parliamentary necessity. Russell, Sir Charles Wood, Sir William Molesworth, and Sir George Grey (soon to be brought into the cabinet) regarded the change as the first step in the eventual consolidation of all the departments of military administration under the secretary for war. The Peelites accepted it for the opposite reason, that it was an expedient that would give only "the supervision of one recognized authority" over the military departments while leaving them largely undisturbed. Newcastle believed that consolidation should be an open question in the future, as Russell insisted, but Aberdeen assured the queen that he and the duke acceded to the change only as a way of postponing consolidation and that they were "determined not to break down the present arrangements" in their implementation of the readjustments. Aberdeen was even more emphatic to Russell a few days later, saying that further study of the military departments must be delayed until after the new secretary of state for war could study the matter.[19]

In proposing the administrative change, Russell was motivated by both public and private concern. He complained of the cabinet's reluctance to prosecute the war with vigor. He had little confidence in the administration as it then existed and believed that a reorganization of the cabinet, starting at the top with him replacing Aberdeen as prime minister, was necessary for the good of the public service. As soon as the creation of a fourth secretary of state was agreed upon, he suggested that Palmerston take the War Office, Newcastle retain the Colonies, and Sir George Grey be brought in to assume the Home Office. Aberdeen thought that this arrangement under the existing circumstances would be unjust to Newcastle. Russell concurred, but justified the change on the ground that Newcastle had recently expressed indifference as to which of the two offices he took. Aberdeen agreed to ask the duke which office he preferred and to consult Russell on the person to be named to the other. This was done. Newcastle chose the War Department; Aberdeen, after again consulting with Russell, accepted Sir George Grey for the Colonial Office. Russell then consented to take office as president of the council.[20]

The reorganization of the cabinet rekindled the fires of partisanship between Whigs and Peelites. Gladstone thought that the whole transaction was "much more worthy . . . of a set of clowns than of an English Cabinet."[21] Several of the Whig leaders took the occasion to attack Newcastle and Gladstone privately for their "Puseyite" tendencies. Admitting Sir George Grey to the cabinet, Lord Panmure explained to Sir Charles Wood, "would give your pudding a good Whig plum of which it had too few from the beginning." Wood readily agreed. With Russell taking office and Sir George Grey joining the cabinet, Wood surmised to Lord Grey, the Whigs would be better able to "counteract the Puseyite propensities of the government and to keep Johnny steady." The new arrangement, he told Russell, would "give us the consistency and character of permanency which your not being in office deprives us of."[22]

But the addition of another Whig supporter of Russell to the cabinet did not sit well with some of the Peelites, particularly with Gladstone, who blamed Lady John for bringing her husband "to a pitch of wilfulness."[23] Aware of this Peelite reaction to the proposed arrangement, Aberdeen at the last moment suggested to Russell that Sir George Grey's appointment to the cabinet be postponed to the end of the session and that Granville be moved to the Colonial Office, leaving vacant the presidency of the council for Lord John. Ending on a note of partisanship, Aberdeen added, "I do not for a moment look to anything like Party in the Cabinet; but if a new member should be introduced I am not certain that Cardwell and Canning might not feel aggrieved." In objecting to the proposal, Russell stated that he did not think that Cardwell and Canning or the other Peelites could object to George Grey's accession to the cabinet, for it would "go but a small way to compensate the partiality of the original distribution of offices."[24] Aberdeen gave in, and the Peelites were forced to welcome Sir George Grey to the cabinet. Nonetheless, the affair had greatly increased Peelite resentment of Russell and his Whig friends.

The new arrangement, however, did not entirely please Russell or the public. In the estimation of Lord Dudley Stuart, who spoke in the Commons on 29 June, the reorganization had cast the parts so that "all the square men were in round holes, and all the round men were in square holes."[25] While he recognized Newcastle's merits, he expressed his great disappointment, one shared widely by his countrymen, that the War Office had not been placed in Palmerston's hands. In and out of Parliament, Newcastle was blamed for allowing personal ambition to stand in the way of public good by not stepping aside for Palmerston. Russell had certainly wanted to see the change, but in the cabinet the prevailing feeling was relief that Palmerston had remained where he was. Thus, although he was not the first choice of many in the cabinet, Newcastle was selected for the War Office.[26]

Newcastle was aware of the general feelings concerning the new arrangement and of the extra burden that those feelings placed upon him. "The public, I know, think I ought not to be War Minister," he confided to Aberdeen.[27] He also realized the risks involved in accepting the new position. "In leaving the Colonial Office," he wrote to his friend Abraham Hayward, "I am well aware what I have done. I know that in this new department, whatever success shall attend our arms I shall never derive any credit; and this, too, I well know, that if there shall be disaster, upon me alone will come the blame and the public indignation."[28] But even with such sobering thoughts, he believed that it was his duty to accept this great responsibility. With his capacity for hard work and his supreme self-confidence, there was little doubt in his own mind that he would overcome the burdens and meet the challenges of the office. Unfortunately—thus befitting the theme of his life—he picked an unlucky hour and an unlucky course through which to satisfy his ambition and fulfill his duty.

IV

The experience of providing for the army during the summer of 1854 proved to Newcastle that the military departments were defective. In particular, he was dissatisfied with the Ordnance, Commissariat, and Medical departments as well as with the system of sea transport. His dissatisfaction stemmed from a combination of factors. Part of the problem arose from the inexperience of all concerned in mobilizing the nation for a distant European war after nearly forty years of peace. The parsimony practiced by Parliament since Waterloo left the country with an inadequate army Medical Department and without a Commissariat and land transport system. These had to be created anew at the start of the war.

The general picture was one of hopeless disorganization among the departments; the result was a remarkable lack of coordination throughout the whole administrative structure. Newcastle labored throughout the summer and autumn of 1854 to overcome these problems and to anticipate the immediate needs of the army in the East. He was in constant communication with the various departments on matters both minute and general in his effort to see that the army was as well equipped and well prepared as the capabilities of Great Britain allowed. With the exigencies of the moment, however, it was impossible for him to devote any time to a major reconstruction of the system of military administration, a reconstruction he knew was badly needed.[29] Therefore, he was forced by the pressures of war to endeavor to make a bad system work well enough to enable the British army to undertake a major campaign against the Russians. He was also confident that Lord Raglan would act to remedy some of the major shortcomings of the system at the front.

The lack of coordination between the Ordnance and Commissariat was one of the duke's greatest concerns. He constantly inquired whether the Ordnance had supplied lists of shipments to the Commissariat or to the other appropriate departments for the material procured on contract. In August, certain that those particulars were not being strictly carried out, he specifically directed the Ordnance to send copies of the manifestos directly to Lord Raglan. He also repeatedly pressed upon that department the necessity of establishing a storekeeping system separate from the Commissariat, but his suggestion was consistently resisted by leading Ordnance and Commissariat authorities. Thus, despite his efforts, a division of duties remained between these two departments in the purchase and distribution of war materials that seriously affected the supply of the British army.[30]

The problems of the medical service were even greater than those of the Ordnance. Subordinate to at least five other authorities, the army medical service was a mass of confusion, and no one within the department showed the competence or the initiative to cut through the confusion and rise above a system that discouraged efficiency and diffused responsibility. Since the Medical Department previously had been under the authority of the secretary at war, Newcastle depended heavily upon Sidney Herbert for the direction of that department. Nonetheless, he took the initiative early in the war on several important matters. In one case, he ordered Herbert to establish an ambulance corps consisting of Chelsea pensioners. The plan was fully endorsed by Lords Hardinge and Raglan, the latter of whom vigorously objected to the use of able-bodied soldiers as stretcher-bearers.[31] In addition, the duke greatly increased the number of staff and regimental surgeons. He also issued instructions through the Admiralty to Admiral Dundas, commander of the British fleet, to provision a large steamer as a hospital ship for the evacuation of the wounded; and on the eve of the Crimean invasion he requested Lord Stratford de Redcliffe, British ambassador to Turkey, to induce the Porte to transfer the entire Scutari Barracks to the British for hospital facilities and winter quarters for part of the British army. Early in September, he ordered a large increase in the quantities of port wine, arrowroot, and other medical comforts for the hospitals in the East and asked Dr. Andrew Smith, director-general of the Medical Department, to explain why he and his staff had allowed those supplies to dwindle.[32]

The administration of the Commissariat presented another major problem for Newcastle. Trevelyan's and Gladstone's dogged determination to maintain the Commissariat under Treasury supervision prevented the transfer of that department to the newly established War Department until late December 1854. Thus most of the decisions that affected the operations of the Commissariat until that time were made at the Treasury, and particularly by Trevelyan, Newcastle's old nemesis. The duke had become apprehensive about some aspects of that department's operations well before it was transferred to the War Office.

As early as the previous June, Lord Raglan had reported the unsatisfactory state of the Commissariat. Besides insufficient land transport, he noted that a shortage of experienced officers and subordinates hampered its operations. Furthermore, the army was supplied by contractors in whom he had little confidence. Newcastle asked Raglan for details, especially with regard to the fitness of Commissary-General Filder, but Raglan's only comment was that the Commissariat was in its infancy and that Filder was an old man who labored from morning to night.[33]

Despite their vagueness, Raglan's complaints about the Commissariat forced Newcastle to intercede with the Treasury. The duke strongly urged the Treasury to appoint men selected from among the Irish Constabulary and the Metropolitan Police Establishment to serve as storekeepers and issuers for the Commissariat. Reluctantly, the Treasury officials agreed to this suggestion, and on 8 August, Newcastle reported with relief to Raglan that officers for the Commissariat were on their way and that more would follow shortly.[34]

Newcastle also turned his attention to the problem of land transport. In mid-August he concurred with the Treasury's sanction of the purchase of five hundred mules in Spain, and about a fortnight later he requested Trevelyan to inform Commissary-General Filder of the availability for purchase of two thousand mules that had been used to construct the railway from Turin to Genoa.[35] By this time, however, Filder's needs had changed. With the Crimean expedition now firmly set, he no longer required the vast number of animals and wagons that he would have needed for the movement of the army through Bulgaria to the Danube. For the time being, therefore, the decision to invade the Crimea resolved the problem of insufficient land transport. Thus Filder saw no need then to purchase additional transport animals for the Commissariat, a decision that was welcomed by the economy-minded lords of the Treasury.

Insufficient sea transport early in the war was even a greater problem for Newcastle than inadequate land transport. Although it had the largest naval and merchant fleets in the world, Great Britain could not provide enough shipping to carry all the available men, equipment, and stores to the theater of war without long delays. The allocation of space aboard the transports became a critical factor in many supply decisions. In July the pressure on sea transport was particularly severe, and consequently the Treasury, with Newcastle's full endorsement, scaled down Commissary-General Filder's requests for biscuit, salt meat, and pressed hay from England. Filder was instructed instead to rely more upon fresh bread, meat, and hay procured from contractors in the East.[36]

The lack of sufficient sea transport also prevented Newcastle from sending out troop reinforcements to Lord Raglan as rapidly as he would have liked. The matter became so critical that on 8 July the duke requested the Admiralty to use all available space aboard steam transports for conveyance to Turkey of two cavalry regiments, the remaining troops of the Rifle Brigade, and some infantry regiments, as well as the second siege train of forty-two guns as soon as additional steamers were available.[37] When he made that request, several British steamers were reserved for the conveyance of ten thousand French troops from Calais to the Baltic. This commitment to the French delayed the shipment of the second battering train, and it was not until 3 August that the first part of it was sent out on the *Medway*.

With requests for space aboard the transports pouring into the Admiralty from all the major departments, it was virtually impossible to produce order without granting the War Office a greater degree of central direction over sea transport. Newcastle was aware of the confusion, and very early in the war he advised the reconstitution of the Transport Board under the supervision of the minister for war. The Admiralty, however, repeatedly rejected his suggestion until after the disclosure early in January 1855 of several instances of delay and muddle; and though the Transport Board was eventually revised, the lord commissioners of the Admiralty refused to surrender authority over it to the War Ministry.[38] Therefore, although there was some improvement, the lack of coordination between the Admiralty and the War Ministry remained unresolved.

Although lack of coordination among the military departments remained a source of difficulty, the major trouble came from a lack of initiative within the departments. Newcastle was hampered by departmental subordinates who failed to execute the government's intentions properly because they did not understand their duties. There was not "that thorough cooperation and understanding, from the highest to the lowest, which ought to exist," Newcastle later reported.[39] Through bitter experience, he discovered that he could not limit his superintending authority to department heads and depend upon them alone to carry out his wishes. The most serious administrative failures that were to cause so much hardship for the army during the winter months resulted from the inability or the unwillingness of upper-level administrators to superintend and coordinate activities within their own areas. A notable example of this was the failure of Dr. Andrew Smith and the Medical Board to issue specific instructions for the administration of the hospitals, particularly the hospital at Scutari, even though Newcastle had directed the board to draw up such instructions. The confusion that resulted from the absence of guidelines for expenditure and staff responsibilities later provided abundant excuses for the medical authorities in Turkey and the Crimea to justify the misfortunes that occurred.[40] Gradually, as Newcastle extended his authority over the departments, many of these problems were rectified. But it took time. With all the pressures of war and with the system so inadequate, it was to the duke's credit that he was able to resolve most of the major problems as quickly as he did.

Still, it has been argued that a more forceful person would have surmounted these deficiencies in means and remedied the difficulties of military administration more rapidly. The duke, according to his critics, lacked imagination, administrative skill, and perception, particularly with regard to selecting subordinates. Although he brought indefatigable industry, much knowledge of public business, zeal, good common sense, rapid judgment, courage, and supreme confidence to the position, the critics argue, he was deficient in statesmanlike vision and tact and in ability to delegate authority—qualities that his office required. For these reasons, it has been suggested that either Sidney Herbert or Lord Palmerston was better suited for the post of war minister.[41]

The criticisms of the duke have not always been just; nor have the assessments of his personality and ability been entirely accurate. Historians have long depended upon Lord Blachford's and Goldwin Smith's opinions of the duke.[42] Although both men knew him well later when he again became colonial secretary, they were not always in the best position to judge these matters, especially with respect to Newcastle's administration of the War Department. They did not fully appreciate the difficulty of reconstructing the War Office while the country was engaged in a war three thousand miles distant. Without an adequate and sufficiently experienced staff, Newcastle faced a most difficult situation; and Treasury restrictions on the appointment of a second under-secretary and a staff of clerks made the duke's task even more difficult. The clerks he had were selected for him from the Colonial, secretary at war, and Ordnance offices, but the rapidly multiplying workload soon overwhelmed them. Furthermore, the lack of an official residence for the new War Office until early autumn was one of the excuses that the Treasury gave to delay the enlargement of the duke's staff and the transfer of the Commissariat to his jurisdiction. Therefore, Newcastle for some time following the separation of War and Colonies was minister for war without a capable ministry. Although he had the requisite authority, he lacked sufficient means to administer his department effectively.[43]

It would take many years and several ministers of war to reorganize the War Department thoroughly and reform the military system. In the more immediate sense, however, Newcastle was caught in a spiraling web of circumstances that would have trapped any person who held the position of secretary of state for war in 1854. The factors that created near disaster in the Crimea were largely beyond his control. Many of them were caused by the failure of the military to execute the objectives of the Crimean invasion in the manner anticipated by the home authorities both in London and in Paris.

V

Despite these problems and administrative shortcomings, the army at the time of the Crimean invasion was more than sufficiently supplied and equipped. In a speech at the opening of Parliament on 12 December 1854, Newcastle defended the government against Lord Derby's charge of inadequate preparations for the campaign. Never in any former war, the duke stated, were two battering trains sent out in so complete a state of efficiency or with so large a supply of ammunition. After consulting with Lord Hardinge and other authorities on the amount of ammunition and other stores that should be sent out, the duke doubled and sometimes trebled the amounts they had recommended. He confidently claimed that "no army ever was better fed than this army has been."[44] In July and August, he observed, large quantities of clothing, blankets, and other bedding items were shipped. Supplies continued to flow to the Crimea, and despite the great fire at Varna in mid-August that destroyed a large amount of valuable stores, the army remained abundantly provisioned.[45]

There was, then, with the exception of the matter of troop reinforcements, no aspect of military preparations at the time of the Crimean expedition that appeared to be so deficient as to cause Newcastle serious apprehension. The absence of an adequate reserve of troops, however, plagued the duke for the rest of the year. He ordered out the reserve division of seven thousand men under the command of Sir George Cathcart, along with an additional two companies of artillery and two regiments of cavalry, as soon as the decision was made to invade the Crimea. Most of these troops had been withdrawn from the colonies at the outset of the war. Their places in the reserve had to be filled by volunteers, recruits from the embodied militia, and troops obtained by additional withdrawals from the colonies. In each case Newcastle faced serious difficulties.

Although the number of recruits for the regular army was higher than usual between March and November, the increase was not enough to meet the needs of the country. Late in September, Newcastle admitted to Russell that they were still far short of the number of troops voted by Parliament.[46] The government, however, did not take measures to encourage more recruitment from the militia until after the news of the costly battle of Inkerman early in November. Therefore, Newcastle was forced to rely mainly upon the ineffective system of enlistment and upon additional troop withdrawals from the colonies for reinforcements needed in the Crimea.

Even the withdrawal of troops from the colonies was not an easy matter. Newcastle's proposal to withdraw troops from North America was delayed for two months because Lord Clarendon and the queen did not feel that it was safe or wise while relations with the United States remained unsettled. In August, in light of the improved Anglo-American relations, the queen finally consented to the proposal, with the understanding that the withdrawal was temporary. The consideration of defense in the Ionian Islands also prevented Newcastle from withdrawing the 97th Regiment from Corfu until late in October, when he could replace it with a regiment from Malta. By mid-September Newcastle had managed to order only eight additional regiments home from the colonies and two from the service of the East India Company. These were the troops he expected to employ at the opening of the next campaign following the anticipated fall of Sebastopol.[47]

Very early in the war Newcastle had seen the difficulty of supplying the number of troops that Raglan thought necessary for the invasion of the Crimea. He thus had urged the commander to use Turkish troops under English officers as much as possible. He was particularly interested in employing the Bashi Bazooks, a Turkish irregular cavalry force commanded by Lt.-Col. William Ferguson Beatson of the Bengal Cavalry, whom the British Foreign Office had commissioned with the consent of the Porte to organize the irregular bands of the Turkish army.[48] Throughout the summer, Newcastle continually impressed upon Raglan the importance of attaching Turkish troops like the Bashi Bazooks to the British army and of introducing English half-pay officers or officers from the service of the East India Company into the Turkish army. Raglan, however, being prejudiced against officers with Indian experience and being quite aware of the Bashi Bazooks' reputation for savagery, demurred. "There is no reasonable ground," he wrote of the Bashi Bazooks, "to hope that men who have contracted such irregular habits . . . and have led the wildest of life from their very infancy, could be brought under proper subjection, and even, in course of time, become efficient soldiers."[49] He would be sorry indeed to be accompanied to the Crimea by a band of men who decapitated the wounded enemy and used their heads as trophies. Despite this resistance, the government persisted with the plan to organize irregular Turkish forces, particularly as the British army was then critically short of cavalry units of any description. Thus Colonel Beatson and his small party of unattached Bashi Bazooks accompanied the British force to the Crimea, although, as Raglan had anticipated, they proved to be more trouble than they were worth.

Newcastle conferred closely with Lord Hardinge on all aspects of recruitment and reinforcements. The same was true for all matters concerning the royal prerogative as vested in the office of commander-in-chief at the Horse Guards. Appointments to high command fell within this prerogative. Although as secretary of state for war Newcastle claimed ultimate responsibility for the appointment of all higher officers, these appointments were actually made by Lord Hardinge, usually after consultation with Lord Raglan. In accordance with accepted practice, the appointments were generally submitted to Newcastle for his sanction before they were forwarded to the queen for her approval.[50]

Military patronage was a most delicate matter, and frequently the decisions made by Newcastle and Hardinge abused the pride and principles of men accustomed to the ritual and routine of the traditional military system. In typical Peelite fashion, Newcastle and Hardinge insisted that merit rather than social status or seniority be the basis for promotions. Such was the case when Newcastle advised the queen to give Sir George Cathcart rather than Sir George Brown, his senior in rank, the dormant commission to succeed to the command of the army in the event of Raglan's death or illness. Lord Raglan, who favored Brown, resented the commission, and the subsequent poor relations between him and Cathcart perhaps affected the decision to besiege rather than to assault Sebastopol. Cathcart was the only major British officer in favor of an immediate assault upon the fortress, while Brown, whom Raglan continued to favor, adamantly opposed such a move and argued instead for a systematic siege.[51]

The appointment of Sir Hew Ross as lieutenant-general of the Ordnance, made necessary by Lord Raglan's absence from England, also was contrary to the traditional consideration of seniority. Sir John Burgoyne, who had just returned from his inspection tour in Turkey, was senior to Ross at the time of the appointment, but Newcastle wanted the former to return to service with the army in the East. Burgoyne, however, felt slighted and resigned his appointment as inspector-general of fortifications in order to relieve himself and his subordinates in the Corps of Engineers from "the effects of the slur that the arrangement entails upon us." Newcastle failed to mollify him with a flattering letter of explanation, but Lord Hardinge prevailed, and Burgoyne, though convinced he was making "the greatest of all sacrifices," withdrew his resignation and joined Raglan in Turkey.[52] Newcastle learned from this experience that Burgoyne was a difficult and obstinate man.

Although Newcastle was directly involved in questions of merit and leadership, he rarely interfered in matters of military discipline, which he generally left in the hands of Lords Hardinge and Raglan. However, once the duke intervened on the side of the soldier against the pedantic traditions of the army. His concern was with the soldiers' comfort. "*De minimis non curat* a Secretary of State!," he wrote to Raglan:

> Perhaps this is a sound maxim, but I fear you have already found me unmindful of it.
>
> I am not going to write to you about the colour or tightness of Cardigan's cherry pants, nor about the tooth-brush to be carried in each man's knapsack, but I am going to plead on behalf of the soldiers' necks and chins.
>
> I have been in the East myself, and if I were called upon to say what two things were most conducive to my bodily comfort, I should name the absence of a neckcloth and the presence of a beard.
>
> I really think you would endear yourself to the men under your command if you would abolish two articles in their kit, the stock and the razor. I dare say the spruce parade appearance would be deteriorated, but their comfort, and I feel confident their health, would be greatly improved.[53]

But even these moderate changes were not accepted without considerable resistance from officers of the old school such as Sir George Brown, who continued to insist upon the leather stock, the high collar of the parade uniform. Even Lord Raglan was a stickler for tradition; he would not concede that the British uniform was more suited to the parade ground than to the battlefield. "Why should not all the Cavalry be in Scarlet?," he asked Newcastle in November.[54] As for shaving, the commander believed that it was the first requirement for cleanliness among the lower classes in England. It mattered little to him that his officers wanted to copy their French counterparts, who returned bearded from campaigns in Algeria. "I am old fashioned," he wrote, "and I cling to the desire that an Englishman should look like an Englishman, though the French endeavour to make themselves look like Africans, Turks and infidels."[55] Eventually the trials of the Crimean winter did far more than official recommendations from London to break down archaic military formalities. Nonetheless, Newcastle could justly claim, as he did in the House of Lords on 12 December 1854, that during his short administration of the War Department the character as well as the general lot in life of the British soldier had improved greatly.[56]

Although conscious of the army's stubborn resistance to change and of the general inadequacies of the military departments, Newcastle still was confident that the British expeditionary army was the finest the country had ever produced and that the immense preparations undertaken by the government would enable that force, in conjunction with the British navy and the military and naval forces of the French, to meet the Allied objectives in the war. Under normal circumstances the duke's confidence would probably have been justified, but the cloud of misfortune that consistently hovered over him now threatened to engulf the whole nation.

9. Invasion of the Crimea

In sending the expeditionary force to Turkey, the government's primary objective was to secure the defense of Constantinople and the Dardanelles. The ministers did not intend, however, to keep the army in a purely defensive position longer than was necessary to achieve that objective; and on 23 April 1854, the duke of Newcastle instructed Raglan to consider sending a portion of his force, assisted if possible by a detachment of the French army, to Varna in Bulgaria. There could be no doubt, he noted, that this troop movement would encourage the Turks, discomfort the Russians, and perhaps induce Austria to take a more active part against Russia. "All this I leave to your judgment on the spot," he continued, adding, however, "We must endeavour to do what is both militarily and politically *right*."[1]

Another month passed before the Allied commanders decided to advance by sea to Varna in support of the Turks. Even at the last moment, Marshal St. Arnaud, the commander of the French army, attempted to change the plan with the plea that the armies were not yet ready to take the field. Raglan remained politely firm, and on 10 June, St. Arnaud finally gave way. Raglan lost no time in forwarding most of the British troops to Varna; but since neither the French nor the British armies possessed adequate cavalry and artillery or sufficient transport for ammunition and provisions to enable them to take to the field at once, the move was designed primarily as a diversion in favor of Silistria, whose Turkish defenders appeared to be near defeat. Somehow that garrison held out, and on 23 June, ten days after the arrival of the British First Division at Varna, the Russians suddenly raised the siege and retreated across the Danube.

The news of Silistria reached London by telegraph a few days later. With a new aspect of the war before them, the ministers met immediately to consider plans for the next operation. In a private letter dated 28 June, Newcastle informed Raglan that the cabinet unanimously believed that the Allied armies should invade the Crimea and lay siege to Sebastopol for the purpose of reducing the naval fortress and capturing the Russian fleet.

The cabinet's decision to sanction the invasion of the Crimea and the attack upon Sebastopol was not made hastily; the ministers had carefully considered the plan for several months. Even before the declaration of war there were advocates of the Crimean expedition within the cabinet and among the French authorities, and Newcastle apprised Raglan in person of these opinions before the latter left London to take up the command of the British army. About a month later Newcastle again referred to Sebastopol and the Crimea in a secret dispatch to Raglan of 10 April. The duke instructed the commander to lose no time in making secret inquiries into the size and condition of the Russian force in the Crimea and the strength of the Sebastopol garrison. The destruction of the naval fortress, he added, might become essential for the attainment of the objectives of the war and for the maintenance of peace in the future. "No blow which could be struck at the Southern extremities of the Russian empire," he concluded his remarks, "would be so effective for this purpose as the taking of Sebastopol."[2]

During April and May the duke's eagerness for an attack on Sebastopol increased, and the move of the Allied armies to Varna did not dash his hopes for the venture. "We must never forget," he wrote to Raglan early in May, "that mere[ly] driving the Russians out of the Principalities without crippling their future means of aggression upon Turkey is not *now* an object worthy of the great [efforts] of England and France." A few days later, in expressing serious doubts about a proposed attack against the Russians in the Dobrutscha on the Bulgarian frontier, the duke argued that an attack upon Sebastopol would have great political and military advantages. But he added that Raglan's judgment on the military aspects of the operation must be left completely unfettered.[3]

Information about the defenses of Sebastopol and the Russian forces in the Crimea was very difficult to obtain through normal channels. Raglan was too much of a gentleman to use unscrupulous means to get the necessary information, and Lord Stratford de Redcliffe was of little help. On 5 June, Raglan confessed his failure to obtain any accurate information on the subject and his inability to discover any channel by which he could acquire the necessary intelligence. His only information was contained in a letter he forwarded from Admiral Dundas dated 10 May 1854, in which Sebastopol was described as a second Gibraltar containing thirty thousand troops, with an additional ninety thousand men in the Crimea. Newcastle found such numbers incredible. "Do not believe the Admiral's story about 120,000 men in the Crimea," he replied.

> I do not believe there are more than 30,000, and that there are about 18,000 more in Odessa. At the same time do not suppose I want to urge you to the siege of Sebastopol against your and the Admiral's judgment. All I say is that in a political point of view this is the thing to do, and unless we destroy Russia's Black Sea fleet I do not see my way to a safe and honourable peace.[4]

After personally interviewing the recent British consuls at Odessa and Kertsch, Newcastle later raised his estimate to forty thousand or forty-five thousand men in Sebastopol, with an additional twenty-two thousand men in Bessarabia and Odessa.[5] These were the estimates of Russian force in and near the Crimea accepted by the ministers at the time of the Crimean invasion. The ministers further believed that the Allies could cut off the Crimea from the mainland and thus prevent Russian reinforcements from reaching Sebastopol by occupying the Isthmus of Perekop with a small force (mainly Turkish) and by patrolling the Sea of Azov with ships from the fleets. When the Crimean expedition was sanctioned, the government sent instructions accordingly to Admiral Dundas and Lord Raglan.[6]

In the spring and summer of 1854, Newcastle's enthusiasm for the Crimean campaign never slackened. Yet Kinglake's assertion that the invasion of the Crimea was inspired by Newcastle and by the *Times* is untrue. Although, as Kinglake noted, Newcastle was a "man of sanguine eager nature, very prone to action,"[7] several other influential members of the ministry had joined him from the outset of the cabinet's deliberations on war strategy in advocating the invasion of the Crimea and the attack upon Sebastopol. Palmerston and Graham were equally as forceful as the duke in pressing the matter even before the declaration of war, and Russell was not far behind them. Without question, the force of public opinion strengthened their hands and helped them to bring such men as Aberdeen and Gladstone into line. Newcastle shared the feelings of most people in England when he encouraged the attack upon Sebastopol, but neither he nor those within the cabinet who initially agreed with him were driven forward by the frenzied feelings of the country. The members of the government had already given considerable attention to the project long before 15 June, when the *Times* launched its campaign for the invasion of the Crimea. The influence of the *Times*, therefore, did not stir the ministers to action; however, the pressure of public opinion as reflected in the columns of that paper made it virtually impossible for them to turn back from this forward position once the decision had been reached.

The ministers were convinced that Sebastopol could be captured and that its destruction and the capture of the Russian fleet would be "the knock-down-blows" that would produce victory with the greatest certainty and in the shortest time. Therefore, despite the general apprehension of the project that prevailed among most of the military and naval officers, they pressed unanimously for the invasion, even though they were uncertain of Sebastopol's strength or the numbers of its garrison. Orders authorizing the invasion were sent to Lord Raglan in the fateful dispatch of 29 June, which Newcastle had read on the previous evening to a sleepy cabinet after dinner at Pembroke Lodge, Russell's house in Richmond. Kinglake placed undue significance on this incident of the sleeping cabinet. The "Cogency in the wording of the Despatch which could hardly have failed to provoke objection from an awakened Cabinet," he wrote, "was the very cause which governed events." Unwittingly, he argued, the sleeping cabinet allowed Newcastle to confine Raglan's discretion "with a precision scarcely short of harshness" to an extent that made it impossible for Raglan to prevent the fateful campaign.[8]

Actually it mattered little that many of the ministers fell asleep, to the annoyance of the duke, while he read his draft, for they had discussed and agreed upon the substance of the dispatch the day before. Therefore, the reading of the draft at Pembroke Lodge was merely the formal ratification of a cabinet decision already reached; and the terms of the dispatch, although cogent, left Lord Raglan some discretionary authority. His concurrence with the feasibility of the campaign was required to put the instructions into effect. The dispatch ordered Raglan to halt operations in Bulgaria and to undertake the invasion of the Crimea with the full cooperation of the French and Turkish allies, unless he saw that the plan was beyond the powers of the combined forces. The ministers assumed collective responsibility for ordering the invasion, but left the final determination of the military feasibility of the plan to Raglan and the military authorities at the seat of the war. They did not intend to overrule Raglan's discretion or compel him to undertake a task that he knew was militarily unwise; at the same time, however, they wanted to state explicitly to Raglan their conviction that only the capture of Sebastopol and the destruction of the Russian fleet could achieve "the great object of a just war, the vindication of national rights, and the future peace of Europe."[9]

Even with this dispatch, the ministers did not believe that the die had been cast; therefore, the next few weeks were filled with anxious moments. Their anxiety was divided between fearing one moment that a Russian withdrawal from the Principalities in accordance with the Austrian summons of 3 June would result in conditions for peace, and the next moment that Russia's refusal to evacuate the Principalities would induce the French to withdraw their assent to the Crimean venture in favor of a campaign on the Danube. On 15 July, Newcastle brought the matter of the Crimean expedition to the attention of the cabinet once again. Palmerston, Clarendon, Russell, and Herbert joined him in pressing for the Crimean attack and in opposing the suspension of hostilities during the course of new peace negotiations. On the latter point, Russell's attitude was shared by the majority of the cabinet. "The only answer we can give," he wrote in response to the Austrian communication about possible peace terms, "is that having sent at a vast cost our fleets and armies to Turkey we cannot withdraw them without the signature of preliminary articles of peace."[10] Nor, Russell might have added, could they be withdrawn without first capturing Sebastopol. Clearly, then, the mood of the cabinet was to push on with the war and the Crimean expedition, even though in July and early August the main objective of the Anglo-French intervention seemed close to being achieved. And in a confidential letter of 18 July, while still leaving an out for Raglan, Newcastle again expressed this desire to the British commander.[11]

On the day that letter was sent, Lord Raglan and Marshal St. Arnaud held a council of war with the British and French admirals to consider the directives they recently had received from Paris and London. After more than four hours of deliberation, they determined that the Crimean operation should be undertaken as soon as naval arrangements for the transport of men, horses, and guns were completed. That conclusion was reached after the officers resigned themselves to the strong determination of their governments to lay siege to Sebastopol. Raglan clearly conveyed this attitude in his response to Newcastle:

> Having stated to your Grace the result of the discussion which took place
> yesterday, and which was carried on in a matter quite satisfactory to all
> parties present, it becomes my duty to acquaint you that it was more in
> deference to the views of the British Government, as conveyed to me in
> your Grace's despatch, and to the known acquiescence of the Emperor
> Louis Napoleon in those views, than to any information in the possession
> of the naval and military authorities, either as to the extent of the enemy's
> forces or to their state of preparation, that the decision to make a descent
> upon the Crimea was adopted.[12]

Newcastle realized that Raglan's acquiescence in the campaign came from a sense of duty rather than conviction:

> I cannot help seeing through the calm and noble tone of your announcement
> of the decision to attack Sebastopol that it has been taken in order to meet
> the views and desires of the Government, and not in entire accordance with
> your own opinions. God grant that success may reward you and justify us!
> . . . The cause is a just one if any war is just, and I will not believe that in
> such a cause, British arms can fail.[13]

Taught by Wellington to consider the government's wishes as if they were commands, Raglan believed he had no choice but to throw caution to the wind in an attempt to win the military victory that the ministers thought was necessary to achieve Great Britain's political and diplomatic objectives in the war. Strategically, the invasion of the Crimea to attack Sebastopol was sound, but everything hinged upon the execution of the plan.

II

Although the decision reached in London and Paris to attack the Crimea was accepted by the Allied commanders at Varna, there still was considerable doubt whether the invasion would ever be launched. Russia's initial rejection of the Austrian summons to evacuate the Danubian Principalities clouded the future of the Crimean operation, and Marshal St. Arnaud and most of the

French generals continued to harbor major reservations about the invasion of the Crimea during that year. Cholera also ravaged the Allied armies and navies, making many of the commanders in both camps lose what little remaining enthusiasm they had for the proposed expedition. The rumors of councils of war and telegraphs of all kinds kept Newcastle in a state of nervous anxiety in London, a condition shared by the queen and the other ministers. "I find a fear springing up here that the expedition is virtually abandoned," the duke told Lord Raglan on 29 August. Newcastle refused to believe it, but the fear became greater after it was learned that even the French authorities in Paris were having second thoughts. In London the resolve remained as firm as ever. The expedition, the queen stressed to Newcastle, "*ought* most positively to be attempted this year." The duke, of course, strongly agreed, and he admonished Lord Raglan that after making such magnificent preparations upon a scale hitherto unequaled, it would be most prejudicial to England's prestige throughout the world and especially in the East to close the campaign without first striking a blow. Even the pacific Lord Aberdeen worried about the attitude of the French authorities. "If we could but hear that they [the Allied forces] had sailed, I should be satisfied," he told Newcastle.[14]

The problems surrounding the expedition were finally resolved, and the Allied forces sailed from Varna to the Crimea on 7 September. But news of the expedition's sailing did not reach London for several days, and while the ministers waited in painful suspense, Newcastle accompanied Prince Albert to Boulogne to visit Emperor Napoleon III. The main purpose of the trip was to strengthen the alliance. After four days of frank discussion between the prince and the emperor that touched on most of the topics of the day in both countries, Newcastle judged the Boulogne camp to have been a complete success. The emperor and the prince, he told Raglan, were favorably impressed with one another, a factor, he thought, that foretold considerable political consequences. As for the prospect of the war, there were mixed feelings at the camp. "All here," he noted,

> are counting the hours which must intervene before we hear of the debarkation. I must say, however, there is a marked difference between the English and the French. *We* are all confidence, *they* are as anxious, but more doubtful. The Emperor agrees with us that you *will* succeed, but talks of a longer time than I think it will cost you.[15]

Capturing Sebastopol would take less time than was generally expected, Newcastle told Palmerston, unless, of course, "our Allies insist as is usual with them, upon doing everything *secundum artem*."[16]

Newcastle received the news of the successful landing of the Allied troops at Calamita Bay by telegraph from Vienna on 21 September. With a tremendous sense of relief, he forwarded the news to the queen at Balmoral and wrote letters announcing the happy event to ministers who were out of town. His letter to Russell was quite optimistic:

> Up to the present time all the arrangements have been good and successful and whatever may be the results of this great Expedition (which is under the control of higher powers than that of Government or Press) I am confident that neither the Country nor the Ministry will have any reason to be ashamed. I have no fear however of a speedy as well as a successful result.[17]

For the next few days, the duke's life was a "strange mixture of excitement and intense distress," as he awaited each successive telegraph and dispatch from the East.[18] The emotional strain was great, and it was evident that excessive work and constant anxiety concerning the war had already borne heavily upon him. Those who saw him noted his haggard appearance. His old heart complaint returned, and he could not get up a staircase without considerable pain. "He is killing himself with work and anxiety," Abraham Hayward told Sir John Young.[19] Newcastle spent each day until well into the evening at the War Office, overwhelmed with the business of his position but unable to decrease it by delegating lesser matters to subordinates. And during much of the autumn he was left alone in London to deal with matters of first importance, for all of his ministerial colleagues had joined the exodus from London as soon as the parliamentary session had ended. Except for the short trip with the prince to Boulogne, the duke did not leave his post in London throughout 1854. Understandably, the pressure of the situation was almost unbearable. Early in October he told Gladstone, "I have been for 7 weeks *entirely alone* in London, and it begins to be almost more than the spirit will bear."[20]

Not all of the news about the Crimean expedition was good, a fact that added to Newcastle's discomfort. He was particularly distressed by the contents of Lord Raglan's private letter of 11 September, written aboard the *Caradoc* on the eve of the Crimean landing. Raglan informed the duke that some of the French generals had presented Marshal St. Arnaud with a petition urging the postponement of the attack on Sebastopol until the following year. St. Arnaud, who was dying from cancer, requested a council with Lord Raglan and the leading officers of both armies and fleets. Although the marshal and General Canrobert, second in the French command, ultimately stood behind Lord Raglan's decision to press on with the attack, the indisposition of some of the most influential French generals to the expedition was a serious obstacle to the success of the campaign. In his dispatch of 12 September, Lord Raglan pessimistically drew the duke's attention to that point and to other difficulties that imperiled the operation.[21]

Even though he knew of the safe landing of the Allied armies by the time this correspondence reached him, Newcastle was still outraged by the French "protest." He immediately penned his indignation to Lord Aberdeen: "Whilst the armies were on the sea, an attempt was made by our *gallant* Allies to turn tail,—they literally *funked*, and wanted by shabby pretexts to put the whole affair off to next year. Luckily both Raglan and all our officers stood firm, and they are now in for it." But he was afraid that the "faint-hearted" French generals had the support of the military men in Paris, most of whom antici-pated the failure of the expedition. Bitterly, he added, "We have many red-coated, but white-livered croakers here too; and it requires some encouraging telegraph to keep up one's pluck, though I have not lost mine *yet*."[22]

Although he was still confident of quick success, Newcastle assured Raglan that he did not underrate the magnitude or the difficulties of the expedition. He was certain that the cause deserved success and that the Allied armies were capable of achieving it before the onset of winter. The duke wrote in response to Raglan's dispatch of 12 September:

> You and your brave army will be able to pass a merry Christmas and be
> able to enjoy the comfortable reflection that in the coming new year there
> will be every prospect of returning home to a grateful country, full of
> honours, having won a peace which, with the blessing of God, we may
> fairly hope to be enduring. Most earnestly I pray that this letter may find
> you so situated as to participate in these hopeful prospects. You can hardly
> imagine, being on the scene of all our thoughts, how anxious is the longing
> of all here for the next telegraph. We have had none for five days.[23]

Two days later, on 30 September, Newcastle received the telegraph message that he had long awaited. The message, sent by Robert J. Colquhoun, British consul at Bucharest, reported the fall of Sebastopol. The duke, uncertain of the report's authenticity, feared a mistake. But the arrival of a second message from Constantinople that same day gave plausibility to the first. To Sidney Herbert he wrote:

> God be thanked! I stop to say that a telegraph has this moment come from
> Stratford—a great battle on the 20th on the Alma—the Russians driven
> in on Sebastopol with heavy loss—our loss killed and wounded 1,400—
> French the same. Victory complete. I now am convinced Sebastopol HAS
> really fallen. Again thank Heaven![24]

On 2 October, after receiving yet another telegraph reporting the Allied victory at the Alma, Newcastle triumphantly noted to Raglan:

> The happy results which have so far attended the progress of the great
> undertaking entrusted to your Lordship, justify Her Majesty's Government
> in the sanguine expectation that those difficulties and obstacles which so
> naturally have presented themselves to your Lordship's mind, will long ere
> this have vanished, and lead us to indulge the fervent hope that Providence
> may be pleased to crown with success the great object of the expedition—
> the capture of the fortress of Sebastopol.[25]

Still convinced that Sebastopol had fallen, Newcastle wrote again on the following day to inform Raglan that the ministers were preparing instructions in conjunction with the French authorities concerning the works and fortifications at Sebastopol and to request him to forward recommendations for sealing off the Crimea and establishing winter quarters there.[26]

The report of the fall of Sebastopol was widely believed, for almost everyone in England had expected a quick assault upon the fortress and a speedy verdict in the war. The ministers shared the jubilation of the nation over the news. While bells were rung all over the country, ministers exchanged congratulatory letters. Palmerston was among those who wrote to congratulate Newcastle on the "auspicious beginning of the Crimean campaign."[27] Throughout the country Newcastle was held in high esteem. But when news arrived on 5 October that Sebastopol had not fallen and that the Allies had executed a flank march around the fortress to Balaclava on the southern coast of the Crimea, the disappointment in the country was devastating. From this moment the public began to turn against the ministry, and particularly against the minister of war.[28]

III

Although the ministers had put extreme pressure on Raglan to undertake the Crimean invasion, the fateful decisions that determined the outcome of the battle were not of the ministers' making. The most important of these, the decision to forgo an immediate assault upon Sebastopol from the north in favor of a siege of the fortress from the south, was the most crucial and controversial decision of the war. Strong evidence exists that an assault from the north would have succeeded had it been attempted immediately after the decisive defeat of the Russian army on the Alma.[29] Lord Raglan was inclined to such an attack, but Marshal St. Arnaud demurred. The marshal, supported by Sir John Burgoyne, instead pressed for a flank march around Sebastopol to the south side to lay siege to it in systematic fashion. On 24 September, Raglan reluctantly concurred with the marshal, and on the following morning the flank march was begun.

On the second day of that march, the British forces entered the tiny fishing village of Balaclava with its small, long, twisting, and almost landlocked harbor, which Lord Raglan, upon the recommendation of Admiral Sir Edmond Lyons, decided to use as the British supply base. The decision, although it seemed inconsequential at the time, contained all the elements of disaster. The harbor was hardly adequate and the town was badly situated for maintaining effective communications with the plateau, "the Upland," where the troops took up positions in front of the southern defenses of Sebastopol. The investment of the fortress from the south confined the army to a small stretch of rocky ground, from which they could not forage, seal off the Russian garrison from the north, or block the lines of communication between the Crimea and the Russian interior. Large numbers of Russian reinforcements, therefore, slipped into the Crimea virtually unopposed. By allowing the French army to occupy the Chersonese peninsula to the west, Raglan committed the British army to the task of defending the land flank of the Allied armies from Russian attack while attempting at the same time to lay siege to Sebastopol. Only later was it discovered that in the face of many unforeseeable difficulties, the British force was far too small to accomplish both tasks with success.

But these matters had grave implications only in the event of a protracted siege, which few in the British camp, including Lord Raglan, then anticipated. Indeed, convinced that the armies could accomplish their mission long before the disadvantages of their situation threatened to entrap them, Raglan pressed for an immediate assault on Sebastopol before the Russians could strengthen their defenses. But General Canrobert, who had taken over the French command from the dying Marshal St. Arnaud, was appalled by the thought of an immediate assault without the support of heavy guns. He also was concerned by the threat of an attack by Prince Mentschikoff against the Allied flank. Sir John Burgoyne shared those apprehensions and agreed with Canrobert that an unsupported assault before the defenses of Sebastopol were reduced by a heavy artillery bombardment was unjustifiable. In a few days, perhaps in a week or two, he told Raglan, the fire from the heavy siege guns would batter the walls and defensive works of the fortress sufficiently to allow the Allies to storm it with greater certainty of success.[30]

For a second time since the battle of the Alma, Lord Raglan found himself at odds with Sir John Burgoyne and the French commander, and for the second time he gave way, even though he sensed that he was right and they were wrong. In both instances his prime concern was to preserve the alliance with the French. Thus for the sake of the alliance and with the assurance from Burgoyne that the siege would not be prolonged, Raglan on 28 September ordered the landing of the siege guns. That same day he wrote to Newcastle: "We are busily engaged in disembarking our siege train and provisions, and we are most desirous of undertaking the attack of Sebastopol without a loss of a day."[31] The dispatch did not mention the disagreements between the Allied commanders over tactics, nor was there any mention either in this or in the dispatch of 3 October of insurmountable obstacles that would prevent the Allies from capturing Sebastopol in the near future.

Although greatly disappointed that Sebastopol had not been taken immediately, Newcastle put the best face possible on these military decisions. "The dissipation of three days [*sic*] sanguine hopes was indeed a heavy blow," he wrote Russell, "but in all that we now know of what has been done there is little to regret and much to admire. So far as my very limited knowledge of such matters goes the attainment of Balaclava appears as a most skilful and strategic move." Any success on the south side, he told Graham, "will be conclusive—on the north it *might* have been so." And to the queen he noted, "The possession of Balaclava is strategically of such vast importance and so materially changes the whole aspect of future operations for the better, that the Duke of Newcastle feels very hopeful that the tantalizing rumour of a week ago will soon assume an authentic shape." [32] He congratulated Raglan on the "glorious" victory at the Alma and the brilliantly conceived and executed flank march. He published Lord Raglan's Alma dispatch in an extraordinary *Gazette* on Sunday morning, 8 October, and the following day he penned a short acknowledgment of it to the British commander and again praised the gallant efforts of the army. [33]

But despite his expression of gratitude and praise, the duke was deeply troubled by certain aspects of the Crimean operation, and none more so than that involving Admiral Dundas. Reports that reached him by early October convinced the duke that the admiral was guilty of culpable negligence. On 5 October, alarmed by these reports, disillusioned by the news received earlier in the day that Sebastopol had not fallen, and depressed by his official solitude in London, Newcastle wrote a "disagreeable" letter to Sir James Graham at Balmoral. Through negligence, he asserted, Dundas had failed to prevent the withdrawal of the Russian garrison from Anapa and to maintain an effective blockade of the Russian ports on the Black Sea and the Sea of Azov. The consequence was the addition of eighteen thousand Russian troops and considerable stores to the Crimea, an addition that the duke feared could be crucial. He believed that the responsibility of leaving Dundas in command of the fleet was now greater than ever, for "if we have a siege of 4 or 5 weeks this man's incapacity may cause great disaster and I really feel more anxious about it than I can express." The duke suggested sending someone to the East with an order of supersession in his pocket to deliver or not at his own discretion, and he offered to go himself if Lord Aberdeen agreed with the suggestion. "Pray think over maturely what should be done," he concluded his letter to Graham. "After all I heard on Monday morning I do indeed feel the responsibility of leaving the fate of 40,000 Englishmen and the honor of our country in such hands to be most serious." [34]

With that letter Newcastle put Graham in an uncomfortable position. Like the other members of the cabinet, Graham had little faith in Dundas and preferred Sir Edmund Lyons, second-in-command, whom Graham had selected specially to prepare the way for the Sebastopol operation, to the man who commanded the Mediterranean station at the outbreak of the war. Graham admitted Newcastle's complaints against Dundas, but he rejected the duke's remedies as impractical and very dangerous to naval authority. Furthermore, since Dundas was scheduled to relinquish his command at the end of the year, Graham believed that Sir Edmund Lyons could continue to "exercise a salutary influence and control over the conduct of Admiral Dundas, and practically diminish the public danger which might arise from the errors of his Judgement." The following day Graham was relieved to find that Aberdeen entirely concurred with him, a concurrence that he believed would strengthen his hand and prove "to the Duke of Newcastle the necessity of proceeding with caution and forbearance in the treatment of Naval and Military Commanders, even when they are less fortunate than ours have been in the Black Sea."[35]

Newcastle believed that his two colleagues had misunderstood him. Although he had complained of Dundas's inactivity with regard to the garrison of Anapa, he informed Aberdeen, he had by no means urged the admiral's recall for that reason alone. "I felt that such a step was necessary—not as a measure of punishment, but of precaution—and every day convinces me more and more of the serious responsibility attaching to us whilst he remains." He was most anxious for the safety of the army; although he would "be ashamed of advising the degradation of an officer for a mere act of omission of duty," he confessed that his sympathy for one man was not very great when he believed that the lives of forty thousand men were imperiled by the incapacity of that individual. In reply, Aberdeen stood his ground: "Dundas may be remiss and incapable, but I could never agree to his recall on general accusations of incapacity without any proof or special charge brought against him." Such a course of action would be most unjust, and Lyons would be the first to protest against it. Besides, Aberdeen added, Dundas could return with half the fleet as soon as the Allies took Sebastopol, "as I presume we shall do in a few days."[36]

The matter had caused Newcastle such great anxiety that even without the sanction of his colleagues, he had instructed Lord Raglan in a most unusual letter to induce Lyons to disobey any of Dundas's orders that unnecessarily imperiled the army. Although he was unwilling to encroach upon the province of the Admiralty, he wanted it understood in the Crimea that in the event of a serious disagreement between Raglan and Lyons on the one hand and Dundas on the other, he would strongly support the former pair. "I can only pledge *myself*," he wrote to Raglan,

> but such is my confidence in you and him in such an emergency—in your discretion as well as in your boldness—that my existence and position as a Minister will be embarked with you. With you both I will sink or swim. I know the irregularity—may be [*sic*] even the impropriety—of this communication to you, but I feel the emergency to be great, and I should be a coward if I shrank from any act which appeared to me necessary to meet it.[37]

Lord Raglan shared the duke's general opinions of Dundas and Lyons. He and Lyons had become close personal friends and were constantly together at

British headquarters during the early days of the Crimean invasion. Raglan respected Lyons's views and recommendations and hardly ever asked Dundas for his. He showed Newcastle's letter of 9 October to Lyons, who revealed that he had received letters from Graham to the same effect but with the fervent wish that all scandal be avoided. "I am quite satisfied," Raglan wrote in reply to the duke, "that this is in the highest degree desirable, and I do not think anything can occur to make it necessary to take any such extreme step as you authorize the adoption of." [38] Indeed, by the time this letter was written, Raglan and Lyons had already proved that they could prevail over Dundas, when, on 15 October, they forced him to agree to the participation of the Allied fleets in the initial bombardment of Sebastopol. Subsequently, Graham strengthened Lyons's hands even more by corresponding with him behind Dundas's back. In late October, Graham wrote, "I rely on you for the infusion of some fire and energy into their [the Allied fleets'] movements." [39] Therefore, although Dundas was not recalled as Newcastle had advocated, his authority was virtually withdrawn even before he relinquished his command to Lyons and returned home in December.

The Dundas affair was not the only critical matter that occupied Newcastle's attention during his lonely vigil at Whitehall early in October, for the published reports of William Howard Russell, war correspondent for the *Times*, put him in the center of a storm of public indignation over the alleged state of the military hospitals in the East. In describing the deplorable conditions of the hospitals and the treatment of the sick and wounded, Russell wrote, "It is with feelings of surprise and anger that the public will learn that no sufficient preparations have been made for the care of the wounded." There was, he charged, not only a deficiency of surgeons and nurses, but also of linen for bandages and "the commonest appliances of a workhouse sick ward." [40] These revelations shook the country and gave the public its first really notorious scandal of the Crimean War.

Without accepting the absolute veracity of the reports, Newcastle and Sidney Herbert, who as secretary at war was largely responsible for the operation of the medical service, acted immediately. On 14 November, Herbert issued new instructions to define the responsibilities of the medical officers in Turkey and the Crimea and to remove any restrictions over expenditure for medical purposes. The duke readily accepted Herbert's suggestion of organizing and sending to Turkey a corps of female nurses superintended by Florence Nightingale. With Newcastle's firm support, Herbert gained the unanimous approval of the cabinet for this bold experiment, and on 21 October, Miss Nightingale with her party of thirty-eight women left London for Constantinople via Paris and Marseilles. [41] A few days earlier, even before the last of William Howard Russell's three sensational reports on the hospital arrangements was published in the *Times*, Newcastle had requested Lord Clarendon to authorize Lord Stratford de Redcliffe to procure in Constantinople whatever was necessary for the hospitals without regard to expense. "I cannot but hope that the statements which I have seen are much exaggerated," he wrote, "but it is hardly possible to believe that they can be wholly without foundation."[42] Despite repeated denials by the military authorities that anything was wrong, Newcastle a few days later appointed a Hospitals Commission consisting of three distinguished men—Peter Benson Maxwell, a well-known barrister, and doctors Alexander Cumming and Thomas Spence—to investigate the charges and to make recommendations for the medical service. The real object of the commission, Newcastle told Lord Stratford de Redcliffe, "is not of course to bring individuals to account unless indeed it should turn out that there has been criminal negligence, but to rectify errors."[43]

Although the duke had acted forcefully to meet the "pressing emergency," he later admitted that he had remained for a long time under the delusion that the state of the hospitals was far better than it actually proved to be. For that reason and also because he was concerned with possible civilian interference with military authority, Newcastle discouraged the use of money from the *Times* Fund for hospital purposes.[44] The fund was opened on 13 October by Sir Robert Peel, the third baronet, to take subscriptions for the purchase of medical provisions supposedly needed in the military hospitals in the East. Dr. Andrew Smith, director-general of the Army Medical Department, contending vehemently that there were no shortages, objected to the use of private money for medical provisions and tried to prevent the fund's agent from entering the hospitals. Newcastle was inclined to agree, but in the end he adopted Sidney Herbert's more moderate course of admitting Mr. Macdonald, the fund's agent, to the hospitals with the strict understanding that he would not be allowed to interfere with the management of the hospitals or to dispense money from the fund without the full assent of the medical men on the spot. Repeating Herbert's advice, Newcastle informed Lord Stratford that to shut Macdonald "out of a great public institution would not only be giving just cause of offense but would raise a very fair suspicion that there was much that would not bear the light."[45]

Newcastle's advice was given with confidence that the crisis was over, or soon would be when the commissioners and Miss Nightingale arrived in Constantinople. Little did the duke suspect that so much in the hospital arrangements could not bear the light, and that the real crisis was before rather than behind them.

10. Autumn Apprehensions and Winter Troubles

A crisis was also fast approaching in the Crimea. As early October passed, the military balance changed from an Allied advantage to more nearly an equilibrium between the opposing sides. The Allies had greatly underestimated the difficulties of preparing for the siege. Landing the heavy guns and siege equipment and moving them to the heights above Balaclava was a slow, laborious operation, and the guns were still not in place ten days after the preparations were begun. The Russians took advantage of their reprieve to strengthen their defenses and to make up losses suffered at the battle of the Alma. Directed by a brilliant young engineer, Lt.-Col. Franz Ivanovitch Todleben, men, women, and children within Sebastopol worked day and night to construct new works and arm them with heavy artillery. They did in a few days the work of months; and with the addition of twenty-eight thousand new troops, the Russians were soon prepared to threaten the British, whose position was far too extensive for adequate occupation by battalions decimated by sickness and losses at the Alma.

There were other problems for the British as well. The ground that they occupied was rocky and difficult to entrench and was intersected with deep ravines that seriously impeded communication between divisions and increased the difficulty of approach. The divisional commanders were unanimously opposed to advancing infantry battalions without cover in support of the engineers, and the engineers were convinced that they could not establish the cover without the support of the infantry. Thus Lord Raglan was forced to conclude that the Allies were committed to a very gradual operation. They had to reduce Russian fire from the ships in the harbor and the Malakoff Tower by long-range guns before they could construct the advances necessary for pushing the siege guns closer to Sebastopol.[1]

Even so, Raglan was still committed to an attack from the British position on the right as soon as the fire from the Allied guns effectively reduced the Russian defenses. But even this view was now challenged by Sir John Burgoyne. Sanguine at first, Burgoyne had gradually concluded that the British force was inadequate for such an attack. Therefore, he urged Raglan to use the British position principally for bombardment in support of a French attack on the left. Raglan immediately consulted with General Canrobert on Burgoyne's plan, and the two commanders agreed that the French would make the major effort in the attack with whatever assistance the British could give them.[2]

Raglan's letters concerning these developments reached Newcastle on 23 October. The duke sent them to the queen and summarized their contents for Russell. To the latter he wrote, "I think the general result of these despatches is that there is much cause for anxiety, but I think none (humanly speaking) for apprehension of an unfavourable issue—the task is a difficult one, but I feel assured it will be accomplished." There was no reason to anticipate worse consequences than a more protracted operation and, he feared, heavy casualties. The British position was a strong one—a Torres Vedras, but with shorter lines and a much larger and better equipped army to defend them. He trusted, he wrote Lord Raglan, "that the formidable character of the undertaking will eventually only prove to Europe that the walls of Sebastopol are not more impregnable than the heights of Alma."[3]

Beneath this air of confidence, however, there was great concern. With the prospect of a protracted siege, Newcastle ordered out all five thousand drilled recruits that were ready, even though Lord Raglan had not specifically requested reinforcements. The duke's major problem was lack of steam transport, but by late October about half the drafts were on their way to the Crimea and the remaining were scheduled to embark during the first two weeks of November. Newcastle augmented these with three additional regiments, the 97th from Corfu, the 62d from Malta, and the 90th from Ireland.[4] After receiving a telegraph containing a brief reference to the heavy loss of cavalry during the battle of Balaclava on 25 October, Newcastle wrote hastily to Lord Dalhousie, governor-general of India, to implore him to dispatch the 10th Hussars of cavalry to the Crimea as soon as possible. "Now pray do all you can," he wrote. "In all human probability we are only at the beginning of a great and deadly struggle, and the honour of the country requires that we should make every possible exertion to come out of it with glory—and, if consistent with success, to terminate it speedily."[5]

Newcastle during the last days of October and early November was concerned with supplying the army during the coming winter and preparing for a spring campaign. Although a large supply of warm clothing was already on the way aboard the *Prince*, the *Golden Fleece*, the *Jason*, and other vessels, Newcastle and Sidney Herbert arranged to send out even larger quantities of winter clothing of all kinds by the steamers that were to convey the reinforcements to the Crimea. Besides these extra articles of clothing, a complete new uniform was to be supplied to each man early in November as soon as space was available aboard the steamers. The duke instructed the Ordnance officials to furnish Lord Raglan with regular accounts of articles shipped as well as the embarkation dates and names of the vessels in which the provisions were shipped. He also urged Lord Raglan to have his adjutant-general, Gen. James Bucknall Estcourt, correspond with Sidney Herbert concerning any other clothing requirements.[6]

The duke was also anxious about the supply of ammunition and siege equipment. On 3 November he informed Lord Raglan that he would send out a third battering train as soon as he could procure two additional steamers. He also instructed Sir William Reid, governor of Malta, to forward as much ammunition as possible to the Crimea and to furnish the Ordnance Department with a complete list of what was needed in the form of shot and shell and bulky field equipment to replenish the depots in Malta for the next campaign. The duke proposed to charter sailing ships to carry those items to Malta during the winter.[7]

A similar procedure was to be followed for biscuit and salt meat, although Newcastle firmly believed that the Commissariat would be able to procure large quantities of fresh meat and flour from many quarters around the Black Sea during the winter. Nonetheless, to assure complete safety, the duke arranged with the Admiralty to have a continuous stream of these articles flowing throughout the winter to depots in Malta and Constantinople, from which they could be conveyed to the Crimea if needed.[8] A few days later, after Sir Charles Trevelyan had informed him of Commissary-General Filder's request for two thousand tons of pressed hay and a monthly consignment of one million pounds of biscuit from England, the duke stressed to the Admiralty the importance of compliance with the request. Unfortunately, however, the Treasury officials had other views concerning Filder's requirements for pressed hay from England. With the high cost of shipping the commodity and the insufficiency of sea transport, the Treasury officials believed that Filder should procure most of the needed forage from the Black Sea area. Following Trevelyan's advice, the Treasury, therefore, sanctioned the shipment of only a fraction of the amount of pressed hay that Filder had requested repeatedly in his letters that autumn.[9] It was a fateful decision that left the Commissariat woefully short of hay during the critical winter months when additional transport animals were desperately needed for the conveyance of huts, ammunition, food, fuel, and other stores to the troops at the front. The shortage of forage was later singled out, though somewhat incorrectly, as the most important cause of the failure of land transport in the Crimea during the winter. Once again Trevelyan's zeal for public economy came to haunt Newcastle.

In making these preparations for the army, Newcastle was still confident that the Allies would capture Sebastopol before the onset of winter. However, he now realized that even with the fall of Sebastopol, it would be impossible for the British army to carry out the additional offensive operations that he had planned in late September. Consequently, he instructed Raglan to make plans for wintering the army in the south of the Crimea behind defensive lines that would include Sebastopol itself. From informed sources he had learned that the winter climate of the southern shores of the Crimea from Sebastopol to Kaffa was mild and salubrious, not unlike that of Genoa, and that the harbor of Balaclava never froze over even during the severest winters. Therefore, he believed that the army could safely winter in the Crimea and prepare for a spring offensive to drive the Russians from the peninsula. With that contingency in mind, he asked Raglan to provide at his next moment of leisure

> timely notice of any preparations for next year which you may wish to be made. My anxiety is to leave you nothing to desire in March next but (tho' assuredly I think of nothing else) I am well aware that many things will be likely to escape the provision of one so unused to warlike operations as myself.[10]

Unfortunately, that moment of leisure never came for Raglan.

II

Events in the Crimea in the meantime had greatly reduced the chances of an early Allied victory against Sebastopol. After slow and difficult preparations, the Allies commenced the bombardment during the early hours of 17 October. The fire from the Allied batteries was devastating until the French guns were silenced for the day at about ten a.m. by a Russian shot that exploded a powder magazine, causing serious damage to the French batteries and killing over fifty artillerymen. The naval bombardment later in the day failed to take up the slack caused by the silent French guns or to inflict any material damage on the stone fortifications facing the harbor. Raglan's carefully planned assault on the fortress had to be postponed.[11]

In the following days the pattern of the bombardment was established. By day the Allied guns would knock down the Russian defenses, and by night the Russians would repair and rearm them. For over a week the bombardment continued without the desired effect. Consequently, each day the assault had to be postponed.[12]

By 23 October, Raglan realized how critical the situation was, and he wrote to Newcastle to dispel any lingering notions of an early and easy victory over the Russians at Sebastopol or, if the fortress did fall, of the possibility of further operations against the enemy before the onset of winter. He reminded Newcastle that in the Crimea the Allies held only the ground upon which they stood. They had no intercourse with the rest of the country and no command of its resources. The winters, he had been told, were severe, with "bleak winds, heavy rains, sleet, snow and bitter cold." Therefore, he believed that the Allied armies could not take up winter quarters either in Sebastopol should it fall or in the southern part of the Crimea. The British army, he stressed, desperately needed rest, and he suggested that it be withdrawn from the Crimea before winter, as soon as possible after Sebastopol had been captured and destroyed.[13]

In another private letter to Newcastle of the same date, Raglan forwarded a memorandum from Burgoyne on the difficulties of the siege as well as papers relating to the state of the British infantry effectives before Sebastopol. In the latter, it was noted that there were only about sixteen thousand effectives, leaving fewer than three thousand men to join a slightly larger force of Turks to defend Balaclava after guards and working parties for the trenches were drawn from their ranks. "I put these documents before you," Raglan wrote, "simply that you may know the real state of the case, with no desire to dispirit you, but on the contrary with the full determination to do all that is possible to overcome difficulties and to achieve the object for which the Allied Armies came to the Crimea."[14]

The British position became even more critical two days later when the Russians advanced toward Balaclava with force. Although the Russian advance was checked by the famous "thin red line" of the 93rd Highland Regiment and by the charge of the Heavy Brigade led by Gen. Sir James Scarlett, the Russians took the Causeway Heights and the very important Woronzov road, which ran along the top of the ridge. Though the British had saved their position before Sebastopol, they had lost the only good road that linked the camps and siege works on the Upland with the harbor of Balaclava below. It was now impossible to conduct the campaign according to the wishes of either the duke of Newcastle or Lord Raglan.

Whether or not Lord Raglan then realized it, the Allies following the battle of Balaclava were destined to spend the winter in the small corner of the Crimea they had occupied before Sebastopol. They were now the besiegers besieged, unable to escape their fate either by taking the fortress or by retreating beyond the sea to safe winter quarters. With each day's bombardment, Sebastopol seemed to become stronger, and the British force was now far too inadequate either to increase the effectiveness of the siege or to storm the defenses. The divisions employed in the trenches were overworked and scattered over a frontier that was too extensive. The defense of Balaclava was too meager, and the six thousand Turkish troops at Lord Raglan's disposal were unreliable either as support troops in the trenches or in the redoubts before Balaclava. In letters of late October and early November to Newcastle, Raglan decried the deficiency of his force and expressed his vexation over General Canrobert's unwillingness to keep him abreast of the French plans for the attack upon Sebastopol. All these matters made him extremely apprehensive, particularly about the vulnerable British position.[15]

Raglan's apprehensions were well justified. Early in the morning of 5 November, the Russians launched a massive attack upon the Allied positions, with the main attack directed against the exposed British position on the Inkerman Ridge. Throughout the morning and into the afternoon, in drizzling rain and dense fog, the Russians advanced against the British. Although greatly outnumbered, the latter, with great tenacity and the timely intervention of General Bosquet's French Corps of Observation, held their own and gradually turned the tide against the Russians. The Russians withdrew shortly after midday, leaving the whole of the Inkerman Ridge in the hands of the Allies.[16]

The battle of Inkerman is remembered as one of the most glorious in the history of the British army. It was the bloodiest, most fiercely contested battle of the Crimean War, and in the long run it was the most decisive, for it assured the Allies of ultimate victory. But the military situation immediately after the battle was a stalemate, with both sides lapsing into a defensive mood. The Russians could not dislodge the Allies from their positions before Sebastopol, nor could the Allies, without large reinforcements, leave those defensive positions to assault the town. At a council of war at Raglan's headquarters on 7 November, the Allies agreed to suspend any further offensive action until reinforcements arrived. They also agreed to strengthen the defensive positions along the right flank that had been attacked with such force two days before. These decisions meant, as was then generally recognized, that the Allied armies would have to winter in the Crimea, probably in their present insecure positions. Therefore, it was resolved to send vessels to Constantinople, Sinope, and other places to procure wood and other materials for the construction of shelter for the troops.[17]

The decision reached at the council of war was not altogether popular among the British military authorities, who were far from being of one mind regarding their situation. Even though the British had suffered tremendous losses at the battle of Inkerman, Raglan still argued for the original plan to assault Sebastopol. Some of the divisional commanders, however, advised him to abandon the siege and either evacuate the Crimea or pull the British army back to the heights around Balaclava. Sir John Burgoyne took a position somewhat between these extremes. Although he believed that further attempts at that time to take Sebastopol were hopeless, he opposed purely defensive operations and vigorously stressed the importance of advancing the trenches and other siege works closer to the fortress. But his views were opposed by both the French leaders and the British divisional commanders, prompting him to complain to his friend Colonel Matson back home of the many advantages lost to the "over-caution" of the Allied commanders.[18]

Burgoyne continued to press his views day after day during the next few weeks, but the purely defensive mood prevailed by and large following Inkerman, advocated most strongly by Canrobert and other French leaders. The fire from the siege guns soon slackened and then ceased altogether. The French made good progress on the new defensive works on the right flank, but the British troops were too fatigued by their constant duties in the trenches and on the pickets to undertake additional defensive, siege, or communications works. The first of the reinforcements sent out after the battle of the Alma arrived on 13 November, along with about five hundred recovered men from Scutari Hospital, but these did not go far in filling the voids left in the ranks by mounting casualties and increased sickness. What Raglan really needed were fresh, fully officered battalions, something he knew the duke of Newcastle had very few of within his immediate reach. Thus, unable to use British troops, Raglan and Burgoyne were forced to rely upon thoroughly inefficient Turkish working parties for the construction or repair of vital facilities. The situation was ripe for disaster.

The most vital matter to British interests was the road from Balaclava harbor to the divisional camps on the Upland. Lord Raglan was well aware of the importance of the road, which was, after the loss of the Woronzov road to the Russians on 25 October, the only route for supplies between the harbor and the troops nine miles away. The road was unmade, a mere track over clay without a trace of stone on it, and heavy traffic in October had already cut the surface considerably before the rains set in. The rains of early November quickly degenerated the road into a quagmire. On 13 November, Commissary-General Filder informed Raglan that the poor state of the road made it extremely difficult to transport the required supplies to the front. It was, he stressed, indispensable that the road be repaired.[19]

Lord Raglan had already foreseen the necessity of repairing the road. On the day after the council of war on 7 November, he issued orders for the purchase in Constantinople of stone hammers and other tools necessary for the work. A work force of four hundred Turks was employed a few days later to collect stones for the road and to dig drains, but heavy rains set in before much progress was made. The work force quickly dwindled to one hundred fifty from sickness and death, and the hired workmen later brought in by the hundreds died by the scores as soon as they were landed. The work was given up; the road remained unmade and soon became impassable by wheeled vehicles.[20]

For defensive reasons, Raglan had not felt justified in withdrawing British soldiers from the trenches to make the road. To recede from the field and siege operations, even for a short time, he believed, would have invited the Russians to launch another massive attack upon British positions. Yet Raglan realized that there were plenty of French troops available to take the place of the British soldiers in the trenches. At the time when Raglan needed manpower for the repair of the road, General Bosquet's men of the Corps of Observation were already employed on the British right constructing defensive works that Raglan and Burgoyne regarded as unimportant. Nevertheless, Raglan, although he recognized the necessity of the road, failed to press the matter forcefully with the French. Once again he was reluctant to push Canrobert and the French beyond a point he thought prudent for the maintenance of good relations. Perhaps pride and his fear that a recognition of the relative weakness of the British army would elevate the French to a position of intolerable dominance over the British also prevented him from asking relief for his troops from their purely military operations.

Lord Raglan first mentioned the bad state of the road to Newcastle in a private letter of 13 November.[21] On the following day a terrible storm swept across the small harbor at Balaclava and hit the British camp with terrific force. It was the most violent tempest Raglan had ever witnessed, attended with extremely high winds, heavy rain and hail, and later in the day snow. The damage was fearful. The tents in all the camps were blown down, and the men, even the sick and wounded, were exposed to the rain, snow, and bitter cold that followed the hurricane-force wind. The camps soon were in a dreadful state of mud, and the roads were impassable for vehicles of any kind. Most serious of all, however, was the loss of shipping. Twenty-one ships in or near Balaclava harbor were destroyed; another eight were badly damaged. The *Prince*, one of the finest steam transports in service, the *Resolute*, the *Kennilworth*, and the *Wildwave* were all driven upon the rocks and smashed to pieces, with most of the crew members and all the cargoes lost. The *Prince* alone contained forty thousand greatcoats and almost enough boots for the entire army, as well as other items of winter clothing, medicines, and surgical instruments—in short, Raglan noted, everything that was most wanted and "all that the foresight of the Government could devise for the equipment and comfort of the troops." Over ten million rounds of Minié ammunition was lost in the *Resolute*, and twenty days' supply of pressed hay and other provisions were lost aboard three destroyed Commissariat ships. The day after the storm Balaclava harbor and the nearby coastline were strewn with wreckage, ruined supplies, and corpses.[22]

Winter had set in with vengeance. An already grim situation had now become desperate. The privation suffered by the troops after the storm was heart-rending. Most of the transport animals were either dead or too weak to work; and the men, suffering again from the reappearance of dysentery and cholera, were compelled to carry stores and ammunition on their own backs through the deep mud from Balaclava to the camps. The loss of most of the forage in store, combined with the Treasury's failure earlier to sanction the shipment of two thousand tons of pressed hay from England for a reserve in Constantinople and with Commissary-General Filder's inability to provide the same, portended a catastrophe of the first magnitude.

Lord Raglan felt the misfortune deeply. On the morning after the storm he wrote to Newcastle to recommend the expeditious shipment of ammunition, forage, and new supplies of winter provisions. On 18 November, after he and Quartermaster-General Airey had gone to Balaclava to inspect the damage, Raglan again wrote to the duke. "You cannot send us too many supplies of all kinds," he stressed, adding that Filder's great concern was forage for the horses.[23] That same day Raglan instructed General Estcourt to write to Sidney Herbert about clothing and other winter supplies and dispatched Captain Wetherall to Constantinople to obtain what warm clothing he could. "I earnestly recommend," he added as a precaution in his letter to Newcastle, "that this should not prevent your Grace from forwarding from England a large supply without delay."[24]

Yet even as these requests were being made, there were supplies of all kinds in the stores of Balaclava and in the holds of ships waiting for days to be unloaded. Nobody was quite sure what was in store or what had arrived in the ships. There was total confusion in the harbor and on the quayside, where thousands of tons of food, charcoal, cases of ammunition, bales of clothing, and planks from Sinope for wooden huts were heaped together in the stores or piled randomly in the muddy streets. But without sufficient transportation, the supplies remained where they were dumped. "Our horses are dying fast," Lord Raglan wrote to the duke on 28 November, "but until we are sure that we can feed them, I would not recommend that they should receive any addition here."[25] Early in December, Raglan again wrote to Newcastle on the army's winter troubles. The weather continued to be bad, and the horrible state of the roads prevented them from bringing down the sick from the trenches or sending up necessary supplies and heavy artillery.[26]

Thus by early December, British military operations had virtually stopped. The breakdown of the land transport service due to bad roads and lack of forage and shelter for the animals had brought the army to the brink of ruin. Moved by the pitiful situation of the soldiers and by anger over what he sensed was gross incompetence and callousness, William Howard Russell on 25 November began his dispatch home for the *Times* with the following words:

> It is now pouring rain—the skies are black as ink—the wind is howling over the staggering tents—the trenches are turned into dykes—in the tents the water is sometimes a foot deep—our men have not either warm or waterproof clothing—they are out for twelve hours at a time in the trenches—they are plunged into the inevitable miseries of a winter campaign—and not a soul seems to care for their comfort or even for their lives.[27]

From the reporter's vantage point, it was clear that Raglan and his staff subordinates were responsible for the deplorable situation.

III

Newcastle learned the real extent of the Crimean tragedy in common with the rest of his countrymen in Great Britain from the pages of the *Times* and from informants who had recently returned from the scene of the war.[28] He did not gain the information from Lord Raglan's letters and dispatches. These were studied exercises in understatement, carefully worded to shelter the home authorities from the dangers of undue apprehension. Although Raglan had made no secret of the needs of the army, his soldier's prejudice against any form of lamentation in speaking and writing frequently led those unaccustomed to his temperament to misunderstand the true import of the facts he conveyed.[29] Thus he failed to explain adequately all that went wrong or to propose specific solutions for the difficulties his army encountered, and at times his letters contained incorrect or misleading information. Such was the case of his private letter and dispatch to Newcastle of 11 and 13 November on the condition of the hospital at Scutari. To the best of his knowledge, he wrote in response to Newcastle's dispatch of 23 October, there was no want of medical comforts, surgeon's appliances, lint, or bandages, nor had there been at the time of the newspaper reports in October. Therefore, instead of condemnation for neglect, he believed the medical officers as a body were entitled to his best acknowledgments for their unceasing exertions and attention to the wounded. He conceded that there had been confusion and suffering after the battle of the Alma, but no more than usual following a major battle: "In all such cases 'Johnny Raws' will not be wanting."[30]

By the time those letters reached him, Newcastle already had information that belied their contents. People who had gone out officially and unofficially to Turkey to investigate the hospitals were now reporting back home, and their reports recorded experiences that were indeed horrendous. The contents of these letters and reports pained the duke beyond expression, and he concluded from them that there was a total want of system in the hospitals in the East. The letters also shattered his hope that the reports in the *Times* had been greatly exaggerated and raised his suspicion of the information he received from military authorities in the East. Since late October, the duke told the queen, he had written to the medical authorities in the strongest terms but "with little other result than a denial of charges the truth of which must now be considered to be substantiated." Dr. John Hall, chief of medical staff of the British Expeditionary Army, whom Raglan would eventually censure for neglect and indifference, had answered the duke's dispatch of 12 October about the report of a want of bedsteads and simple medical comforts at Scutari by stating that the reports in the *Times* were either gross exaggerations of real occurrences or else tales of fiction.[31] But the private letters to Newcastle were corroborated by Miss Nightingale's reports to Sidney Herbert, and the ministers were forced to conclude that the reports in the *Times* and the letters from private individuals were far more reliable than some of the information received from military authorities in Turkey and the Crimea who obviously had much to cover up. From this moment the ministers began to be far more skeptical of the official reports; they also began to lose confidence in the military authorities, including Raglan, even though they showed their gratitude for the victory of Inkerman by conferring the rank of field marshal upon him.

The condition of Scutari Hospital kept Newcastle in constant anxiety the rest of the year, and he began to act on many of the points raised in the private letters and in Miss Nightingale's reports. He believed that Major Sillery, commandant of the hospital, was greatly overworked and had too little influence for the tasks that he faced. Therefore, Newcastle advised Lord Hardinge to draw up measures to guarantee greater supervision of the medical staff at Scutari and to appoint a general officer of superintendence for the hospital. In an effort to alleviate the overcrowding at Scutari, he asked Lord Stratford through Lord Clarendon to obtain additional buildings for hospital accommodations and to send a medical officer to Smyrna, in Turkey, in order to establish a convalescent hospital there. The duke also broadened the scope of the Hospitals Commission to empower the commissioners to investigate the mode of conveyance of the sick and wounded from the Crimea to Scutari. "What we want," he told Benson Maxwell, "is a full enquiry and one fair to all, but especially and above all fair to those who are the sufferers by any neglect or mistakes."[32]

Newcastle acted on many other matters during the late autumn in response to Raglan's official dispatches and private letters. The problem foremost in his mind, as well as in the minds of Prince Albert and Sidney Herbert, was that of finding additional troops to send to the Crimea. Lord Raglan's announcement of the extensive losses from battle and sickness and his stress upon the need for replacements in his dispatches of late October and early November, along with intelligence gained through French sources of massive Russian troop movements from the Danube to the Crimea, produced within the cabinet a growing sense of urgency, a feeling that a great catastrophe might be looming in the Crimea unless reinforcements were sent to Raglan's army at the earliest possible moment. Prince Albert and Sidney Herbert especially pressed this upon the cabinet.[33] By late November the ministers were ready to take additional steps to meet Raglan's demands for reinforcements.

The cabinet accepted Herbert's proposals to increase the number of embodied militia regiments from eighteen to sixty-one to permit recruitment from these regiments into the regular service to the extent of one-quarter of their current strength. The quota was later raised to one-third. On 24 November the cabinet approved Prince Albert's project of raising a foreign legion and agreed to submit legislation to Parliament when it was summoned for a special session on 12 December to permit enlistment of foreigners for preliminary training in England. At the same cabinet, it was also agreed to introduce legislation to authorize the dispatch of six to eight militia regiments to Gibraltar, Malta, and the Ionian Islands for garrison duty to relieve regular troops for service in the Crimea. On the last day of November the cabinet adopted a plan of army organization recommended by a committee consisting of Albert, Newcastle, Herbert, and Lord Hardinge. The plan would increase each of the forty-four regiments under Raglan's command from twelve to sixteen companies. Of those sixteen companies, eight were to be in active service with the army, four in training in England, and the remaining four in advance training in a new depot to be formed in Malta to hold an army reserve of 16,000 men. A third battalion was to be added to the Rifle Brigade. An additional 880 officers were to be provided for the army, some drawn from the militia on the condition that they each bring 200 men with them. These plans required the addition of 20,000 men to the service, half of whom were to come from the militia.[34]

While these plans were being made, Newcastle was at work desperately trying to find as many drilled troops as he could to send to Lord Raglan. On 25 November the *Royal Albert*, a fast, magnificent new three-decker, sailed with the English reserve of 1,000 troops.[35] After consulting with Lord Hardinge, Newcastle ordered the 90th Regiment from Dublin, four regiments totaling 3,400 infantry from Gibraltar and Corfu, and three companies of artillery to proceed to the Crimea. The regiments from Gibraltar and Corfu were to be replaced by depleted regiments that had recently returned from North America. On 22 November, anticipating the passage of the bill to allow the use of volunteer militia regiments for colonial service, Newcastle ordered four regiments, two from Malta, one from Gibraltar, and one from England, to join Raglan's force. With these troop arrangements, a total of 7,037 reinforcements were ordered out to the Crimea in November. The effort, Newcastle told the queen, had strained the reserve to such an extent that it would be several weeks before additional reinforcements could be sent.[36]

These reinforcements and the French offer early in November to supply 8,000 additional troops if the British transported them to the Crimea necessitated considerable reallocation of shipping. After some heated debate among the ministers on the French proposal, it was decided in cabinet on 13 November to accept the offer only when it was ascertained that some of the ships needed could be obtained through the assistance of Samuel Cunard. But the problem of shipping became even more acute a few days later when Newcastle requested steamers for the conveyance of the enormous quantities of huts, materials for huts, ammunition, and warm clothing that he had requisitioned for the army in response to the storm in the Crimea.[37]

On 18 November, the day he received the news of the battle of Inkerman, Newcastle issued orders to the Ordnance to contract for the expeditious construction of sufficient huts to accommodate twenty thousand men and for the purchase of one thousand small stoves for the huts. On the same day, he sent word both by telegraph and dispatch to Lord Stratford to purchase lumber in Constantinople for a company of sappers and miners that he was sending out on the *Royal Albert* to construct huts in the Crimea. He also issued orders for the purchase of materials and supplies for huts in Trieste and Malta.[38]

At this same time Newcastle received news by telegraph of the loss of the *Prince*, the *Resolute*, and other ships in the storm of 14 November. Without waiting for confirmation of the loss of the valuable cargoes, the duke immediately ordered the Ordnance to send agents into the manufacturing districts to purchase all the warm clothing they could procure at any cost and without delay. So rapidly was that order executed, he later told the Roebuck Committee, "that when we received the despatch which made the loss certain, a great part of those articles were already in London, and were shipped in vessels which had been prepared for other purposes, within a day or two afterwards."[39] On 4 December the *Adelaide*, which had been scheduled to take out the 82d Regiment, sailed with a large supply of clothing and blankets similar in character and amount to that lost in the *Prince* and one million rounds of Minie ammunition. The *Charity* soon followed with another one million rounds of ammunition and one thousand barrels of gunpowder, and a third supply of clothing and ammunition was ready within a few days. In announcing these arrangements to Raglan, the duke observed:

> I am greatly concerned at the very serious loss of ammunition, and if possible even more so at that of the large supply of warm clothing and I cannot help thinking that some blame must attach either to the Commissariat or some other Department for leaving the "Prince" in the open roadstead for seven days without discharging any portion of her valuable cargo—especially when that cargo was so immediately wanted by the troops.

He made the same assertion four days later when he asked Raglan to conduct an inquiry into the matter.[40]

When he wrote these letters, Newcastle was unaware of the deplorable state of the harbor at Balaclava, the rapidly disintegrating land transport service, and the critical shortage of forage in the Crimea. He was aware, as of very late November, of the poor condition of the main road from the harbor to the camps on the Upland. By the time Raglan's letter of 13 November reached him revealing that the road was ruined by the heavy rains, the duke had already considered a plan presented to him by Samuel Morton Peto, partner in a railway contracting firm with Thomas Brassey and E. L. Betts, for a railway from Balaclava to the heights around Sebastopol. Newcastle accepted the proposal on 30 November, and the cabinet sanctioned the project the next day. The chief engineer for the railway, James Beatty, arrived at Balaclava on 19 January 1855, and men and materials soon followed. Work began on the line on 8 February, and on 26 March the railway was open for the transport of shot and shell as far as the headquarters summit.[41]

Another project approved by the duke late in 1854 was the laying of a submarine cable between Balaclava and Varna to complete the telegraphic communications between London and the Crimea. The task was entrusted to Messrs. R. S. Newall and Company and was to be completed by 8 February 1855. The completion of this line of communication, Newcastle told Raglan, would alleviate to some degree "that great and almost overwhelming state of anxiety with which the French and English Nations now look for intelligence from the seat of active warfare in which both are at present engaged."[42]

Many other details were attended to by the duke in the brief time before the special session of Parliament in December. He announced to Raglan that the queen would confer the Crimean Medal with clasps for the battles of the Alma, Balaclava, and Inkerman upon all officers and soldiers who had taken part in the campaign. He instructed the Ordnance to send out in sailing vessels to Malta as quickly as possible guns, ammunition, gunpowder, entrenching tools, and camp equipment of all sorts for a reserve force of fifty thousand men. He also asked the board to send out additional storekeepers to operate the general depot at Malta. He sanctioned the plans drawn up by the Treasury to recruit 350 drivers from the Irish Constabulary Force for the Commissariat transport service in the Crimea. He instructed the Treasury to send out one thousand pounds of preserved uncooked meat as an experiment, and he sent orders to the consul at Venice to charter a vessel for the shipment to the Crimea of three hundred tons of vegetables that were to be purchased in Italy. He also arranged for the shipment of a cargo of special articles, including wine, brandy, cigars, and tobacco, that were provided privately by Fortnum and Mason and Messrs. Cunningham for the comfort of the soldiers and officers.[43]

In still other business, the duke suggested to Lord Hardinge that a small commission be appointed consisting of an officer of the line, an engineer, a surgeon, and a Commissariat officer to review the French military arrangements, with particular attention paid to the depot de la guerre, in which, the duke noted, "we must acknowledge ourselves to be utterly deficient." After talking with Austen H. Layard, who had recently returned from the Crimea, the duke wrote to Raglan about the need to appoint a sanitary officer for each division to make sure the camps were kept clear of offal, dead horses, imperfectly buried bodies, excrement, and other matter dangerous to the troops' health.[44]

Although he was convinced that the ministers had done all in their power to meet the exigencies in Turkey and the Crimea, Newcastle was apprehensive on the eve of the special session of Parliament early in December. He had perceived the changed mood of the country following the failure of the Allies to take Sebastopol quickly. This new feeling the duke expressed to Raglan upon receiving the telegraph telling of the battle of Inkerman:

> I will not conceal from you that intense anxiety—I will not say as yet depression—prevails in all classes here, forming a strong contrast to the cheerful tone of all private letters received from your army. It is right you should know this, for if success does at last crown your efforts, it will indeed be highly appreciated. The follies of over-confidence in the beginning of October have given way to very different feelings.[45]

A few days later the duke informed Raglan that Parliament would meet on 12 December and that the members probably would share the anxious mood of the country. "The greatest enthusiasm will prevail in favor of the war—how much in support of the Government remains to be seen," he noted.[46]

11. *The Government Divided and Besieged*

The cabinet faced Parliament in December 1854 in a divided condition. As the disappointment of the Crimean situation deepened, Lord John Russell became more querulous and bent on, as Newcastle put it, "the revival of personal projects tending to his own aggrandizement."[1] In mid-November Russell urged upon Lord Aberdeen certain changes in the administration of the war. He proposed the abolition of the secretary at war by combining the function of that office with those of the secretary for war under a minister in the House of Commons. Since only Lord Palmerston in his opinion combined all the characteristics necessary for the control of other departments and the vigorous direction of the war, he proposed putting him in Newcastle's place as secretary for war. In making the suggestion, Russell told Aberdeen the next day, his intent was to strengthen the authority of the secretary for war rather than to throw blame on Newcastle in the conduct of the war. "Indeed," he added with respect to the duke, "I think he deserves very great credit for the exertions he has made. But he had not the authority requisite for so great a sphere, and has not been able to do all that might have been done with larger powers of control."[2]

Although the suggestion to end the division of authority between the secretary for war and the secretary at war was a sensible one that was adopted the moment the Aberdeen ministry fell, the entire plan smacked of pure political maneuver when Russell proposed it. Lord Clarendon thought it was an intrigue got up for the purpose of breaking up the government and getting Russell back as prime minister. The prince thought so, too. "It is evident," he wrote in a memorandum, "that the whole intrigue is aimed at Lord Aberdeen and to realize Lord John's old wish to be Prime Minister again, Lord Palmerston having been disposed of by fixing him in the War Office." Clearly Russell wanted to replace Aberdeen, whose heart had never been in the war, far more than he wanted to alter the departments concerned with the war, a charge which later at a cabinet dinner he did not deny.[3]

Aberdeen showed Russell's letter to Newcastle and Herbert, as Russell had desired. The duke was "deeply mortified at the heartless manner" in which

Russell contemplated ruining his "reputation and public position."[4] He suspected that Russell still resented his attempt to undermine the Whig ministry in 1852, and, more currently, he knew full well that Russell regarded him as a strong competitor for the succession to Lord Aberdeen. Nonetheless, he joined with Herbert to urge Aberdeen to do what was best for the public service. The prime minister, however, regarded Russell's proposals as neither advantageous nor desirable for the time being, and he believed that the proposed changes would reflect unjustly upon Newcastle. Besides, Aberdeen told Russell, he could not advise the queen to entrust the laborious and complicated duties now discharged by two much younger men to a man of Palmerston's age.[5]

Russell refused to let the matter rest. He attacked each of Aberdeen's objections with acidity and complained once again of the lack of vigor in the prosecution of the war. "I think it is clear," he wrote, "that the Prime Minister must be himself the active and moving spirit of the whole machine, or the Minister of War must have delegated authority to control other Departments. Neither is the case under the present arrangement." He argued that Newcastle's inability to overcome the obstacles that the various departments had put in his way had resulted in confusion in the Crimea and the loss of the advantage that Lord Raglan might have enjoyed against the enemy. There was no clearer lesson than this, he continued, that a cabinet, while it could make suggestions, could not administer. "What you want therefore, I repeat," Russell concluded with emphasis, "is a Minister of War of vigour and authority."[6]

Aberdeen held his ground and defended Newcastle. He denied that the duke lacked authority or was guilty of negligence. The question, therefore, was simply one of personal preference. In his opinion, Newcastle had discharged the duties of his office "ably and honourably," and "in the absence of any proved defect, or alleged incapacity," he could see no sufficient reason for change, which he believed was forbidden by a sense of justice and good faith.[7]

Russell promised to bring the matter before the cabinet and stated that he expected to resign on it. Aberdeen showed Russell's letters to his Peelite colleagues, who were all highly indignant, and Graham and Gladstone advised Aberdeen to turn Russell out at once. Newcastle, however, "begged most earnestly to let himself be removed" if this was the only way to keep the cabinet together.[8] After Russell raised the subject at the cabinet meeting on 4 December, Aberdeen circulated the correspondence among the other ministers in preparation for a discussion at a cabinet dinner at his house on 6 December. The atmosphere of the meeting was tense. At the outset Aberdeen stated that since Russell's proposals really pointed to a change in the head of government rather than in departments, he would not stand for a moment in Lord John's way if the latter "could get the Cabinet, or any Cabinet, to join him."[9] But it was obvious that Russell could find no support from any of his

Giving the Office. Johnny Russell: "I say, Abby, my old-un, the Vestminster sessions is fixed for the 12th. If you ain't prepared with your defence, you'd better cut." (From *Punch*, 9 December 1854.)

colleagues, who were, according to Lord Clarendon, all "profoundly disgusted" with his "selfish and unpatriotic conduct." Observing Russell's behavior at the meeting, Clarendon wrote:

> John Russell was wrong in his facts, insolent in his assertions and most ill-tempered in his replies. No spoilt child could be more perverse or inaccessible either to kind or firm words, and his look was as if he had plied himself with wine in order to get courage for doing what he felt was wrong, for he several times compared himself to the juryman who complained of the eleven obstinate fellows in the box with him. Everybody was dead against him, though some said nothing. . . . Aberdeen's conduct was a most remarkable contrast and there the matter rests.[10]

Indeed, everybody in the cabinet was against Russell's recommendations.[11] Palmerston argued forcefully for the retention of the office of secretary at war and refused to blame Newcastle for the problems in the Crimea. At the same time he suggested that the duke hold periodic meetings of the heads of the military departments.[12] Lord Lansdowne observed that Newcastle could not leave the War Department so soon after his colleagues had entrusted him with such arduous duties without a slur upon his character and conduct. Like most of the Whigs, he preferred the popular and suave Sidney Herbert to the more egotistical and brash duke, but all agreed that the time to make a change in departments was long past.[13] Sir Charles Wood brought that point home forcefully to Russell and reminded him that six months earlier he had concurred with those who preferred Newcastle to Palmerston in the newly separated War Department. "I certainly understood at the time," he wrote, "that on full consideration you were satisfied that the *best* arrangement was Newcastle's remaining there. This being so, we who made the machine were bound to do our best to make it work well." They must share the common responsibility for any deficiency. To refuse to stand behind Newcastle now would be a confession to blunder that "would be destruction to us all." To break up the government now, he reiterated in another letter a few days later, "would be little less than high treason."[14]

The knowledge that he would be deserted by his own party induced Russell to retract his threat to resign over the issue. For the time being, therefore, he gave up his effort to replace Lord Aberdeen and to oust the leading Peelites from the Cabinet. He attended cabinet meetings on 8 and 9 December and helped prepare the speech from the throne. On 15 December he told Aberdeen that as a result of a conversation with Lord Panmure, a convinced military reformer, he had decided that it was not the proper time to pursue his proposed changes.[15] Thus the political storm dissipated almost as quickly as it had gathered. However, almost everyone believed that it would eventually return to threaten the coalition government.

II

The queen opened the special session of Parliament on 12 December with a speech containing a brief outline of the war measures that the ministers believed were necessary. Lord Derby ignored the plea for national unity by delivering a severely critical rebuttal, which the *Times* described as a party attack founded on "misrepresentation and captiousness."[16] "My complaint against the Government is this," Derby told the Lords,

—that they have from the commencement, and before the commencement of war, lived, as it were, from hand to mouth; that they have never anticipated in due time the contingencies of the struggle in which they were about to engage, that they never considered the greatness of the undertaking upon which they were entering, and that they never made adequate and timely provision to meet, not the contingent exigencies of the day, but those exigencies which the fortune of war rendered inevitable.[17]

The charge was plausible, especially since it was obvious that the government had reacted only very recently to the altered circumstances in the Crimea. Newcastle later admitted that no ample provision had been made at first for a winter campaign in the Crimea and that the government had responded to that eventuality with the features of a more permanent siege—huts, the Balaclava railway, and the electric telegraph to Varna—only after it became certain that the army was committed to a winter campaign against Sebastopol.[18] Yet the government's case was not weak. Lord Raglan had poorly informed them of the prospects for the siege and of the Allied commanders' strategy. Until the battle of Inkerman, neither Lord Raglan nor the ministers contemplated a winter campaign in the Crimea; Inkerman produced the stalemate that made the campaign inevitable. Until Inkerman, the ministers had continued to expect the fall of Sebastopol before the onset of winter, and all that they heard from Raglan did not dispel that notion. They had not calculated on the inability (or unwillingness) of the Allied armies to assault Sebastopol before the Russians could bring up substantial reinforcements.

In a long speech, which to Greville and Lord Broughton was pompous, dull, and futile, but to the *Times* "ingenious, candid to the verge of indiscretion, and conclusive on many points urged against his administration,"[19] Newcastle reviewed every aspect of the government's war policies. He defended the decision to invade the Crimea and explained the reasons for the delay of the invasion. He cited numerous statistics respecting troops and supplies sent to the Crimea. There had been defects, he admitted, particularly in the distribution of the enormous amount of supplies the government had sent out. But the government, he added, had already acted to correct the defects and to supply huts, additional warm clothing, new uniforms, and extra rations of meat, spirits, and vegetables. Although he admitted that mistakes had been made, the duke denied Derby's charge that the army was half-starved and argued instead that no army had ever been better fed than the present one. As for the defects in the medical service, he stated that they were "consequent on that ill-judged economy which prevented an efficient medical department being kept up in time of peace." There had been considerable suffering, but he denied that the government could be blamed for any want of care or forethought in these matters. He praised the army and lauded Lord Raglan: "I believe the records of war do not show greater deeds of valour, greater constancy, greater endurance, greater patience under privation and suffering, and greater courage in the moment of action." The government, he confessed, had erred in overconfidence regarding Sebastopol, but he promised that with the confidence of Parliament the ministers would "prosecute the war with a firm resolve and with unflinching perseverance."[20]

Newcastle's speech, filled as it was with facts and figures and reasoned arguments, was not well designed to allay the growing despair and spreading panic within the country. Nor was it calculated to meet successfully the opposition's main assertion that everything done had been done too late. Therefore, Lords Derby, Ellenborough, and Grey continued to criticize Newcastle and the government severely.[21] In the House of Commons, Sidney Herbert made a vigorous, straightforward defense of the government in answer to Sir John Pakington;[22] but, like the duke in the Lords, he was unable to satisfy the most determined critics. Nonetheless, the two secretaries of the War Office were convincing enough to gain the support of the majority in each House. The ministers thus were permitted to introduce their measures for the future conduct of the war.

On 15 December, Newcastle moved resolutions for a vote of thanks to the armed forces and their commanders in the Crimea. The motions were carried unanimously in both Houses that same day. On the previous day Newcastle had introduced the foreign enlistment bill in the House of Lords; the measure would allow the government to recruit foreign troops for the war in the Crimea and to train up to fifteen thousand of them at a time in England. Newcastle noted that Great Britain had neither a sufficient body of troops in the Crimea to carry on the war with efficiency nor a sufficient reserve to support the army in an emergency. He emphasized the historical precedents for the bill and argued that since Great Britain did not have a system of conscription it had always been necessary to recruit foreigners in the initial stages of a major war.[23]

The Conservative opposition in the Lords, led by Derby and Ellenborough, was strong enough to force concessions on the measure from the ministerial bench. To meet one of Derby's greatest concerns, Newcastle agreed to alter the bill to make it absolutely clear that the foreign legionnaires could not be used in the place of English troops for garrison duty in Great Britain. He also

Remanded. Johnny Russell: "Well, old boy, what luck?" Aberdeen: "Weel, I'm just remanded till next sessions." (From *Punch*, 23 December 1854.)

accepted an amendment to reduce the maximum force on British soil at any time from fifteen thousand to ten thousand men.[24] With these and a few other minor changes, the bill was passed in the Lords by an unimpressive majority of 55 to 43.

There was far more extensive and acrimonious debate on the bill in the House of Commons, where it was introduced by Russell on 19 December. The Conservative leaders, namely Disraeli, Stanley, Pakington, and Bulwer-Lytton, sensing that the bill was controversial enough to bring down the Aberdeen ministry, made a concerted effort to defeat the measure, which they characterized as impolitic and degrading to the country. They noted the insular prejudice in England against "condottieri and mercenaries" and warned the ministers that they were leaving the impression that the country was on the verge of exhausting its military resources. Instead of the adoption of the measure, they urged the government to intensify domestic recruiting. Herbert, Palmerston, and Russell, however, persisted with the bill and persuaded an unenthusiastic majority to accept it as an unpalatable necessity. The bill was carried 173 to 135 on the third reading. The heavy pressure exerted by the government whips perhaps made the margin of victory a comparatively safe one.[25]

III

The militia bill, the other major item of the special session, passed easily through both Houses, and Parliament adjourned for a month on 23 December. Although the Aberdeen ministry had survived another session, its future was still quite bleak. The general public was upset over the Foreign Enlistment Act and disturbed by letters and reports from the Crimea published in the press. More ominous still for the government and Newcastle was the tone of "the Thunderer," the *Times*.

Until the middle of December, the attitude of the *Times* toward the progress of the war had been generally optimistic and patient. Suddenly, however, the tone of the paper changed dramatically. The hundreds of letters that poured in from officers and men in the Crimea telling of the total disorganization of the army and the jeopardy in which it was placed from "its own utter mismanagement" compelled the editors, they stated, to publish this evidence of the "stern realities of the case" rather than to "cling to old hopes or idle conventionalities."[26] "Our duty is to ascertain, if we can, where the fault of all this waste of life, of time, and of resources lies, in order, if possible, to apply a remedy," read a leader of 19 December. The paper returned to this tone in subsequent days, and on 23 December, the day Parliament was adjourned, it published a strident editorial on the deplorable condition of the army in the Crimea, concluding that the "noblest army England ever sent

THE QUEEN VISITING THE IMBECILES OF THE CRIMEA.

From *Punch*, 3 February 1855.

from these shores" had been sacrificed to "incompetency, lethargy, aristocratic hauteur, official indifference, favour, routine, perverseness, and stupidity."[27] Leaders condemning the mismanagement of the war appeared frequently. The British army organization was compared unfavorably with the French, and the backwardness of British military science was deplored. Lord Raglan and his staff were accused of incapacity, callousness, and neglect of the army, and on 30 December the editorialist asserted that it would be a crime for the war minister "to permit an officer to remain for a single day in the nominal discharge of duties the neglect of which has brought a great and victorious army to the verge of ruin."[28]

The *Times*, with a circulation of sixty-one thousand, was the largest daily paper in Great Britain. It had immense influence, and it received a phenomenal amount of attention by bringing the war home to thousands of households throughout the country. For the most part, however, the *Times* reflected rather than guided public opinion, particularly the opinion of the middle class. To-gether the middle-class public and the *Times* concluded late in December that the British army was failing in the Crimea because its aristocratic leaders were hidebound by precedent and tradition, or "routine." According to this view, the war was being bungled by an aristocracy that failed to adopt modern methods. The attitude of the *Times* and many of its readers crystallized into a middle-class attack upon the aristocracy. The *Times* became the organizer of "bourgeois efficiency," and the war became a test of the aristocracy's ability to rule in a modern world.[29] The ministers were not immune to this attack when public excitement regarding the war began to infect Parliament late in Decem-ber. In particular, there was a strong feeling in the country against Newcastle as war minister.[30]

IV

The ministers were quite anxious over the changed attitude of the *Times*. After reading the article of 23 December, Granville told Russell that he would be sorry to attempt to answer it, especially after talking with Layard and seeing General Canrobert's reports. Granville hit on the point that had all the ministers perplexed—Raglan's letters and dispatches did not paint as dismal a picture as did either the letters printed in the *Times* or the accounts of those recently returned from the Crimea. Raglan continued to write of the bad state of the road, of the necessity of sending hundreds of men down to Balaclava to carry up shot and provisions, of short rations issued to some of the battal-ions, of continued sickness, especially among the newcomers, and of young, green recruits, many little more than sixteen years old, who were being swept away like flies. Characteristically, however, he coupled these bad tidings with observations that were far more optimistic. On 13 December, for example, after writing of the bad condition of the road, he added, "We however make some progress daily in the movement of heavy guns from Balaclava." And the men, he observed, were delighted with the issuance of warm clothing, which was "hailed as a great boon, and a receipt in full for all privations and hardships."[31] Thus the curious wording of Raglan's dispatches and private letters to Newcastle, with the juxtaposition of the bad with the good reports, confused and perplexed the ministers. They did not know from their com-mander the true state of things in the Crimea or the long-range plans for the siege. "Raglan's private letter (as usual) adds little to his public dispatch," Clar-endon told Palmerston on 23 November; that complaint was common among the ministers late in 1854. A month later Granville noted to Russell:

> The War Office and the Cabinet derive no assistance from their general in
> the East. The extreme meagerness of Lord Raglan's despatches to Newcastle
> is unsatisfactory. When the secret of his views and intentions are so well
> kept it almost leads us to suspect that there is no secret to be divulged.[32]

   Stung by the criticism of the administration in Parliament and the press and
assailed by a host of people with accounts from relatives and friends in the
Crimea, Newcastle, urged on by his ministerial colleagues, requested Raglan
on 18 December to inquire into the operation of the quartermaster-general's
department and to report more fully on the general condition of the army.
On 22 December the duke again referred to the complaints pouring in about
the lack of organization that prevailed in all the departments of the camp and
in Balaclava harbor. He had heard that this confusion was causing the horses
of the British army to die from starvation, the soldiers to lie knee-deep in
mud in their tents, and many of the ships to return to Constantinople still
laden with their cargoes, two even returning to England with much of their
cargoes still on board. He assured Raglan that these matters were causing a
sensation in England and that unless some great improvement were made, the
government would face motions of inquiry when Parliament met late in January that would be irresistible. He strongly urged Raglan to provide more
supervision over the military departments in the Crimea.[33]
   On Christmas Day the duke wrote again to Raglan about the private letters
he had just received from the camp that spoke of the tremendous suffering of
the troops from lack of supplies. Again Newcastle implored Raglan to make
the "vigorous corrections" necessary to end the "carelessness amongst the
higher departments" of the army.[34] But complaints came to the duke "so
thickly and so strongly" during the next few days that he was compelled "to
sing the same song again" on 29 December, especially since his colleagues at
every cabinet complained "that more is not done to remedy the defects complained of." With considerable asperity, the duke observed that most of the
complaints appeared to be wholly attributable to the failure of the quartermaster-general and the adjutant-general and their staffs. "The truth is," he
wrote, "General Airey and General Estcourt are much complained of as not
being up to their work, and those under them appear to be little capable of
supplying their deficiencies." He advised Raglan that more officers for these
departments would soon be on their way; but as quality rather than quantity
was most wanted, he advised Raglan to allow the least efficient of those now
serving to return to their regiments when the new officers arrived. He also
urged the commander to approach General Canrobert about the possibility of
the French taking over some of the British trenches. The duke believed that
the reduction of the English lines would remedy a pressing problem that was
constantly mentioned in the letters from the Crimea, of British soldiers being
required to spend longer periods of time in the trenches than their health and
strength could bear.[35]
   On 1 January 1855, Newcastle wrote his strongest letter yet to Raglan. He
was sure that an inquiry into the prevalence of sickness among the newly
arrived troops would "bring to light fresh cases of neglect and want of precaution." There was, he stressed, growing irritation produced by the stories

of horses dying of starvation while the hospital at Scutari abounded with chopped straw, of men on short rations while live cattle were kept aboard ships at Balaclava for five days without forage or water, and of the deplorable manner in which the sick and wounded were evacuated from Balaclava. These stories were

> creating a ferment in the public mind which will soon find a vent in a burst
> of unreasoning violence. I shall, of course, be the first victim to popular
> vengeance, and the papers, assisted by the Tory and Radical parties united,
> have pretty well settled my fate already. To this I am as indifferent as a man
> who has done his best and worked zealously ought to be; but more victims
> will be required. You and I will come first; but those who are most to
> blame will not escape. Their names are already in the mouths of everybody.

The names of course were Airey, Estcourt, Filder, and Burgoyne; of those, the duke was most concerned with Airey and Estcourt. He told Raglan the gossip he had heard about Airey finding time to write to at least six fine ladies in London while neglecting his duties in the Crimea, and about an incident on the *Sydney* in which 3,300 wounded and sick were embarked without the assistance of a single medical officer. Although it pained him to write as he did, the duke believed that he could not remain silent "till either remedy is found, or some other person relieves me of the painful duty of *trying* to cure such evils."[36]

Although Newcastle was to be judged severely for these letters to the commander,[37] he acted responsibly in pressing Raglan, who had failed to keep him adequately informed, for a complete explanation of all that was going wrong in the Crimea. To have ignored the corroborating reports submitted to him would have been irresponsible, for, although some of the complaints of mismanagement proceeded from rash generalizations, incorrect fact, or the captious spirit of disgruntled relatives of officers, other reports to the duke commanded respect. Rather than condemning Raglan outright without first hearing his comments, Newcastle recited what he had heard in order to have Raglan explain or contradict the reports.[38] Only in this way could the ministers find out what was really going on in the Crimea. With these letters, however, Newcastle left the impression that he was anxious "to expiate the sins of Whitehall by finding victims in camp" to offer as scapegoats to the angry public.[39] Certainly, the duke was anxious to defend himself against public and parliamentary attacks, but his main motive in writing these critical letters to Raglan was not to save himself but to save an army.

V

The ministers at the end of 1854 could hardly have been in a more difficult position. They were confronted with the enigma of an army rapidly disintegrating in spite of the enormous exertions they had made to supply it with all its needs and to put it on a sound footing. Most of the ministers were satisfied that the government had done all in its power to provide for the army. Raglan agreed with this assessment. "You seem to have left no stone unturned to provide us with warm clothing, huts, and whatever is required for our better equipment, as well as with reinforcements as far as your means will allow," he wrote to Newcastle on 23 December. On the previous day General Estcourt wrote similarly to Herbert: "The efforts you are making, I must repeat again, are most generous, and when the articles come which you are sending, no doubt the men will feel a very great benefit."[40]

Such statements as these led the ministers, confident that they themselves were not at fault, to give added credence to the reports of alleged misman-agement that reached them from the East. Thus they concluded that the great distress of the army was caused mainly by the negligence of important officials in the Crimea and Turkey. In some cases the criticism of military leadership extended to Raglan himself. "It is quite clear," Palmerston told Newcastle on 4 January 1855, "that in many essential points Raglan is unequal to the task which has fallen to his lot, but it is impossible to remove him, and we must make the best of it, and endeavour to point his attention to things which he has neglected." However, Palmerston added, it was possible to replace the incompetent Airey and Estcourt with better and more active men. In a matter so important, he continued, "personal feeling and delicacy towards individuals ought not to stand in the way" of doing what was necessary to save the lives of brave men and the honor and vital interests of the country. Great blame, he warned, "will justly be thrown upon the Government at home, if aware of the enormous evil, and conscious of its principal causes, the proper steps are not taken for establishing a better order of things."[41]

Even Russell, while still severely rebuking Aberdeen and Newcastle for not prosecuting the war with more vigor, conceded that some of the shortcom-ings were due to negligence or mismanagement in the Crimea. Late in De-cember he prepared a comprehensive memorandum for the cabinet enumer-ating the principal military problems they faced and suggesting possible solutions.[42] Sidney Herbert carefully studied the paper and commented on it at length. He observed that some of Russell's proposals had already been adopted. Newcastle, for instance, had already urged Lord Raglan to arrange a reallocation of responsibilities and a redistribution of ground with the French as a way to relieve the burdens on the British troops. Herbert also noted that Newcastle had begun to establish a separate land transport service, and that he himself had started a separate hospital corps.

As for the other major points Russell raised, Herbert observed that a large quantity of clothing had been sent to the Crimea and that he hoped to hear soon that complaints on that head had been removed. He found the death of horses from want of forage "unaccountable," although he suspected that the causes were a lack of men with ability and experience on the Commissariat staff and the failure to place sufficiently large orders for forage at Constantinople. Herbert recommended the recruitment of a corps of experienced men from the mercantile houses to augment the Commissariat staff. The shipment of huts to the Crimea, he observed, had been materially delayed by the loan of steamers to the French, but huts for thirteen thousand men had passed Malta, and another quantity for twenty-three thousand men had left Trieste and would soon reach the Crimea. He trusted that the changes already made in the naval and military staff at Constantinople would expedite the transmission of stores of all kinds.

Concerning the demand for the dismissal of incompetent officers, Herbert was circumspect. It was, he noted, impossible for the ministers at home to determine incompetence with accuracy and justice. However, he suggested that Russell's memorandum be made the basis of a public dispatch to Raglan, with additional points concerning the failure of the army either to build a road from the harbor to the camp or to create divisional depots, and with instructions to him to replace any senior officers whom he judged incompetent with men of talent on the spot.[43]

The duke of Argyll, Sir George Grey, Sir Charles Wood, and Lord Clarendon all concurred with Herbert's views. Furthermore, they argued that Raglan should be called upon to give a full report of the causes that had led to the deplorable suffering of the army. Molesworth and Gladstone took an even stronger line. Molesworth emphatically laid the blame for the Crimean troubles on the adjutant-general and quartermaster-general and stated that tenderness of heart in refusing to dismiss the most incompetent officers at such a time would be a public crime. To Gladstone it was "heartrending" to read the fresh evidence that burned "as if written in letters of fire" of the total insufficiency of those in the Crimea upon whom the government depended. He believed that the government should send out competent men and instruct Lord Raglan to employ them in mastering, arranging, and using the materials that the government had so profusely supplied.[44]

Notwithstanding the increasing pressure upon him in the cabinet, Newcastle was not yet ready to demand the recall of Airey and Estcourt, especially as the move could be construed as a desperate means of saving himself. He answered Palmerston:

> I am ready to advise the dismissal of anybody, nay, everybody on the Staff
> in any command, if I can have the hope of saving the lives or the health
> of the men, but what I confess I am not prepared to do is to recall men
> against whom there is a newspaper clamour, and for whom I have no better
> substitutes, merely to save myself. No doubt two small tubs to the whales
> as Airey and Estcourt might save me from playing Jonah. I am not ambi-

tious of being swallowed alone on the 23rd [the day Parliament was to
resume], but I had sooner share that fate than escape it by a dodge.[45]

The duke at first opposed the suggestion that he include the complaints
against the principal members of Raglan's staff in an official dispatch to the
commander. However, he found the ministerial pressure upon him too great
to resist, and in a private letter to Raglan of 8 January he confessed his submission to the will of the cabinet on this matter. "If anything could add to the
pain of writing anything which could give you annoyance," the duke lamented, "it would be the fact that I am called upon to do so at a moment
when you have been so unfairly and ungenerously attacked by the ruffianly
Times," with which, he stressed, he had no sympathy.[46] Thus, Newcastle
wrote the famous official dispatch of 12 January 1855 at the cabinet's will in
order to put the government's position and concerns formally before Raglan
and, if necessary, the nation at large. He acted responsibly, honestly, and hon-
orably for a ministry anxious to ascertain the causes of the failures and privations in the Crimea and to take action against them. The duke shared the
conviction of his colleagues and many of his countrymen that until the administrative problems were resolved in the Crimea, all the policies and
changes initiated in London would have little or no effect in the field. The
dispatch of 12 January, therefore, was the cabinet's bold attempt to stir Raglan
to action on the matter.

The cabinet approved Newcastle's dispatch to Lord Raglan at a meeting on
11 January, the day before it was officially sent. The dispatch was based on the
memoranda of Russell and Herbert and the recommendations of other ministers. In it Newcastle once again referred to the numerous reports of deficiencies and deplorable conditions in the Crimea that had reached the ministers from various quarters. These reports, Newcastle wrote, even allowing
for the bad state of the roads and the weather, made the ministers "painfully
apprehensive that there had been either a want of foresight or of ability" on
the part of some of Raglan's staff that had "led to an amount of suffering and
sickness . . . which might and ought to have been avoided." The ministers,
therefore, demanded that Raglan conduct an inquiry into the internal arrangements of the camp, the means of supply, and the care of the sick and wounded.
The duke promised that whatever additional aid and expenditure Raglan
needed for reforms in the military departments would "be cheerfully supplied
by a country which has the deepest sympathy with the army and the noblest
reliance in its commander."[47]

The queen enthusiastically approved the dispatch, although she regretted
that her name had not been mentioned when reference was made to the sympathy of the "People of England" with the army in its suffering. She thought
that the dispatch was "so delicately worded that it ought not to offend," although its content would most certainly be "painful to Lord Raglan." For that

very reason Newcastle had omitted her name from the document. "When censure has to be passed," the duke explained to her, "he has spoken in the name of Your Majesty's Government; but when praise has to be given he has spoken in the name of Your Majesty."[48]

For the ministers, however, or at least those most responsible for the conduct of the war, there was a more immediate problem than Raglan's displeasure with that dispatch. They, and particularly Newcastle, had to face the growing clamor of public opinion over the Crimean crisis and the attack in the *Times*, which reached a crescendo on the eve of the resumption of Parliament. "We have a storm brewing against the working of the military departments," Herbert told Newcastle on 8 January, "and if we intend to outlive it we must make vigorous use of the fortnight between this and the meeting of Parliament." They had "a terrible arrear to make up in this fortnight," for the work hung with all of them and important things were left undone or undecided. They had no right to complain of the mismanagement at Balaclava until their own house was in order. Herbert mentioned several matters that required immediate attention: they must press the Admiralty and the Ordnance to conduct an immediate inquiry into the manner in which stores were packed, loaded, and shipped to the East; they must send out efficient men to Balaclava to serve as storekeepers and issuers; they must press Graham at the Admiralty to do something about a harbormaster for Balaclava; and they must send out huts for the hospitals and settle the question of an order of merit.

To accomplish these items of business before the opening of Parliament, Herbert believed, Newcastle and he needed to meet more regularly with the heads of departments. "If we can succeed in giving our meetings the regularity of a Board," he wrote on this point, "we shall in a great degree meet the difficulty, not only the Parliamentary but the practical difficulty." He believed that copies of the minutes of the board meetings should be sent to the prime minister and to the leader of the House of Commons. "It seems to me," he added for good measure, "that for your own sake you should make much greater use of the Cabinet than you do, and of Lord John likewise. People to be carried with you must be kept *au courant* of what is being done, and made parties to it by giving their assent." In this way, Herbert explained, Newcastle would not only get valuable advice from Lord John, but, more importantly, "a very full and hearty defence in Parliament" as well. "The *amour propre* of Lord John" would be satisfied and his "foibles enlisted in favour of instead of against the public service."[49]

That was sound advice, but it came too late for Newcastle to repair his relationship with Russell, and much of what Herbert suggested was already under orders for implementation or under final consideration. Even the board that Herbert suggested existed on an informal basis. Meetings attended by Newcastle, Herbert, Lord Hardinge, and Sir Hew Ross, the lieutenant-general of the Ordnance, were held at the War Department on 3, 10, and 20 January to review the steps that had been taken to complete the establishment of the depot at Malta, to send additional supplies to the East, and to establish a medical staff for the convalescent hospital at Smyrna. Herbert's proposal to formalize these meetings through the establishment of a board under the secretary of state for war and including the secretary at war, the commander-in-chief, and the master-general of the Ordnance gained cabinet approval on 20 January 1855. It was hoped that this move would at least partially meet Lord Grey's demands for changes in the administration of the army without touching the powers of the commander-in-chief or the royal prerogative of patronage.[50]

Besides these matters, Newcastle was busy with many other administrative details associated with the conduct of the war, many of which were urged upon him by Prince Albert along the lines suggested by Herbert.[51] He instructed Lord William Paulet, newly appointed military commandant in the Bosphorus, on ways to improve the hospitals and the medical service in general. Paulet was told to spend whatever he deemed necessary for this "sacred duty," for "expense," the duke wrote, "can not be balanced against lives, and you are at liberty to use my authority for saying so." Paulet was to work closely with the members of the Hospitals Commission in developing improvements of the whole medical establishment.[52]

There was much other business as well for Newcastle. As soon as he became aware of the critical shortage of forage in the Crimea, the duke arranged for the purchase and shipment of large quantities of pressed hay for the army in the East and for the establishment of a reserve depot at Malta. He organized a corps of bakers and purchased a steamer to serve as a floating bakery at Balaclava. He also appointed an officer to serve as dockmaster at Balaclava, selected men from the customs department to serve as Commissariat storekeepers, and appointed a corps of laborers to erect iron warehouses and to land the stores and supplies at the harbor.[53]

The deplorable situation in the Crimea also convinced Newcastle of the need to establish a separate land transport service, a task he began early in January with Prince Albert's strong encouragement. He relied heavily upon Lieutenant-Colonel McMurdo, who had already drawn up a plan for a new service under military control. On 19 January he asked Herbert to prepare the draft of a royal warrant establishing the Land Transport Corps, and on the following day he informed Lord Raglan of the action.[54]

Doubtlessly, in taking the first step to organize the Land Transport Corps, Newcastle reacted as much to the precarious political situation at home as to the military crisis in the Crimea. There was a strong impression in all the duke's feverish activity early in 1855 of a race against time to set things right before the meeting of Parliament. The tide of business threatened to overwhelm him mentally and physically. "You will have to class your business according to its importance," Prince Albert advised the duke, "and keep the important one alone for your personal transaction. I know that this must be repugnant to an active mind like yours but turns out beneficial in the end as carrying out the . . . principle of division of labour."[55]

Despite this wise advice, the duke, suffering from the strain of overwork, perplexity, and anxiety, pressed on with the business of his office. He was dissatisfied with the existing system of rewarding meritorious service in battle, which, if the recommendations of Lord Raglan and the divisional generals were followed, would reduce the three grades of the Order of the Bath "to a mere appendage to certain ranks" of the army in the field. Nor was he in favor of adding to the three classes of the Order of the Bath. Instead, he proposed the institution of an entirely new order of merit that would be open to all ranks.[56] Newcastle's proposal, which was eventually accepted, was the origin of the highly honored Order of the Victoria Cross.

Besides the problems of merit, supply, transport, and recruitment, both for the British army and the foreign legion, Newcastle faced the task of making specific plans for the future reform of the whole military system. In this area much depended upon the outcome of the inquiries that the government requested Raglan to institute into the operation of the military departments in the Crimea, and upon Raglan's own recommendations. Newcastle awaited that information with considerable anticipation.

VI

Lord Raglan received Newcastle's critical communications of late December and early January with "feelings of deep regret and mortification." The irregularity in the issue of rations and the periodic inadequacies in supply, he explained, were due to the want of sufficient means of transport. The winter troubles were also caused in part by difficulties in inducing the French to occupy some of the ground held by the British. He had not pressed the issue to the breaking point with the French, for the advantage of keeping on good terms with them was "too obvious to require discussion." He emphatically denied the reports about his principal staff officers and angrily denounced Newcastle for giving credence to what was stated in private letters and the letters printed by newspapers. He assured the duke that he was in a far better position than the writers of those letters to pronounce upon the merits of his officers, and he saw no grounds whatever to remove them from their appointments. The duke's adoption of the imputation against these officers, Raglan continued, reflected indirectly on himself and indicated that the ministers did not consider him capable of judging the merits of his departmental officers, the chief of whom took their orders directly from him. He was surprised to find his staff officers accused of "aristocratic hauteur, incivility, and God knows what besides," for they were all perfect gentlemen, "extremely intelligent, zealous beyond everything, and most courteous to all."[57]

Raglan became even more disdainful of the accusations against Airey in his letter to Newcastle of 20 January. "I really cannot understand any gentleman venturing to intrude upon you such an insinuation," he wrote in reference to the charge that Airey had taken time from his duties to write home to several "fine" ladies. "I cannot say how all these attacks annoy me and add to my anxieties, and these are far from being few." He also denied that he had not kept Newcastle fully informed. "I passed a part of the night before last in reading over the correspondence with you since the month of October," he wrote,

> and I perceived that I had set before you all the difficulties by which the army was surrounded, and that I told you the serious consequences of the state of the roads, and of the deficiency of transport, and that I asked your attention to a report of Mr. Cattley's on the climate, and to the opinion he gave that nobody could withstand the cold unless properly sheltered.[58]

On 30 January, Raglan responded to Newcastle's official dispatch of 12 January. He warmly defended the character and reputation of his staff officers and repudiated the charges against them. He lectured the duke on the organization of the army in order to show that the military departments had nothing to do with the supply, care, or conveyance of provisions, which services, he stressed, rested exclusively with the Commissariat. There had been considerable deficiency and irregularity in the issue, he lamented, but he denied that the irregularity and deficiency were due to the negligence or want of foresight of his staff officers. The failure of land transport was the root of the troubles, he argued, and he could do little to remedy it so long as an insufficient supply of forage prevented him from procuring additional horses and mules to replace the transport animals that had been destroyed by the bad weather and bad roads.

Although he had been constantly concerned with the welfare of his troops, he confessed that the means within his reach to assure the smooth operation of the army in the field were inadequate. He realized that the army was imperfectly organized for field operations, and he knew that it compared unfavorably with the French army, which could rely upon conscription to provide trained men for the hospital, ambulance, commissariat, artillery, and engineer services. He was fully aware that reform was needed, but it had not occurred to him that the government was anxious to form military establishments upon a larger scale while a campaign was in progress. But even with substantial changes in the military system, he argued, the ministers must realize that the British service establishments would remain inferior to those of the French army unless there was a major reorganization of the whole system and a fundamental change in national attitudes toward the military in England.[59]

A note of fatalism sounded throughout this long dispatch. Raglan believed the army's position had been dictated by fate, by the government's fateful decision to send the army to the Crimea. He thought therefore that the deplorable conditions with which the army had to contend were beyond his or any other person's control. On this point the ministers at home and the military officers in the Crimea disagreed. Here was a major difference of temperament between Newcastle and Raglan, between a Peelite administrator who sought solutions for problems and a military traditionalist who lacked imagination and disliked innovation. The government was too far away from the seat of the war to pinpoint the source of the problems in the Crimea with any accuracy, and Raglan and his staff officers gave the ministers very little direction on this score. For the most part, they failed to make specific recommendations to the government either for the resolution of pressing problems or for the long-term improvement of the military system. They recognized the system for what it was and accepted the difficulties as a matter of course. Generals Airey and Estcourt and Commissary-General Filder all functioned reasonably well within the traditional military system, and for this Raglan praised their efforts and strongly defended them against charges of mismanagement and lack of foresight. Yet their perspective was narrowly confined within the limits of the "aristocratic establishment" for which they were vigorously attacked in the *Times*. Undoubtedly they had neither the ability nor the imagination to make a defective system work during a crisis.

Clearly much that was complained of in the Crimea pointed to something essentially wrong in the organization of those departments over which Airey, Estcourt, and Filder presided; and Newcastle was convinced that the worst evils of the defective system could be corrected only by the appointment of men of proved fitness to replace those in the departments whose incompetence could be verified. From a distance of three thousand miles, he told Raglan on 22 January, it was impossible for him to decide whether Airey or Estcourt or any individuals acting under them were at fault. That responsibility, therefore, devolved upon Raglan, and the duke urged him "to take this matter in hand at once and deal with it vigorously." Newcastle urged the commander not to "allow seniority or any other consideration but efficiency" to influence his selection if he found it necessary to replace any staff members.[60]

But Lord Raglan was neither willing to part with Airey and Estcourt nor institute a thorough investigation of the quartermaster-general's and adjutant-general's departments. Replacing Airey as quartermaster-general, Raglan told Newcastle, would inflict "a very great injury . . . on the service and on myself personally."[61] The duke, who firmly believed that he had "not written heedlessly or on insufficient information," was surprised by Raglan's adamant support of his staff officers. "On my part," he wrote on 26 January,

> I feel great concern at the unequivocal terms in which you express entire approval of the Quarter-Master-General's Department. The present condition of the army—wet, cold, and hungry, within seven miles of warm clothing, huts, fuel, and food, must be caused by the improvidence of somebody. Who is it?

In writing this letter, Newcastle was not moved by "ugly motives" based on Raglan's refusal to sacrifice Airey to save the government, as Kinglake asserted.[62] The duke's position was no longer in doubt, as the rest of the letter proves:

> The storm at home which some time ago I told you was inevitable is about to break. Lord John Russell has quitted the Government. To-night a motion for enquiry into the conduct of the war comes on in the House of Commons. It is almost certain that the Government will be beaten. If so, we shall of course all resign. But if not, it is impossible that I can remain in office. The public feeling against me is so strong that I should only be impeding the public welfare if I attempted to resist it. I must therefore make way, God grant it may be for somebody more capable, though certainly not more anxious or devoted to the cause of this country—whatever may happen to others.[63]

What troubled the duke was Raglan's refusal to institute a thorough investigation of the military departments in the Crimea and to take whatever action was necessary to save the army in the field. Raglan continued to disdain Newcastle's concern as founded on erroneous reports by journalists and by private letter writers who wrote "simply to gratify vindictive feeling and love of rancourous abuse."[64] Newcastle, on the other hand, believed that Raglan was protecting personal friends at the expense of efficiency and thus endangering the entire army and the Allied operation against Sebastopol.

VII

Newcastle's concern took another turn on 23 January, the day that Parliament reconvened. On that date Russell submitted his letter of resignation from the government after John Arthur Roebuck gave notice of a motion for a committee of inquiry into the conduct of the war. When Aberdeen showed him Russell's letter the following morning, Newcastle, who was already prepared to make a "sacrifice" to "appease the public," offered to resign his office immediately in favor of Palmerston. He renewed his offer at the cabinet meeting that afternoon, and Palmerston, who was most critical of Russell's resignation, agreed to take the War Department as a way to keep the government from dissolving, although he told Aberdeen that he did not believe he could administer it half as well as Newcastle.[65] The Peelites were incensed over Russell's resignation, which they regarded as another sign of his personal ambition. They refused to consider Clarendon's suggestion that Russell be asked to withdraw his resignation in view of Newcastle's departure. While they were willing to sacrifice the duke to the wishes of the country, they were vociferously opposed to sacrificing him to Lord John. Although inclined to resign, the ministers, acting in deference to the queen, decided on 25 January to fight Roebuck's motion in the Commons.[66]

There was little doubt as to the outcome of the vote on the motion. The Commons had been greatly infected by the temper of the *Times*. The attacks in the paper had intensified as a new Parliament neared, and on 20 January an editorial prophesied the annihilation of the army. "A torpor and lethargy seems to have fallen on the spirit of our rulers," the leader read; "they go on mechanically sending out men and stores to the fatal harbour of Balaclava, without seeming to advert to the fact that men and stores under the present circumstances of the British army are only sent, one to perish, the other to be wasted." The army was the plaything of the aristocracy, another leader stated three days later, and not even the ablest minister could save it from a foul system.[67]

The House of Commons was in an angry mood over the conduct of the war, and it was far readier than the *Times* to attach blame to specific individuals for what was widely termed the "disaster" in the Crimea. Russell helped to focus the blame on Newcastle in his speech explaining his resignation from the government. He told a very attentive House that he could not oppose Roebuck's motion in clear conscience, for he had been unsuccessful in his efforts to convince Aberdeen and the cabinet to accept the changes in personnel and in the machinery of administration that he had advocated persistently since the previous October.[68] Although Palmerston, Gladstone, and Sir George Grey gave truer accounts of the unhappy situation, it was clear to Gladstone and Herbert that Russell had carried the House with him.[69] Russell had made certain that his former colleagues had no chance of surviving the Roebuck motion.

The debate over Roebuck's motion began later that day, with Sidney Herbert making a strong reply to the motion on behalf of the government. He admitted that the army's administrative machinery had not functioned efficiently after forty years of peace. He reviewed what the government had done to correct the difficulties and to improve the system, and he observed that the ministers had corresponded with Raglan about the apparent failures in the Crimea. There was no reason for a select committee, he concluded, for the government already knew what was wrong and was acting to rectify the faults.[70]

When the debate resumed a few days later, Gladstone vigorously defended

Newcastle's administration of the War Department and denounced the concept of a select committee as a constitutional absurdity. It was "hard and heavy
work," he noted of the speech, "especially as to the cases of three persons:
Lord John Russell, Duke of Newcastle, and Lord Raglan."[71] It was a forceful
speech and he was greatly applauded for it. The House divided after Palmerston summed up the case for the government and Roebuck contributed a brief
statement. The motion was carried by a vote of 305 to 148. After a moment
of silence in the House, members on both sides burst into laughter. The enormous majority against the ministers, Gladstone observed, "not only knocked
us down but sent us down with such a whack, that one heard one's head
thump as it struck the ground."[72]

Before leaving for the House of Lords earlier in the day, Newcastle wrote
a short letter to Raglan to report on the parliamentary proceedings:

> The House of Commons will divide to-night on Mr. Roebuck's motion,
> and my impression, though it is not generally entertained, is that the Gov-
> ernment will have a majority. If it has not, of course we shall all resign,—
> but at any rate I shall tender my resignation tomorrow morning. All my
> little means of public usefulness are cut from under me by the popular men
> against me, and particularly by the ungenerous conduct of Lord John Rus-
> sell, and of course I have no wish to retain *any* office when this is the case.

His last official act, he noted, would be the painful one of recalling Lord
Lucan, whom the duke believed could no longer remain as commander of the
Cavalry Division after he had publicly attempted to exculpate himself from
all blame for the fatal charge of the Light Brigade during the battle of Balaclava
the previous October.[73]

In the House of Lords later in the day, the duke spoke on Lord Grey's
motion for consolidation of the various military departments. Although he
denied that the distress of the Crimea was due to the existing organization of
the departments, Newcastle readily admitted that extensive changes were necessary. He agreed with Grey that the medical service had broken down and
that substantial alterations in the service were needed. He also agreed with
Grey that there was a need for greater coordination among the departments
and a more extensive authority for the secretary of state for war. Nevertheless,
he opposed Grey's plan for joining the duties and functions of the military
departments under one roof. The secretary of state for war, he stated, was
already overburdened by details, leaving little time for his paramount duties.
Even with the bitter experiences of the past year, Newcastle still believed that
the best way to conduct the business of the army was by a board with the
minister of war at its head, as had been done with considerable success in
recent weeks. Therefore, he strongly urged the extension of the practice by

the official creation of a board with supremacy granted to the secretary of state for war.

Newcastle also agreed with Lord Grey that much of the army's suffering was caused by the improper training of the soldiers and officers, and added that the deficiency of arms and the unsatisfactory testing of scientific improvements at Woolwich had seriously impaired the army. The duke stressed that he had wanted vast improvements in the British military system, but he reminded the House that the work of army reform was slow and weary. It should not be surprising, he added, "that during the last nine or ten months they had not made vast progress in amending the errors of the past, which, for twenty years, every successive Government had found plenty of fault with, but has never been enabled properly to correct." Still, he hoped that he had been instrumental in correcting some of the system's worst evils.[74]

Newcastle's speech on Earl Grey's motion was an appropriate final comment on his administration of the War Department. On the following day, 30 January 1855, he resigned, along with the other ministers of the Aberdeen Coalition. On 1 February, in a most unusual procedure, Newcastle addressed the Lords in a full House immediately after Aberdeen announced the ministers' resignation. Lady Frances Waldegrave, "looking splendid in black & red," appeared in the gallery to show her sympathy for the duke.[75] Newcastle cited confidential transactions and correspondence of the late cabinet to repudiate several statements Russell had made in his speech to the Commons on the previous Friday. In particular, he attacked Russell's claim that his resignation was made necessary by the cabinet's refusal to adopt his views on the newly created army board. As for himself, the duke noted that he had approved Russell's proposal and had resolved not to interfere with the general views of the cabinet on the matter. In fact, he told the Lords, he had decided shortly before Parliament met to give way to Russell on all counts and to resign office as soon as he had faced the ordeal of censure in the House of Lords and submitted his conduct of the administration of the War Department to the judgment of the House of Commons.

In his lengthy speech, Newcastle also referred to the public charges made against him. As for incapacity, he would leave the verdict to others, but the other charges of indolence and indifference, which hurt him deeply, he would deny with all his strength. "My Lords," he stated,

> as regards the charge of indolence, I have only to say that the public have had, at all events, every hour and every minute of my time. Not one hour of recreation or of amusement have I presumed to think I was entitled to take. My Lords, the other charge, that of indifference, is still more painful to me. Indifference, my Lords!—to what? Indifference to the honour of the country—indifference to the success and to the safety of our army! My Lords, I have myself, like many who listen to me, two dear hostages for

my interest in the welfare of the military and naval services of the country
to allow of such a sentiment. I have two sons engaged in those two services,
and that alone, I think, would be sufficient to prevent me from being
indifferent; but, my Lords, as a Minister—as a man—I should be unworthy
to stand in any assembly, if the charge of indifference under such circumstances could be truly made against me. Many a sleepless night I have
passed, my Lords, thinking over the evils which the public think and say I
could have cured; and which, God knows, I would have cured if it had been
within my power. Indolence and indifference are not charges that can truly
be brought against me. I deny the charges; and I trust that my countrymen
will before long be satisfied, whatever they think of my capacity, that
there is no ground for fixing this unjust stigma upon me.[76]

The *Times* pronounced the speech "a manly and becoming defence," which
no man could read without feeling sympathy and respect, and an overwhelming refutation of Russell's statement. Not one man in a hundred, the paper
postulated, would hesitate to choose Newcastle "who had fallen at his post"
over "a politician who has terminated his official career by flight, and sheltered
that flight under a misrepresentation." No one could impugn the duke's "jealous industry in the public service, his generosity, or his honour," while no one
could help but cast scorn on Russell's "sordid personal calculation," his "petty
but incessant attempts . . . to supplant the Chief Minister and to obtain a
position over his colleagues."[77]

Most members of Parliament reacted to the situation in much the same way
as did the *Times*. Lord Broughton recorded that he had met only one man at
Brooks's who did not condemn Russell. Generally, he observed, it was felt
that Newcastle had been ill treated, like Palmerston in 1851. Newcastle's defense of himself, Broughton further noted, was "as good as circumstances
would permit and his exposure of John Russell's conduct complete. The
whole house seemed to think so too—for the duke was cheered more than
any one I ever heard in that house . . . by men on all sides." All the duke's
colleagues had been nearby to cheer him repeatedly.[78] Even Lord Grey, long
the duke's adversary, praised Newcastle's speech and noted that among the
numerous persons assembled in the House there was little difference of opinion as to how severely Newcastle's statement had damaged Russell. "It con-
victs him," Grey wrote in his journal, "not only of having behaved very ill to
his colleagues but also of pat want of candour in his own statement on Friday
last."[79] According to Colonel Phipps, Newcastle's speech had shown that the
duke "had been sacrificed to misfortunes, and not by his own fault."[80] No
servant of her majesty, Edward Ellice had earlier told Col. Charles Grey, could
"have devoted more untiring industry, zeal or ability to the service than Newcastle; but it was his misfortune to have confronted an anomalous army administration."[81]

The Dirty Doorstep. Palmerston (an active lad): "Well! This is the greatest mess I ever saw at anybody's door." Little Jack Russell: "Ah! I lived there once—but I was obliged to leave—it was such a very irregular family." (From *Punch*, 14 April 1855.)

The country as a whole, however, was not in a sympathetic mood. Newcastle, even more than Lord Aberdeen, was a convenient target for public wrath. It was far easier for the public to blame him than an impersonal military system for the Crimean troubles. The public demanded that somebody pay for the suffering the troops had endured throughout the winter. And the political maneuvers of the Conservatives and the supporters of Russell against the Aberdeen Coalition exposed him all the more to the public's attack. The price the duke paid for the failure of the Allied armies to take Sebastopol before the end of 1854 was not only the loss of office in 1855, but also the loss of a bright political future. Not surprisingly, there was much bitterness in his heart.

12. Political Isolation

Lord Panmure candidly stated that "the barometer was steadily on the rise" when he took over the War Department from the duke of Newcastle. He confessed that he had little to add to the measures that had already been initiated by his predecessor for improving the condition of the British army in the Crimea.[1] Despite his disclaimer, it was to him and to Lord Palmerston, the new prime minister, that credit was given for the improvement that had been made in the state of the army by the spring. Newcastle, for a time at least, continued to be pilloried by the press for the failures that had brought near disaster in the Crimea during the previous winter.

As the spring progressed, the measures that Newcastle had taken in December and January gradually began to benefit the troops in the East. The Balaclava railway, for which the duke had contracted early in December 1854, began in March 1855 to haul stores, shot, and shell up to the headquarters summit. Plentiful supplies both of clothing and food were now issued regularly, and the huts that had arrived in Balaclava in late December and early January were in place by late February. The Land Transport Corps that Newcastle had authorized in January finally began operations in the Crimea by late summer. The Hospitals Commission helped to repair deficiencies in the medical service, and the relief granted to the British soldiers in the trenches by the extension of the French lines greatly contributed to the restoration of the army's health and morale.

Although the condition of the army was greatly improving, the new administration took added steps to remedy the shortcomings of the system both in the Crimea and at home. Lord Panmure appointed sanitary commissioners to find ways to keep the camps and hospitals in sanitary condition. A corps of scavengers was recruited from Constantinople to remove the filth in the harbor at Balaclava and in the camps. Civilian doctors were temporarily enlisted in the Medical Department and sent to the East. Sir John Burgoyne was recalled, and Sir John McNeill and Col. Sir Alexander Tulloch were appointed to inquire into the operation of the Commissariat. Maj.-Gen. Sir James Simpson was sent out to the Crimea as chief of staff to convey Lord Raglan's orders to the staff and to see that they were quickly and implicitly obeyed. He also was to serve as an inspector to report to the secretary of state on the manner

216

in which the staff officers performed their duties. A Sea-Transport Board was established at the Admiralty to coordinate military transport with the War Office. The post of secretary at war was abolished, and the secretary of state for war received considerably greater powers over the civil administration of all the military departments. In May 1855 the Board of Ordnance was abolished, with its military functions transferred to the commander-in-chief and its civil functions to the secretary of state. Later in the year Panmure overrode military prejudice and sent civilian laborers of the newly organized Army Work Corps to the Crimea.[2]

Newcastle had long advocated some of these important measures, but it took the pressures of crisis and Roebuck's Select Committee to get them past "old-fashioned departmentalism" and army and navy obstruction. Even with their adoption, however, confusion continued to prevail in the reorganized War Department. The changes had all the earmarks of hasty expedients adopted by ministers anxious to still popular clamor. As such, they did not meet the real needs of the country. Much more reflection during calmer times was needed to produce a more rational organization of the military system.[3] Nonetheless, the measures succeeded in quieting public agitation and restoring confidence in the government.

Public attention had shifted from the Crimea to the committee room where the Select Committee on the Army before Sebastopol took evidence. Newcastle went before the committee late in April. The *Times* recorded that he showed amiable—if not altogether admirable—qualities, a good temper, fair memory, and some ability to relate information to the committee.[4] The duke's evidence, the paper concluded, proved that as secretary of state for war, "There was hardly a difficulty, physical or moral, he had not to encounter." Newcastle had tried to produce directness and unity of action amid warring departments, the writer argued, but he had had neither the requisite authority nor the vigor to improve substantially a bad system.[5]

Newcastle's testimony drew a strong protest from Elizabeth Herbert, who believed that he had not done justice to her husband's indefatigable exertions at the War Office. Deeply wounded, the duke replied to Lady Herbert's letter by stating that Sidney was the last man under the circumstances whom he would knowingly have hurt. He assured her that he was especially gratified by Sidney's assistance during the peak of the crisis. "The only requital I could make," he explained, " . . . was to assume to myself the whole weight of obloquy which attached to the conduct of the War."[6]

Elizabeth Herbert's sharp rebuke increased Newcastle's feeling of estrangement from some of his former Peelite colleagues who, he believed, had not done enough to exonerate him from the failures in the Crimea during the previous winter. Newcastle also disagreed with their political attitude toward Palmerston, whom the queen early in February asked to form a government after Derby and Russell (who could get neither Clarendon nor Sir George Grey to join him because of his treatment of the Peelites) had failed. The duke strongly urged Graham, Gladstone, and Herbert to accept Palmerston's invitation to join the new government; they reluctantly agreed after Aberdeen told them to put their country's interests before their personal feelings.

The relations between Newcastle and his former Peelite colleagues worsened when the Peelite trio resigned from Palmerston's government only two weeks after joining it and when Graham and Gladstone adopted an extremely pacific attitude toward the war. As the spring progressed, the distance between them and Newcastle widened perceptibly over the war issue. Palmerston and Clarendon, the foreign secretary, were quick to thank the duke for his continued support. After Newcastle spoke in the Lords defending the management of the war, Clarendon wrote to Aberdeen, "My regret at the course taken by Gladstone and Graham is as sincere as my satisfaction with respect to Newcastle's conduct. The public has been doing him justice for some time past, but his speech on Friday seems to have raised him in everybody's estimation."[7] Consequently, Palmerston asked Newcastle to go to the Crimea to report on the state of the army; the duke agreed, even though Aberdeen remonstrated that to go in face of the pending resolution on the Sebastopol Committee Report would be taken "as an act of indecent defiance, or of pitiable cowardice." Gladstone also was both astonished and grieved to learn that Newcastle intended to leave the country at such a critical time.[8]

The pending resolution concerned the proposed censure of the members of the late coalition government for mismanagement of the war. Although the Sebastopol Committee Report blamed the Crimean difficulties on the whole system rather than upon specific individuals, John A. Roebuck, the committee's chairman, carried an amendment in committee censuring the administration in England for having undertaken the Crimean expedition without sufficient planning and information and concluding that the poorly conceived expedition "was the first and chief cause of the calamities that befell the Army."[9] Justified by the adoption of this additional paragraph to the original report, Roebuck in June brought forward a motion of censure in the Commons against the members of the late administration. Both Aberdeen and Gladstone believed that Newcastle should stay to help resist the motion.

Newcastle was not insensitive to the difficult and humiliating situation that the report and Roebuck's motion presented to him and his former colleagues in the Aberdeen government. He was greatly perturbed that the report had not found Generals Airey and Estcourt, Commissary-General Filder, and Admiral Boxer more specifically responsible for the logistical failures in the Crimea, and he was deeply angered by Roebuck's motion censuring the past administration for conducting the war without sufficient care and forethought. Nevertheless, perhaps to justify his own case and to help him prepare his own defense, he was anxious to leave for the East to see for himself the state of the army in the Crimea and the hospitals in Turkey; although he delayed his departure once at Aberdeen's request, the postponement of Roebuck's motion until early July forced him to leave the country at a moment most painful to himself.

II

Newcastle left London by the 8:30 train on 27 June 1855 and steamed out of Dover harbor for Calais at 11:00 the same morning. Bothered by a violent headache, he rested a day at Cologne before traveling on by rail through Germany and Austria to Vienna, arriving on 3 July. While there, he conversed at length with Count Buol, the Austrian foreign minister, who expressed his fear of a protracted war between the Allies and Russia. In Vienna also, news arrived of Lord Raglan's death. The duke received the information with sadness. "I had hoped once more to shake him [Raglan] by the hand and dispel, if it existed, the idea that in the performance of my official duties I had treated him harshly," he wrote in his journal that evening.[10]

From Vienna the duke traveled to Trieste and boarded there a Lloyd's steamer for Constantinople. He stopped off at Corfu to visit his old Peelite friend Sir John Young, to whom he expressed some dissatisfaction with his current status. He described the treatment he had lately received at the hands of Palmerston and "his coxcomb colleague," Vernon Smith, who, in spite of the India Board's recommendation, had passed him over in favor of Lord Canning for the governor-generalship of India.[11] From Corfu the duke proceeded to Smyrna, where he inspected the British Hospital. While passing through the Dardanelles to Gallipoli, he conversed with Calvert, the British consul, learning valuable information about the excellent progress being made in supplying the Land Transport Corps with horses and drivers. Calvert also told the duke "of the extraordinary and culpable vacillation" of Commissary-General Filder in respect to hay during the previous summer. Filder had ordered a large quantity of hay through Calvert's office, but later had counter-ordered it before it was cut. Still later, Filder again changed his mind and reordered the hay, but the season was over and the French had bought most of it previously. "This is providence! and this *economy* forsooth!," the duke exclaimed.[12]

Newcastle arrived at Constantinople on 15 July. He went immediately to the Scutari Hospital, the scene of much suffering and confusion during the previous autumn and winter. The place was now far different. The duke believed that the condition of the hospital was excellent, at least superficially. Still he seriously doubted the competence of Dr. Cumming, the hospital's head, and he wrote home to urge the government to supersede him immediately. His views were strengthened during his long conversation with Florence Nightingale and Charles and Selina Bracebridge on hospital matters. Before leaving Scutari, he visited the military cemetery that covered a large field overhanging the sea. "This melancholy receptacle of so many brave men," he observed, "is a sad record of last winter's sufferings. There are already 5,000 bodies buried in it."[13]

The duke reached Balaclava early on 27 July. The coast was one of the boldest and most beautiful he had ever seen, and the little harbor was far more striking than he had expected. The cleanliness of the harbor and base camp also surprised him. That evening he visited Gen. Sir James Simpson, the new British commander, at headquarters and slept in the room in which Lord Raglan had died. The following day he met General Airey. "I feared our meeting would have been unpleasant in consequence of the severe remarks I had felt it my duty to make respecting him to Lord Raglan," the duke wrote in his journal, "but to his credit I must say such was far from being the case."[14] In the afternoon he rode with General Barnard, the new chief of staff, to Cathcart's Hill, where he pitched his tent.

With only occasional absences to visit such places as Eupatoria, the duke remained encamped on Cathcart's Hill for nearly two months. The camp was easily within range of the Russian guns, and occasionally round shot fell near his tent. During the days, the duke indefatigably visited the trenches and the battlefields, frequently while under Russian fire, to observe the progress of the siege; during the evenings, he talked with English and French officers over cigars and brandy. On 3 August he examined the plain of Balaclava, the scene of the famous charge of the Light Brigade in October of the previous year. "It is wonderful that any man could have been rash enough to order such a forlorn hope, and not less wonderful that a single man returned alive," he observed. "Unlike Inkerman, this plain seems to be destined by nature for the great contests of man—it might be chosen for a battle-field either by the Attacker or Defender and certainly by the Spectator, for an amphitheatre of high hills surrounds it."[15] On 17 August, the duke walked over another field that was still covered with dead from the great battle of the Tchernaya the previous day. "The sight," he wrote in his journal that evening, "must always be horrible and disgusting, and the reflections, even after a victory, not only painful but reproachful—but I cannot say that I experienced those sickening sensations from the aspect of so many mangled and distorted bodies of one's fellow creatures which I fully expected."[16]

During his close inspections, the duke found much about which to complain to both the civil authorities at home and the military authorities in the Crimea. There was, for example, a severe shortage of ammunition. "Surely the reformed Ordnance ought to be able to do what its condemned predecessor always contrived under serious difficulties to effect last year!," he exclaimed to Lord Clarendon. He was not satisfied with the execution of the railway from the harbor to the camps on the heights above. There had been neither the time nor the opportunity to build a roadbed, and the duke believed that unless measures were taken, the horses used to pull up the cars would be knee-deep in mud and the rails broken by the rains. The new Army Works Corps had arrived, but the duke commented that he had not as yet seen any of its members in a state of sobriety; although he hoped it would do some good in making roads, he feared that the corps would not meet expectations. He observed that his "bantling," the Land Transport Corps, was progressing but had suffered great misfortune with the death from illness of many officers and men. As for supplies, it was evident to him that no steps had been taken either in the Crimea or at home to prevent the recurrence of the misfortunes of the previous winter.[17]

His observations on the spot convinced him more than ever that General Airey and Commissary-General Filder were mainly to blame for these serious problems, as he told Clarendon: "Mr. Filder, who has fortunately for the public service just gone home on sick-leave, has never departed from his lamentable system of living from hand to mouth. He has no stores—no store-houses—no depots in Camp." It was insanity not to provide for the certainty of wintering in the Crimea, he continued, but "whilst the French and even the Sardinians have accumulated vast mountains of hay and barley and piles innumerable of fuel our Commissariat does not seem to have a week's supply of anything." He urged the immediate establishment of divisional depots with at least a month's or six weeks' supply of forage, fuel, salt meat, biscuit, and rum. He also urged General Barnard to order immediately a vast supply of huts, which he believed would be needed with the onset of winter.[18] On the whole, he found General Barnard receptive to his suggestions. "Whether they will be adopted here or at home is another matter," he added.[19]

Newcastle also passed judgment on questions of military personnel and strategy. At headquarters, relations between Generals Airey and Barnard soon became strained, and General Simpson lacked the firmness necessary to settle the difficulties. The duke thought that Simpson, although an amiable gentleman, was an incompetent commander. But he found the state of the French command little better. General Pélissier, he believed, differed from Simpson only in that he was not a gentleman. On 10 August, the duke had a long conversation with Admiral Sir Edmond Lyons and found that he agreed with him as to the prospects of the war and the bad strategy of the Allied commanders. "I wish," he commented in his journal, "the Admiral could take command for a month—I believe in that case the South side would fall within that time; as it is, luck may achieve a favourable result—generalship certainly will not."[20]

In contrast, Newcastle praised the Sardinian army and its commander, General La Marmora. "La Marmora," he wrote Clarendon, "is a real soldier, and the superiority of everything one sees in his camp is as humiliating to our National vanity as it is calculated to raise our estimate of the Country to which that Army belongs and to form anticipations of its future greatness." The duke believed that the Sardinian army was far ahead of both the English and the French armies. They had executed excellent defenses and redoubts and constructed admirable roads that put the work of the English engineers to shame. Had La Marmora commanded the armies on the Tchernaya, the duke opined, the Allied victory would have been far more decisive.[21]

Newcastle's letter to Clarendon provoked responses from Prince Albert and several cabinet members. "I am sorry that the Duke ever wrote this letter," the prince wrote to Clarendon:

> It is at all times hazardous for a civilian going into a camp and picking up information from this or that person, and listening to the different stories flying about there, to give an opinion upon plans of operation, military system, the merit of the different men in command, but was particularly so for the Duke, who fell quite into the ways of our Correspondent, from very much the same causes.

In particular the prince thought the duke's contrast between the Sardinian and British armies and his severe criticism of Simpson and Pélissier were most unfair. The problems in the army, the prince argued, would "not be remedied by the abuse of military men in difficult and responsible situations, such as the Duke (who is a thorough John Bull upon that question) deals out."[22] Three days later, Palmerston told Panmure that he had seen Newcastle's letter from the Crimea and that he totally agreed with Panmure's observations upon it. Newcastle, he wrote, "saw things with the eyes of a disappointed politician, and he retailed the opinions picked up by a traveller from the idle gossipers of a camp." Panmure's criticisms were even more severe. Newcastle, he believed, had descended from the role of a minister to that of spy in order to make political capital for himself. In retaliation, Panmure tried to use the military to destroy the duke's credibility. "You have never mentioned Newcastle in any of your letters," he wrote to General Simpson; "Tell me how he and Airey met, and what His Grace did in the camp, for I am rather anxious to know the opinions your soldiers entertained of him, knowing as I do what he has written of you."[23] Granville observed to Clarendon that Newcastle's letter showed none of his good qualities. It was impossible, he added, "not to have a sad feeling after reading the account given by a man of his calibre and truth."[24]

Clarendon, however, defended the duke. He told Palmerston that Newcastle was incapable of spying. "He has many faults besides a bad temper but he is a thoroughly honorable man, without an atom of party spirit, & has the public good at heart." Clarendon considered the duke's testimony valuable, although not at all agreeable, and he urged Panmure to review it carefully: "You may think him all wrong in his observations, but depend upon it that he has stated nothing but what he believes to be true."[25]

Newcastle's letter brought some results. Largely through Clarendon's urging, the government began to take notice of some of the army's deficiencies in supplies. Both the prince and Palmerston, even though they thought Newcastle's judgment of Simpson was hasty and harsh, agreed with the duke that the general was not quite up to the command of the army and that he should be replaced by a younger, more dynamic man. Thereupon, Gen. Sir William Codrington, whom Newcastle earlier had reservedly recommended, became the new British commander on 10 November 1855. The prince also agreed with Newcastle's plan of operation for sending a large Allied force against Simpheropol in an attempt to invest the Russian army on the heights north of Sebastopol and to cut their communications with the Russian mainland. But, the prince observed, "the [French] Emperor puts his veto upon it even now!!"[26]

The prince's last point referred to the changed circumstances in the Crimea. On 8 September the Russians had evacuated Sebastopol following the successful French assault on the Malakov. The duke witnessed the momentous events of that day from a vantage point that gave him a full view of the French and British assaults on the Malakov and the Redan. It was a strange experience for him finally to see occur what he had awaited with nervous anxiety nearly a year before.

Even after the fall of Sebastopol, the duke continued to criticize the Allied commanders for their lack of élan. "Caution is good, but without dash great deeds will never be done," he wrote in his journal.[27] He believed that the Allies could have driven the Russians out of the Crimea and thus have derived the basis for peace on English terms within a month had they launched an offensive immediately after the fall of Sebastopol. But, he complained to Clarendon, a paralysis had come over headquarters, and Simpson and Pélissier had gallantly resolved to do nothing.[28]

Thoroughly disgusted with the Allied inactivity, the duke left the Crimea on 27 September. He sailed aboard the *Highflyer* from Balaclava to the eastern coast of the Black Sea to visit the Circassian chiefs and to encourage them in their resistance to Russia. He went onshore at Anapa and rode twenty-five miles inland to see Sefir Pasha, the leading prince, and the chiefs, who were assembled for a council of war. For the ride he had doffed the grey shooting coat that had formed his costume in the Crimea and "mounted a plain blue military frock-coat with cavalry sword and an ample Turkish sash, a red fez cap, a pair of high yellow boots and heavy spurs, a brace of revolvers in my girdle, and a field-glass slung over my shoulders." After being received by

Sefir Pasha "with barbaric ceremony and great cordiality," the duke encouraged the chiefs to unite against all foreigners and to fight for the freedom of Circassia. He also promised to plead their cause upon his return to London.[29]

Newcastle spent nearly six weeks in Circassia and in the northern part of Georgia. From Constantinople on 18 November, he wrote to Abraham Hayward to announce that he was on his way home and that, after a delay of three or four days at Malta and two in Paris while he met with Napoleon, he hoped to be in London by the end of the first week in December. He added his thanks for a newspaper cutting Hayward had sent him from the *Liverpool Daily Post*, which stated that the duke would be a welcome addition to any ministry and that it was certain he would become the next premier. "I fear the opinion," he continued,

> very flattering—and too favourable—is much further from being that of the country than you suppose. Never in my recollection was the whole London *daily* press so dishonest, and never had a man who seeks no interest but that of his country so little chance of fair play; whilst the great mass of the people, having neither leisure nor mind to form their own opinions, found their political judgment upon the trash they imbibe with their tea and coffee, or their gin and bitters, as the case may be.[30]

Hayward had been greatly angered by the public clamor against Newcastle early in 1855 and had done all that he could, including writing an article on the Crimean campaign, to vindicate the duke and to put him back on the path to the premiership. Hayward also conferred with Alexander Kinglake, who was about to commence his history of the campaign, to stress the point that the Crimean expedition was well planned as a *coup de main* and would have succeeded had it been carried out by the military as planned. Another of the duke's friends, Peter Benson Maxwell, also took up his pen in defense of the duke's administration of the War Office. He sent Newcastle a copy of his pamphlet *Whom Shall We Hang* while the duke was still in the Crimea. The pamphlet was written in response to the Roebuck Committee Report and Roebuck's motion of censure of the Aberdeen ministry's conduct of the war.[31] These statements supporting Newcastle and citing the improved conditions in the Crimea undoubtedly helped remove some of the rancor against the duke by the time he returned to England.

An offer of the Garter awaited Newcastle upon his return. The duke, however, immediately refused the offer; he believed accepting it would compromise him politically. He told Aberdeen that he found himself at the moment "as much a matter of discussion and speculation as the great question of peace itself." It was widely reported that he had a book in press criticizing Panmure and the generals and that he was "brimfull of thundering attacks ready for the

31st of January," when Parliament reconvened. Therefore, he explained, "if neither the book appears, nor my speech is sufficiently acrimonious, what cause so conclusive to the present generation of politicians as that I am muzzled by a Garter?" But there was an even more fundamental reason for his refusal. He could not accept the Garter from a government that contained some of the Whigs who had supported Russell earlier in the year. "I cannot forget whence came the principal rancour of the Cabal against me a year ago," he told Clarendon. "I knew it not then, but know it now."[32]

III

Still bitter over his past treatment and to some extent separated from his old political friends, the duke of Newcastle semiretired from politics in 1856. He declined an invitation from Herbert to attend a pre-Parliament conference of Peelites early in the year primarily because of his divergence from his former colleagues on the subject of peace negotiations with Russia and because he was opposed to any meetings that were intended to keep up the notion of a Peelite party. Although he assured Aberdeen that no personal estrangement from any of his friends entered into the reasons for his conduct, the duke nonetheless found himself at political odds with Gladstone, Herbert, and Graham.[33] But he also had strong personal reasons for wanting to stay aloof from politics. Estate and family matters pressed in upon him, and he more assiduously turned his attention to Lady Frances Waldegrave, whom he hoped to marry when she was widowed once again.

After his return from the Crimea, the duke was regularly in the company of Lady Frances, and his affection for her was widely discussed in society. On 1 February 1856, she held an intimate dinner for him during which he regaled the guests with an account of the final assault on Sebastopol. In April she gave another dinner for him, this time a much larger party, to which she invited the Gladstones and several other leading political figures. During the party she "stood up to Gladstone about the Lucan case" by expressing her support of the general, whom she had visited almost daily at Chelsea Hospital during the hearings of the Board of General Officers. Gladstone deplored the reverence with which she treated the much-maligned Lucan. He remained quiet, however, during a heated discussion concerning the rude treatment of the Peelites at the Carlton, for he still harbored thoughts of joining Lord Derby and the Conservatives. Newcastle, on the other hand, expressed a fervent desire to try "the hardness of his fist" on the faces of some Conservatives.[34]

The gulf between Newcastle and his old Peelite friends, particularly Gladstone, widened during the rest of the year, even after the Treaty of Paris of March 1856 ended the Crimean War. The duke moved cautiously closer to

Fifth Duke of Newcastle, by George Richmond, 1856.
Courtesy of the National Portrait Gallery, London, by permission of the Trustees of the
late 7th Duke of Newcastle.

supporting Palmerston, while Aberdeen, Graham, Herbert, and Gladstone continued to fear the prime minister's foreign policy. In November the duke accepted Palmerston's offer of the lord-lieutenancy of Nottinghamshire, the office from which his father had been dismissed seventeen years before. Newcastle explained to Aberdeen that in accepting the office he had in no way sacrificed his political independence and that he did not entirely concur with Palmerston's foreign policy. Although skeptical of Newcastle's pledged independence, Aberdeen and Graham endorsed the duke's acceptance of the lord-lieutenancy. A refusal after his rejection of the Garter, Graham told Aberdeen, would have seemed "churlish." "But," he added, "the Scripture maxim is quite true as to Patronage, 'it is better to give than to receive.' The Minister always has the best of it in cases such as this." [35]

By the end of 1856, the Peelite party was thoroughly disorganized and nearly defunct. Both Graham and Aberdeen strove to keep Gladstone from joining the Conservative opposition under Derby, and to keep Cardwell and Newcastle from supporting Palmerston. But there was no apparent leader under whom the Peelites could rally. In the twilight of their careers, neither Graham nor Aberdeen wished to lead. Instead, they pressed the claims of Russell as a possible alternative to Derby and Palmerston. But holding up this shopworn political leader as the man to follow drove the younger Peelites into deeper confusion and despair.

Lord Aberdeen visited Newcastle at Clumber early in 1857 before the opening of the parliamentary session. He found the duke very hostile to Russell and not very friendly toward anyone. Writing to Gladstone, Aberdeen noted that the duke

> appears to be well satisfied with his local position, and believes that a great change respecting him has taken place in the opinion of the Country generally. He is not friendly to the Government, but I think still less so to the Conservatives. He evinced, as was natural, a good deal of personal animosity against Lord John. Although holding a language of comparative indifference to political matters, he always spoke as being identified with his old friends. Of yourself I need not say that he spoke as warmly as ever; but he seemed to think that your position in the country was greatly changed in consequence of the part taken by you during the war.

The duke also concurred with Aberdeen that Gladstone was risking great danger to his character and consistency by talking with Derby about political union. Any approach to Derby was out of the question, he believed, as long as Disraeli maintained his position within the Conservative party. [36]

Gladstone, of course, did not agree with Newcastle on these matters, and a few days before a scheduled meeting with Derby he told the duke that Palmerston was the worst possible prime minister. Newcastle strongly disagreed. He admitted that there were points in Palmerston's character that placed him below Russell in the scale of ministers; but the latter, he believed, would indisputedly bring a change for the worse if he were to replace Palmerston. "I see little in Lord John but the impersonation of low selfishness," he wrote; Russell was only an expedient politician, "as dangerous as Palmerston in his foreign policy tho' from a very different impulse and far more unsafe in all matters of domestic interest except perhaps Reform of Parliament." The duke saw in Derby the same political purpose that he saw in Russell. Therefore, at least for the present, he believed that there was no good alternative to the government, and he warned Gladstone that if they upset Palmerston but failed to form another government, Palmerston would return to power "with lessened strength for good but increased means for the perpetuation of that mischief for which you desire his removal."[37]

Disregarding Newcastle's strong warning, Gladstone, hoping to bring about the defeat of Palmerston's ministry and the reunion of the Peelites and Conservatives, negotiated with Derby and Disraeli early in February on resolutions attacking the government's budget. Consequently, Newcastle felt compelled to write to his friend once again:

> I must not leave you to suppose that I wish those who are nick-named
> Peelites to remain a separate body. I have long seen that our position was
> alternately useless and absolutely mischievous and I think you will remem-
> ber that 3 or 4 years ago I held this language and repudiated the name
> though proud of its original meaning. I said then that both Whigs and
> Peelites must merge in some broader combination if we were to act together
> and I also said and still maintain that the latter are far more liberal in all
> their principles than the former.

For this reason, he continued, they could never act continuously and honestly with the Derby party, and if they were to be of any further use to the country, they must retain or regain "the sympathy of the *sound* portion of the Liberal Party." He was convinced that Gladstone would have neither the confidence nor the good will of the rank and file of Derby's party and that they would openly break with him in less than a year.[38]

Gladstone was undaunted. Whiggism and Peelism, he replied to Newcastle, could never merge in a broader party as long as Palmerston was in charge and had the support of the country. He stood behind his agreement to join Disraeli against the budget, a proposal that reversed his 1853 budget by raising the duties on tea and sugar to relieve the wealthier classes from the income tax.[39] But the dual attack by former chancellors of the Exchequer was not enough, as the government won a narrow victory. A few days later, however, an unnatural combination of Radicals, Conservatives, Peelites, and a few Liberals defeated the government on the China issue. Wisely, Palmerston took his case to the people. The 1857 general election was a resounding victory for him and

Viscount Palmerston, by John Partridge, 1844–1845.
Courtesy of the National Portrait Gallery, London.

a rout of the Peelites and Radicals. The position of the Peelites who survived was more ambiguous than ever.

During the election, Palmerston asked the duke of Newcastle to go to China as a plenipotentiary with full powers of war or peace and with complete discretionary authority to negotiate with the Chinese government on terms drawn up by the British government. The queen particularly wanted Newcastle to accept the mission. "His conduct," she wrote of the duke to Clarendon, "has been ever since he left office—so judicious and prudent and forms a bright contrast (alas!) to that of most of his friends—that it would gratify the Queen much to see him undertake this (no doubt) arduous mission."[40] Aberdeen, however, was unusually scathing in his comment on the offer to his son Arthur Gordon. Palmerston the great war minister, he wrote, "was the other day obliged to go to the rejected Duke of Newcastle, and ask him to carry on a war for him at the other end of the world, singly and without assistance, although it was supposed he was unable to carry on the War with Russia, assisted by his colleagues."[41] Aberdeen need not have worried, for Newcastle had already declined the offer on the ground that for the present he did not want to leave his daughter, whom, with the help of Lady Waldegrave, he was launching into society. A month later he turned down another offer of the Garter, even though the queen very much wanted him to have it. Again, as with the first offer eighteen months previously, the duke felt honor bound to maintain his political independence.[42]

Newcastle did not consult his old Peelite friends on these matters, nor did they confer with him on the future course of the Peelites in Parliament. Gladstone and Graham, however, corresponded with the duke on the divorce bill in 1857, a matter that caused the greatest pain to the former. Newcastle, who strongly favored the bill, cautioned Gladstone not to take any step that might increase his unpopularity and excite the bitter spirit that had recently been expressed against him in the country.[43] Ignoring the duke's advice, Gladstone, believing that Parliament should not take upon itself the authority to determine religious and spiritual matters, fought the bill with holy wrath. As a result, he was taunted in the Commons for insincerity. His 1849 mission to Italy in pursuit of Lady Lincoln was recalled both in the House and in the press. It was apparent, according to the *Morning Post*, that he "would . . . deny to the poor that relief which he himself was the principal means of obtaining for a noble and wealthy colleague."[44]

Much to Gladstone's regret, the marriage and divorce bill became law despite his spirited battle against it. By permitting divorce and remarriage without special act of Parliament, the measure marked one more stage in the secularization of the state. To the duke the whole affair was a grim reminder of the past, coming at a time when he was increasingly apprehensive about his daughter, who he feared might follow the same path as her mother.

IV

The duke's endless domestic misfortunes had seriously affected his health and character. His fear that his children might inherit their mother's morals caused him to tyrannize over them. The eldest, Henry, Lord Lincoln, popularly called Linky, had already rebelled, spending his time and money on racing and gambling. His indecorous behavior increased the duke's determination to watch his daughter Susan even more carefully. Throughout the 1857 season he regularly took her on his visits to Lady Frances Waldegrave at Nuneham, Strawberry Hill, or Carlton Gardens, for he was most anxious that she get to know and like Lady Frances. To his delight, Susan's devotion to Frances soon almost equaled his own. Lady Waldegrave returned the affection.

Lady Waldegrave thought highly of the duke's political abilities, and she ardently hoped to see him premier of a future Liberal administration. With Russell's unpopularity in the country and Gladstone's inclination to join the Conservatives, she viewed Newcastle as the likeliest successor to Palmerston, and she worked fervently to achieve that goal. During one of her Strawberry Hill parties in June, she took all her guests across the river by boat to Pembroke Lodge in an attempt to reconcile the duke and Lord John; she partially succeeded.[45] That autumn she and her husband visited Newcastle at Clumber. Abraham Hayward and John D. Cooke, a former editor of the *Morning Chronicle* and founder in 1855 of the *Saturday Review*, also were guests at the party. It was a perfect opportunity for Lady Waldegrave to obtain the great influence of the *Saturday Review*, with its staff of brilliant writers, and of Hayward, whose articles in the *Quarterly*, the *Edinburgh Review*, and *Fraser's* commanded enormous respect, on behalf of her protégé. Hayward, perhaps the best informed man politically of his time, was already in the duke's camp, and Lady Waldegrave's success with Cooke was phenomenal. A few weeks later she boasted to Lady Clarendon, "Lady Palmerston and I are two Delilahs. She has cut the hair of *The Times*, and I of the *Saturday*."[46] Thus the "Peelite hostess" pursued her plan for the promotion of Newcastle to the Liberal premiership.

For a brief time Newcastle enjoyed good health and was again in fine spirits. Early in October he and Susan visited Aberdeen at Haddo House. He was, Aberdeen told Graham, "very friendly and cordial," believing with the reported illness of Lord Canning that his appointment to India was still possible.[47] Chichester Fortescue recorded in his diary a month later, "The Duke says (to Lady Waldegrave) 'He has been leading the hounds better than he did at five and twenty, and almost persuades himself he is as young as she sometimes tries to convince him he is,' referring, she said, to her advice to him to marry a young woman. I believe it meant more than that." Lady Waldegrave had tried hard during the summer and autumn of 1857 to marry the duke to

Miss "J. L.," whose identity is now unknown.[48] But as Fortescue feared, Newcastle was determined to wait until Lady Waldegrave was widowed again before making a move toward marriage.

Whether or not he could lead the hounds "better than he did at five and twenty," the duke while out hunting late in November 1857 dislocated his left shoulder in a bad fall from his horse. It was some time before he could use his arm again. John Cooke was quite alarmed over the duke's accident: "For Heaven's sake, take great care of yourself, and be sure to avoid cold, or we shall have you laid up, when we can so ill spare you in the present very critical state of public affairs." A very anxious and serious session of Parliament was about to begin, he noted, and he did not think Palmerston could survive the dangers of finance, reform, India, China, and national distress. "Do, therefore, take the greatest care of your . . . health, for I have not, or has the *Saturday Review*, the least intention to let you escape office if Pam goes, and I think he must, to pot."[49]

Newcastle had predicted shortly after the general election that Palmerston would soon come to grief in the new Parliament. Therefore, he was not surprised when the government was defeated on 19 February 1858 on the second reading of the conspiracy to murder bill. Palmerston had introduced the measure in order to strengthen the law after the attempted assassination of the French emperor and empress by a man who used bombs made in England. Palmerston for once had badly misjudged public sentiment, and Peelites, Radicals, and Conservatives joined to defeat the government by 234 votes to 215 for truckling to the French. Palmerston resigned the following day. The duke wrote to Hayward as soon as he received the news at Clumber, begging Hayward to send him the latest gossip: "Being only an outside passenger, I shall not go to Town but as a looker-on I am *still* interested."[50]

On the same day, 21 February, Newcastle also wrote a long letter to Aberdeen in London expressing his concern over the ministerial crisis and the prospect of Peelite consultations:

> As your library will sure to be [sic] filled with once familiar faces during the next few days, and consultations as of old may be held there, I think it may not be otherwise than convenient for me to let you know that happening to be out of town when the crash has come, I do not propose to go into it till the dust has blown away.
>
> As I have never been taken into Council by my old friends in the Commons since you and I quitted office, I should not wish to appear to thrust my opinion upon them now, and still less to make myself responsible for any decision they may come to in the not improbable contingency of their being asked to take part in the new arrangements.
>
> Do not suppose I put this in the way of complaint. I only state a fact. I never felt that I had any prescriptive right to continue in the Councils of my

friends, and perhaps, when so much odium and unpopularity fell to my
share, they were wise not to encumber themselves with me.

Since he was not wanted in the Peelite council and since he was not a candidate
for any office, he would not come to town, unless Aberdeen were called upon
to form a government. In that case he was ready to help to any extent in his
power. "I need hardly to say," he concluded, "I am writing in ignorance of
everything beyond Lord Palmerston's resignation. I presume Derby will be
sent for, and my opinion is that he will *form a* Government. The Whigs will
soon rally round Johnny, but at this moment I do not see where is his material." [51]

But before the ink was dry on the stationery, a special messenger surprised
Newcastle with a letter from Derby asking him to come to town to confer
concerning office. Although the duke in reply virtually declined the offer of
office, he agreed to meet with Derby in London the following day. The interview led to nothing, even though Derby had asked the queen herself to try to
persuade Newcastle to join him in the new government. [52] Politically, the duke
was wise not to bind himself to an administration that could not last long,
particularly as Gladstone also refused to join. Whatever they might think of
Derby, neither man could tolerate Disraeli as leader of the House of Commons.

V

Lady Waldegrave also saw that the Derby government could not last long.
In the spring of 1858 she set out to unify the divided Liberal ranks and to
promote Newcastle as the next prime minister. She worked to reconcile Clarendon and Russell and to stop Gladstone's backsliding toward the Conservatives. Upon her urging, Abraham Hayward and John Cooke also were busy
on the duke's behalf. Hayward implored Newcastle to be a modern-day Cin-
cinnatus, ready at a moment's notice to exchange the plow for the helm.
Cooke informed Newcastle in May 1859 that he hoped the duke would be
the next prime minister, and in the way of promotion, he stated that he would
have "a go" at him in the *Saturday Review*. Although he would feign to be
impartial, he would deal with him "as Walton did with the worms—put the
hook into you as if I loved you, but still put the hook in." [53]

Goldwin Smith also urged Newcastle to end his political isolation. Following the duke's appearance in the Lords in May 1858 in support of Canning's
policy of clemency in the aftermath of the Indian Mutiny, Smith encouraged
the duke to resume his role in politics and national affairs: "Let me venture to
express my earnest hope that having once returned to Parliament you will stay
there, instead of going to Clumber again." The duke, being a man of high
character and independent position, Smith observed, could perform a great

service by vindicating "English political life from the reckless aspersions that have been cast upon it." He could help restore a "more gentlemanly tone" in the debates of Parliament and in the conduct of the country's business.[54]

By this time, the duke had in fact recovered his appetite for politics, and he took an active part in the debates during the rest of the session. He supported such causes as the abolition of property qualification for membership in Parliament, the establishment of an agency with substantial powers to deal with the deplorable state of the Thames, and the constitution of a new government for New Caledonia. Although he favored the principle of abolition, he voted against the church rates abolition bill because it failed to provide a substitute for the rates.[55]

During the course of 1858, other matters gradually drew Newcastle back into public life. The duke became chairman of the Royal Commission on Education, despite his belief that Sir John Pakington's motion for the appointment of such a commission was carried with the understanding on all sides that it was to be an "imposture."[56] He accepted the task only after Lord Salisbury, lord president of the council, agreed to place on the commission those members whom the duke recommended. Newcastle immediately asked for the appointment of Goldwin Smith, the Rev. William Charles Lake, and Sir John Coleridge. Since the difficulty over religion had been the greatest impediment to all former plans of education, the duke requested that the commission not be dominated by the Church of England. He insisted that representatives from the secular interests and the Nonconformist denominations be included in the appointments.[57]

Newcastle was granted most of what he wanted, and in the summer of 1858 the commission began its task of inquiring into the state of popular education in England and of recommending measures for the extension of sound and cheap elementary instruction to all classes. As a basis for comparison, the commission sent assistant commissioners to inquire into the operation of schools in other countries as well as in England. Matthew Arnold, for instance, was sent to report on the French, Dutch, and Swiss systems. Unfortunately, the commissioners had little means of judging the efficiency of private schools, and they largely ignored charity and poor-law schools. Still, extensive information was gathered.

After much consultation, deliberation, and argument, with Newcastle performing well his role as moderator, the commission issued its report in 1861. Although it was estimated that only 4.5 percent of school-age children did not attend school, the commissioners found that most working-class children left school at the age of eleven without receiving systematic training and with few learned skills, even elementary ones. Only one child in twenty among the poorer classes received any education after the age of thirteen. To counter these problems, the commission recommended the establishment of local boards of education with the power to levy rates, to examine children in reading, writing, and arithmetic, and to pay grants to the schools based on the results of those tests. The commission did not recommend compulsory education or establishing a school-leaving age, nor did the commissioners suggest that the school boards have authority over the appointment of teachers or the right to interfere with the management of schools. Thus the commissioners skirted the issues of religion and compulsion, questions on which they disagreed.[58]

Not all the commission's recommendations were adopted, and some that were adopted were effected in ways the commissioners had not intended. Palmerston's last government, which was in office when the report was issued and of which the duke was a member, was unwilling to face the sectarian storm over local school rates. The government, therefore, did not establish the local school boards recommended by the commission, but Robert Lowe, head of the Education Department, endorsed the principle of payment by results and tied it to the existing system of national inspection. To the economy-minded government and nation, Lowe's Revised Code of 1862 was the cheapest way of ending the neglect of the rudiments of education. During the next decade, the system of payment by results raised the standards of the worst schools but defeated all endeavors to improve elementary education at all levels.

The Newcastle Commission's recommendations had been too far in advance of public opinion in England. It would take the world-wide events of the 1860s to convince the English public of the need for a national system of education that would incorporate and extend some of the basic recommendations of the 1858–1861 Royal Commission on Education. It was appropriate, however, that Gladstone's Liberal government in 1870 incorporated at least some of the progressive steps delineated by the Newcastle Commission nearly a decade earlier.

The Education Commission was not the only public matter that captured Newcastle's attention during the last part of 1858. From his convalescent bed in October 1858, where he was recovering from smallpox, Newcastle advised Gladstone, who had sought his advice, to accept Lord Derby's offer to go to the Ionian Islands as a special commissioner to report on the constitution and the state of the Protectorate.[59] Gladstone undertook the mission with the hope of perpetuating the British Protectorate over the islands through constitutional reforms. But the strong Ionian desire to join Greece doomed his mission from the start, and Newcastle, along with the majority of the Peelites and many of the Liberals, criticized Gladstone for assuming the office of lord high commissioner for the Ionian Islands soon after his arrival there. The duke regretted his friend's course of action, which he described as an act of self-immolation that did no compensating good to the public.[60] After the Ionian Assembly rejected his reform proposals, Gladstone, deeply disappointed, surrendered his office and returned to England in 1859.

Gladstone reached England in time to participate in the debate over the government's parliamentary reform measure. On 31 March 1859, the government was defeated on the bill, and Derby dissolved Parliament immediately. In the general election that followed, the Conservatives gained about thirty seats, but the government remained a minority. Nonetheless, with the opposition badly divided, it appeared as if Derby could continue indefinitely. Newcastle certainly thought so, as he told Lady Waldegrave:

> My belief is there will be no motion to remove the Govt. which will suc-
> ceed, because honest men (I do not mean the extreme men) feel that they
> have a right to know before they displace one Govt. whether a *stronger* can
> be formed, and even if Palmerston and Lord John Russell can come to
> any agreement (& this seems doubtful) they see on all sides amongst the
> *junior* Whigs so much selfishness and intrigue that they can place no reliance
> upon what is to come.[61]

The duke, however, was wrong. Derby resigned on 10 June following the defeat of the ministers on a confidence motion in the Commons. The queen, unable to decide between Russell and Palmerston, considered the merits of three other men, Granville, Clarendon, and Newcastle. All were favorites at Windsor, with the first two particularly liked by the queen, and Newcastle by Prince Albert, who had even wept in sympathy with the duke's continued domestic misfortunes.[62] When Granville failed to form an administration, however, the queen summoned Palmerston, who returned to power at age seventy-five.

Newcastle was again asked to join the cabinet. Although the queen preferred him to the duke of Somerset for the Admiralty, Palmerston thought the latter was abler and more energetic, and feared that "the clamour raised, though unjustly," against Newcastle about the defective arrangements for the army in 1854 might be revived if he were put at the head of the Naval Department.[63] Thus Newcastle was offered the position of colonial secretary, which he accepted after Palmerston assured him that the government would introduce a political reform measure, the details of which were to be open for discussion in the cabinet, and that no measures affecting foreign relations would be taken until they had been approved by the cabinet.[64] Chichester Fortescue also returned to the Colonial Office as under-secretary. Palmerston probably took malicious pleasure in placing the two great rivals for Lady Waldegrave's hand in the same office. It was an amusing situation for everyone except the two individuals most concerned.[65]

13. *Colonial Secretary*

From cramped quarters in a pair of dilapidated seventeenth-century buildings at numbers 13 and 14 Downing Street, the duke of Newcastle directed the colonial affairs of Great Britain from late 1852 to mid 1854 and again from mid 1859 to the spring of 1864. He was well suited for the Colonial Office. Since the late 1840s he had taken a keen interest in the empire and had studied it extensively. He was particularly interested in the possibility of promoting emigration to the colonies as a means of removing and assisting the unemployed population of Ireland, and he was an active member of the Canterbury Association, which had colonized part of New Zealand. Although he was not a member of the Colonial Reform Society, he largely concurred with the society's views. His severe criticism of Earl Grey's policies and his opposition to convict transportation had marked him as one of the most zealous advocates of a liberal colonial policy.

During his second tenure at the Colonial Office, Newcastle was assisted by several capable men, including Sir Frederic Rogers, later Lord Blachford, the permanent under-secretary; Henry Taylor and Thomas Frederick Elliot, assistant under-secretaries; and Chichester Fortescue, parliamentary under-secretary. Rogers was a very intelligent administrator who would become one of the greatest civil servants of the Victorian era. Taylor also had great intellectual prowess and was highly respected by both superiors and subordinates. Elliot, although lacking the brilliance of Rogers and Taylor, was experienced and painstaking. Fortescue, who handled colonial affairs during the duke's absence in British North America and the United States in 1860, played an increasingly important role at the Colonial Office late in 1863 and early 1864 when the duke's health deteriorated. Newcastle, however, placed little confidence in him, and he was passed over in favor of Edward Cardwell when the duke resigned in 1864.

The relationship of these men to the duke was generally one of polite reserve. Their opinions of him were influenced by differences in social rank and temperament. Rogers, for example, although an impressive administrator, was egocentric, somewhat overconfident, and overly critical. He described Newcastle as a thorough gentleman who had moderate abilities and inflated ambitions, but who readily accepted the conclusions of subordinates and was clear in his own direction. The duke also was careful "never to throw back on a subordinate any shadow of responsibility for advice that he has once accepted," a characteristic Rogers respected highly. The duke was, Rogers continued, dilatory about patronage and indecisive when faced with conflicting advice. "He seems to hesitate at making the plunge, and goes on letting the idea simmer in his mind."[1] Although Rogers did not suggest it, the duke's administrative habits were typically Peelite.

Although some nineteenth-century colonial secretaries may have been more efficient administrators, few were as sympathetic and benevolent in their attitude toward colonial affairs as the duke. He represented a new spirit in the Colonial Office. Early in 1860 he urged Palmerston to include a favorable reference to the colonies at the opening of the parliamentary session: "The Colonies have rarely been mentioned in a Queen's Speech, unless when they have incurred a censure for some rebellious indication. I cannot but think it would be wise to introduce the innovation of a little praise and sympathy, and I am sure it would gratify them much." Palmerston agreed, and in her speech the queen stated that she was gratified to observe the spirit of loyalty and contentment that prevailed throughout her empire.[2]

Newcastle was on friendly terms with several colonial governors, and in his private correspondence with them he left the impression of punctiliousness and politeness.[3] Many of the governors appreciated his kindness and personal attention. In 1869 George Higinbotham, the attorney general of state of Victoria, expressed what many others remembered about the duke:

> It would be fortunate, not only for these colonies, but for England, I believe, if other Secretaries of State were men of the same rank of class and character. The distinguishing characteristics of the despatches of that nobleman is their perfect straight-forwardness, simplicity and sincerity. He was always able to speak his mind without reserve, and at the same time, so far as I know, without giving offence on a single occasion. He spoke explicitly, but with such real and hearty good will, as to disarm even the strongest expressions of any offensive or disagreeable effect.[4]

In the estimation of such Canadian leaders as Francis Hincks and Joseph Howe, it was the duke's "singular sweetness of manner, nobleness of mien and earnest amiability, more than any broad or bold range of policy" that made him the most popular minister ever to occupy the Colonial Office chair. Likewise, the absence of those attributes made Lord Grey, "with all his vigorous energy and sound Colonial views, personally the most unpopular."[5]

During a time when a new concept of empire was slowly evolving, it was indeed fortunate for Great Britain and the colonies that Newcastle presided over the Colonial Office for over six and a half years. Through good will and farsightedness, he contributed significantly to the process of nation building overseas within the framework of the British empire.

II

Shortly after Newcastle returned to the Colonial Office in 1859, a special envoy from the Canadian legislature arrived in England with an invitation to the queen to visit her subjects in North America and to dedicate the Victoria Bridge on the St. Lawrence River at Montreal. Although she declined the offer for herself, the queen agreed to be represented by her eldest son, the prince of Wales. She accepted the suggestion that the royal state visit be extended to include all the North American provinces, and she also accepted an invitation from President Buchanan for the prince to pay a private visit to the United States. Early in 1860 the court arranged for Newcastle to accompany the prince as an official adviser and leader of the entourage.

The prince and his party, including the duke, Lord St. Germans (the lord steward), and General Bruce (the prince's governor), sailed from Plymouth aboard the *Hero* on 10 July 1860 and reached St. John's, Newfoundland, on 23 July. Large crowds turned out to greet the nineteen-year-old prince, who, in almost perpetual motion over the next few days, received addresses at levees, inspected local companies of the Volunteers, rode horseback into the country, and attended luncheons, dinners, and balls. Newcastle, wearing the scarlet uniform with silver facings of a lord lieutenant, bedecked in diplomatic colors and glittering with decorations, stood by the side of the prince at the levee in St. John's.[6] While the people were enthusiastic, the press was complimentary in reflecting upon the importance of the prince's visit. The *Royal Gazette* (Newfoundland), for instance, stated that the visit foreshadowed a new era about to dawn upon the colonies. With strengthened ties of loyalty binding them closer to the mother country, the colonies henceforth would be looked upon "as integral portions of the British Empire."[7]

After three days in Newfoundland, the prince and his party went on to Halifax, and from there to St. John, New Brunswick, and then to Fredericton. After a short visit to Charlottetown on Prince Edward's Island, they sailed up the Gulf of St. Lawrence to Gaspé Bay, where they were met by Sir Edmund Head, the governor-general of Canada, who escorted them to his house near Quebec, where they stayed for five days before going on to Montreal. Everywhere the crowds were large and the prince was received with enthusiastic loyalty.[8]

It appeared that the prince had completely won the hearts of the people, but news foreboding trouble reached the duke at Ottawa early in September. The extreme Protestant Orange Society threatened to demonstrate during the prince's visits to Kingston and Toronto. The duke immediately remonstrated with Sir Edmund Head, but to no avail. Upon arrival at Kingston on 4 September, the duke could see from the deck of the ship that the main street up which the prince was to pass was completely occupied by an immense force of Orangemen with a band and that at the top of the street the arch under which the prince was to pass was covered with "devices the most offensive to the Roman Catholic population."[9] After failing to resolve the matter with the mayor, Newcastle gave orders the next morning to weigh anchor and proceed to Belleville at the head of the Bay of Quinté. But the Orangemen at Belleville, inspired to action by members of the Kingston society, decorated the arches and streets with emblems and banners. Again, both on colonial and imperial grounds, the duke made a stand, realizing, as he told Palmerston, that many would condemn him on both sides of the Atlantic.[10]

Both Palmerston and the queen strongly endorsed Newcastle's action. They believed that he had handled the affair of the Orangemen adroitly, and both were pleased with the reception given to the prince. It was fortunate, Palmerston responded, that the prince "had with him a good Head like yours," and although the duke undoubtedly felt a great strain on mind and body, he would, Palmerston thought, be satisfied that his sacrifice of personal comfort in going with the prince would promote the interests of both the empire and the royal family. The queen was also pleased with the duke's reports of the prince's excellent demeanor. She and Prince Albert, she told the duke, realized that the trip was a great trial for the prince of Wales, and both were very pleased with the excursion.[11]

At Toronto the prince was again enthusiastically welcomed by huge crowds, though there was one minor incident at the "Orange Arch," from which was hung a transparency of William III. The duke protested vehemently and pursued the matter to a showdown with the mayor and other city authorities. Although he regretted that the prince was subjected to the annoyance of being made a party to religious and political struggle, Newcastle told Palmerston that he was sure the prince had lost nothing by it and had gained a useful lesson. "The whole affair," he wrote, "has created a great stir both in Canada and the United States, and the newspapers are full of it." The general tone of the provincial press, he added, "is satisfaction at the Orangemen being beaten, but they have not courage to back me warmly."[12]

The following day in London, Ontario, both the prince and the duke were warmly cheered; it was "the first time," the duke observed to Palmerston, that "my name has been noticed throughout the journey."[13] The trouble with the Orangemen was over, and the duke was satisfied that he had contributed to the future good of Canada by teaching the respectable majority not to be afraid of a violent and overbearing minority. The strain on him, however, had been tremendous. Often his health had been near the breaking point. But he refused to leave his post even for an hour, and, he confided to Lady Waldegrave, "the result was the triumph of will over head and stomach and heart and nerves." Although he did not expect public credit for it, privately he knew that his zealous attention to every detail of the trip had "conduced to the éclat with which the Prince has left the Colonies."[14]

Newcastle pronounced the tour "a most remarkable success." He was convinced that it had done immense good by cementing the North American colonies to the crown of Great Britain for many years to come. It had shown other nations how useless it would be in case of war to tamper with the allegiance of the North American provinces, had raised the level of national consciousness among the colonists, and had drawn them closer together in a spirit of generosity and cooperation. And, the duke told the queen, it had strengthened monarchy and contributed significantly to the development of the prince's own abilities.[15]

On 20 September 1860, the party crossed into the United States at Windsor. From Detroit, the prince and suite traveled to Chicago; after two days' shooting in the prairies of Illinois, they went on to St. Louis, where the annual agricultural fair was in progress. Each city held an enormous crowd of curious people straining to get a glimpse of the prince. Occasionally, the prince was exposed to a bit more roughness of manner than he was accustomed to, but on the whole he was impressed by the kindly spirit with which he was received.

From St. Louis the party traveled eastward through Cincinnati, Pittsburgh, Washington, and Philadelphia to New York City. Newcastle was most impressed with President Buchanan's reception at the White House and with the enthusiasm of the five or six hundred thousand people who assembled in New York City to honor the prince. Still elated over the American reception, the duke wrote to Palmerston from New York to say that they would leave the United States "a faster friend to our country than they have been since their separation."[16] Although the duke exaggerated the depth and permanence of the good impression produced by the prince's visit to the United States, it was fortunate for Great Britain that during the crisis that followed the outbreak of the American Civil War in 1861 there was a reserve of good will left by the prince's visit of the previous year. The duke's knowledge of the personalities and politics of the American continent acquired during the tour was also invaluable to his government during the period of strained relations with the United States.

The prince and his party visited West Point and Albany before going on to Boston and then to Portland, where they embarked for England on 20 October. Among Newcastle's friends there was a sense of relief; they were happy that the "evil genius" that dogged him throughout his life had stayed at home. "I am so glad the Prince of Wales has arrived," Emily Eden exclaimed. "I always thought they would have to put Jonah, Duke of Newcastle, overboard before the ship could make any way." King Leopold of Belgium also was surprised that "the poor Duke of Newcastle got home without accident."[17] The queen was delighted with the success of the tour, and, without waiting for a vacancy to occur, she offered the Garter to the duke to express her appreciation publicly for his services.[18] A vacancy was not long in coming. On 14 December 1860, the duke received the sad news of the death of Lord Aberdeen. It was a fitting touch to the duke's life to receive the Collar of the Order of the Garter formerly worn by his late friend and political associate.

III

Newcastle took the Colonial Office in 1859 at a time when the whole question of empire was under extensive examination. The mounting economic and political attacks upon the old colonial system during the early Victorian period had produced a general review of the constitutional structure of the empire and had forced a debate in the country on the purpose and future of the colonies. The acceptance of a free-trade commercial policy in Great Britain had undermined the rationale for colonies inherent in the mercantilistic economic system and had caused an increasing number of British taxpayers to demand relief from the financial burdens of colonial government. And the increased colonial resentments of the paternalistic strictures of the old system, as witnessed in the Canadian Rebellion of 1837, reinforced the belief that British settlement colonies (predominantly white colonies) were developing nations that would mature and eventually become self-governing. Together, economic changes and political reality produced a liberalizing climate of opinion in England toward the empire. By the 1850s the administrators and politicians had endorsed self-government and greater self-reliance in the more politically advanced settlement colonies as solutions to the problems caused by economic and political changes.

Although his views on colonial self-government and self-reliance were extremely liberal, Newcastle was still a decided imperialist at a time when the separatist opinion reached its height. He believed that the colonies could be retained "by bonds of mutual sympathy and mutual obligation,"[19] and throughout his tenure as colonial secretary he was more concerned with colonial welfare and security than with British convenience and selfish interests. "If any fault is to be found with his administration," the *Times* noted shortly after the duke's death,

> it will certainly not be on the ground of harshness or repression, but rather
> that he has carried the desire to conciliate and avoid every possible cause
> of collision between the mother country and the colonies to an extent which
> may result in the advancement of claims and pretensions to which it will
> not always be possible to yield.[20]

Although Newcastle proclaimed in 1862 that the attachment between Great Britain and her colonies was strong enough to endure any efforts to sever them, there were "theoretical gentlemen," as Palmerston called them, in the Colonial Office who, like the separatists, believed in the inevitability of imperial disintegration. "I had always believed," Sir Frederic Rogers wrote, "that the destiny of our colonies is independence; and that in this point of view the function of the Colonial Office is to secure that our connection, while it lasts, shall be as profitable to both parties, and our separation, when it comes, as amicable as possible." In 1864 Henry Taylor told the duke that "our American possessions were a sort of *damnosa haereditas*." He regretted that the duke and the prince of Wales during their visit to North America in 1860 had so successfully conciliated the colonists and tightened their bond to Great Britain.[21]

But separatism, the anti-imperialism of the Radical Manchester School of John Bright and Richard Cobden, neither became the majority opinion in Britain nor governed the actions of the ministers. Even Rogers and Taylor in the Colonial Office thought more in terms of loosening imperial ties than of dismembering the empire, and they, like the duke himself, were far too busy dealing with the problems of empire as they arose to develop a consistent policy either of separation or retention of the colonies. The introduction of responsible government had left many undefined spheres of responsibility, such as control of commercial policy, conduct of native affairs, colonial contributions to imperial defense, and the limitations on colonial and imperial legislation. In meeting these problems, the Colonial Office under Newcastle adopted a liberal policy of advocating the minimum of interference in colonial affairs. It was an attitude that allowed the maximum of nation-building within the framework of the empire. This attitude and the duke's liberal view of empire provided many valuable precedents for the eventual transition from empire to Commonwealth.[22]

IV

While interest in the empire quickened in the country, Parliament remained generally indifferent to the colonies during most of the 1860s. Newcastle faced little difficulty in the Commons, where Palmerston was a strong and popular defender of colonial policy, and only moderate difficulty in the Lords, where Earls Derby and Grey and Lord Taunton showed the most critical interest in colonial affairs and policy. Discussions in the cabinet on colonial matters were quite infrequent, and Newcastle's communications with ministerial colleagues concerning the empire were relatively sparse. The duke, therefore, was virtually free from either ministerial guidance or hindrance on most matters affecting the empire.[23]

However, occasional difficulties occurred between the Colonial Office and other departments. Newcastle did more than any of his immediate predecessors to assert and maintain the position of the Colonial Office relative to the other departments, which in the past had been overbearing and frequently condescending.[24] During the early 1860s, Newcastle carried on an extended argument with the War Office over the size of the military forces and over obtaining arms for colonial forces. He blamed most of his difficulties with the War Office on John Robert Godley, the under-secretary of state for war, who was intent upon reducing Britain's military commitments and forces throughout the world. But Newcastle's greatest difficulty came from his old nemesis, the Treasury, which was once again under the direction of Gladstone. Frequently the duke found it necessary to remonstrate with Gladstone about the "improper conduct" of the Treasury in resisting or even vetoing Colonial Office plans. In 1862 he stated that the Treasury's "assumption of right to interfere in the *policy* of the Colonial Department" could never "be submitted to without very evil consequences."[25] At least in matters of "piddling economy," Newcastle began to take upon himself the responsibility for requisitions by presenting *faits accompli* to the Treasury.[26]

One of Newcastle's last communications with the Treasury was over the status of colonial governors. Under the duke's direction a new professional class of civilian colonial governors began to emerge. Men of talent and long service were sought, especially those who had "shown a specialité for the government of mankind."[27] His list of applicants was always long, and he often had to put experienced men "on the shelf" for lack of openings. The problem became increasingly critical, and shortly before he resigned from office, Newcastle wrote to Gladstone in an attempt to obtain a pension for retired or unemployed governors of long service.[28] The Treasury moved slowly on the matter; not until 1865 was an act finally passed to provide modest pensions for governors of at least twenty years' service.

Fundamental differences of opinion over imperial policy also produced periodic confrontations between the Colonial and Foreign offices. Twice during Newcastle's second tenure at the Colonial Office, diplomatic rather than colonial considerations guided the British government in decisions affecting the empire. Newcastle and the Colonial Office played almost no part in the cession either of the Bay Islands to Honduras or the Ionian Islands to Greece. In each case, the decision was made in the Foreign Office without prior consultation with the Colonial Office.

The case of the Bay Islands caused much friction between the two offices. Early in 1860 the Foreign Office abruptly informed the Colonial Office that the islands were to be ceded to Honduras in order to improve Anglo-American relations. The announcement caught Newcastle and his staff completely by surprise and elicited from them a strongly worded protest against the proposed treaty of cession. Lord John Russell, the Foreign Secretary, immediately returned the letter to the Colonial Office with the comment that it was "hardly decent." Responding heatedly, Newcastle stated that it was not only decent but right and necessary for the Colonial Secretary to express his objections to terms of a treaty that seriously affected the British guarantees of liberty and free institutions to the people of the Bay Islands.[29] The Foreign Office stood firmly behind its decision, explaining that the Bay Islands colony, established in 1852 in violation of the Clayton-Bulwer Treaty, was a great source of tension with the United States. Although the duke again protested against the way in which the Colonial Office had been ignored on the matter, he could not reverse the decision. Late in March he expressed to the Bay Islanders, who had objected to the cession, the crown's great regret that "paramount motives of State Policy" had necessitated the separation.[30]

Similarly, the Ionian Islands were ceded to Greece in 1864 for diplomatic reasons. The islands were ceded on the conditions that Greece accept constitutional monarchy, fill the vacant throne with a king acceptable to Britain, and pledge not to undertake any aggressive measures against Turkey.[31] Newcastle accepted the cession, although he did not attend the cabinet on 8 December 1862, which endorsed the terms under which the cession of the islands would be made, for Russell had not informed him that the object of the cabinet was to take up the subject of the Ionian Islands.[32] Newcastle's absence from the cabinet, however, was not particularly critical, for Palmerston knew that the duke had long favored the transfer of the islands to Greece provided that the fortifications at Corfu were demolished to prevent them from falling into the hands of France or Russia in time of war. Thus there was no interdepartmental difficulty over this matter.

The lack of interdepartmental conflict concerning the transfer of the Ionian Islands was more than made up by arguments over policies in West Africa. The British colonies in that part of the world, consisting of Gambia, Sierra Leone, and the Gold Coast, produced more conflict among the principal departments of state than any other region of the empire. The Treasury under Gladstone demanded the greatest economy in the administration of the three West African colonies. On the other hand, the Foreign Office under Russell insisted upon the forceful use of British power on the coast to secure and to extend trade in the region. The Foreign Office also advocated the annexation of Lagos and the unification of the governments of the three colonies. Assailed from both sides, Newcastle and the Colonial Office attempted to chart a course for West Africa that, although closer to the Treasury's position, was between the two extremes. The duke opposed unifying the colonial governments or annexing Lagos; he favored keeping British territory to a minimum and restricting British interference in the internal affairs of the neighboring African states. He also advocated the strictest economy.[33]

Contrary to the views of territorial expansion and colonial federation that he developed in regard to the settlement colonies, Newcastle generally opposed extension of territory in the tropical colonies unless there were overriding strategic, commercial, or philanthropic reasons. For the most part, the duke accepted extension in the nonsettlement colonies only if the expansion was likely to help maintain peace and security, to promote the welfare of indigenous peoples, or to achieve economic retrenchment. Normally, expansion in these colonies meant heavy expenditure from London and conflict with indigenous peoples; therefore, Newcastle opposed most applications for extension of territory in the tropics, including West Africa.[34]

Newcastle realized that his policy in West Africa was contradictory. While insisting upon strict economy and the confinement of British interests, he was willing to permit some extensions of territory to counter the slave trade, which to him was the prime reason for maintaining a British presence in an unhealthy, unprofitable region. He also believed that it was necessary to exercise force occasionally against uncooperative chiefs to maintain British influence in the region. Nevertheless, in 1861 the duke concluded that the governors were becoming too fond of expeditions against the "barbarous chiefs" and that the suppression of the slave trade was leading Britain into serious territorial complications on the coast of West Africa.[35]

Still, the pattern in West Africa remained the same for the next two years. The governors felt compelled by the instability of the region to intervene in the internal areas to settle disputes among the native African tribes and to annex small, apparently insignificant, territories in order to suppress the slave trade or to prevent them from falling into French or Portuguese hands. Newcastle reluctantly accepted these "insignificant" extensions of territory and occasionally sanctioned military expeditions against refractory chiefs who were mistreating British merchants. He sensed the helplessness of his position, and he believed that his only recourse was to urge the governors to use "moral influence" where they could and to warn them that the home government had no intention of adding to the civil and military estimates for West Africa.[36]

Faced with such a situation, the West African governors were not inclined to heed Newcastle's caution. Even at home in the cabinet, the duke met opposition to his policy of limiting British expansion in West Africa. He found the pressure of Lords Russell and Palmerston for the annexation of Lagos too great to overcome. Russell believed that the annexation of Lagos was necessary to protect the population from the slave traders, to develop the important trade of the area, and to exercise an influence on the surrounding tribes that he hoped would be permanently beneficial to the African people. Palmerston hoped that assuming direct British sovereignty would preclude French interference and promote stability, and he was particularly interested in encouraging the cultivation of cotton in West Africa for export to Great Britain.[37]

Unable to prevent the annexation of Lagos, Newcastle attempted to limit the dangers of the move. He tried to scale down the philanthropic program of the Foreign Office. Regarding the new colony merely as a naval rendezvous and commercial entrepot rather than as a base of operations against inland slavery, the duke enjoined the new governor, H. S. Freeman, not to engage in hostilities except in self-defense without permission from the Colonial Office.[38] Responding to the governor's request for more troops to restore peace in the area, the duke noted categorically:

> You must distinctly understand that if you can not prevent native Tribes from destroying each other, even within a few miles of Lagos, without involving the British Government in war, you must not resort to armed interference to prevent the consequences of their own barbarous habits. In the present instance I should be very glad to hear that you had been able to terminate the war between the Egbas and the Ibadans by moral influence.[39]

Although the duke never defined "moral influence," he preferred it to "chastisement" of the tribes. If they were to retain the questionable possession of Lagos, he noted on one of Freeman's dispatches, they must resort to means other than "bush fighting."[40]

But despite the duke's efforts, the same pattern was followed in Lagos as elsewhere on the western coast of Africa: the intervention by British arms between warring tribes. "Where was it to end?," Thomas Frederick Elliot asked at the Colonial Office. The British had enlightened motives, but, he warned the duke, "We are insensibly sliding into a new policy . . . of trying to stop the slave trade by means of soldiers instead of sailors."[41] The duke was quite aware of the situation. In August 1863, when British commitments had become greatly extended, Newcastle prohibited any further expansion. Although he admitted privately that he had "little hope of permanently averting this mischief [intermeddling by force of arms]," he was determined to make every effort to do so. In the future, he told the West African governors, the Colonial Office would prohibit all extensions of territory and veto all plans for military intervention.[42]

Newcastle's doctrine was relatively successful in Sierra Leone and Gambia, but it led to unfortunate consequences in the Gold Coast. Even as the Colonial Office was working out its new policy against expansion and interference, the powerful Ashanti king was preparing for war against the Fanti tribes and their British allies in that colony. In April 1863, the Ashantis, shortly after Gov. Richard Pine of the Gold Coast had warned the Colonial Office of the impending war, descended upon the "Protectorate." They plundered and killed at will before retiring in complete triumph at the start of the rainy season. Governor Pine immediately asked for reinforcements and permission to march on Kumasi, capital of the Ashanti nation, to retaliate.[43]

Notwithstanding Governor Pine's urgent pleas, the Colonial Office was determined to enforce Newcastle's policy of restraint. The duke himself found the system of protecting certain native tribes on the West Coast of Africa "painful and embarrassing." He appreciated the difficulty of Governor Pine's position, but he found the governor's proposed actions too impetuous. He was convinced that the result of military intervention in the Ashanti kingdom would be either a prolonged and costly war or an expansion of British influence by new annexations. The militant tone of Pine's dispatches appalled the duke, who observed, "The 'Pomp and circumstances of glorious war' heightened by Garibaldian costume is somewhat turning this man's head."[44]

Nonetheless, rumors of another Ashanti invasion and news of Ashanti sacrifices of Fanti prisoners compelled Newcastle to ask the War Office to send reinforcements to the Gold Coast and to give Governor Pine conditional permission to advance on the Ashanti nation.[45] The request for reinforcements, however, was delayed in the interdepartmental channels between the War Office and the Horse Guards. For a time the two departments could not agree on arrangements for raising the new regiment, which was to come from the West Indies. Neither department was inclined to prosecute the West African matter with vigor. Even after agreement was reached on raising the new regiment, further delay was caused by the Admiralty's insistence upon a systematic redistribution of the remaining British troops in the West Indies before the new regiment was conveyed to the Gold Coast. Consequently, the urgently needed reinforcements did not arrive at the Gold Coast until 9 April 1864, four days after Governor Pine had been forced to call off the proposed expedition against the Ashantis.

Governor Pine had regarded Newcastle's conditional permission to advance into Ashanti territory as an unqualified approval of a march on Kumasi. Newcastle, however, had intended no such approval; he intended only to remove a prohibition from advancing into Ashanti territory on the condition that the move was thought safer, less costly, and more decisive than waiting for another Ashanti attack upon the "Protectorate."[46] Pine, however, was so intent upon a march to Kumasi that he ignored the highly qualified terms of the dispatch and took upon himself the responsibility of a forward policy. Therefore, upon the receipt of the dispatch, he established a British post at Prasu on the Pra. From this post he intended to launch his invasion into Ashanti territory as soon as the reinforcements arrived from the West Indies. The delay caused by Whitehall dilatoriness proved fatal to his plans and nearly fatal to the Palmerston government. Severe sickness decimated the ranks of the British troops at Prasu, and that brought on a motion of censure in the Commons and forced the government late in May 1864 to order the evacuation of the troops to the West Indies.[47]

By this time Newcastle was no longer in office. Failing to recover from the serious illness that had struck him the previous November, the duke resigned on 2 April 1864. His incapacity, which had caused his absence from the Colonial Office during the first three months of the year, had seriously affected official business relative to the Ashanti crisis; Whitehall dilatoriness was in part caused by the absence of strong leadership from the Colonial Office. Thus the government had allowed the Ashanti affair to drift to crisis status. The fault was not Newcastle's, however. He had proffered his resignation in January 1864, but Palmerston had urged him to continue in office in the hope that he would recover his health. It was a forlorn hope, and while he lingered on, neither the Colonial Office staff nor the ministry filled the vacuum in administrative leadership left by his absence. Consequently, departmental confusion in Whitehall led to vacillation in the Ashanti affair.

However, ministerial indecision and reluctance to pursue a forward policy in West Africa did not produce the disaster alone. The divergence between the policy formulated in Whitehall and that implemented by the officials in West Africa also helped to make the whole Ashanti affair, in General Lord Wolseley's greatly exaggerated view, one of the most "scandalous episodes" in British imperial history.[48] In June the ministerial representatives had a difficult time dispelling the impression of gross neglect and mismanagement, and the government escaped censure by only seven votes. Although Newcastle was removed by illness from the official limelight at the time of the vote, the unfortunate incident cast a shadow on the last phase of his career.

14. *Colonial Nation Building*

Despite the misgivings of some Colonial Office officials, the fundamental mechanism of self-government and ministerial responsibility was established in most of the settlement colonies during the 1850s. Responsible government, as the concept and practice of self-government came to be called, had the two-fold merit of appearing to be both an infallible remedy for colonial discontent and a logical extension of British political and economic philosophy. It also had the advantage of widespread support in and out of Parliament and ready acceptance in the colonies. The question, therefore, was not whether concessions should be made to the settlement colonies, but how quickly and to what degree they should be made.[1]

Opinions differed considerably among administrators as to the timing and degree of these concessions. Newcastle, for example, being a sincere advocate of responsible government in its most liberal and extensive form, wanted a rapid extension of responsible government. On the other hand, Lord Grey, previously colonial secretary in the Russell administration, accepted the inevitability of responsible government in the settlement colonies but believed that self-government was a privilege rather than a right and could be earned only after a period of political apprenticeship. Even after the political maturation of a colony warranted the grant of responsible government, Grey argued, the crown should retain control of commercial policy, public lands, and native policy.

With such stringent views, it is not surprising that responsible government was awarded only to Nova Scotia and Canada during Grey's tenure at the Colonial Office. Increased pressures from Australia and New Zealand, however, soon forced further concessions from the Colonial Office. In December 1852, Sir John Pakington, Grey's successor, conceded the demands of the Legislative Council of New South Wales for a constitution similar to Canada's. He invited each of the colonies of New South Wales, Victoria, and South Australia to submit draft constitutions establishing an elected assembly and a nominated upper chamber. Shortly thereafter, Newcastle replaced Pakington at the Colonial Office and immediately yielded even more to the pressures for responsible government. The spread of self-government thus was greatly accelerated. During his first tenure of a year and a half at the Colonial Office, Newcastle contributed significantly to this transfer of power, a process that has been termed "the most important change in British colonial policy during the nineteenth century."[2]

Newcastle went far beyond either Lord Grey's or Pakington's view of responsible government. In confirming the latter's decision concerning the Australian colonies, the duke even withdrew the solitary restriction that the colonists should establish nominated chambers and explicitly stated that the new constitutions should provide for responsible government. The colonists themselves were allowed to decide upon the form of their legislatures through their legislative councils.[3] It mattered little to Newcastle that the Colonial Office concessions actually outstripped the colonial demands for responsible government. "It appears to me," he wrote to Sir Charles Fitzroy, governor of New South Wales, " . . . that while public expectation is as yet but little excited on the subject of Responsible Government, it is very desirable that we should prepare ourselves to regard its introduction as a change which cannot be long delayed, and for which the way should be smoothed as far as possible by the removal of unnecessary impediments."[4] He wrote in nearly the same vein to Sir H. E. F. Young, lieutenant-governor of South Australia:

> I am convinced there is little use in endeavouring by government influence, or the weight of your own popularity to retard the attainment by the Colony of what is called "responsible Government." The state of Society in South Australia may not be fit for it, but it will in my opinion be better to face the evil of its premature adoption than to encounter the certain mischief of a long democratic struggle to attain it. The first is soon cured, but the latter engenders permanent social disorder.[5]

A few impediments, however, temporarily blocked the extension of responsible government to some of the settlement colonies. The survival of convict transportation, for example, had prevented Pakington and Newcastle from including Van Diemen's Land in their instructions on new Australian constitutions. But with the passage of legislation in July 1853 abolishing transportation to that colony, Newcastle instructed Lt.-Gov. Sir William Denison to allow the Legislative Council of Van Diemen's Land to draft a constitution containing provision for responsible government. In supporting the transportation bill in the Lords, Newcastle emphasized how anomalous transportation was with the granting of representative institutions and how difficult it was to withhold political privileges from one colony when they had been conceded to neighboring ones.[6]

Halfway around the world from Van Diemen's Land, Newcastle used the same argument in extending responsible government to Newfoundland. "Shall we or shall we not continue to refuse to Newfoundland what has been given to the smaller Colony of Prince Edwards Island?," he asked Gov. K. Baillie Hamilton. Even though Newfoundland, with the constant threat of conflict between the predominantly Protestant merchants and the Irish-Catholic lower class, seemed unprepared for responsible government, the duke believed that the change should be made "before such a degree of animosity and antagonism has been produced as must always add far greater dangers to the attainment of popular rights."[7] But the governor warned that responsible government would "constitute this island a misruled Papal diocese" and would not promote the peace or prosperity of the colony.[8] Nevertheless, with the colonial assembly threatening to cut off supplies unless there was an extension of responsible government to the colony, Newcastle saw no alternative but to comply with the popular demand. "It is perhaps the severest test to which 'responsible government' can be exposed," he wrote.[9] He was right about the difficulty, but in the long term the colony passed the test.

Another severe test of responsible government awaited in Cape Colony, where the extension of representative institutions had been delayed by the outbreak of the Seventh Kaffir War. With British public opinion crying out against the incessant costly wars in South Africa, the Colonial Office was anxious to extend representative government to the colony without surrendering all responsibility over the natives. The task was left to Newcastle, who sent out the new constitution in March 1853 as soon as the war ended. It was, the duke informed Sir George Cathcart, governor of Cape Colony, "one of the most liberal constitutions enjoyed by any of the British possessions," granted for the purpose of "appeasing the jealousies of sometimes conflicting races" and of promoting "the security and prosperity, not only of those of British origin, but of all the Queen's subjects."[10] Liberal though it was, the constitution still did not provide for responsible government, a concession that would not be granted for nearly twenty years.

The extension of responsible government to the settlement colonies was seldom trouble-free; when he returned to the Colonial Office in 1859, Newcastle found many adverse accounts of the system in operation. Chichester Fortescue shuddered at the thought of inexperienced, frequently corrupt colonists controlling local affairs. Colonial governors complained often about the lack of talented men capable of forming stable governments, about corruption in the elections, and about the conduct of public affairs in a spirit of personal animosity. Nonetheless, Newcastle's confidence in responsible government remained unshaken, and his visit to British North America in 1860 strengthened his convictions. He believed self-government was a process of learning through mistakes, and he was willing to take risks in its application. In granting responsible government to settlement colonies, he told Sir George Bowen, governor of Queensland, the Imperial Government was fully aware that the power they granted must occasionally be used amiss. But they have trusted that the errors of free government would cure themselves, and that the Colonists would be led to exert greater energy and circumspection in legislation and government when they were made to feel that they would not be rescued from the consequences of any imprudence, merely affecting themselves, by authoritative intervention of the Crown or of the Governor.[11]

And to Sir William Denison, who had complained of the low character, moderate attainments, and immoderate vanity of most members of the Legislative Council of New South Wales, Newcastle expressed his hope that through the process of "natural fermentation," men of education and property would soon take the political lead and prove that the descendants of Englishmen were fit "for that self-government which appears to be the peculiar Anglo-Saxon inheritance."[12]

Although responsible government was working ill in many of the North American and Australian colonies, Newcastle in 1859 confidently introduced ministerial responsibility into the newly created Queensland. In 1861 he successfully resisted Lord Grey's demand for the suspension of the New Zealand constitution for the duration of the Maori rebellion. Such an act, he stated in the Lords, "under any circumstances, and certainly under the present, . . . would be one of the most impolitic acts which a British Minister could commit."[13]

Without precise statutory or legal definition, responsible government developed pragmatically in the various colonies in accordance with local circumstances. This evolutionary process was exactly what Newcastle desired, to give each colony a just and impartial government adapted to particular needs and capacities. He set only a few rules for the governors to follow in the practice of responsible government, but the governors could circumvent these rules in exceptional circumstances. Therefore, much depended upon the personality of the colonial governor and the local operation of the party system in the autochthonous development of responsible government.[14]

For the most part, the role of the governor in the self-governing colonies was difficult. Sir William Denison, governor of New South Wales, complained that "in the responsible governments one sees much going on which is objectionable, yet one is powerless to do good or prevent evil."[15] Newcastle did not agree. Although in matters of purely local politics the governor was bound, except in extreme cases, to follow the advice of the colonial ministry, which possessed the confidence of the legislature, he was not to be merely a cipher. "The *form* of power and influence [of colonial governors] is much changed," the duke wrote to Sir John Young, "but it is his own fault if it does not exist and work much good."[16] Newcastle exhorted the governors to use their influence to check the evils of an immature society. In a colony where no other corrective existed, he told Denison,

> there are but two palliatives that can be brought into immediate action—the Governor and the Secretary of State; and these can only operate by precept and example and not by the exercise of power. If they can check the current, we must trust to education and the progress of Religion for the future and more important amelioration.[17]

But in exercising this influence, Newcastle repeatedly cautioned the governors to play the role of constitutional monarchs. In a constitutional colony the governor must not appear the "sovereign of a party," or refuse to accept as advisers any persons whom the parliamentary proceedings might force upon him. Most importantly, the governor was to remain neutral in purely local affairs and above all personal conflicts.[18]

Nonetheless, Newcastle subscribed to the doctrine that a governor must uphold the law and reject unlawful proceedings, and he realized that to do this governors must have discretionary powers. Writing to Governor Gore Browne in New Zealand in 1861, the duke noted that it was not possible in time of war "to regulate affairs by didactic despatches which require more than two months for their transmission."[19] A month later, when informing Sir Alexander Bannerman in Newfoundland that the governor did not have the constitutional authority to proclaim martial law, Newcastle observed that in all but the most extreme cases, it was far better to seek legislative approval for emergency gubernatorial powers when civil tumult threatened. But in an extreme case, "a man in authority must dare anything that his sense of duty dictates rather than risk the safety of the country."[20]

Even though Newcastle's attitude toward gubernatorial power in self-governing colonies was clear and precise, he and his subordinates at the Colonial Office were quite tolerant of governors who occasionally acted contrary to the accepted view of responsible government. The duke realized that the working of responsible government depended largely upon the stability of the local political leadership and the existence of a reliable administrative system. Therefore, when in the absence of such stability a strong-willed governor flagrantly contravened the concept of responsible government, he usually escaped censure from the Colonial Office while Newcastle was secretary of state. The Colonial Office generally deplored such actions but reacted pragmatically. Downing Street did not want to destroy the little independent authority that governors of responsible colonies still retained. Sir Frederic Rogers argued that the governors at their own peril ought, in extreme cases, to be able to act as they thought necessary to redeem a deplorable situation. Newcastle, the sincere advocate of responsible government, argued similarly in reacting to Sir Alexander Bannerman's controversial dismissal in 1861 of

Newfoundland's Executive Council while it still possessed a majority in the House of Assembly. "I fear," the duke wrote in a minute, "Sir Alexander Bannerman has acted in this matter under the impulse of temper and rashly. Nothing can justify this extreme step except that which is generally held to justify strong measures—success." [21] To the satisfaction of Bannerman and the relief of the Colonial Office, Hugh Hoyles's conservative ministry obtained a majority in the elections. Bannerman's bold action, by helping abate sectarian animosities in party politics, paved the way for stability in Newfoundland. [22]

Extreme cases of this sort were relatively few, and the power of the colonial governors continued to decline during Newcastle's tenure at the Colonial Office. Much the same occurred with respect to the remaining imperial powers, as Newcastle willingly cooperated with the colonial authorities in loosening the ties of empire. Several important matters were settled during the duke's first stay at the Colonial Office. In 1853 Parliament passed the Canadian Clergy Reserves Act, which transferred responsibility over lands in Canada that had been set aside for the support of the clergy from the Imperial Parliament to the Canadian legislature. The measure was an important test case of responsible government, and Newcastle stressed that point in introducing it in the House of Lords. No matter what use the Canadian legislators chose for the lands in question, the duke argued, the Imperial Parliament must act upon the principle of colonial freedom in all questions relating to the internal administration of colonial affairs. He appealed to the Lords "to leave the colonists of this empire to arrange their own church affairs" and implored the bishops not to engage the Church of England in a contest in which "colonial freedom will in the end prevail." [23] It was a forceful speech, and both Aberdeen and Elgin gave full credit to Newcastle for the easy rejection of Derby's hostile amendment. The duke hoped that the act would demonstrate to the people of Canada how strong the feeling was in the Imperial Legislature for the colonies and how little sympathy there was with those who wanted to dismember the empire. [24] Whether or not it accomplished that objective, the acceptance of the Canadian Clergy Reserves Act clearly showed that the majority in Parliament agreed with the duke's view that responsible government meant freedom in religious matters also.

In the following year Parliament supported Newcastle on another important issue. The duke argued that Britain should not interfere in questions of constitutional changes in the colonies. Upon Elgin's recommendation, he introduced the legislative council (Canada) bill, which would enable the Canadian legislature to amend the constitution in order to permit an elective upper chamber. The measure was opposed by Derby, who wanted to check the torrent of democracy at home and in the colonies, but Newcastle's effective rebuttal to the opposition in the Lords provided a substantial margin for the bill. The duke argued that the nominated upper chamber had not checked the democratic tendencies of the elected lower house and had steadily fallen into disfavor in Canada. Far from causing an early separation of Canada from Britain, the duke claimed, the change would strengthen the union by removing another source of irritation. Parliament, he advised, "ought to legislate for a principle, and not for a colony."[25]

Granting to the settlement colonies the right to amend their constitutions and freedom to govern their own church affairs were two important principles established during Newcastle's short stay at the Colonial Office in 1853–1854. During the duke's second tenure in 1859–1864, the imperial government relinquished to colonial control several other matters earlier regarded as outside the scope of colonial self-government. One of these was the imperial trusteeship of the native races. Newcastle realized that England had only a shadow of power in the distant colonies in this matter. Therefore, he handed the care of the Indian population in Canada over to the colonial government in 1860, and that of the Maoris to New Zealand in 1862. The surrender of native trusteeship was partly one of economy, but the duke was convinced that the colonists would treat the natives more prudently and temperately if they shaped their own policy and bore its consequences.[26]

Newcastle was also reluctant to disallow colonial legislation. He believed that the colonists themselves best understood their own interests, and he wanted to leave the colonial legislatures as free as possible from imperial interference. The foundations for the Colonial Laws Validity Act of 1865, the only great statute of general imperial constitutional law passed in the nineteenth century, were laid during the Newcastle years at the Colonial Office. The act clearly defined the doctrine of repugnancy by declaring that a colonial law was invalid only if it was repugnant to an imperial statute extending to the colony, and it confirmed the powers of colonial legislatures to amend their own constitutions.[27]

Even imperial control of colonial trade was greatly restricted during Newcastle's second term at the Colonial Office. Although he deprecated the tendency to protection in many of the colonies, the duke conceded that the principle of self-government was even more important than the principle of free trade. Reluctantly, therefore, he accepted the Canadian tariff of 1859, which raised the import duties on several manufactured items. As colonial secretary, he believed that the only recourse left to him in matters of finance and commerce was to lecture the colonists on the virtues of free trade.[28]

Thus many of the great powers hitherto reserved to the imperial government were relinquished without serious friction. Robert Lowe might grumble that "from a muddling tyrant the Colonial Office has sunk into a parasite of the colonies,"[29] but to Newcastle it was in the best interests of Great Britain to foster powerful communities overseas and to tie them to the mother country with bonds of mutual affection and interest. He constantly worked toward that end by promoting the constitutional progress and economic welfare of the colonies. At times it was a thankless task, for Newcastle frequently found it easier to transfer powers than duties to the self-governing colonies.

II

Newcastle agreed with Gladstone that one could not separate the benefits of freedom from its burdens. Reflecting the overwhelming sentiment of the British nation, both men believed that the duty of self-support was coextensive with the right of self-government and that self-defense was a corollary of responsible government. Thus they agreed with the popular demands for the withdrawal of imperial troops from the self-governing colonies and for increased colonial contributions to imperial defense.

Unlike Gladstone, however, Newcastle's main reason for these beliefs was not economy. The duke was far more concerned with maintaining effective defense than with cutting military expenditures. Along with Assistant Under-Secretary Thomas Frederick Elliot, Newcastle dissented from the majority report of the 1859 interdepartmental committee on military expenditure in the colonies, which recommended that self-governing colonies determine the number of imperial troops required and share a fixed proportion—perhaps half—of the total burden for the garrison. Newcastle believed that the report had the interests of the British Treasury rather than those of the colonies at heart. He and Elliot were opposed to a uniform rate of colonial contributions irrespective of local conditions. Instead, they favored giving discretionary powers to the colonial secretary to negotiate with the colonial ministers on the number and composition of troops and the amount of colonial contribution toward the cost of the imperial garrison. Newcastle strongly favored military reorganization in the colonies to achieve greater imperial defensive strength, but he did not want to overburden colonial resources in the process merely to satisfy the British taxpayers.[30]

The Colonial Office had no intention of following the interdepartmental committee's majority recommendations. Instead, the office under Newcastle's leadership proceeded with military reorganization in the colonies using well-established policies. Between March 1859 and March 1861, twenty percent of the imperial garrison was withdrawn from British North America; nearly forty percent of the Australian imperial garrison was withdrawn in 1860; and substantial reductions were achieved at the Cape and the West Indies. However, these reductions were more than offset by the increase of 8,455 troops sent to New Zealand, Mauritius, St. Helena, the Bahamas, and the strategic Mediterranean bases of Gibraltar, Malta, and the Ionian Islands. Except for the reinforcements sent to New Zealand at the outbreak of the Anglo-Maori Wars in 1860, these troop movements generally corresponded with Newcastle's policy of reducing imperial garrisons in "colonies proper" and concentrating the imperial military reserves in strategic bases. But Newcastle's achievements were not appreciated by those who wanted a net reduction in military expenditures.[31]

It became clear in the wake of the interdepartmental report that the Colonial Office's pragmatic approach to imperial defense was anathema to the officials at the Treasury and War Office. Pressure from those two departments and from Parliament forced Lord Palmerston to appoint a select committee in 1861 to report on colonial defense and expenditure. The committee was chaired by Arthur Mills, a noted colonial reformer, and contained some of the ablest and most knowledgeable men on colonial and military affairs in Parliament. Their outlook, however, was dominated by the idea of self-reliance, and some were conspicuous for their desire for imperial disintegration.

Newcastle was apprehensive about the committee inquiry. Among other things, he feared that the committee might serve as a mouthpiece for John Robert Godley, under-secretary of state for war, who had important connections with Charles B. Adderley and other empire disintegrationists. During the previous year, the duke had frequently complained of the "pieces of screwing economy" from Godley and of the "modus Godleiamus" by which the War Office intended to reduce British military commitments.[32]

In his evidence before the committee, Newcastle emphasized the importance of imperial sentiment. He argued that the complete withdrawal of imperial garrisons would make the difference between colonial and independent status "infinitesimal." For the time being in British North America, he observed, there was little chance for reducing imperial forces beyond what had already been done. Since the Cape was an important bastion on the route to India, he was strongly in favor of maintaining a large imperial reserve there. He agreed with the majority of the committee that naval protection was the most appropriate form of defense for Australia and New Zealand, and he concurred with the prevailing opinion that additional troops should be withdrawn from those colonies as soon as circumstances permitted.[33]

To Newcastle's great relief, the committee report was far more acceptable to the officials at the Colonial Office than to Godley and the extreme colonial reformers. Indeed, for the most part the report merely reiterated principles that the government had already adopted. It did not formulate any rigid rules. While it recommended that British troops be withdrawn gradually from the self-governing colonies, the "colonies proper," and concentrated in military bases at the heart of the empire, it left the colonial secretary considerable administrative flexibility in the matter. Newcastle and subsequent secretaries of state, therefore, retained ample discretionary authority to pursue the ideal of colonial self-defense and self-government.[34]

During the next few years, Newcastle achieved considerable success in following the policy of the select committee with regard to the Australian colonies. In a draft circular dispatch of July 1863, he informed all the colonies except Western Australia that in the future they must pay £40 for each man of the 1,300 imperial troops they were to be allotted. Any additions to this force were to be supplied, if available, at £70 per head. The dispatch made clear that while Great Britain would employ the Royal Navy to protect the colonies in the event of war, the colonies would be held responsible for the defense of their own cities and ports.[35] The plan was fully accepted in March 1864.

Similar details were gradually worked out for Hong Kong, the West Indies, Ceylon, and Mauritius. Newcastle was willing to reduce imperial garrisons and demand higher colonial contributions when he thought it was possible without impairing imperial defense and putting too great a burden on colonial resources. But unlike the more doctrinaire Treasury and War Office officials, Newcastle never made economy the primary objective of his defense policy.[36]

III

In other parts of the world, though, Newcastle's plan of military reorganization was in jeopardy as a result of the outbreak of the American Civil War and the resumption of the Maori Wars in New Zealand. Anglo-American relations deteriorated rapidly after the outbreak of the American Civil War in April 1861. British statesmen suspected American motives and particularly feared that William H. Seward, the American secretary of state, might be willing to pick a fight with Britain if it suited his purposes. Lord Lyons, the British ambassador in Washington, urged the government back home to be on its guard, and Palmerston requested Newcastle and Herbert to work out the details for sending reinforcements and a large quantity of arms and accouterments to Canada. In response to Palmerston's request, Newcastle wrote, "I quite agree with you as to the danger to be apprehended to our North American Colonies from the unscrupulous and bullying conduct of Seward and I equally agree that a bold front and a show of preparation are the best means of preventing such acts on his part as might render war inevitable."[37]

Yet Newcastle cautioned against overreacting to Seward's conduct; he wrote to Sir Edmund Head, governor-general of Canada, "I entirely concur in what you say in your letter of the 18th of May about Mr. Seward's speculations and unfriendly views towards Canada, but I think you hardly make sufficient allowance for his hyper-American use of the policy of bully and bluster." The greater danger to Canada, the duke believed, would come from the existence of a large American army composed of "the scum of all nations" that might be diverted against Canada at the close of the Civil War by American politicians seeking safety for themselves and security for American institutions. But in whatever aspect the possibility of war with the United States was regarded,

Newcastle assured Head that the force in Canada would be increased immediately by three regiments of infantry and a battery of field artillery of Armstrong guns. He hoped that "this manifestation of our determination to defend
Canada will, in the first place, make our neighbours a little more cautious,
and, in the second, encourage the Canadians in their loyalty, and induce them
to make corresponding efforts for their self-defence."[38]

The troops were hurriedly sent out from England on the *Great Eastern*, then
the largest ship in the world. Their arrival had the desired effects of boosting
the spirits of the Canadians and allaying their fears about an American invasion.[39] Nonetheless, Palmerston insisted that the *Great Eastern* make two more
trips to North America with three additional regiments before the onset of
winter. With a "swaggering, bullying set of men" in Washington and an influential war party in the North that would "rather court than shun a quarrel
with England" as a way to pair failure against the South with success in Canada, he argued, it was necessary to increase the regular force in British North
America to ten thousand men. By so doing, he concluded, "we should keep
the United States Government in check, give spirit and confidence to our own
people in the Provinces and take the best chance for the continuation of
peace."[40]

Newcastle strongly dissented from Palmerston's view. Although he dis-
trusted Seward and the Washington ministers as much as Palmerston did, he
did not believe an American attack on Canada was imminent. He argued that
the course of events since the outbreak of the Civil War, particularly the decisive victory of the South at Bull Run, had rendered it virtually impossible
for the North to direct their warlike tendencies toward Canada for at least
another seven or eight months. He also feared that additional reinforcements
might dampen the ardor of the Canadians and deter them from preparing for
self-defense. Therefore, he suggested that the troops be kept in a high state of
discipline at home and that only military stores and artillery be sent over
during the winter.[41]

Reluctantly, Palmerston gave way to Newcastle, and no further reinforcements were sent to Canada for the time being. Nevertheless, the prime minister complained bitterly of "the theoretical gentlemen" in the Colonial Office
who, in their desire to get rid of the colonies as soon as possible, had allowed
the defense of the North American Provinces to fall into such an imperfect
state as to endanger them greatly.[42] Palmerston's charge of inadequate preparations ruffled Newcastle's feathers. In response he assured the prime minister
that he had always advocated adequate military preparations for British North
America and that he would meet with indignation the views of the "supposed
theoretical gentlemen" in the Colonial Office if they contemplated the disruption of the empire through the act of a hostile power. As for the British North
Americans, the duke asserted that they would be more than willing to accom-

modate the additional imperial troops and, in the event of war, would fight to the death for the mother country—if only Gladstone would guarantee him an intercolonial railway.[43]

Meanwhile Newcastle appointed Lord Monck to succeed Sir Edmund Head as governor-general of Canada. It was fortunate for the duke that he placed his confidence in a man of Monck's ability, for at the time of the appointment the *Trent* affair had brought England and the United States to the brink of war. Early in November 1861, two Confederate envoys were seized from the British steamer *Trent* in international waters and hauled aboard a United States warship. Although by restraint on both sides war was avoided and the affair was successfully concluded with the release of the two Southern envoys, the British ministers had prepared for the worst eventuality.

The *Trent* crisis forced Great Britain to put the North American Provinces on a wartime footing. With "Seward at the helm and the mob and the press manning the vessel," Newcastle expected war with the United States. He urged Monck and Lord Mulgrave (governor of Nova Scotia) and Arthur Gordon (lieutenant-governor of New Brunswick) to make every preparation to defend the provinces from invasion. "We are doing all that the season of the year will allow here," he wrote to Monck on 5 December. "A ship with 30,000 stand of arms and a battery of Armstrong guns sails to-morrow. Two regiments will sail in a few days for Rivere du Loup. More will follow through Nova Scotia. Officers for organizing the militia will go out at once." Two days later he announced to Mulgrave and Gordon that two regiments and 5,000 stand of arms would be sent to Halifax and a regiment to St. John's on its way to Canada. A week later he urged Monck and Gordon to use their existing militia laws to call out as many regiments as possible at the first sign of war and to introduce amendments to the militia laws at the beginning of the next session of the provincial parliaments. "Pray bear in mind," he wrote to Monck, "that even if war is deferred it may not be wholly got rid of and your preparations will not be thrown away. This is a golden opportunity in any case to induce people to prepare for defence, and the new Military organization of your neighbours renders this very necessary."[44]

With the troop reinforcements following the *Trent* crisis, the imperial garrison in British North America reached 17,599 by spring 1862. Large amounts of stores and weapons continued to pour into the provinces, and the War Office agreed to lend arms to the colonial militias. The quick arrival of the British troops after the beginning of the crisis and the willingness of the imperial government to help supply and arm the militias helped silence those in the provinces who had proclaimed England to be indifferent to the safety and welfare of the colonies.[45]

The threat of war with the United States prompted the Canadians to reassess their own defenses, a reassessment for which Newcastle had long pressed.

A Militia Commission was appointed to reorganize the militia. But colonial defense preparations subsided rapidly once the immediate threat of war was removed by the peaceful resolution of the *Trent* affair. In May 1862, the Canadian militia bill, which embodied the recommendations of the Militia Commission, was defeated in the Canadian Parliament. Its defeat reflected several cross currents at work in the province; opposition was especially strong toward the specter of compulsory military service and direct taxation. The opposition was able to seize upon the unpopularity of the measure to turn the Cartier ministry out of power.

Newcastle reacted strongly to the rejection of the measure. The Canadian ministers, he noted disgustedly to Monck, had greatly strengthened the anti-colonial sentiment in England. The English people, he warned, would not tolerate any further aid to the Canadians under such circumstances. "If our Parliament should be obliged to meet in November on account of the distress in Lancashire" arising from the cutting off of imports of raw cotton from the Confederate States, he continued,

> I can easily imagine many circumstances which may call forth angry and
> anti–Canadian debates if nothing is still done to support the 12,000 men
> whom our starving workmen are helping to pay and whose isolated position
> in the event of war I assure you many military men in the Country think
> would be very dangerous during the months that the St. Lawrence is closed.

He realized that Canada suffered from a large deficit and that the people strongly opposed direct taxation. But, he suggested, a bold ministry that proposed both a well-organized system of defense and an improved plan of finance would triumph over prejudice and the national aversion to taxation. "I am convinced the time is come when a great change in the system of taxation is necessary for the prosperity of Canada, and it will never be so easily accomplished as when proffered in conjunction with measures for improving the defences."[46]

In August 1862, Newcastle forwarded a long public dispatch to Monck in which he stressed the need for Canada to take more active steps for self-defense by organizing an extensive militia. Again he argued that colonies possessing responsible government should provide for their own defense. He urged Monck to consult with the lieutenant-governors of Nova Scotia and New Brunswick to create a union of the North American colonies for defense.[47] But the duke's message fell on deaf ears, as the Canadian ministers continued to reject his ideas; and throughout the rest of the year they exchanged increasingly pungent notes with the colonial secretary through Monck. The ministers in Quebec continued to insist upon an imperial concept of defense that entitled Canada to substantial assistance from the British Treasury if the colony became the theater of a war resulting from imperial policy.

They refused to accept Newcastle's dictum that the defense of Canadian territory must depend mainly on the Canadian people themselves.[48]

Although the Canadian government passed two measures in August 1863 to strengthen the militia, the basic issue between the Quebec statesmen and the Colonial Office remained unresolved while Newcastle was in office. Nevertheless, the duke continued to show considerable forbearance. The imperial garrisons in North America were maintained throughout the critical years of the American Civil War. But in the face of persistent colonial reluctance to provide for self-defense, Edward Cardwell, Newcastle's successor as colonial secretary, began to withdraw the imperial garrisons to spur the Canadians into action. Still, it was to the duke's credit that the issue over defense in British North America was brought to a head.[49]

IV

The resumption of the Maori Wars in New Zealand in 1860 presented Newcastle with his greatest problem in implementing the policy of withdrawing imperial troops from self-governing colonies. With the renewal of hostilities, Governor Gore Browne asked the home government to send three additional regiments of infantry and one of artillery to New Zealand. The ministers, however, were reluctant to supply the troops requested. Both Newcastle and George Cornewall Lewis, the secretary of state for war, were convinced that the white settlers had provoked the Maoris to resume the war, and both were angered by the unwillingness of the New Zealand ministers to contribute to the expense of the troops they demanded. But when Gore Browne continued to press for more troops, the home government in July 1860 finally consented to dispatch one regiment to New Zealand. Lewis warned the governor that in the future, requests for military assistance would be weighed in light of the colonists' willingness to share the burdens of self-defense.[50] For his part, the duke, on the eve of his departure for North America with the prince of Wales, advised the governor that a spirit of generous reconciliation between the colonists and the natives should be the first order of business once the "rebellion" had been suppressed. When he returned to England, Newcastle again urged Gore Browne to seek a permanent peace based on justice and honor, with security for the natives.[51]

Additional reinforcements were sent to New Zealand in the autumn, and it was finally agreed that the colony would contribute £5 per officer and soldier toward maintenance costs. By March 1861 the number of imperial troops in New Zealand had risen to 5,354. Nonetheless, the war went on. The early victories of the Maoris encouraged other native chiefs to join the resistance against British encroachment. As a result, full-scale rebellion broke out early in 1861.

As the crisis deepened, Newcastle became exasperated with Gore Browne and General Cameron, commander of the imperial troops in New Zealand, who both wanted to enlarge the military operations against the Maoris. Newcastle refused to sanction the expeditions they proposed and criticized them for yielding to the antinative feeling of the white settlers. He still urged the governor to end the hostilities and to negotiate with the Maoris.

Newcastle's opinion of Gore Browne had gradually changed over the year, and he at last bowed to the Colonial Office staff's belief that the governor was personally incapable of resisting the pressure from the settlers or of working with the Maoris to begin reconciliation in the colony. Therefore, since the governor's term was about to expire, Newcastle accepted Chichester Fortescue's suggestion to send Sir George Grey, currently governor of the Cape, back to New Zealand, where he had been Gore Browne's predecessor from 1845 to 1853. Sir George Grey was in good standing with the natives, and the Colonial Office hoped that he would initiate a new plan that would include, at the least, the conferring of authority upon paid native chiefs who would work with white magistrates and police officers in the native districts.[52]

In accordance with Newcastle's general instructions, Sir George Grey made several important concessions to the Maoris shortly after his arrival in New Zealand. He extended ministerial responsibility over Maori affairs, and he established a system of Maori government through councils of chiefs and assessors assisted by British resident magistrates and civil commissioners.[53] But despite these concessions and initiatives, the conflict between the settlers and the Maoris was not resolved, even though a truce had been arranged. Grey had lost his credibility with the Maoris, who continued to be suspicious of everything he attempted, and the New Zealand ministers and House of Representatives refused to accept full responsibility for the affairs of the natives, a matter upon which Newcastle strongly insisted. Furthermore, the ministers agreed to pay only half the cost of the new Maori scheme of administration, with the stipulation that the remaining £25,000 be deducted from the money that the colony paid for the maintenance of the imperial troops in New Zealand. Although it was contrary both to his and to the home government's views, Grey accepted the plan without prior authorization from the Colonial Office.[54]

Newcastle was upset by these rebukes to his own policies and by Grey's acceptance of a plan that was "ingeniously contrived so as to throw the whole burden on the Mother Country."[55] With this turn of events, the duke's patience was understandably almost exhausted with the governor and the New Zealand ministers and legislators. Still, he felt compelled to accept the plan, and after a delay of two months he finally convinced the Treasury to accede to it. In announcing the decision, the duke warned the governor that both the Treasury and the House of Commons were weary of the military expenses in

New Zealand: "I confess I am not surprised at it for both the Colonial Government and the Legislature are constantly doing things and expressing opinions which indicate an intention to pull more and more on the English purse and to do less and less for themselves." He reminded Grey that the crown had now given up the administration of the natives as well as almost everything else to the colony; but, he added, power has "its duties as well as its rights." The duke was increasingly concerned about the growing hatred of the native race in New Zealand, and he suggested that Grey issue a proclamation on the subject and try everything within his power to avoid the resumption of war. The objective, he stressed, should be to seek a demographic rather than a military solution. The natural increase in the white population and the continual decrease in the native population would soon render war impossible.[56]

From this moment, Newcastle became much more critical of the conduct of New Zealand's affairs. Henceforth, he vigorously resisted every attempt of the colonial government to exact further financial aid from the British Treasury. He was determined not to allow the colonists to wage war in defense of their own property at Great Britain's expense, and he was determined to show the colonists that self-government carried with it the correlative of self-defense. In an official dispatch of 26 February 1863, the duke stated that Great Britain was not compelled to educate, govern, or civilize all the "savages" among whom British subjects chose to plant themselves. For the first time he acknowledged that the present trouble was brought on by the determination of the British commander of the imperial troops to act with the white colonists against the natives. In a private letter of the same date the duke complained of the "disingenous and hardly creditable" actions of the colonial ministers: "I see too frequently attempts made in the colony to overreach the Home Government, and these attempts I must and will withstand." He vowed to persevere in resisting the colonists' bid to have self-government with imperial protection. The home government, he stressed, would pull the colony through its present troubles, "but when once this is done it [the colony] must be left in great measure to take the consequences of any false steps it may make."[57]

The duke carried out his threat to resist New Zealand's unwarranted claims upon the imperial Treasury. Sir George Grey became quite agitated by the "harsh" tone of Newcastle's official dispatches and private letters and complained of unjust treatment and of being undercut by the Colonial Office in his attempts to negotiate peace with the natives. He charged Newcastle with possessing a "hostile spirit" toward him and everything he did, a charge the duke denied.[58] The exchange of several frank letters on these matters did not clear the air, and the relations between colonial secretary and governor remained tense for the rest of Newcastle's term in office.

Although Newcastle had hoped that the resumption of war could be avoided, he supported the New Zealand government's decision to invade the Waikato in 1863. He believed that this act of firmness was necessary to show the Maoris that the government did not intend to allow them to destroy what was good for both settlers and natives.[59] The invasion, however, caused the Maoris to renew the war with increased vigor, and the resumption of the war put Newcastle in a difficult position at home. With great difficulty, he gained the sanction of the British cabinet to send two more regiments to New Zealand, even though a storm of protest in Parliament was anticipated over the action. In justifying the cabinet's decision, Newcastle told the Lords that although he had established the general principle that the colonies should provide for their own defense, he had never stated that all assistance from the home government would be withdrawn from New Zealand during this time of crisis. Although the principle should be maintained in the future, he added, present circumstances did not allow it to be enforced in New Zealand. Thus Newcastle's great concern for colonial security overrode his desire to implement the policy of colonial self-defense. Although he accepted self-defense as a corollary of self-government, he believed it was his duty to see the New Zealanders through the present crisis on the clear understanding that the troops would be withdrawn as soon as the Maori threat subsided.[60]

The government's decision to send more troops to New Zealand was unpopular in England. Lord Grey strongly criticized the policy and Newcastle in the Lords. Even in New Zealand, it soon became evident that Gov. Sir George Grey and his ministers did not appreciate the home government's generosity. The New Zealand government continued to refuse increasing financial support of the imperial troops, leaving Newcastle little recourse but to send another severe rebuke to Grey and to announce a hardened attitude on the matter. In a strongly worded minute of September 1863, the duke stated that he was "quite disposed to withdraw shortly from the colony Regiment by Regiment as the local Government fails to fulfil each of the fair requirements placed upon them from home."[61]

Newcastle's sharp warning had a moderating effect. By the end of the year, he was generally satisfied with New Zealand's efforts against the Maori rebels. "The Colony seems to be now exerting itself nobly and in earnest," he wrote to Grey on Christmas Day. "The account you sent me shows nearly 10,000 Colonial troops under arms and as there are upwards of 10,000 British soldiers in the Islands besides the naval force, I hope your sanguine expectations of ending the war before the end of the summer may be realized."[62]

Unfortunately, those sanguine expectations were not realized. Matters in New Zealand worsened, and there was little prospect for peace when ill health forced Newcastle to retire from office. The New Zealand government's policy of confiscating rebel Maori land caused the miserable struggle to spread, as Newcastle had feared. With his policies for New Zealand in shambles, the duke was thoroughly frustrated by the colony's intractable problems; the worsening situation in New Zealand may well have aggravated his illness and hastened his death.

In the five years after the duke's death, the British government and Parliament tired even more of the incessant fighting in New Zealand. The Maori Wars had proved that imperial protection of native interests was incompatible with colonial self-government. The majority of the settlers welcomed a war of native extermination as long as it was financed by the British Treasury. Although sincere in his desire to protect the rights and the lands of the Maoris, Newcastle had been entirely too generous to the white interests in New Zealand. Under the direction of Edward Cardwell and Lord Granville, Newcastle's successors at the Colonial Office, the British government began to withdraw the imperial troops from the colony; by 1870 the last British regulars had gone. With only militia volunteers left to fight the Maori chiefs still under arms, the war quickly came to an end. Gradually thereafter, Newcastle's ideal of an assimilation of the Maoris into New Zealand society and culture was generally achieved.

V

During his final term in office, Newcastle realized that the political and military aspects of colonial nation-building were interrelated. Confederation of the British colonies in North America, South Africa, and Australia into powerful communities that were capable of defending themselves and existing independently was the logical sequence of colonial self-government and self-defense. In accepting these views, he departed from the opinions of those who preceded him. In 1858 proposals for federation in North America and South Africa had been presented to the Colonial Office. Sir Edward Bulwer-Lytton, then colonial secretary in the Derby government, strongly rejected the two proposals and even recalled Sir George Grey, governor of the Cape of Good Hope and British high commissioner in South Africa, for defying Colonial Office instructions by advocating federation of the Cape and Natal with the Boer Republics of the Orange Free State and the Transvaal. Upon entering office in 1859, Newcastle rescinded Grey's recall, but with the strict understanding that the governor would not espouse his federation schemes.[63]

Although he upheld the censure passed upon the governor, Newcastle was far more impressed than his predecessor by Grey's arguments for expansion and federation in South Africa. Grey was uncompromisingly opposed to the policy of the Conventions, which the British government had followed since 1852 and to which the duke had assented in 1853 and 1854. Under the Conventions, Britain abandoned sovereignty over the Boer Republics and accepted restraints upon the expansion of the British frontiers. But early in his second tenure at the Colonial Office, Newcastle realized that complete separation between affairs within and affairs beyond the colonial border could not be maintained forever. Thus he believed that the Conventions and their restraint upon further British expansion must ultimately be abolished or modified. "It is really a question of time," he wrote in a minute dated 28 January 1860. "We are not a free agent in the final issue. . . . Annexation is an ugly word, and ugly deeds have been done under it—but the word ought not to frighten us and the deeds by no means need be repeated."[64]

With this minute, Newcastle laid the groundwork within the Colonial Office for a change of policy toward South Africa. Gradually he made the points with his subordinates that Britain was on the verge of another phase of expansionism in South Africa and that the tendency to extend the frontiers could be modified but not prevented by the actions of the Colonial Office. Later in the year he supported Governor Grey's plan of extending the Cape frontiers and British influence throughout the length of Kaffraria to the border with Natal. And in new instructions to Gov. Sir Philip Wodehouse, who had replaced Grey at the Cape, and to Gov. John Scott of Natal, Newcastle revealed the extent to which he had departed from the policy of the previous seven years. He granted permission to the Cape Colony to annex the land between the Kei and the Bashee, and permission to Natal to annex the portion of Kaffraria that lay between the Umzimkulu and the Umtanvuma rivers as a way to control the Zulu tribes in the area. The sanction of the extension of the frontiers, however, was contingent upon the willingness of the Cape and Natal themselves to undertake the necessary expenditure and responsibility for government. Newcastle made it clear that colonial expansion would not be allowed at the home government's expense.[65]

Newcastle had departed from previous British policy in South Africa for several important reasons. The first was necessity. He firmly believed that expansion into the Transkei was necessary to maintain peace and protect the welfare of the African inhabitants. Accomplished at colonial expense, expansion into the Transkei also promised to lift a great financial burden from the shoulders of the British government. Strategically, it was important for Great Britain to check the advance of the Transvaal to the sea and to thwart Portugal's claims to Delagoa Bay by asserting prior rights to the bay, annexing parts of Zululand, and closing the coastline between the Cape and Natal. Lastly, but not least in importance, Newcastle regarded the extension of territory as the first step toward the union of all the British South African colonies in one powerful government that would be strong enough militarily and politically to face any threat from Zulus, Basutos, and Boers.[66]

Newcastle's policy was one of strength through unity. It was designed to extend British leadership, but not sovereignty, throughout South Africa in order to maintain peace between the European and native races. But the colonists in South Africa were not ready to dance to the new tune from London. The government in Cape Colony refused to accept the responsibility of federation and the burdens of self-defense envisaged by Newcastle and his immediate successors at the Colonial Office. Political and constitutional deadlocks in South Africa blocked federation and prevented complete self-government for many years. Thus Sir George Grey's and Newcastle's dream of avoiding war between the two European sections of the population, as well as between them and the black natives, failed to materialize. It was a tragic failure for which neither man was responsible.

Federation materialized much earlier and more smoothly in British North America than it did in South Africa. Newcastle was an early advocate of federation for the British colonies in North America. His celebrated visit to the American continent with the prince of Wales in 1860 had allowed him to study the matter firsthand; he left more convinced than ever that a federal union of the North American Provinces was not only possible but highly desirable for economic, political, and military reasons. Early in 1862 he wrote for the benefit of the British cabinet that he could not "imagine an object more clearly marked out for a British statesman to aim at than to secure the continued separation of Canada and the United States and the eventual formulation of a powerful state out of the now disjointed and feeble British North American provinces." He urged that a strong Canadian federation would be a valuable ally to Great Britain and an essential makeweight in the balance of power on the American continent.[67]

Although he pledged the British government's support for federation, Newcastle informed the North American governors that the proposals would have to emanate in the first instance from the provinces, and that they would have to work out the arrangements for such a plan themselves.[68] He was certain, however, that the formation of a legislative union of the Maritime Provinces and the linking of them with Canada by an intercolonial railway were prerequisites for the federation of all the British provinces in North America. He continued to urge the governors of the Maritime Provinces to work for the legislative union, and he supported a plan to build a railway link between the bankrupt Grand Trunk Railway in Canada and the short lines of Nova Scotia and New Brunswick. By linking the Grand Trunk with the settled regions and ice-free ports of the Maritimes, he firmly believed that an avenue would be provided for increased interprovincial trade. Newcastle also shared the hope of Edward E. Watkin, the principal agent of Messrs Baring Brothers, the most important London financiers behind the Grand Trunk, of further reviving the railway by extending communications westward to the Pacific and thereby encouraging settlement of the west, producing increased trade in the region, and forming the shortest route between Western Europe and the Far East. Therefore, the duke was convinced that the intercolonial railway was not only inextricably bound up with confederation but also with the economic, social, and political development of all British North America.[69]

In December 1861, Newcastle proposed to the cabinet that the British should help construct 350 miles of the intercolonial railway between Halifax and Quebec. Gladstone adamantly opposed the plan, which, notwithstanding the duke's strong advocacy, was substantially rejected by the cabinet in the spring of 1862. The cabinet was only willing to give an imperial guarantee of interest toward raising a public loan. In reporting the decision to Governor-General Monck, the duke stressed that it was not a refusal of all assistance, and, he added,

> if you knew how strong was the repugnance of the Cabinet to give *any* aid you would be satisfied how strongly I have fought in order to obtain the concession now made. . . . I hope the offer will not be rejected lightly . . . for I do not think better terms are likely to be obtained. . . .
>
> You have no idea what an unfortunate influence upon this question has been exercised by your high tariff on British manufactures both in the Cabinet and amongst the Public.

Newcastle believed that he could have obtained approval for the proposal from both the cabinet and the House of Commons had it not been for "this insuperable obstacle," the Canadian tariff, and he appealed to the colonial ministers through Monck to revise the tariff in Britain's favor.[70]

Newcastle's appeal to the colonial ministers had some effect. In Canada, Alexander Galt, minister of finance, although plagued by a chronic shortage of revenue, consented to a small reduction of the tariff on manufactured articles. He also agreed to raise money to meet a budgetary deficiency and the outlays for the new militia through a graduated stamp duty and increased duties on tea, sugar, spirits, and tobacco. The Canadian ministers also agreed to host a conference at Quebec in September to work out details concerning the intercolonial railway and to discuss political union with representatives from Nova Scotia and New Brunswick.

Although the concept of political union was not ripe, the colonial representatives at the Quebec conference reached a satisfactory agreement concerning the intercolonial railway. They approved a new plan for sharing the burden of building the railway and decided to send delegates to England to confer with Newcastle and Gladstone on implementing the loan guarantee.[71]

Difficulties arose early in the discussions between the colonial delegates and the British ministers. While the delegates from Nova Scotia and New Brunswick were interested mainly in securing an intercolonial railway across the Appalachian upland, the Canadian delegates, following instructions from their government, insisted upon including in the negotiations a proposal for extending communications westward to the Pacific, a project more popular than the intercolonial railway with most Canadians. They also wanted the British government to consider any Canadian expenditure on the intercolonial railway as a contribution toward imperial defense. At the last minute the Canadian delegates also rejected the sinking fund stipulated by the British government as a prerequisite for guaranteeing the provincial railway loan. In Quebec the Canadian ministers upheld the actions of their delegates and later repudiated the plan established at the Quebec Conference for a division of railway expenses among the provinces.[72]

It was a disheartening moment for the duke, who saw all his plans for the British North American provinces jeopardized by the Canadian government. "The fact is," he complained bitterly to Monck, "your Government—afraid of losing their places—only wish to get rid of any question which entails trouble or difficulty."[73] It was a temporary setback, however, as powerful forces were soon at work to change the adverse situation. The formation in 1864 of a coalition government in Canada favorable to the railway scheme and to federation, the spread of nationalism throughout British North America as a result of the American Civil War, the increased pressures brought by that war for a stronger defense against a hostile United States, and the trade uncertainties in the Maritime Provinces all converged to pave the way not only for the intercolonial railway but also for general confederation. In Quebec in October 1864, the month of Newcastle's death, delegates from the three Maritime Provinces, Newfoundland, and Canada drafted and approved a series of seventy-two resolutions for federation.

The Quebec Resolutions, including a provision binding the federal government to undertake the railway communication between the Maritime Provinces and Canada, later became the basis for the federal constitution of the Dominion of Canada, which came into being with the enactment of the British North America Act in 1867.[74] Clearly, contrary to his fears late in 1862, Newcastle's labors were not in vain. Although he did not live to see their fruition, he contributed significantly to the building of a nation in British North America that would eventually become politically, economically, and militarily strong.

15. Final Misfortunes

The tragic theme of Newcastle's life was played out to the end. Family matters and poor health continued to plague him; perhaps as a way to smother the agonies of his private life, he undertook more public responsibilities than his health could withstand. His many years of personal misfortune left him at the end of his life a broken, desperate man, greatly pitied by his friends and the queen.

By the late 1850s, the duke's daughter and eldest son had become two of the principal causes of his domestic unhappiness. In 1858 Lord Lincoln piled up large racing debts, which, to the duke's great embarrassment, Lincoln tried unsuccessfully to have settled through Lady Waldegrave's influence. For over a year thereafter, Newcastle refused to see his son. Also in 1858, Lady Susan fell in love with Lord Adolphus (Dolly) Vane-Tempest, the favorite son of Frances Anne, second wife of the marquess of Londonderry. Lord Adolphus was a complete wastrel. He had gambled away his money and was generally believed to be nearly insane. Nevertheless, Lady Susan was determined to marry him; Newcastle was just as determined to prevent her. He forbade any correspondence between them, but his interdiction was useless, as Lady Susan continued to see Dolly Vane at every opportunity.

During these family crises, Newcastle never missed a chance to consult with Lady Waldegrave. In 1861 Chichester Fortescue, whose own fond feelings for Lady Waldegrave doubtlessly influenced his tone, complained angrily to his diary that Newcastle told her "every conceivable thing, about himself, his family, his money matters, his will etc."[1] But nothing could stop the flood of misfortune that burst upon the duke. Early in 1860 Susan, Newcastle's divorced wife, married her Belgian courier, Jean Alexis Opdebeck. The news of the marriage seriously affected the duke's health. An old eye infection that had nearly left him blind late in 1858 returned to one of his eyes, and his mental state also deteriorated. He raged about his daughter's infatuation with Dolly Vane, and the terrible scenes between father and daughter became public, knowledge. The situation became nearly intolerable for the duke when, on 23 April 1860, Susan, against the advice of her governess and Lady Waldegrave, left her father's house at Portman Square in a cab paid for with borrowed money and drove to St. Mary's Church, Bryanston Square, to marry Lord Adolphus. Only a witness for the bridegroom and Lord Lincoln, who gave his sister in marriage, were in attendance.[2]

Scarcely two years earlier, Lady Susan had been bridesmaid to Victoria, the princess royal; the queen was shocked to learn of Susan's marriage to Dolly Vane. To think, the queen wrote to her daughter, that "one of your brides-maids & really a clever, agreeable, handsome girl should do such a thing." "It was most sad," the queen wrote again a few days later, "for I fear Susan will pay dearly for it and her poor father is heartbroken about it. Lord Adolphus is a good creature . . . but between drink and his natural tendency to madness there is a sad prospect for Susan." A few days later the queen repeated what she had heard from Lady Selina Vernon: "Think how horrid—they say that Lord Adolphus Vane is already gone mad and shut up." During the honeymoon, he had thrown a decanter, knives, and forks at his wife; yet Lady Susan told the duchess of Marlborough that she had never had so happy a week in her life![3] Writing to the duchess of Manchester, Lord Clarendon observed that Lady Susan "must be among the most foolish. . . . They have not made a penny of settlement on her so that if that fellow dies in one of his fits she may find herself on pavé, unless her father took her back."[4]

Newcastle escaped from his domestic problems only briefly in the summer and autumn of 1860 while he accompanied the prince of Wales on the tour of Canada and the United States. But the "evil genius" which Lord Selborne claimed "followed him in all the relations of life" awaited him upon his return.[5] He found that Lincoln had been forced to flee the country for failing to pay his racing debt, which had reached the staggering amount of £230,000. While in Nice later in the year, Lincoln fell in love with the beautiful Henrietta Hope, the illegitimate daughter of millionaire Henry Thomas Hope of Deepdene, Surrey, and contracted to marry her. Newcastle was aghast at the thought of such a marriage, which, it was rumored, had been arranged in part by Lincoln's mother, the former Lady Lincoln and present Mrs. Opdebeck. The Hopes, on the other hand, favored the marriage, which, Lady Londonderry observed to her son Lord Adolphus, was soon much "talked of in England, & not pleasantly, as it is known that illegitimacy & gambling debts made the *fond* for the barter of Wealth and Rank, & it is thought the young Lady has been sold for a ducal coronet."[6] Lady Londonderry was exactly right. The price for the ducal coronet was the understanding that Hope would pay Lincoln's debts and settle £10,000 or £12,000 a year upon his daughter, with an additional £50,000 a year for the couple after his death. "The match," Lord Stanley observed in his diary, "is not brilliant as to rank, certainly, but it saves the dukedom from ruin, otherwise inevitable."[7]

The marriage took place in Paris on 11 February 1861. Lady Susan and her husband Lord Adolphus were there, along with Lincoln's and Susan's mother Susan Opdebeck, who was then living in Paris, and their uncle Lord Charles Pelham–Clinton, who lived in Brussels with his wife and children. While in Paris, Susan spent more time with her mother than with her husband, and Dolly Vane consequently was able to consume brandy and liqueurs on the sly. On the night of Lincoln's wedding, Dolly became extremely intoxicated and went out "to a House the nature of which you will understand," Lord Charles told Lord Vane, Dolly's elder brother; after insulting and hitting a gentleman at the Café Anglais, Dolly was put into police custody, from which Susan's mother and Henry Hope eventually recovered him. For three successive nights, much the same occurred. Vane became more and more violent, and on the third night it took three men to subdue him.[8]

The situation became worse when Dolly and Susan returned to England. Susan had a miscarriage after one of her husband's violent outbreaks. In March he was arrested for creating a disturbance in Coventry Street and remanded for medical examination. He was later committed to an institution, but because he was Lady Londonderry's son and a member of Parliament, he was enabled to leave the institution once the charge had been dropped. Meanwhile, Susan, Lord Vane regretfully informed Lady Londonderry, "is generally under the influence of opium & hardly knows what she does or says."[9]

By this time Arthur, the duke's third son, also had proved himself to be totally irresponsible. He had become liable for nearly £15,000 in debt, and there were rumors of his sexual deviation. Writing to Dolly about his brother who was at Versailles at the time, Lincoln noted that Arty wrote on "*mauve scented paper with his initials in red & a coronet in gold*" and had run up a bill for 130 francs "to a coiffeur!!!"[10] It was a portent of worse things to come.

Newcastle continued to pour out his heart to Lady Waldegrave, pleading that "he couldn't live without seeing her."[11] He also talked openly with Abraham Hayward, who in turn spoke to Lord Stanley of the duke's family quarrels, his habit of complaining of ill luck, and his lingering bitterness about being passed over when the last vacancy for the governor-generalship of India had occurred.[12]

Gradually, the duke came to accept Lincoln's marriage, although he never forgave him for giving Susan away in marriage to Dolly Vane, particularly when it became known that the latter had promised surety for large sums of money that Lincoln had owed. The duke met his new daughter-in-law in March 1861, but he refused to see Lincoln until later in the year. Lincoln, however, was present when the prince of Wales stayed at Clumber in October. Dolly Vane, meanwhile, had gone to America for a few months in search of health. But he was madder than ever, "quite maniacal," when he returned.[13] His return proved that the duke could never escape from his troubles for long.

II

Estate matters also remained a constant source of anxiety for Newcastle. The duke embarked upon the arduous task of restoring prosperity to the estates shortly after succeeding to the dukedom. He was able at least to stem the tide and to prevent the further sale of property. Through financial inducement in the form of reduced rents, he encouraged his tenants to adopt more efficient agricultural techniques. He became a model landlord, working with his tenant farmers in extending drainage works, improving the state of the buildings on the estates, establishing schools in each village for the children of the laborers and farmers, and improving the condition of the cottages in order to provide adequate housing for all classes.

Newcastle's approach to the restoration of his finances and his estates rested squarely upon a paternalistic desire to promote the welfare of his tenants and to induce them to become more productive farmers. When at various times he reflected on the changing social climate, he expressed a desire to initiate a new relationship with his tenants, one that stressed cooperation and mutual obligations rather than rights and privileges. Early in February 1851, realizing that discretion and moderation were now necessary in the exercise of political influence, he announced in a letter to his Newark agent that he would break with his late father's electioneering practices. Although he would never hesitate to state his preferences, he observed, he would never coerce his tenants to vote for any particular candidates.[14] In December 1851, he told a large group of his tenants assembled in Clumber's magnificent dining hall that he considered himself the head of one vast family with duties and responsibilities devolved upon him from God. In trying to perform those duties and meet those responsibilities, he said, he would listen to all the tenants and, if possible, entertain their wishes and observations.[15] He was sincere, and he eventually won the love and respect of his tenants. They deeply mourned his death in 1864.

Through the duke's efforts, the financial condition of the estates gradually improved, although they were still in serious disarray at the time of his death. In 1859 these improvements were quite discernible to Lord Clarendon. "I was last week at Clumber," he wrote to Aberdeen,

> and had the opportunity of understanding how the last Duke ruined himself by his more than Sardinian desire for territorial aggrandisement. The present Duke, with small means, administers his vast property in a manner to inspire general respect and esteem. I was delighted with all that he had done and is doing.[16]

In 1861 Newcastle redecorated the mansion at Clumber on a palatial scale in preparation for a visit by the prince of Wales in October. The effect was,

View of Clumber, Newcastle estate in Nottinghamshire,
as it looked in 1861. *Illustrated Times*, 19 October 1861.

according to Sir Frederic Rogers, "all a kind of George III. grandeur—imposing without much interest." [17] Goldwin Smith, who visited the estate on several occasions, described Clumber as a great historic house full of historic treasures and gifts. He was present at the banquet given in the state dining room in honor of the prince of Wales and was impressed by the size of the household staff, which, he conjectured, must have cut deeply into the duke's revenue. Several mayors of neighboring towns also were invited to the banquet. At the occasion, ice, which had just come into fashion, was served to

The Prince of Wales arrives at Clumber. *Illustrated Times*, 26 October 1861.

cool the wine, and one of the mayors mistook it for an entree. After getting the ice on his plate, he first tried to cut it, then he scooped it up to his mouth with a spoon. An observant servant quickly whipped it away, greatly to the embarrassment of the befuddled mayor.[18]

The prince's visit gave Newcastle a chance to show off his collieries at Shireoaks. Those collieries in Nottinghamshire had become one of the principal sources of investment for the duke in his endeavor to restore the fortunes of the Newcastle estates. Between 1854 and the spring of 1859, he spent nearly £70,000 to sink two pits at the location under the direction of the engineer John Lancaster. The duke was just beginning to realize a modest return on his large investment at the time of the prince's visit. During 1860, 90,351 tons of coal and slack were raised at a net profit of £2,252.[19] But the market became depressed later in the year, and the managers of the Great Northern Railway, who found the hard coal of the Shireoaks pits generally unsuited for locomotive engines, reduced the quantity of their order from sixty to twenty tons a day. The duke's colliery agent, Charles Tylden Wright, was forced to raise softer coal from veins nearer the top of the mines. The soft coal was far more satisfactory as steam coal, and early in 1862 the Shireoaks coal was placed on the Admiralty list. Within a short time, the collieries were supplying a thousand tons of coal daily to steam vessels plying in the Baltic region.[20] Even with increased operational costs because of higher wages and deployment of new machinery and underground tracks, the pits continued to provide considerable revenue for the duke. Still, financial matters remained one of his greatest anxieties.

III

Newcastle's domestic troubles continued in the last years of his life. In 1862 Lord Lincoln infuriated his father-in-law, Henry Thomas Hope, by again running up fantastic racing debts. Lady Waldegrave was prophetic in suspecting that Hope, who was near death late in the year, would leave nearly his whole property to his widow, for "he was wary as to giving too much into Lincoln's foolish hands. How annoyed the Duke would be! Another case for martyrdom."[21] Early in the year Newcastle moved to No. 5 Carlton House Terrace to be near the thrice-widowed Lady Waldegrave (George Granville Harcourt, her third husband, had died the previous year), who lived a stone's-throw away at No. 7 Carlton Gardens. The duke lost no opportunity to see Lady Frances, to the great irritation of Chichester Fortescue, who also continued to seek her company. Following a Colonial Office dinner given by the duke at his new house in April, Fortescue tactlessly reminded his host that Fortescue had first met Lady Waldegrave in the very room in which they were then sitting and discussing the British North American intercolonial railway. Fortescue sensed afterwards "that there was some change in his manner with me—something constrained."[22] The great rivalry between the two men for Lady Waldegrave's hand forced her to make an early decision about marriage. She chose Fortescue, and it was partly her great fondness and deep sympathy for Newcastle that prompted her to decide before she had intended. She wanted to avoid a proposal from the duke in order to spare him the embarrassment of a refusal.[23] From the moment he heard of Lady Frances's engagement, Newcastle seemed to lose all desire to live.

The duke's health deteriorated rapidly after Lady Frances's marriage to Fortescue in 1862. Late in November 1863, he was stricken by a serious illness that nearly incapacitated him for the rest of the year. Gladstone offered the duke the use of the ground-floor rooms of his house at Carlton House Terrace. Newcastle declined the offer, although his condition continued to worsen. On 3 December the queen, still deeply mourning the loss of her own husband, Prince Albert, wrote sadly to her uncle Leopold, king of the Belgians, about the recent death of several outstanding men and the illness of two others:

> This terrible account of Lord Elgin will, I am sure, shock you *very* much. I
> fear ultimate recovery is out of the question, *if* even he lingers on! He is

only 52! The Duke of Newcastle is also in a very precarious state; here are two again of our young men, very able, honest, and personal friends of ours, likely ere long to be removed, and I, unprotected, unaided, unadvised, uncheered, will *soon* be left with *none* of *our personal* friends on whom I *relied* more than *ever before* even; Lord Dalhousie, Lord Canning, Lord Elphinstone, Lord Herbert, and Sir C. Lewis, ALL *gone within* three years, and two more on the brink of the grave; and this already alarmed my beloved Angel so much (although *then* Lord Canning and Sir C. Lewis were alive), but with *him* by my side, I needed, so *far less*, all assistance and advice; but NOW? I *hope* and *think* that I shall *not* long *require any*, for I hope I am *gradually* nearing the end of my sad and wearisome journey.[24]

By late December, however, the duke's health had improved to the extent that he was able to travel northward to Clumber for Christmas. But the journey brought on a relapse, and he was unable to attend the cabinets and the opening of Parliament early in 1864. His closest friends urged him to retire from the cares of office.[25] Even his old friend Henry Manning, now a leading Catholic prelate, wrote from Rome advising the duke to seek a well-deserved rest:

> To a man who loves work, and has lived for it as you have, to be ill is a trial in many ways more sensible than the illness itself. But you have one great consolation, which is that for the last thirty years your life has never been at rest. It is a great thing to wear out, and I never can think any man to have cause for regret, in this sense, who wears out early and in full work. *Terar dum prosim.* It seems to me but the other day when we were all starting from Oxford into active life, little knowing what a future was before us, and how our paths would part asunder. I have always looked upon yours as one of the most useful and consistent public lives of those who began so full of hope thirty years ago.[26]

Despite these pleas for his retirement, Newcastle retained office at Palmerston's request. Gradually he improved, and early in March the queen expressed her gratification that he seemed to be recovering. "How the Queen wishes she cd. alleviate these sorrows," which were the cause of his long suffering, she wrote. "But trials like the Duke's seldom fall to the lot of man!"[27]

Newcastle's improved condition was short-lived, however. On 19 March, he suffered a relapse that nearly proved fatal. On 2 April, after consulting his doctors, he submitted his resignation to Palmerston. The prime minister accepted the letter with deep regret. He assured the duke that he and his colleagues in the cabinet would "long miss that clearness of head, that political sagacity, that nobility of presence, and that straitforward honesty of purpose which have endeared you to your Colleagues."[28] Several other members of the cabinet followed with kind notes. Lord Russell, still Lord John to his friends, wrote:

> I cannot part with so good a colleague without expressing my regret that a return of illness should have made this separation from the Ministry a matter of necessity. Your sound & firm views of public policy have always made me listen with attention & weigh with deference the opinions you gave in the Cabinet, & I am sure we shall all feel the loss of so enlightened & judicious a colleague.[29]

Above all the duke cherished a note from the queen, which he acknowledged in a letter to Sir Charles Phipps:

> I have this morning received a letter from the Queen accepting my resignation, so gracious and kind to me, and so beautiful in itself that it would amply repay all the suffering which has rendered it necessary. It will take its place among my greatest treasures with two others written to me when I was hunted out of the Queen's service in January 1855.[30]

Although the duke rallied briefly from time to time, his general condition worsened steadily. Late in May, Edward Cardwell, who had replaced the duke as colonial secretary, found it impossible to speak to him on official matters. In fact, only occasionally was the duke able to speak at all.[31] In June he slipped even further. He lost all memory of names, although not of the persons or places they represented. Thus, Lord Stanley observed, "he spoke to Fortescue of N. Zealand as 'that large island where we are at war with the natives' and of Gladstone as 'that very able man—my friend—who made that odd speech lately.' Such are the eccentricities of brain disease."[32] Lady Waldegrave and Fortescue were frequently with the duke in June, and Queen Victoria came up from Windsor with Arthur Stanley, dean of Westminster, to take her farewell when she heard of the hopelessness of his condition. "Though looking drawn & pinched," she wrote in her journal, "the countenance was unaltered & he gave me a look of the kindest recognition which I shall not forget! I took hold of his hand saying 'God bless you' & told him what a kind friend he had been to us both."[33] During the next month, the queen sent no fewer than ten telegrams to inquire of his health and to express her concern, and she visited him again on 2 July. The prince of Wales also demonstrated his appreciation for the duke by a visit to his bedside.

There was some solace for the duke in the news of Lord Adolphus Vane-Tempest's death. "I forgot to tell you," the queen told her eldest daughter, Princess Victoria, "that poor Susan Vane's dreadful husband died . . . I believe in a struggle with four keepers when he burst a vein in his throat. She is left penniless. Is this not retribution? He tried to kill her last week and also the child—so that I believe it is to her a real release too."[34]

By August the duke was well enough to travel to Clumber. His homecoming was an occasion for great rejoicing throughout Nottinghamshire. The bells of the Abbey Church were pealed, and in Worksop the principal tradesmen decorated their premises in honor of his arrival. On 18 August, a large group of influential Nottingham residents adopted an address expressing gratification for the duke's partial recovery and the hope that he would soon be able to resume the duties of the lord lieutenancy.[35] But the duke remained in a languid state the rest of the summer.

Two of his children were with him at Clumber during his final days. Lady Susan and her infant child had taken up residence there after the death of Lord Adolphus, and late in August, Lord and Lady Lincoln arrived for an extended visit. In September, Lady Lincoln gave birth to her first son, the future seventh duke of Newcastle. Another piece of family news was kept from the duke, however. Lord Albert, the youngest of the children, the baby for whom Prince Albert had stood godfather, had deserted from the navy and was in Paris merrily amassing a huge debt. The family solicitor would have informed the duke of the matter had the duke's condition not worsened. At 6:25 in the evening of 18 October 1864, at the age of fifty-three, the duke suffered a sudden and devastating attack. He died seven minutes later. The massive cerebral hemorrhage brought a "very merciful" end to a tragic life.

The day of the funeral, 27 October, brought "a deluge of rain."[36] Yet thousands of tenants, local townspeople, and friends of the late duke assembled at the Markham Clinton Church following the private service to walk behind the coffin draped in crimson Genoa velvet as it was carried to a mausoleum a few miles away. During the afternoon, hundreds of the thousands who were present filed past the coffin in the vault. Late in the evening the tomb was closed upon one who had been "beloved by his Queen, honoured by his countrymen, and held in the highest esteem by all to whom talents of the highest order are felt and appreciated."[37]

Conclusion

Gladstone stayed at Clumber for a few days after Newcastle's funeral in his role as one of the executors of the estate. His task was most difficult; it would take years to unravel the finances of the estate. However, the late duke's dissolute younger sons presented Gladstone with an even more immediate and difficult problem, one that he was unable to resolve satisfactorily. Lord Arthur, who had deserted from his ship shortly before his father's death, was dismissed from the navy without any declaration of disgrace in November 1864. But thereafter his personal dissipation increased, and he died six years later from scarlet fever while awaiting trial at the Central Criminal Court on the charge of appearing in public in women's attire. Lord Albert, the youngest of the duke's five children, also caused Gladstone grave concern. He continued to be in danger of arrest for debt. In 1870 he married Frances Evelyn, widow of Captain Edward Stotherd, who later shut herself up in a Roman Catholic convent in Kensington for a time before moving in with the corespondent in the divorce case that dissolved the marriage in 1877.[1]

The story of Lady Susan, the duke's only daughter, exemplifies the family theme of misfortune. In 1867 she became one of the many mistresses of the prince of Wales and later bore one of his many illegitimate children. Following the birth of the child in 1871, Lady Susan lived out her life in London in very poor health and circumstances. She died in 1875, leaving very little record of her last few miserable years.[2]

Of the duke's children, only Lord Edward was saved from the misfortunes that had afflicted the family. Born in 1837 shortly before his mother's fateful infatuation with his uncle, he completed a successful army career before becoming master of the household during Queen Victoria's last years and a groom-in-waiting to King Edward VII.

Very little is known of the mother, Lady Susan, formerly Lady Lincoln, after her marriage to Jean Alexis Opdebeck in 1860. Shunned by London society for activities that were considered flagrant even in the more lax moral atmosphere of the aristocracy, Lady Susan chose to remain on the Continent. She lived in Paris for awhile, to the disgust of her brother, Lord Douglas, eleventh duke of Hamilton, who also lived there until his death in 1863. She returned to England sometime in the 1880s and lived the rest of her life in rooms in a large red brick house at Keymer, near Burgess Hill in Sussex. She died on 28 November 1889, the anniversary of her marriage to Lincoln. Her grave in St. John's cemetery, Burgess Hill, is marked by a gravestone that may have been erected by either Lord Edward or Horatio Walpole, her surviving sons. The latter, whom Lady Susan had called her "pickle," was reared by nuns in Italy and educated at Heidelberg University. His father, Lord Walpole, succeeded as the fourth earl of Oxford in 1858 and lived as a notorious misogynist until 1894, with every link with Susan severed soon after her divorce from Lincoln in 1850.[3]

Linky, Lord Lincoln, who succeeded his father to the title as the sixth duke of Newcastle-under-Lyme, died in 1879, ten years before his mother. He had done nothing to restore the fortunes of his family. Upon his death, the title and estate passed to his son Henry Pelham Archibald Douglas, seventh duke of Newcastle, who was born less than a month before his grandfather's death in 1864. Although the seventh duke was not very active politically, he did much to restore grandeur to the title and estate. In 1890, he sold Worksop Manor, which the fourth duke had purchased in 1843, for £106,020. After a fire in 1879 destroyed twenty rooms at Clumber House, he had it rebuilt on plans drawn up by the younger Charles Barry. Although it was not the largest of stately homes, Clumber was magnificent. It contained a vast collection of treasures, including paintings by Rembrandt and Rubens in the state dining room. The drawing room was elegantly decorated and richly furnished with items obtained from the Doge's Palace in Venice; and the library, perhaps the finest apartment in the mansion, contained many fine books, including volumes of rare engravings by Vandyke, Hogarth, and Holbein.[4] The September 1908 issues of *Country Life* featured the mansion and gardens.

In 1928, Henry Francis Hope Pelham-Clinton-Hope succeeded his brother as the eighth duke of Newcastle-under-Lyme. Under the terms of the seventh duke's will, however, Clumber House went to the late duke's nephew, Henry Edward Hugh, earl of Lincoln, who became the ninth and present duke of Newcastle in 1941 when he succeeded his father. With the increase in taxation, Lord Lincoln found it necessary to sell by auction many of the contents of Clumber House. In 1936 Christie's obtained £43,396 from the sale of pictures, silver, objects of art, and furniture; and during a seven-day sale on the premises at Clumber in October 1937, Christie's sold most of the remaining contents of the mansion, including marble mantelpieces, crystal chandeliers, antique and modern statuary, and a varied collection of furniture and porcelain. The total from the Christie auction at Clumber was £15,714. The books and manuscripts from the library were sold at Sotheby's between June 1937 and February 1938, bringing a total of £64,000.[5]

Except for one wing, the old study, Clumber House was completely demolished in 1938. The Nottinghamshire County Council purchased the paneling and carved oak mantelpiece from the Oak Room of the mansion for the apartments of the new County Hall. The congregation of St. Bernard bought nearly three hundred thousand handmade, 150-year-old bricks from Clumber for the facing of their new church in Sheffield. During World War II, Clumber Park served as a vast and closely guarded munitions dump. In 1946, after issuing a national appeal for £45,000, the National Trust purchased the thirty-eight hundred acres of Clumber Park from the ninth duke of Newcastle for permanent preservation as a public park under the supervision of the Clumber Park Management Committee. With its natural beauty and romantic associations with Sherwood Forest, Clumber Park is one of the most popular public parks in England today.[6]

Following the sale of Clumber Park, the duke of Newcastle purchased Boyton Estate in Wiltshire and established the Newcastle Estate Office in Warminster. After selling the Boyton Estate in 1961, the duke purchased several farms comprising nearly three thousand acres in Gloucestershire and Bishopstone's Estate of five thousand acres in Kent. Currently, the ninth duke of Newcastle-upon-Lyme resides on a small private estate in Somerset.

II

The fortitude with which the fifth duke of Newcastle had borne accumulated misfortune and torturing disease touched the hearts of those who knew him. His death brought a profound sense of loss. "It is always very touching to see a strong man fail—to see him tugging at the oar while there is a spark of life in him—and relinquishing his toil only because he has killed himself with work," read the obituary notice in the *Times*:

> An energetic man like the Duke could ill be spared at any time, but his loss
> now that the Liberal party has within the last few years been cruelly shorn
> of its strength by the decease of some of its best men has been most severely
> felt. Personally, too, he was held in such regard and liking that it is less
> easy to reconcile ourselves to his loss than to the loss of perhaps a much
> abler man. There was in his friendship a loyalty that made him one pecu-
> liarly to be trusted; and if it was not given to him to dazzle the eyes of
> his countrymen by the brilliancy of his talents, he could at least win our
> confidence by his sound sense, by his good faith, and by his zeal in the
> public service.[7]

It was an appropriate tribute to a man whose many significant contributions were made even more remarkable by the misfortunes and tragedies of his personal life.

Although short-lived, Newcastle's political career was significant in several ways. He was instrumental in formulating the Peelite concept of "conservative progress," which called for the enactment of moderate reforms to bring greater efficiency in public administration and to place the country on firm financial and economic foundations. Through a program of steady but cautious movement forward, the Peelites hoped to strike a balance between the extremes of radicalism and ultraconservatism, between tradition and progress. In their view, to do nothing about abuses in society would encourage revolutionary activity and the growth of democracy in its most radical form.

Newcastle's political opinions were at the heart of the Peelite political concept of conservative progress. He stressed the need to meet the threat from democracy by a substantial extension of the franchise and a more equitable system of parliamentary representation. He argued vigorously for an income tax that would be used as an engine for social reform, and he staunchly advocated the extension of free trade. He was one of the chief spokesmen for a large program of social and economic regeneration for Ireland. Although a High Church man, he was a strong proponent of religious liberalism, and his contempt for reactionaries was well marked by his condemnation both of Tory religious intolerance and resistance to change.

In political principles as well as in administrative policies, Newcastle was influenced greatly by Sir Robert Peel. Most of the duke's views were derived from his mentor. Newcastle and Sidney Herbert, who were clearly Peel's favorites, fulfilled all of Peel's early expectations. Despite the difference in their ages, Peel and Newcastle became close friends. Peel wrote to Newcastle in an easy, informal style that he rarely used with any other person. After Peel's death, Newcastle continued to be one of the major spokesmen of Peelite political philosophy, and he in turn influenced Gladstone considerably.

Newcastle's influence on Gladstone was twofold. During the 1850s, the duke frequently urged his friend to sever his Conservative ties and to move toward liberalism on such issues as parliamentary reform and the income tax. Furthermore, Newcastle helped to convince Gladstone that the goals of extending free trade, retrenching public finance, effecting administrative reform, and securing religious toleration could be achieved only through a Peelite-Whig juncture. But he stressed that in joining with the Whigs, the Peelites must take the lead. To gain the leadership of the Liberals, the duke believed that the Peelites must outbid the Whigs on reform, demonstrate their skills in administration, and appeal more directly to the people. He denounced Whig exclusiveness in very strong terms. He vigorously opposed Lord John Russell's many attempts to recruit Peelite talent as a way of bolstering and retaining Whig leadership of the Liberal party, and he repeatedly told Russell that traditional Whig leadership based upon social prestige and narrow public support alone was not sufficient in an age of expanding democracy. Thus Newcastle pressed for a national party that would be preeminent in administration, dedicated to moderate reform, and secured in power by wide popular support in the constituencies. What he envisaged was very like the party and political movement that came to fruition later in the form of Gladstonian Liberalism.

Like his fellow Peelites, Newcastle stressed excellence in public administration, although his own official career was tarnished by events largely beyond his control during the first year of the Crimean War. Although the duke cannot be exonerated completely, an objective review of his administration of the War Office clearly reveals that no individual was solely responsible for the failures in the Crimea. The mistakes and miscalculations of the civilian authorities in London were compounded by the mistakes and miscalculations of the military men in the Crimea. But it was more a failure of strategy and military execution than a failure of logistics that brought near disaster. There was, however, no denial that the administrative system was weak and corrupt, and that the weakness of the system was graphically exposed by the stress of war. It was Newcastle's misfortune to be placed at the head of that system without having either the authority or the opportunity to make it more workable. Even a man of more vision and vigor than the duke probably would not have been much more successful in administering the War Office at that particular time. But early in 1855 a frustrated and angry public sought both villains and heroes, and the duke seemed to fit the role of the first as perfectly as Lord Palmerston did that of the second.

Throughout his career, Newcastle followed two main administrative principles. He believed that officials in London must rely heavily upon information and advice from subordinates in the field, the "men on the spot," to guide them in policy formulation and implementation. He also stressed the need to give administrators discretionary authority to meet local circumstances. In most instances of administration, the duke was more pragmatic than doctrinaire; he stressed flexibility within the framework of a few general rules. In the case of Irish famine relief early in 1846, Newcastle (then Lord Lincoln) believed that as chief secretary he was the principal "man on the spot" whose appeal for discretionary authority was resisted by the doctrinaire officials at the Treasury. In colonial matters, the duke was well aware of the difficulties and dangers of dictating instructions from London, of ruling the empire by "didactic Despatches." He always tried to take local needs into consideration. He even tolerated colonial governors who occasionally for local reasons contravened the concept of responsible government, even though he was a sincere advocate of responsible government in its most liberal and extensive form. At times, as the duke himself recognized, he became too dependent upon the men on the spot, which frequently created difficulties. That was the case in 1854. Newcastle discovered belatedly that the information supplied to him from the theater of war was frequently incomplete, incorrect, or misleading. The result was Newcastle's greatest failure in administration.

Although he was an astute political observer, Newcastle's greatest weakness was his inability to adjust well to the rough game of politics. His political problems in 1854–1855 stemmed in part from the lingering animosities and temporary disunity between the older, traditional Whigs like Lord John Russell and the younger Peelite and Liberal leaders. The failure of the Whigs and Peelites to fuse completely during the early 1850s was evident to both groups, and the struggle over the successor to Lord Aberdeen as prime minister and leader of the Liberal coalition aggravated both the tensions between Whigs and Peelites and Newcastle's political difficulties. The rift between Newcastle and Russell was caused to some extent by the question of future Liberal leadership, and the crisis of early 1855 severely damaged the political reputations of both men. The duke was a victim both of political maneuver and his own political weakness.

Newcastle recovered his health and political stature sufficiently by 1859 to permit him to take the Colonial Office seals, an official position for which he was eminently well suited. With declining health, a tragic family life, and past political disappointments forming a dismal backdrop, the duke as colonial secretary would play his greatest role as a statesman. For the next few years, Newcastle supervised the empire with gloved hand and sheathed sword, with "mutual sympathy and mutual obligation" his guiding principles, during a time when there was considerable doubt as to the value of Britain's possessions overseas. He was a decided imperialist who administered the empire with tact and understanding in an innovative way that proved he was an important imperial architect, particularly in the areas of colonial self-government and self-defense. He was one of the most highly regarded colonial secretaries of the nineteenth century.

Newcastle was a liberal imperialist who believed that the continuance of the empire would be assured on the basis of responsible government and local independence, with imperial defense being the main link with Great Britain. The introduction of responsible government in most of the settlement colonies during the 1850s had left many undefined spheres of responsibility, such as control of commercial policy, conduct of native affairs, colonial contributions to imperial defense, and the limitations on colonial and imperial legislation. In meeting these problems, the Colonial Office under Newcastle adopted a liberal policy of advocating minimum interference in colonial affairs, an attitude that allowed the maximum of nation-building within the framework of the empire. Like Gladstone, Newcastle was interested in economic retrenchment, but not at the expense of peace and security or of the interests of the indigenous peoples in the colonies. He also laid the foundations of confederation in British North America, and he initiated a new period of expansion and settlement in South Africa that ultimately would facilitate the union of the colonies in that area. All in all, his administration of the Colonial

Office during these critical years of the nineteenth century when the whole question of empire was under extensive examination provided many valuable precedents in the evolutionary process from empire to commonwealth.

Newcastle's public achievements were quite significant despite poor health and personal misfortunes that plagued him throughout his life. He was alienated from his father for long periods of time; their political and familial struggles provide valuable insight into social and political aspects of England during the 1830s and 1840s. After he succeeded his father to the title in 1851, Newcastle's own strict parental propriety led four of his five children to rebel against him. His eldest son and heir was an utter profligate, and his only daughter made a disastrous marriage to the mad Lord Adolphus Vane-Tempest. The duke suffered yet another personal blow when Lady Frances Waldegrave, whom he had courted for several years, married Chichester Fortescue, his subordinate at the Colonial Office; this additional disappointment may well have hastened the duke's death.

The story of Newcastle's wretched and protracted marital crisis is the material of which Victorian novels were made. But the divorce, although a personal tragedy, did not affect the duke's political and social standing. Through all his personal misfortunes, Newcastle never lost his zeal for public service, and perhaps as a way to lessen the agonies of his private life, he undertook more public responsibilities than his health could withstand. His steadfast loyalty and devotion to duty made him a favorite at court, a friend of the queen, of the prince consort, and of the prince of Wales. Even as late as the early 1860s, he was mentioned as a possible successor to Lord Palmerston as prime minister and leader of the Liberal party. By that time, however, his health was shattered, and his greatest ambition, becoming the prime minister of England, was never fulfilled.

Abbreviations Used in Notes

Aber.	Aberdeen Papers, British Library
Aber. Corres.	*Aberdeen Correspondence*, British Library, privately printed
Bro.	Broughton Papers, British Library
CHBE	*Cambridge History of the British Empire*
Clar.	Clarendon Papers, Bodleian Library
C.O.	Colonial Office Records, Public Record Office, London
DP	Derby Papers, Knowsley (currently in custody of Lord Blake)
Dis.	Disraeli Papers, Hughendon Papers, Bodleian Library
EP	Ellenborough Papers, Public Record Office, London
F.O.	Foreign Office Records, Public Record Office, London
G-G MSS	Glynne-Gladstone Manuscripts, St. Deiniol's Library, Hawarden
Glad.	Gladstone Papers, British Library
Goul.	Goulburn Papers, Surrey Record Office
GP	Grey Papers, University of Durham
Gram.	Graham Papers, microfilm, Bodleian Library
Gran.	Granville Papers, Public Record Office, London
Her.	Herbert Papers, Wilton Estate Office
Hick.	Hickleton Papers, microfilm, Bodleian Library
ND	Diary of the fourth duke of Newcastle, Manuscripts Department, University of Nottingham
NeC	Newcastle Papers, Manuscripts Department, University of Nottingham
Pal.	Palmerston Papers, British Library
Parl. Deb.	*Hansard's Parliamentary Debates*, third series
Parl. Pap.	*Parliamentary Papers*
Peel	Peel Papers, British Library
PP	Palmerston Papers, National Register of Archives
RA	Royal Archives, Windsor Castle
RP	Russell Papers, Public Record Office, London
Stra.	Strachie Papers, Somerset Record Office
TLB	Sir Charles Trevelyan's Letter Book, University Library, Newcastle-upon-Tyne
W.O.	War Office Records, Public Record Office, London

Notes

Introduction

1. Cited Phillip Magnus, *Gladstone: A Biography*, 156.
2. NeC 10,890, fols. 211–15, Newcastle to A. W. Kinglake, 13 November 1862.
3. Quoted J. B. Conacher, *The Aberdeen Coalition, 1852–1855*, 45.
4. George Eden Marindin, ed., *Letters of Frederic Lord Blachford*, 225.
5. John Morley, *The Life of William Ewart Gladstone*, 1:651.
6. John Martineau, *The Life of Henry Pelham, Fifth Duke of Newcastle, 1811–1864*.
7. A. W. Kinglake, *The Invasion of the Crimea*.

Chapter 1: Early Years

1. Sir Leslie Stephen and Sir Sidney Lee, eds., *Dictionary of National Biography*, 4:550, quoting Orderic Vitalis.
2. H. A. Doubleday and Lord Howard de Walden, eds., *The Complete Peerage*, 9:532.
3. John Martineau, *The Life of Henry Pelham, Fifth Duke of Newcastle, 1811–1864*, 2–3.
4. John Golby, "A Great Electioneer and His Motives: The Fourth Duke of Newcastle," 201.
5. Ibid., 203, quoting from Newcastle's pamphlet, *Thoughts in Times Past Tested by Subsequent Events* (1837), xxxi.
6. ND, Ne2 Fl, 73.
7. Besides Lord Lincoln, the children of the fourth duke of Newcastle were: Lord Charles Pelham Clinton, 1813–1894, M.P. for Sandwich, 1852–1857; Lord Thomas, his twin, 1813–1882, 1st Lifeguards; Lord William, 1815–1850; Lord Edward, 1816–1842, Royal Navy; Lord Robert Renebald, 1820–1867; Lady Anna Maria, 1808–1822; Lady Georgiana, 1810–1874; Lady Charlotte, 1812–1886; Lady Caroline Augusta, 1818–1898, m. Sir Cornwallis Ricketts, 2d Bart.; and Lady Henrietta, 1819–1890, m. 1859 Admiral E. C. Tennyson-d' Eyncourt.

8. ND, Ne2 F5, 235.
9. Ibid., F1, 183.
10. Ibid., 201–2.
11. Ibid., 249.
12. Ibid., 223.
13. Ibid., 243.
14. Ibid., F2, 1.
15. Ibid., 85.
16. Ibid., 121.
17. Ibid., F3, 68.
18. NeC 12,922, Lincoln (copy) to Dr. John Keate, no date.
19. Disturbed by the absence of religious teaching at Eton, the duke, shortly after Lincoln left the school, founded the Newcastle Scholarship to reward annually the most successful candidate in an examination in divinity and classics.
20. ND, Ne2 F3, 182.
21. Ibid., Ne2 F2, 215, 230–31, 236–38.
22. Ibid., 19, 67–68.
23. Ibid., 71–72.
24. NeC 5,575, Lincoln to Newcastle, 14 November 1831.
25. ND, Ne2 F4, 97.
26. Martineau, *Newcastle*, 35, quoting Newcastle to Lincoln, no date.
27. The Yorkshire boroughs of Aldborough and Boroughbridge were abolished under Schedule A of the Reform Act.
28. ND, Ne2 F4, 182.
29. NeC 5,700b, Lincoln to Newcastle, 15 June 1832. Some readers will notice that in this letter and in others by both Lincoln and Jonathan Thompson, American rather than British spellings are often used for words such as *honor*; apparently this peculiarity of Thompson's was adopted by Lincoln, his student.
30. NeC 11,773b, Gladstone to Lincoln, 9 July 1832; M. R. D. Foot, ed., *The Gladstone Diaries*, 1:545; John Morley, *The Life of William Ewart Gladstone*, 1:88–89.
31. NeC 11,655, Lincoln (copy) to Gladstone, 9 August 1832.
32. Gladstone honored Lincoln's request. In

his diary entry for 19 December 1832, Gladstone recorded, "Wrote to Lincoln from Newark (under my first frank, given for tomorrow & addressed to the Countess)" (Foot, ed., *Gladstone Diaries*, 1:593).

33. Virginia Surtees, *A Beckford Inheritance: The Lady Lincoln Scandal*, 11–12, quoting Newcastle to Hamilton, 21 November 1832, and Hamilton to Newcastle, 27 November 1832.

34. Ibid., 13–14, quoting Newcastle to Hamilton, no date.

35. Ibid., 14, quoting Newcastle to Hamilton, no date.

36. Ibid., 14–15, quoting Newcastle to Hamilton, no date. On 30 January 1832, Newcastle noted in his diary that he believed Lincoln had selected a person for his partner who was "in every way calculated to make a happy & advantageous union" (ND, Ne2 F4, 98).

37. NeC 5,701, Lincoln to Newcastle, 20 June 1832.

38. NeC 5,706, Lincoln to Newcastle, 12 July 1832.

39. ND, Ne2 F4, 143–44.

40. Cf. Surtees, *A Beckford Inheritance*, 5–8; Stephen and Lee, eds., *Dictionary of National Biography*, 2:82–85, 5:1164. Alexander Hamilton Douglas, tenth duke of Hamilton, 1767–1852, believed that as the descendant of the regent Arron he was the true heir to the throne of Scotland.

41. John Brooke and Mary Sorensen, eds., *The Prime Ministers' Papers: W. E. Gladstone*, II: *Autobiographical Memoranda, 1832–1845*, 65.

42. Cf. Surtees, *A Beckford Inheritance*, 8–9.

43. NeC 11,656, Lincoln (copy) to Gladstone, 13 September 1832.

44. ND, Ne2 F4, 153.

45. NeC 11,656, Lincoln (copy) to Gladstone, 13 September 1832.

46. NeC 5,732 and 5,734, Hamilton to Newcastle, 4, 22 October 1832.

47. ND, Ne2 F4, 92.

48. Ibid., 170.

49. Ibid., 173.

50. Foot, ed., *Gladstone Diaries*, 1:592.

51. ND, Ne2 F4, 184–85; cf. Martineau, *Newcastle*, 21.

52. ND, Ne2 F4, 92.

Chapter 2: Apprenticeship to Peel

1. A. Aspinall, ed., *Three Early Nineteenth Century Diaries*, 340.

2. Glad., Add. MS. 44262, fols. 2–9, Gladstone (copy) to Lincoln, 26 September 1833, and Lincoln to Gladstone, 3 October 1833.

3. Ibid., fols. 15–17, Gladstone (copy) to Lincoln, 9 April 1834.

4. NeC 12,967, Newcastle to Lincoln, 27 September 1834.

5. Peel, Add. MS. 40405, fols. 173–74, Peel (copy) to Lincoln, 13 December 1834; John Morley, *The Life of William Ewart Gladstone*, 1:119.

6. Quoted Phillip Magnus, *Gladstone: A Biography*, 21.

7. The final analysis was: government supporters—290; Radicals—150; Whigs and Stanleyites—218, 40 or 50 of whom Peel hoped to attract to his side. Cf. Norman Gash, *Sir Robert Peel*, 101.

8. Peel, Add. MS. 40410, fols. 24–25, Peel (copy) to Lincoln, 11 January 1835.

9. Glad., Add. MS 44262, fols. 26–29, Gladstone (copy) to Lincoln, 20 January 1835.

10. ND, Ne2 F5, 8–9.

11. Ibid., 9.

12. Ibid.

13. Ibid., 10.

14. Cf. Gash, *Peel*, 121–26.

15. Quoted Morley, *Gladstone*, 1:128.

16. NeC 12,968, Newcastle to Lincoln, 20 April 1835.

17. ND, Ne2 F5, 1.

18. Ibid., 83, 85, and 107.

19. Ibid., 39.

20. NeC 5,761, Newcastle to Lincoln, 27 June 1835.

21. NeC 5,762, Lincoln to Newcastle, 28 June 1835.

22. NeC 5,763, Newcastle to Lincoln, 28 June 1835.

23. Quoted Gash, *Peel*, 143.

24. ND, Ne2 F5, 129.

25. *Nottingham Journal*, 20 January 1837.

26. M. R. D. Foot, ed., *The Gladstone Diaries*, 2:275.

27. Ibid.

28. ND, Ne2 F5, 165.

29. NeC 11,850, Lincoln (copy) to Bonham, 30 January 1837.

30. NeC 5,777, unsigned and undated letter.

31. Cf. Virginia Surtees, *A Beckford Inheritance: The Lady Lincoln Scandal*, 37; Colin C. Eldridge, "The Lincoln Divorce Case: A Study in Victorian Morality," 25–26.

32. NeC 5,822, Lincoln to Newcastle, 18 April 1837.

33. NeC 12,980a, Journal of 1837 Tour.

34. NeC 5,825; 5,826; and 5,827, Lincoln to Newcastle, 4 and 10 July 1837, and Thompson to Newcastle, 8 July 1837.

35. NeC 5,828, Lincoln to Newcastle, 11 July 1837; NeC 5,829, Thompson to Newcastle, 11 July 1837.

36. Cf. Surtees, *A Beckford Inheritance*, 47.

37. *Times*, "Report of the Proceedings of the Tribunal De Premeire Instance," 7 and 14 December 1837.

38. Ibid.

39. Quoted Surtees, *A Beckford Inheritance*, 48.

40. Ibid.

41. ND, Ne2 F5, 258–59.

42. NeC 12,980a, Journal of 1838 Tour.

43. Foot, ed., *Gladstone Diaries*, 2:519–22.

44. ND, Ne2 F6, 67.

45. John Golby, "A Great Electioneer and His Motives: The Fourth Duke of Newcastle," 204.

46. ND, Ne2 F5, 251.

47. Ibid., 284–85.

48. NeC 12,853, Lincoln to Newcastle, 1 February 1841.

49. ND, Ne2 F6, 74, 146–47.

50. Ibid., 4–5. The incident that caused the duke's dismissal arose over a very discourteous letter he wrote to the lord chancellor protesting two of the lord chancellor's nominations to the Commission of the Peace. When Newcastle refused to withdraw the letter and accept the appointment of the two nonconformists to the commission, Melbourne notified him that he had been dismissed as lord lieutenant. Newcastle became quite disconsolate over the whole affair.

51. Cf. Gash, *Peel*, 236–37.

52. NeC 5,577, Lincoln to Newcastle, 1 May 1841.

53. RA C22/21, Peel to Anson, 7 September 1841; Gash, *Peel*, 278.

54. Henry Reeve, ed., *The Greville Memoirs*, 5:268.

Chapter 3: Office under Peel

1. *Parl. Deb.*, LXXXIII, 1737.

2. Peel, Add. MS. 40481, fols. 11–12, Lincoln to Peel, 16 May 1842; NeC 8,823, Lincoln (copy) to Lord F. Egerton, 26 May 1842.

3. NeC 12,074, Lincoln (copy) to Peel, 27 April 1845.

4. NeC 9,019a, Lincoln (copy) to Duke of Cambridge, 16 March 1844.

5. NeC 12,063, Lincoln (copy) to Peel, 4 February 1845.

6. Peel, Add. MS. 40481, fols 83–84 and 108–9, Lincoln to Peel, 15 January 1843, and Peel (copies) to Lincoln, 18 and 21 April 1843.

7. NeC 12,045, Lincoln (copy) to Peel, 11 October 1844. See Norman Gash, *Sir Robert Peel*, 389, for Peel's part in the purchase of Osborne. Peel favored the scheme.

8. G-G MSS, Lincoln to Lady Lincoln, 24 August 1841.

9. ND, Ne2 F6, 210–11.

10. George Peel, ed., *Private Letters of Sir Robert Peel*, 192–93, Peel to Lady Peel, 8 January 1842.

11. Ibid., Peel to Lady Peel, 13 January 1842.

12. ND, Ne2 F6, 216.

13. G-G MSS, Lincoln to Henry Murray, 11 November 1842. The love letter, signed "Winchilsea," no date, remains a mystery. It remains among Lady Lincoln's papers at Hawarden.

14. NeC 5,882 and 5,885, Lincoln to Newcastle, 24 May 1842, and Hamilton to Newcastle, 8 June 1842.

15. ND, Ne2 F6, 241–42.

16. Ibid., 244.

17. G-G MSS, Lady Lincoln to Lincoln and to Newcastle, and Lincoln to Lady Lincoln, 22 June 1842.

18. Ibid., Lady Lincoln to Lincoln, and Lincoln to Lady Lincoln, 29 July 1842.

19. Ibid., Lincoln to Hamilton, 19 August 1842, and Hamilton to Lincoln, 27 August 1842.

20. Virginia Surtees, *A Beckford Inheritance: The Lady Lincoln Scandal*, 62, quoting Madge Orde to Hamilton, December 1842.

21. G-G MSS, Graham to Lincoln, 24 August 1842, and Peel to Lincoln, 22 August 1842.

22. ND, Ne2 F6, 259.

23. Surtees, *A Beckford Inheritance*, 63.

24. Ibid.

25. G–G MSS, Lady Lincoln to Lincoln, 30 November 1842.

26. Ibid., Peel to Lincoln, 3 December 1842.

27. Ibid., Lincoln (draft) to Lady Lincoln, 4 December 1842.

28. Surtees, *A Beckford Inheritance*, 64, quoting Madge Orde to Hamilton, no date.

29. NeC 5,578 and 5,579, Lincoln to Newcastle, 8 and 20 July 1843.

30. Foot and Matthew, eds., *The Gladstone Diaries*, 3:239–40.

31. S. E. Finer, *The Life and Times of Sir Edwin Chadwick*, 239–40.

32. G–G MSS, Lady Lincoln to Lincoln, 2 September 1844.

33. Ibid., Gairdner to Lady Lincoln, 5 and 6 September 1844, and Lady Lincoln to Lincoln, 7 September 1844.

34. Ibid., Lincoln to Lady Lincoln, 10 September 1844.

35. NeC 5,853, Lincoln to Newcastle, 15 September 1844.

36. G–G MSS, Newcastle to Lincoln, 22 September 1844. The duke characterized Susan as "vicious, deceitful, and heartless" in his diary (ND, Ne2 F7, 136).

37. Peel, Add. MS. 40481, fols. 291–94, Lincoln to Peel, 17 September 1844.

38. G–G MSS, Peel to Lincoln, 20 September 1844; Herbert to Lincoln, 14 September 1844; and Thompson to Lincoln, 17 September 1844; Foot and Matthew, eds., *Gladstone Diaries*, 3:410.

39. NeC 5,852, Lincoln to Newcastle, 12 September 1844; G–G MSS, Newcastle to Lincoln, 22 September 1844.

40. Cf. Gash, *Peel*, 438–53; D. R. Fisher, "Peel and the Conservative Party: The Sugar Crisis of 1844 Reconsidered"; Robert Stewart, *The Politics of Protection*, 15–22.

41. Gash, *Peel*, 418–19, 456–57, and 463–65; Stewart, *Politics of Protection*, 19.

42. ND, Ne2 F7, 161.

43. G–G MSS, Lincoln to Thompson, 25 March 1845.

44. ND, Ne2 F7, 174; *Times*, "Duke of Newcastle's Address," 19 May 1845.

45. ND, Ne2 F7, 174–76.

46. *Parl. Deb.*, LXXIX, 727–35; *Times*, 16 April 1845.

47. G–G MSS, Lincoln to Thompson, 19 April 1845.

48. ND, Ne2 F7, 174.

49. Ibid., 182–85.

50. Cf. Gash, *Peel*, 666; John Martineau, *The Life of Henry Pelham, Fifth Duke of Newcastle*, 52–53. Lord Palmerston also noticed the coming young man. In February 1845 he noted that he thought "higher of Lincoln than people in general do" (Evelyn Ashley, *Life of Viscount Palmerston*, 1:488).

51. The 1832 settlement stipulated that the owner of the Haford estate would pay £738 to have the crown's claim to 7,438 acres relinquished. Newcastle paid the total of nearly £1,050 in August 1843.

52. *Parl. Deb.*, LXXVIII, 399–405 and 439.

53. Ibid., LXXXVIII, 729–30; NeC 12,102b, Lincoln memorandum of 9 December 1845.

54. NeC 9,104, Lincoln (copy) to Wellington, 27 March 1845; NeC 12,346, Wellington to Lincoln, May 1845; NeC 9,065, Wellington to Lincoln, 7 April 1845; NeC 9,067, Lincoln (copy) to Wellington, 24 May 1845; and NeC 9,105, "Report of the Commissioners of Metropolitan Improvements," 29 September 1845.

55. *Parl. Deb.*, LXXXII, 1077.

56. R. A. Lewis, *Edwin Chadwick and the Public Health Movement, 1832–1854*, 124–29; Finer, *Chadwick*, 240–41.

57. NeC 9,072, Lincoln (copy) to Peel, 9 June 1845.

58. NeC 9,042a, Lincoln (copy) to Goulburn, 28 August 1845.

59. Peel, Add. MS. 40445, fols. 172–75, Goulburn to Peel, 31 August 1845; fols. 178–80, Peel (copy) to Goulburn, 2 September 1845.

60. Ibid., fols. 188–89 and 202–3, Peel (copies) to Goulburn, 8 and 10 September 1845.

61. NeC 9,075, Treasury Minute, 16 September 1845.

62. NeC 9,078b, Milne and Gore Memorandum on the Northern Receivership and the Geological Survey, 13 October 1845; NeC 9,088b, Treasury Minute, 11 November 1845; and NeC 9,088a, Treasury Minute on Geological Survey of Great Britain and Ireland, 14 November 1845.

63. NeC 9,074, Lincoln (copy) to Goulburn, 5 September 1845.

Chapter 4: Corn Laws and Ireland

1. Norman Gash, *Sir Robert Peel*, 538–39.

2. Ibid., 539–40.

3. Peel, Add. MS. 40481, fols. 322–331, Lincoln to Peel, 5 November 1845.

4. Charles S. Parker, *Sir Robert Peel: From His Private Papers*, 3:232–33.

5. Sir Robert Peel, *Memoirs*, ed. Lord Mahon and Edward Cardwell, 2:163–64; Gash, *Peel*, 541–42.

6. Peel, Add. MS. 40580, fols. 131–32, Lincoln to Peel, 1 December 1845.

7. Foot and Matthew, eds., *The Gladstone Diaries*, 3:500–501; Glad., Add. MS. 44777, fol. 233, Gladstone memorandum of 6 December 1845.

8. Quoted Parker, *Peel*, 3:233.

9. Foot and Matthew, eds., *Gladstone Diaries*, 3:504–6; Glad., Add. MS. 44777, fols. 237–41, Gladstone memorandum of 20 December 1845.

10. Glad., Add. MS. 44262, fols. 64–66, Gladstone (copy) to Lincoln, 16 February 1846.

11. NeC 9, 281a, Lincoln (copy) to Peel, 25 February 1846.

12. G-G MSS, Thompson to Newcastle, 4 November 1845.

13. Parker, *Peel*, 3:338, quoting Peel to the queen, 4 February 1846.

14. *Nottingham Journal*, 20 February 1846.

15. Robert Stewart, *The Politics of Protection*, 57–58; John Golby, "A Great Electioneer and His Motives: The Fourth Duke of Newcastle," 216–17.

16. Lincoln spent a great deal of money on the contest. In May, Lord George Bentinck charged him in the House of Commons with bribery during the election. Lincoln explained the reason for the large expenditure of money, most of which went to his solicitors, but denied spending any of it for bribery. Bentinck later withdrew the charge (*Parl. Deb.*, LXXXVI, 297–99, 419–21).

17. *Times*, 9 February 1846.

18. G-G MSS, Lincoln to Thompson, 31 January 1846.

19. *Times*, 23 February 1846. The nomination was on 21 February.

20. Parker, *Peel*, 3:339, quoting the queen to Peel, 11 February 1846.

21. NeC 12,112a and NeC 12,116, Lincoln (copies) to Peel, 11 and 18 February 1846.

22. NeC 12,110 and NeC 12,111, Lincoln (copies) to Peel, 9 and 10 February 1846.

23. *Times*, 24 February 1846.

24. Ibid., 26 February 1846.

25. Cf. Gash, *Peel*, 572.

26. ND, Ne2 F7, 243 and 248–49.

27. NeC 12,394, "Notes for Speech to Family Tenants," no date.

28. NeC 11,868, Lincoln (copy) to Bonham, 28 February 1846.

29. *Times*, 27 April, 1 and 2 May 1846.

30. Ibid., 4 and 5 May 1846. The result of the poll was Lincoln 506 and Wilson 495.

31. Ibid., 6 May 1846, quoting the *Glasgow Citizen*.

32. *Parl. Deb.*, LXXXVI, 244–51.

33. NeC 9,224, Graham (copy) to Lord Heytesbury, 3 November 1845; Cecil Woodham-Smith, *The Great Hunger*, 48.

34. NeC 9,226, Graham (copy) to Heytesbury, 26 November 1845.

35. NeC 9,228, Graham (copy) to Heytesbury, 15 December 1845.

36. See my article "Charles Edward Trevelyan and Peelite Irish Famine Policy, 1845–1846."

37. Jenifer Hart, "Sir Charles Trevelyan at the Treasury," 99.

38. Quoted Kevin B. Nowlan, "The Political Background," in *The Great Famine*, ed. Robert Dudley Edwards and T. Desmond Williams, 151.

39. *Parl. Pap.*, Trevelyan's statement of 8 March 1846, "Public Works for the Relief of Scarcity in Ireland," *Correspondence Explanatory of the Measures Adopted by Her Majesty's Government for the Relief of Distress Arising from the Failure of the Potato Crop in Ireland*, 274–75 (House of Commons, 1846 [735], XXXVII).

40. Thomas P. O' Neill, "Organization and Administration of Relief," in *Great Famine*, ed. Edwards and Williams, 221.

41. *Parl. Pap.*, Trevelyan, "Public Works," *Corr. Explan. of Measures Adopted*, 274–75 and 277, Trevelyan to Routh, 14 March 1846; TLB, Dep. d. 96, 89–90, Trevelyan to Jones, 11 March 1846.

42. Gram., microfilm 122, Lincoln to Graham, 26 March 1846.

43. G-G MSS, Graham to Lincoln, 22 and 25 March 1846.

44. See Woodham-Smith, *Great Hunger*, 111, for a description of these two men.

45. NeC 12,157/14, Lincoln (copy) to Peel, 25 March 1846; Gram., microfilm 122, Lincoln to Graham, 26 March 1846.

46. G-G MSS, Graham to Lincoln, 30 March 1846; NeC 11,979, Peel to Lincoln, 27 March 1846. Lord Heytesbury also praised Lincoln's energy and activity in effecting the new arrangements (Gram., microfilm 149, Heytesbury to Graham, 26 March 1846).

47. NeC 12,157/15, Peel to Lincoln, 27 March 1846; NeC 9,238, Goulburn to Lincoln, 3 April 1846.

48. NeC 12,157/10; NeC 12,122; NeC 12,123; and NeC 12,130, Lincoln (copies) to Peel, 23, 24, 26, and 31 March 1846.

49. NeC 12,134, Lincoln (copy) to Peel, 4 April 1846.

50. NeC 12,135, Peel to Lincoln, 7 April 1846.

51. NeC 12,145, Peel to Lincoln, 2 June 1846.

52. *Parl. Pap., Corr. Explan. of Measures Adopted*, 293–95, Jones to Trevelyan, 4 April 1846, and Commissioners of Public Works to Trevelyan, 7 April 1846.

53. NeC 12,147, Treasury Minute to the Commissioners of Public Works, 4 April 1846; NeC 12,148, Trevelyan (copy) to Pennefather, 4 April 1846.

54. NeC 12,136, Lincoln (copy) to Peel, 8 April 1846.

55. NeC 12,137a, Lincoln (copy) to Peel, 9 April 1846.

56. Peel, Add. MS. 40445, fols. 317–20, Peel (copy) to Goulburn, 10 April 1846.

57. Ibid., fols. 325–28, Goulburn to Peel, 12 April 1846; Goul., II/20, Peel to Goulburn, 14 April 1846; NeC 12,140, Lincoln (copy) to Peel, 19 April 1846.

58. Cf. O' Neill, *Great Famine*, ed. Edwards and Williams, 215; Woodham-Smith, *Great Hunger*, 69.

59. Woodham-Smith, *Great Hunger*, 70–71.

60. *Parl. Pap., Corr. Explan. of Measures Adopted*, 107, Trevelyan to Routh, 17 April 1846.

61. TLB, Dep. d. 96, 165–66, Trevelyan to Pine Coffin, 13 April 1846.

62. NeC 9,235, Lincoln (copy) to Goulburn, 15 April 1846; NeC 9,284, Lincoln (copy) to Graham, 18 April 1846.

63. Goul., II/20, Peel to Goulburn, 26 April 1846.

64. NeC 9,242, Goulburn to Lincoln, 17 April 1846.

65. Gram., microfilm 149, Heytesbury to Graham, 10, 12, and 15 April 1846.

66. NeC 12,138, Lincoln (copy) to Peel, 11 April 1846. To Goulburn, Lincoln wrote, "Trevelyan is still *privately* corresponding and issuing *his private orders*. Let me beg of you to stop this. Nobody but one who is here on the spot can form an opinion of the mischief it does" (NeC 9,234, Lincoln [copy] to Goulburn, 10 April 1846).

67. Gram., microfilm 122, Graham (copy) to Heytesbury, 27 April 1846. At this same time Peel informed Goulburn that he preferred Lincoln's recent procedure of sending men like Griffith to confer personally with parties on the spot in the distressed areas to make arrangements for works to the Treasury system of regulations and protracted correspondence (Goul., II/20, Peel to Goulburn, 26 April 1846).

68. NeC 9,345, Pennefather to Lincoln, 4 June 1846; *Parl. Pap., Corr. Explan. of Measures Adopted*, 326–28, Treasury Minute, 16 June 1846.

69. NeC 9,331a; NeC 9,345; and NeC 9,356, Pennefather to Lincoln, 3, 4, and 28 June 1846.

70. Gash, *Peel*, 609. A total of £75,000 was spent in relief, public works, and loans during the Peelite administration of Irish famine relief.

71. Lincoln acknowledged that the ministry's relief plans could not have been carried out in Ireland without the cooperation and zealous endeavors of Larcom, Griffith, and Routh, all of whom he continued to praise and thank even after he left office.

72. NeC 9,306, Heytesbury to Lincoln, 10 February 1846.

73. *Parl. Deb.*, LXXXVII, 279–89.

74. These included the ejectment and distress bill, leases (Ireland) bill, and the rateable property (Ireland) bill.

75. The vote was 327 for and 229 against the repeal of the Corn Laws. Of the Conservatives voting, 106 voted for the measure and 222 against. There were six Conservative pairs in favor and three Conservative supporters of the measure who were absent.

76. *Parl. Deb.*, LXXXVII, 143–73.

77. Ibid., 177–84; Gash, *Peel*, 595.

78. Cf. Gash, *Peel*, 595–96; John Martineau, *The Life of Henry Pelham, Fifth Duke of Newcastle*, 80; and Goldwin Smith, *Reminiscences*, 176–77.

79. NeC 9,319, Heytesbury to Lincoln, 22 June 1846.

80. Cf. Martineau, *Newcastle*, 81; Gash, *Peel*, 590, n. 2.

81. Glad., Add. MS. 44777, fol. 246, Gladstone memorandum of July 1846.

82. Ibid., fols. 246–56.

Chapter 5: The Early Peelite Years

1. Norman Gash, *Sir Robert Peel*, 619, quoting Lincoln to Peel, 2 July 1846; NeC 12,699a, Lincoln (copy) to Russell, 2 July 1846.

2. Peel, Add. MS. 40481, fols. 354–61, Lincoln to Peel, 25 and 27 August 1846; DP, 132/13, Bentinck to Stanley, 17 October 1846; and Dis., B/XX/Be/12, Bentinck to Disraeli, 9 November 1846.

3. Theodore Martin, *A Life of Lord Lyndhurst*, 416–26; Peel, Add. MS. 40452, fols. 140–41, Peel (copy) to Graham, 2 July 1846; *Parl. Deb.*, LXXXVIII, 974, Lyndhurst's speech.

4. Peel, Add. MS. 40481, fols. 354–57, Lincoln to Peel, 25 August 1846.

5. J. B. Conacher, *The Peelites and the Party System, 1846–52*, 20; DP, 132/13, Bentinck to Stanley, 10 July 1846. The animosity of the Protectionists toward the Peelites is clearly evident in the correspondence among the Protectionist leaders, who particularly singled out Lincoln and Sidney Herbert as arch enemies. Cf. Robert Stewart, *The Politics of Protection*, 86–87.

6. Charles S. Parker, *Sir Robert Peel: From His Private Papers*, 3:472–74; Conacher, *Peelites and Party System*, 17–18 and n. 18.

7. Aber., Add. MS. 43196, fols. 243–45, Goulburn to Aberdeen, 12 December 1846.

8. Peel, Add. MS. 40445, fols. 386–90, Goulburn to Peel, 19 and 24 December 1846; Goul., II/20, Peel to Goulburn, 20 December 1846.

9. Peel, Add. MS. 40481, fols. 392–97, Lincoln to Peel, 1 January 1847.

10. Ibid., 40598, fols. 62–65, Young to Peel, 23 January 1847.

11. Ibid., 40481, fols. 400–3, Lincoln to Peel, 23 January 1847.

12. John Martineau, *The Life of Henry Pelham, Fifth Duke of Newcastle*, 83, quoting John Peel to Sir Robert Peel, 20 October 1846.

13. G-G MSS, Lincoln to Thompson, 8 December 1846.

14. Peel, Add. MS. 40481, fols. 368–77, Lincoln to Peel, 17 November 1846; NeC 11,990, Peel to Lincoln, 12 December 1846; and NeC 12,178, Lincoln (copy) to John D. Cooke, 5 January 1847.

15. Peel, Add. MS. 40481, fols. 390–91, Lincoln to Peel, 31 December 1846.

16. *Times*, 15 January 1847.

17. G-G MSS, Lincoln to Thompson, 23 January 1847. Lincoln hurt his chances at Manchester by his refusal to pledge himself against grants or endowments to the Roman Catholic clergy.

18. Peel, Add. MS. 40481, fols. 382–85, Lincoln to Peel, 10 December 1846.

19. *Times*, 15 January 1847; Peel, Add. MS. 40481, fols. 386–87, Lincoln to Peel, 14 December 1846.

20. DP, 132/13, Bentinck to Stanley, 2 January 1847; 177/1, Stanley (copy) to Beresford, 30 December 1846; and 149/1, Beresford to Stanley, 30 December 1846. Some of the moderates within the Protectionist camp who regarded Lincoln as a possible leader of a reunited Conservative party in the Commons found Bentinck's and Beresford's attitude toward him galling (Stewart, *Politics of Protection*, 95).

21. DP, 132/13, Bentinck to Stanley, 19 December 1846; NeC 11,688, Lincoln (copy) to Gladstone, 25 February 1847.

22. EP, P.R.O. 30/12/21/3, Ellenborough to Lincoln, 3 January 1847.

23. Ibid., Lincoln to Ellenborough, 5 January 1847.

24. Cf. Stewart, *Politics of Protection*, 103; Wilbur Devereux Jones and Arvel B. Erickson, *The Peelites, 1846–1857*, 64–65.

25. Glad., Add. MS. 44262, fols. 101–2, Gladstone (copy) to Lincoln, 8 April 1847.

26. G-G MSS, Lincoln to Thompson, 17 July 1847. The seats included Dover, Yarmouth, and Cheltenham. North Lancashire also had been offered to him, though not without a contest.

27. Peel, Add. MS. 40481, fols. 408–9, Lincoln to Peel, 16 July 1847.

28. Ibid., fols. 414–15, Lincoln to Peel, 3 August 1847.

29. Glad., Add. MS. 44262, fols. 105–6, Gladstone (copy) to Lincoln, 13 September 1847.

30. Peel, Add. MS. 40599, fols. 121–22, Bonham to Peel, 2 August 1847.

31. Goul. II/20, Peel to Goulburn, 15 July 1847.

32. Dis., BB/XX/Be/35, Bentinck to Disraeli, 2 September 1847. There were anywhere from 199 to 240 Protectionists elected. Bentinck counted 240 nominal followers but doubted their loyalty.

33. DP, 132/13, Bentinck to Stanley, 7 August 1847.

34. Peel, Add. MS. 43065, fols. 322–26, Peel (copy) to Aberdeen, 19 August 1847; NeC 11,918, Graham to Lincoln, 22 October 1847.

35. Peel, Add. MS. 40481, fols. 420–25, Lincoln to Peel, 18 November 1847; Clar., dep. c. 530, G. C. Lewis to Clarendon, 22 November 1847.

36. Glad., Add. MS. 44777, fols. 271–74, "Political Memorandum of the Session 1847–8."

37. ND, Ne2 F8, 61; Osbert Wyndham Hewett, *Strawberry Fair*, 56.

38. ND, Ne2 F8, 53.

39. NeC 11,693, Lincoln (copy) to Gladstone, 23 September 1847; NeC 11,943, Lincoln (copy) to Herbert, 19 December 1847.

40. Peel, Add. MS. 40481, fols. 342–47, Lincoln to Peel, 13 August 1846.

41. Ibid., fols. 366–67, Lincoln to Peel, 12 October 1846.

42. Ibid., fols. 368–77, Lincoln to Peel, 17 November 1846.

43. Ibid., fols. 362–63, Lincoln to Peel, 29 August 1846.

44. Ibid., fols. 366–67, Lincoln to Peel, 12 October 1846; NeC 11,989, Peel to Lincoln, 16 October 1846.

45. Parker, *Peel*, 3:464, quoting Lord Jocelyn to Peel, 13 October 1846, and Graham to Peel, 26 September 1846; Goul. II/20, Peel to Goulburn, 14 August 1846.

46. Peel, Add. MS. 40481, fols. 368–77, Lincoln to Peel, 17 November 1846.

47. Cf. Cecil Woodham-Smith, *The Great Hunger*, 150.

48. Cf. Spencer Walpole, *The Life of Lord John Russell*, 2:78; Woodham-Smith, *The Great Hunger*, 293.

49. Lord John Russell's attitude toward the Irish landlords is of particular significance. His animus against them caused him on a number of occasions to lose sight of the famine (cf. John Prest, *Lord John Russell*, 236–37).

50. Ibid., 249, quoting Russell to Grey, 15 October 1846.

51. Ibid., 250; Peel, Add. MS. 40600, fols. 465–72, Young to Peel, 5 October 1848.

52. Her., Lincoln to Herbert, 4 December 1847.

53. Cf. Prest, *Russell*, 273–74; Walpole, *Russell*, 1:472–73.

54. Peel, Add. MS. 40481, fols. 382–85, Lincoln to Peel, 10 December 1846; G-G MSS, Lincoln to Thompson, 30 March 1848.

55. *Parl. Deb.*, XCV, 348–51.

56. *Morning Chronicle*, 10 April 1848. J. D. Cooke, the editor of the *Morning Chronicle*, consulted Lincoln closely about the editorial line that he should take during the early stages of the Peelite ownership of the paper.

57. Ibid., 19 and 29 July 1848.

58. *Parl. Deb.*, XCVIII, 63–68.

59. Prest, *Russell*, 280.

60. *Parl. Deb.*, C, 772.

61. Cf. Woodham-Smith, *Great Hunger*, 377.

62. Cf. Gash, *Peel*, 642.

63. *Parl. Deb.*, CIII, 294–304.

64. *Morning Chronicle*, 17 February 1849.

65. *Parl. Deb.*, CIII, 179. Only seven out of forty-four Peelites voting supported Viscount Castlereagh's motion to postpone debate on the Poor Law (Ireland) rate in aid bill.

66. Ibid., C, 393 and 772.

67. *Morning Chronicle*, 6 April 1849.

68. Cf. Clar., dep. Irish Box 26, Russell to Clarendon, 28 December 1849.

69. Cf. Prest, *Russell*, 301 and 307–8; Woodham-Smith, *Great Hunger*, 371–73.

70. Prest, *Russell*, 301.

71. Henry Reeve, ed., *Greville Memoirs*, 6:201.

72. Ibid., 201–3; W. F. Moneypenny and G. E. Buckle, *The Life of Benjamin Disraeli, Earl of Beaconsfield*, 3:98; DP, 149/2 Beresford to Stanley, no date [1848]. Lincoln told Thompson in March, "Not only could we [Peelites] throw out the Government at any moment but if we were to retire from the House and leave them to their friends they would be devoured in one night" (G-G MSS, Lincoln to Thompson, 30 March 1848).

73. Glad., Add. MS. 44777, fols. 279–80, Gladstone memorandum of 12 December 1848.

74. Reeve, ed., *Greville Memoirs*, 6:179–84.

75. Clar., dep. c. 532, Clarendon (original) to Lewis, 2 July 1848, printed in Sir Herbert Maxwell, *The Life and Letters of George William Frederick, Fourth Earl of Clarendon*, 1:291.

76. Clar., dep. c. 530, Lewis to Clarendon, 19 February and 30 June 1848.

77. Prest, *Russell*, 287.

78. *Morning Chronicle*, 18 July 1848.

79. *Times*, 12 July 1849. With disgust, Beresford observed to Stanley that the *Morning Chronicle* was also engaged in a war with the *Herald*, one of the major Protectionist organs, which, he concluded, would make it more difficult than ever to reunify the Con-

servative party (DP,149/2, Beresford to Stanley, 9 December 1848).

80. Peel, Add. MS. 40481, fols. 454–57, Lincoln to Peel, 27 January 1849. Peel privately deplored the *Morning Chronicle's* tone toward the Whigs (Gash, *Peel*, 638).

81. Peel, Add, MS. 40481, fols. 460–61, Lincoln to Peel, 13 April 1849.

82. G-G MSS, Lincoln to Thompson, 12 January and 3 February 1849; NeC 11,694, Lincoln (copy) to Gladstone, 4 October 1848.

83. Peel, Add. MS. 40455, fols. 490–92, Aberdeen to Peel, 2 April 1850.

84. Glad., Add. MS. 44777, fols. 283–84, Gladstone memorandum of 15 March 1849. Throughout early March, Lincoln and Gladstone frequently discussed the Navigation Laws and Vancouver's Island.

85. NeC 12,424, Cardwell to Lincoln, 15 October 1849.

Chapter 6: The Lincoln Divorce

1. G-G MSS, Catherine Gladstone to William E. Gladstone, 4 August 1849.

2. Osbert Wyndham Hewett, *Strawberry Fair*, 236.

3. The three youngest children had been sent the day before to Ryde, where the whole family was to have met in a few days for a brief holiday.

4. G-G MSS, Lincoln to Thompson, 18 August 1848.

5. Ibid., and Lincoln to Catherine Gladstone, 28 August 1848.

6. Glad., Add. MS. 44262, fols. 107–8, Gladstone (copy) to Lincoln, 14 August 1848.

7. Foot and Matthew, eds., *The Gladstone Diaries*, 4:59.

8. G-G MSS, Lincoln to Thompson, 18 and 24 September 1848.

9. Hewett, *Strawberry Fair*, 68.

10. NeC 11,695, Lincoln (copy) to Gladstone, 25 October 1848.

11. G-G MSS, Lady Lincoln to Catherine Gladstone, 6 November 1848. Although Lady Lincoln claimed to have gone to Baden to seek medical advice from a specialist, according to Richard Deacon, *The Private Life of Mr. Gladstone*, 50, the "doctor" proved to be entirely fictitious.

12. Virginia Surtees, *A Beckford Inheritance: The Lady Lincoln Scandal*, 77, quoting Lady Lincoln to Hamilton, no date.

13. G-G MSS, Catherine Gladstone (copy) to Lady Lincoln, 4 November 1848.

14. Ibid., Lord de Tabley to Catherine Gladstone, 4 November 1848.

15. Ibid., Lady Lincoln to Catherine Gladstone, 25 November 1848, and Catherine Gladstone (copy) to Lady Lincoln, no date.

16. Ibid., Lady de Tabley to Catherine Gladstone, 29 November 1848.

17. Surtees, *A Beckford Inheritance*, 93–94, quoting Lincoln to Manning, 24 November 1848.

18. Peel, Add. MS 40481, fols. 443–47, Lincoln to Peel, 2 December 1848.

19. G-G MSS, Lincoln to Thompson, 2 December 1848.

20. Foot and Matthew, eds., *Gladstone Diaries*, 4:131.

21. G-G MSS, Catherine Gladstone (copy) to Lady Lincoln, 12 July 1849. Catherine was very near to her sixth confinement and thus was unable to accompany William to Italy.

22. Several recent writers have recounted the story of Gladstone's mission. See, for example, Surtees, *A Beckford Inheritance*, 91–110; Colin C. Eldridge, "The Lincoln Divorce Case: A Study in Victorian Morality"; Phillip Magnus, *Gladstone: A Biography*, 92–94; Deacon, *Private Life of Gladstone*, 50–52; and Georgina Battiscombe, *Mrs. Gladstone: The Portrait of a Marriage*, 73–76. Gladstone's own account is extremely interesting and important (Foot and Matthew, eds., *Gladstone Diaries*, 4:135–48).

23. Foot and Matthew, eds., *Gladstone Diaries*, 4:142.

24. Ibid.; Surtees, *A Beckford Inheritance*, 106–7.

25. G-G MSS, Gladstone to his wife, 31 July 1849.

26. Ibid., Parkinson to Gladstone, 3 December 1849.

27. Foot and Matthew, eds., *Gladstone Diaries*, 4:144.

28. G-G MSS, Gladstone to his wife, 8 August 1849.

29. Quoted Eldridge, "The Lincoln Divorce Case," 37.

30. G-G MSS, Lincoln to Thompson, 19 September 1849.

31. Foot and Matthew, eds., *Gladstone Diaries*, 4:155; Surtees, *A Beckford Inheritance*, 118, quoting Gladstone to Manning, no date.

32. NeC 11,788, Gladstone to Lincoln, 28 September 1849.

33. Battiscombe, *Mrs. Gladstone*, 75.

34. G–G MSS, Catherine Gladstone to Lady Lincoln, 3 November 1849; Battiscombe, *Mrs. Gladstone*, 76.

35. Her., Peel to Herbert, 10 November 1849.

36. NeC 5,909, Lincoln (copy) to Bonham, 23 August 1849.

37. G–G MSS, Lincoln (copy) to Thompson, 19 September 1849.

38. Quoted Norman Gash, *Sir Robert Peel*, 666.

39. NeC 11,696, Lincoln (copy) to Gladstone, 16 July 1850.

40. NeC 11,883, Lincoln (copy) to Bonham, 26 November 1850.

41. ND, Ne2 F8, 254.

42. NeC 5,910 and 5,911, Henderson to Newcastle, 1 and 3 September 1849.

43. G–G MSS, Parkinson to Lincoln, 31 October 1849.

44. NeC 5,919, Hamilton to Newcastle, 23 March 1850.

45. G–G MSS, printed "Minutes of Evidence taken upon the Second Reading of the Lincoln Divorce Bill," 8.

46. Two of Lincoln's brothers, Lord Edward and Lord William, predeceased the fourth duke, Edward in 1842 and William in 1850.

Chapter 7: In Search of a Party

1. NeC 12,425, Cardwell to the fifth duke of Newcastle, 13 January 1851.

2. Clar., dep. c. 530, Lewis to Clarendon, 6 October and 22 November 1850 and 15 January 1851.

3. C. H. Stuart, "The Formation of the Coalition Cabinet of 1852," 55; RA F11/106, Prince Albert memorandum, 10 April 1854; Foot and Matthew, eds., *The Gladstone Diaries*, 4:596. Lord Derby and Disraeli, although they did not think that the duke had sufficient standing in the country, realized in 1854 that the general respect in which he was held in Parliament and at court made him a strong candidate to head the government as Aberdeen's successor (J. R. Vincent, ed., *Disraeli, Derby and the Conservative Party: The Political Journals of Lord Stanley, 1849–69*, 117).

4. NeC 11,699, Lincoln (copy) to Gladstone, 2 January 1851.

5. NeC 12,558, Newcastle (copy) to Herbert, 19 February 1851.

6. Charles S. Parker, *Life and Letters of Sir James Graham*, 2:129, quoting Newcastle to Graham, 23 February 1851.

7. NeC 11,701, Newcastle (copy) to Gladstone, 23 February 1851.

8. Her., Newcastle to Herbert, 23 February 1851.

9. Quoted John Morley, *The Life of William Ewart Gladstone*, 1:406. Gladstone saw Stanley later in the day. Stanley's announcement that he intended to impose a five or six shilling duty on corn decided the question for Gladstone.

10. Henry Reeve, ed., *The Greville Memoirs*, 6:280–81.

11. RA Y96/13, The queen to King Leopold, 4 March 1851. The queen and Prince Albert wanted a coalition government of Whigs and Peelites. The queen attributed the failure of the Whig-Peelite negotiations to Lord John Russell's "unfortunate, dry, reserved as well as indifferent manner," which had the effect of "discouraging and awakening suspicion in the minds of others" (RA Queen Victoria's Journal, 24 February 1851). Russell admitted to the queen that the most natural solution to the existing political problems was "a Coalition sooner or later with the Peel party," but he informed the queen and Prince Albert that his party was very much adverse to it (RA C46/118, Russell memorandum of 3 March 1851; RA C46/117, Prince Albert memorandum of 3 March 1851).

12. Glad., Add. MS. 44777, fol. 326, Gladstone memorandum, 23 April 1851; Aber., Add. MS. 43247, fols. 200–201, Londonderry to Aberdeen, 5 July 1851; Morley, *Gladstone*, 1:407.

13. NeC 11,887, Newcastle (copy) to Bonham, 18 April 1851.

14. NeC 12,234, Newcastle draft memorandum on party matters.

15. NeC 11,702, and NeC 11,704, Newcastle (copies) to Gladstone, 18 August and 17 October 1851.

16. NeC 11,888, Newcastle (copy) to Bonham, 24 September 1851.

17. Stuart, "Formation of Coalition," 60; Her., Newcastle to Herbert, 27 October 1851, printed in Lord Stanmore, *Sidney Herbert, Lord Herbert of Lea*, 1:145–46; NeC 11,706, Newcastle (copy) to Gladstone, 8 December 1851; and Glad., Add. MS. 44777,

fols. 327–29, and Add. MS. 44262, fols. 110–13, Gladstone memorandum, 22 April 1851, and Gladstone (copy) to Newcastle, 22 October 1851.

18. Her., Newcastle to Herbert, 27 October 1851, printed in Stanmore, *Herbert*, 1:145–46.

19. NeC 11,706, Newcastle (copy) to Gladstone, 8 December 1851.

20. NeC 11,890, Newcastle (copy) to Bonham, 14 January 1852.

21. RP, P.R.O. 30/22/9J, part 2, fols. 212–17, Russell memorandum, 31 December 1851. Emphasis in quotation is mine. These words were in the original draft but were left out of the corrected version (RP, P.R.O. 30/22/10A, part 2, fols. 90–94).

22. A. C. Benson and Viscount Esher, eds., *Letters of Queen Victoria*, 2:434–35, the queen to Russell, 15 January 1852; RA F9/44, Prince Albert memorandum of 11 January 1852.

23. RP, P.R.O. 30/22/10A, part 2, fols. 54–57 and 87–89, Newcastle to Russell, 17 January 1852, and Russell (copy) to Newcastle, 19 January 1852.

24. RP., P.R.O. 30/22/9J, part 1, fols. 11–12, Lansdowne to Russell, 5 December 1851; part 2, fols. 132–35, Clarendon to Russell, 24 December 1851; fols. 136–41, Sir G. Grey to Russell, 25 December 1851; Hick., A4/55/1, Lord Grey to Sir Charles Wood, 23 December 1851.

25. RP, P.R.O. 30/22/10A, part 1, fols. 129–30, Minto to Russell, 3 January 1852; fols. 183–89, Sir G. Grey to Russell, 12 January 1852; part 2, fols. 39–43, Lord Grey to Russell, 16 January 1852; and GP, D5/2A, Journal of General Charles Grey, 16 January and 2 February 1852.

26. J. B. Conacher, *The Peelites and the Party System, 1846–52*, 94–95; John Prest, *Lord John Russell*, 338–39.

27. Reeve, ed., *Greville Memoirs*, 6:328–29.

28. GP, D5/2A, Journal of General Charles Grey, 16 January 1852.

29. Clar., dep. c. 530, Lewis to Clarendon, 11 January 1852.

30. Aber., Add. MS. 43190, fols. 264–66, Graham to Aberdeen, 10 January 1852; Parker, *Graham*, 2:152, Graham to Cardwell, 26 January 1852; Conacher, *Peelites and Party System*, 96–97.

31. Conacher, *Peelites and Party System*, 96–97; Foot and Matthew, eds., *Gladstone Diaries*, 4:387–88.

32. Glad., Add. MS. 44778, fols. 5–20, Gladstone memorandum, 25 February to 12 March 1852.

33. Ibid. Graham told Baron Stockmar that Newcastle frequently spoke irritably to Gladstone during the Peelite discussion on their course of action at a dinner at Herbert's house on 25 February (RA C27/54a, Stockmar memorandum of 27 February 1852).

34. NeC 11,712, Newcastle (copy) to Gladstone, 4 March 1852.

35. NeC 11,713, Newcastle (copy) to Gladstone, 8 March 1852.

36. It is a mistake to accept Gladstone's claim that the forty Peelites whom he "drilled" kept Derby and the Conservatives in power in 1852 (cf. Stewart, "Formation of Coalition," 49).

37. Glad. Add. MS. 44778, fols. 23–32, Gladstone memorandum, 25-26 March 1852; Dis., B/XX/S/106 and 109, Derby to Disraeli, (1852).

38. NeC 11,714, Newcastle to Gladstone, 21 May 1852.

39. *Parl. Deb.*, CXXI, 989–1005.

40. Morley, *Gladstone*, 1:429, quoting Gladstone to Aberdeen, 5 August 1852; Glad., Add. MS. 44262, fols. 114–15, Newcastle to Gladstone, 15 July 1852; Aber., Add. MS. 43197, fol. 11, Newcastle to Aberdeen, 2 August 1852.

41. Conacher, *Peelites and Party System*, 113–14, quoting Heathcote to Gladstone, 24 August 1852.

42. NeC 12,462, Newcastle (copy) to Tallents, 15 May 1852.

43. Conacher, *Peelites and Party System*, 118.

44. Aber., Add. MS. 43197, fols. 11–18, Newcastle to Aberdeen, 2 August 1852.

45. Ibid., fols. 7–9, Aberdeen (copy) to Newcastle, 25 July 1852.

46. Ibid., fols. 11–18, Newcastle to Aberdeen, 2 August 1852.

47. Ibid., fols. 21–23, Newcastle to Aberdeen, 3 August 1852.

48. RP, P.R.O. 30/22/10D, fols. 52–53, Aberdeen to Russell, 8 August 1852; Aber., Add. MS. 43066, fols. 93–95 and 99–104, Russell to Aberdeen, 11 and 13 August 1852.

49. Aber., Add. MS. 43197, fols. 27–34, Newcastle to Aberdeen, 21 and 27 August 1852.

50. RP, P.R.O. 30/22/10E, fols. 44–45, Aberdeen to Russell, 16 December 1852.

51. Aber., Add. MS. 43197, fols. 35–36,

Aberdeen (copy) to Newcastle, 31 August 1852.

52. Ibid., fols. 37–38, Newcastle to Aberdeen, 4 September 1852.

53. GP, Sir Charles Wood to Lord Grey, 30 September and 8 October 1852; Hick., A4/55/2, Lord Grey to Wood, 3 October 1852; A4/67, Parkes to Wood, 14 October 1852; and A4/57, Clarendon to Wood, 17 August 1852; RP, P.R.O. 30/22/10D, fols. 80–86, Clarendon to Russell, 1 August 1852; and fols. 67–70 and 101–8, Wood to Russell, 10 August 1852.

54. RP, P.R.O. 30/22/10E, fols. 8–11, Minto (copy) to duke of Bedford, 2 September 1852.

55. RP, P.R.O. 30/22/10D, fols. 183–89, Clarendon to Russell, 31 August 1852; and P.R.O. 30/22/10E, fols. 116–17, Panmure to Russell, 27 September 1852; Clar. dep. c. 532, Clarendon to Lewis, 1 September 1852; Hick., A4/121, Lewis to Wood, 24 September 1852; and A4/55/2, Lord Grey to Wood, 28 October 1852.

56. RP, P.R.O. 30/22/10E, fols. 176–77, Minto to Russell, 4 October 1852.

57. See letters from Clarendon, Wood, and Lewis to Russell, October 1852, Ibid.; Hick., A4/55/2, Lord Grey to Wood, 21 October 1852.

58. Parker, *Graham*, 2:179–80, Aberdeen to Graham, 27 September 1852.

59. Aber., Add. MS. 43197, fols. 41–42, Newcastle to Aberdeen, 30 September 1852; Glad., Add. MS. 44262, fols. 133–34, Newcastle to Gladstone, 3 September 1852.

60. NeC 11,893, Newcastle (copy) to Bonham, 19 September 1852.

61. Parker, *Graham*, 2:176.

62. Henry E. Carlisle, ed., *Selections from the Correspondence of Abraham Hayward*, 1:173. Attending the dinner were Newcastle, Gladstone, Herbert, Frederick Charteris, Henry Fitzroy, Young, Cardwell, and Lord Ernest Bruce.

63. Villiers's amendment was defeated 256 to 336 and Palmerston's amendment was adopted 468 to 53. For references to the Peelite meetings at Aberdeen's house on 16 and 18 November, see Reeve, ed., *Greville Memoirs*, 7:7–8, and Glad., Add. MS. 44778, fols. 56–58, Gladstone memorandum.

64. *Parl. Deb.*, CXXIII, 963–64.

65. *Morning Chronicle*, 3 August 1852.

66. *Parl. Deb.*, CXXIII, 1669; Glad., Add.

MS. 44778, fols. 61–71, Gladstone memorandum, 18 December 1852.

67. *Parl. Deb.*, CXXIII, 1706–8.

68. RA C28/7 and C28/12, Bedford to Stockmar, 17 December 1852, and Phipps to Prince Albert, 18 December 1852.

69. RA C28/13, Prince Albert memorandum, 19 December 1852.

70. Donald Southgate, *The Passing of the Whigs*, 246, quoting Clarendon to Reeve of the *Times*.

71. Cf. J. B. Conacher, *The Aberdeen Coalition, 1852–1855*, 14–21; Prest, *Russell*, 354–55. The duke of Bedford had pressed his brother to join the government and to take the lead of the Commons (RP, P.R.O. 30/22/10F, fols. 85–87, Bedford to Russell, 19 December 1852).

72. Quoted Conacher, *Aberdeen Coalition*, 29.

73. GP, Wood to Lord Grey, 27 December 1852.

74. Gran., P.R.O. 30/29/19/9, fols. 7–10, Newcastle to Granville, 18 April 1855, printed in Lord Edmond Fitzmaurice, *The Life of Granville George Leveson Gower, Second Earl Granville, 1815–1891*, 1:79–80.

75. For a discussion of how the Parliamentary Whig party developed into a national Liberal movement, see J. R. Vincent, *The Formation of the British Liberal Party, 1857–1868*.

76. Foot and Matthew, eds., *Gladstone Diaries*, 5:15.

Chapter 8: Preparations for War

1. PP, GC/AB/293, Aberdeen to Palmerston, 4 July 1853.

2. Cf. J. B. Conacher, *The Aberdeen Coalition, 1852–1855*, 137–74.

3. Kingsley B. Martin, *The Triumph of Lord Palmerston*, 134.

4. Aber., Add. MS. 43069, fols. 122–23, Palmerston to Aberdeen, 7 October 1853; *Aber. Corres., 1852–1854*, 283–84, Aberdeen to Graham, 8 October 1853.

5. Quoted Sir Herbert Maxwell, *The Life and Letters of George William Frederick, Fourth Earl of Clarendon*, 2:26.

6. Glad., Add. MS. 44088, fols. 201–2 and 204–6, Aberdeen to Gladstone, 17 and 20 October 1853.

7. RA G8/6, Aberdeen to the queen, 22 December 1853.

8. W.O. 6/75, fols. 2–7, Newcastle to Hardinge, Raglan, and Trevelyan, 9 February 1854.

9. W.O. 6/69, fols. 22–31, Newcastle to Raglan, 10 April 1854; NeC 9,973, fols. 7–8, Newcastle (private) to Raglan, 13 April 1854.

10. NeC 10,513 and NeC 9,973, fols. 25, Trevelyan to Mundy, 27 April 1854, and Newcastle (private) to Raglan, 28 April 1854; *Parl. Deb.*, CXXXII, 908–14. Sidney Herbert dismissed the charges in a speech in the House of Commons.

11. NeC 10,518a, Trevelyan to Newcastle, 2 May 1854.

12. NeC 10,529, Filder (copy) to Trevelyan, 14 May 1854.

13. W.O. 62/4/96, Filder to Trevelyan, 30 May 1854; *Parl. Pap., Third Report from the Select Committee on the Army Before Sebastopol* (House of Commons, 1854–5 (218) IX. part II), 96, Trevelyan's evidence; NeC 10,523a and NeC 10,529, Trevelyan to Newcastle, 11 May 1854, and Filder (copy) to Trevelyan, 14 May 1854.

14. *Parl. Deb.*, CXXXII, 606–38.

15. Ibid., 639–54. Following in the debate, Lord Hardinge warmly praised Newcastle for the smooth operation of the system and for the very satisfactory assistance he had received from him (Ibid., 654–57). For Herbert's speech on the subject in the Commons, Ibid., 233–45.

16. Ibid., 667.

17. Aber., Add. MS. 43068, fol. 28, Russell Memorandum, 24 April 1854.

18. RP, P.R.O. 30/22/11D, fols. 1099–1102, Russell Memorandum, 20 May 1854.

19. RA G13/61, Aberdeen to the queen, 28 May 1854; Aber., Add. MS. 43049, fol. 123, Aberdeen (copy) to the queen, 30 May 1854; RP, P.R.O. 30/22/11D, fols. 1097–1124 and 1171–74, various memoranda of cabinet ministers on Russell's memorandum of 20 May 1854, and Aberdeen to Russell, 7 June 1854; and Hick. A4/58, Sir George Grey to Sir Charles Wood, 3 June 1854. See also Conacher, *Aberdeen Coalition* 402–5; and Olive Anderson, *A Liberal State at War*, 54–56.

20. Aber. Add. MS. 43068, fols. 62–63 and 72–73, Russell to Aberdeen, 29 and 31 May 1854; RP, P.R.O. 30/22/11D, fols. 96- 97, Aberdeen to Russell, 30 May 1854. Aberdeen supposedly preferred Sidney Herbert to anyone else for Minister of War (cf. Lord Stanmore, *Sidney Herbert, Lord Herbert of Lea*, 1:224).

21. Glad., Add. MS. 44778, fols. 183–84, Gladstone (copy) to Lord Canning, 8 June 1854; *Aber. Corres., 1854–5*, 142, Gladstone to Gordon, 6 June 1854.

22. Hick., A4/65, Panmure to Wood, 3 June 1854; GP, Wood to Lord Grey, 9 June 1854; and RP, P.R.O. 30/22/11D, fols. 101-6, Wood to Russell, 4 June 1854.

23. Glad., Add. MS. 44778, fols. 183–84, Gladstone (copy) to Lord Canning, 8 June 1854.

24. RP, P.R.O. 30/22/11D, fols. 126–27, Aberdeen to Russell, 7 June 1854; *Aber. Corres., 1854–5*, 146–47, Russell to Aberdeen, 8 June 1854.

25. *Parl. Deb.*, CXXXIV, 335–39.

26. Ibid., CXXXVI, 1240, Newcastle's statement upon resignation, 1 February 1855. Sir Charles Wood certainly did not want to see Palmerston become the Secretary of State or War (RP, P.R.O. 30/22/11D, fols. 101–6, Wood to Russell, 4 June 1854). In his *Autobiographic Note* of September 1897, Gladstone disputed that Newcastle took the War Department with the unanimous desire of his colleagues. Gladstone noted that he and those with whom he communicated at the time were very strongly of an opposite opinion. "I believe we all desired that Lord Palmerston should have been war minister" (John Morley, *The Life of William Ewart Gladstone*, 1:651).

27. *Aber. Corres., 1854–5*, 162–63, Newcastle to Aberdeen, 4 July 1854.

28. Henry E. Carlisle, ed., *Selections from the Correspondence of Abraham Hayward*, 1:220–21.

29. *Parl. Pap.*, 1854–5, IX, part II, *Third Report*, 180.

30. Ibid., 126–27.

31. Ibid., 167–68; W.O. 6/75, fols. 82–83, Newcastle to Herbert, 6 April 1854.

32. NeC 10,437 and NeC 10,883, Newcastle (copies) to Stratford, 2 September 1854, and Raglan, 18 August 1854; W.O. 6/76, fols. 200–201, Mundy to Smith, 5 September 1854.

33. W.O. 1/368, Raglan to Newcastle, 24 June 1854; NeC 9,973, fols. 69–70, Newcastle to Raglan, 8 July 1854; and NeC 9,796, Raglan to Newcastle, 14 July 1854.

34. NeC 9,973, fols. 77–79 and 95–96,

Newcastle (private) to Raglan, 22 July and 8 August 1854; see also *Parl. Pap.*, 1854–5, IX, part II, *Third Report*, 131.

35. W.O. 6/76, fols. 183–84, Mundy to Trevelyan, 31 August 1854.

36. Ibid., fols. 36–37 and 68–69, Mundy to Trevelyan, 8 and 18 July 1854.

37. Ibid., fols. 33–36, Mundy to Osborne, 8 July 1854.

38. *Parl. Pap.*, 1854–5, IX, part II, *Third Report*, 126 and 187– 88.

39. Ibid., 203.

40. Ibid., 132, 153, and 184–85.

41. For example, see Conacher, *Aberdeen Coalition*, 488; Stanmore, *Herbert*, 1:224; C. H. Stuart, "The Formation of the Coalition Cabinet of 1852," 55; and A. W. Kinglake, *The Invasion of the Crimea*, 7:254–57.

42. Goldwin Smith, *Reminiscences*, 185–87; George Eden Marindin, ed., *Letters of Frederic Lord Blachford*, 225. Arthur Gordon, Lord Stanmore, Aberdeen's younger son and biographer, with his excessive filial piety, was not always just in his estimate of public men. He was particularly harsh at times on the duke of Newcastle. Thus in his two biographies he frequently praised Aberdeen and Herbert at the duke's expense (cf. Stuart, "Formation of Coalition," 47 and n. 3).

43. *Parl. Pap.*, 1854–5, IX, part II, *Third Report, 180–181,* and part III, *Fourth Report,* 296; Kinglake, *Invasion,* 38–40.

44. *Parl. Deb.*, CXXXVI, 55.

45. Included in the items lost in the fire at Varna were 16,000 pairs of boots, 6,000 blankets, and 350,000 tons of biscuit (NeC 10,883, fols. 103–4, Raglan to Newcastle, 14 August 1854).

46. RP, P.R.O. 30/22/11E, fols. 1451–54, Newcastle to Russell, 21 September 1854.

47. NeC 10,792, Newcastle (private) to Lord Elgin, 11 August 1854; NeC 9,739, the queen to Newcastle, 17 August 1854; NeC 9,973, fols. 55–56, Newcastle to Raglan, 23 June 1854; NeC 10,809, Newcastle to Sir William Reid, 19 October 1854; and NeC 10,973, Newcastle to Hardinge, 16 September 1854.

48. NeC 9,973, fols. 43–44, and 55–56, Newcastle (private) to Raglan, 3 and 17 June 1854; M. E. S. Laws, "Beatson's Bashi Bozooks."

49. NeC 10,883, fols. 111–112, Raglan to Newcastle, 16 August 1854.

50. This was true except in three cases. The appointment of Lord Lucan to the command of the cavalry division and the appointments of Brigadiers-General Torrens and Goldie were made by Lord Hardinge and approved by Lord Raglan without consultation with Newcastle (*Parl. Pap.*, 1854–5, IX, part II, *Third Report,* 110). The appointment of Lord Lucan would have tragic consequences in October during the battle of Balaclava.

51. NeC 9,973, fols. 125–30, Newcastle (private) to the duke of Cambridge and to Raglan, 30 August 1854. The government later decided that Cathcart should give up the commission.

52. NeC 10,785, Newcastle to Burgoyne, 10 April 1854; NeC 10,327, William Monsell to Newcastle, 11 April 1854; and NeC 10,328b, Burgoyne to Newcastle, 11 April 1854.

53. NeC 9,973, fol. 27, Newcastle to Raglan, 28 April 1854.

54. NeC 9,903, Raglan (private) to Newcastle, 11 November 1854.

55. Quoted John W. Fortescue, *A History of the British Army*, vol. XIII: *1852–1870*, 35.

56. *Parl. Deb.*, CXXXVI, 67.

Chapter 9: Invasion of the Crimea

1. NeC 9,973, fols. 21–22, Newcastle (private) to Raglan, 22 April 1854. Newcastle's letter followed closely the wording of the letter he had received two days earlier from Prince Albert about the propriety of sending a portion of the Allied forces to Varna (NeC 9,689, Prince Albert to Newcastle, 20 April 1854).

2. W.O. 1/385, fols. 91–97, Newcastle to Raglan, 10 April 1854.

3. NeC 9,973, fols. 33 and 35–36, Newcastle (private) to Raglan, 9 and 18 May 1854.

4. NeC 10,833, Raglan to Newcastle, 5 June 1854; John Martineau, *The Life of Henry Pelham, Fifth Duke of Newcastle, 1811–1864,* 144–45, quoting Newcastle to Raglan, 8 June 1854. Marshal St. Arnaud estimated the Russian army in the Crimea to be seventy-five thousand strong.

5. NeC 9,973, fols. 59–61 and 87–88, Newcastle (private) to Raglan, 3 and 29 July 1854. According to Kinglake, the total Russian force available for the defense of Sebastopol at the time of the invasion was seventy-

six thousand men (*The Invasion of the Crimea*, 3:129).

6. On 28 September the duke again urged Raglan to use a Turkish force to take possession of Perekop and to destroy the Russian garrison at Anapa and clear the Sea of Azov of all Russian shipping (NeC 9,973, fols. 145–48, Newcastle [private] to Raglan, 28 September 1854). It made very little difference that Admiral Dundas did not carry out his instructions relative to operations in the Sea of Azov, for the existence of a paved road and a bridge unknown to the Allies until later in the year enabled the Russians to reinforce their troops in Sebastopol without going through Anapa.

7. Kinglake, *Invasion*, 2:228.

8. Ibid., 248–50.

9. W.O. 1/385, fols. 309–24, Newcastle to Raglan, 29 June 1854; RA G14/51, Aberdeen to the queen, 29 June 1854.

10. Clar., dep. c. 15, fols. 536–37, Russell to Clarendon, 14 July 1854; PP, GC/NE/96, Palmerston (copy) to Newcastle, 16 July 1854.

11. NeC 9,973, fols. 73–74, Newcastle (private) to Raglan, 18 July 1854.

12. NeC 10,883, fols. 73–75, Raglan to Newcastle, 19 July 1854. Sir George Brown told Raglan that he had better accede to the instructions; for if he would not agree to the invasion of the Crimea, the ministers, having made up their minds to it, would replace him with someone who would.

13. NeC 9,973, fol. 91, Newcastle (private) to Raglan, 3 August 1854.

14. Ibid., fols. 119–21, Newcastle (private) to Raglan, 29 August 1854; NeC 9,741, the queen to Newcastle, 30 August 1854; and NeC 12,518, Aberdeen to Newcastle, 6 September 1854.

15. NeC 9,973, fols. 133–34, Newcastle (private) to Raglan, 8 September 1854; RP, P.R.O. 30/22/11E, fols. 19–22, Newcastle to Russell, 9 September 1854.

16. PP, GC/NE/72, Newcastle to Palmerston, 9 September 1854.

17. RP, P.R.O. 30/22/11E, fols. 1451–54, Newcastle to Russell, 21 September 1854.

18. NeC 11,737, Newcastle (copy) to Gladstone, 27 September 1854.

19. Henry E. Carlisle, ed., *Selections from the Correspondence of Aberdeen Hayward*, 1:228, Hayward to Young, 4 December 1854.

20. NeC 11,738, Newcastle (copy) to Gladstone, 6 October 1854.

21. NeC 9,837a and NeC 10,883, fols. 127–29, Raglan to Newcastle, 11 and 12 September 1854.

22. *Aber. Corres., 1854–55*, 221, Newcastle to Aberdeen, 28 September 1854.

23. NeC 9,973, fols. 145–48, Newcastle (private) to Raglan, 28 September 1854.

24. Her., Newcastle to Herbert, 30 September 1854, printed Lord Stanmore, *Sidney Herbert, Lord Herbert of Lea*, 235; NeC 9,785, fols. 88–89, Newcastle to the queen, 30 September 1854.

25. NeC 10,883, fols. 132–33, Newcastle to Raglan, 2 October 1854.

26. NeC 9,973, fols. 159–62, Newcastle (private) to Raglan, 3 October 1854. Newcastle had had a long conversation with Napoleon at Boulogne concerning the fortifications at Sebastopol, and he agreed with the emperor that they should be destroyed and that the Allied armies should establish winter quarters in Sebastopol. Most of the British ministers were inclined to agree with this position (cf. J. B. Conacher, *The Aberdeen Coalition, 1852–1855*, 463).

27. NeC 10,042, Palmerston to Newcastle, 1 October 1854. Even Gladstone, one of the most pacific ministers, thanked Palmerston for having earlier urged the attack on Sebastopol (PP, GC/GL/9, Gladstone to Palmerston, 4 October 1854).

28. This was the opinion of Sir George Cornewall Lewis. See Sir Gilbert Frankland Lewis, ed., *Letters of Sir George Cornewall Lewis to Various Friends*, 287–89, Lewis to Head, 29 December 1854.

29. Historians and military authorities from that day to this have been divided on this matter. The historiography is far too extensive to enter here; but for some of the standard references, see Kinglake, *Invasion*; Sir Edward Hamley, *The War in the Crimea*; Sir George MacMunn, *The Crimea in Perspective*; and H. P. Collins, "The Fateful Weeks."

30. NeC 9,876 and NeC 9,877, Raglan (private) to Newcastle, 24 September 1854; George Wrottesley, *Life and Correspondence of Field Marshal Sir John Burgoyne*, 2:93–98; Whitworth Porter, *History of the Corps of Royal Engineers*, 1:425–28; Christopher Hibbert, *The Destruction of Lord Raglan*, 125–34; and Kinglake, *Invasion*, 7:95–97.

31. NeC 10,883, fols. 139–41, Raglan to Newcastle, 28 September 1854.

32. RP, P.R.O. 30/22/11E, fols. 188–91, Newcastle to Russell, 7 October 1854; NeC 10,805, Newcastle (copy) to Graham, 5 October 1854; NeC 9,785, fols. 94–99, Newcastle (copy) to the queen, 8 October 1854.

33. NeC 9,973, fol. 157, Newcastle (private) to Raglan, 9 October 1854; NeC 10,883, fols. 141–43, Newcastle to Raglan, 10 and 13 October 1854.

34. NeC 10,805, Newcastle (copy) to Graham, 5 October 1854. Some of the information Newcastle had on Dundas came from A. H. Layard's correspondence with Lord John Russell. Layard, a constant detractor of Dundas, charged the admiral with "apparent complete incompetency and culpable negligence" (RP, P.R.O. 30/22/11E, fols. 1395–1402, Layard to Russell, 16 September 1854). The members of the cabinet also regretted Dundas's caution in not attacking the Russian ships and arsenal while the Sebastopol harbor remained open before the Russians sank vessels across the harbor mouth to block its entrance.

35. Charles S. Parker, *Life and Letters of Sir James Graham*, 2:250–52, quoting Graham to Aberdeen, 7 October 1854; *Aber. Corres., 1854–5*, 246–49, Graham to Aberdeen, 8 October 1854, and Aberdeen to Graham, 8 October 1854.

36. *Aber. Corres., 1854–5*, 252, Newcastle to Aberdeen, 11 October 1854; NeC 10,024, Aberdeen to Newcastle, 15 October 1854.

37. NeC 9,973, fols. 155–56, Newcastle (private) to Raglan, 9 October 1854.

38. NeC 9,896, Raglan to Newcastle, 28 October 1854.

39. Parker, *Graham*, 2:257, quoting Graham to Lyons, 25 October 1854.

40. Quoted Cecil Woodham-Smith, *Florence Nightingale, 1820–1910*, 98. The articles were published in the *Times* on 9, 12, and 13 October 1854.

41. Woodham-Smith, *Nightingale*, 103–8; Stanmore, *Herbert*, 1:337–38.

42. NeC 10,883, fol. 154, Newcastle to Clarendon, 12 October 1854. There is little evidence that Lord Stratford availed himself of this power (cf. Woodham-Smith, *Nightingale*, 119 and 132–34).

43. NeC 10,443, Newcastle to Stratford, 23 October 1854; W.O. 6/77, fols. 73–82, Roberts to Commissioners Benson, Cumming, and Spence, 23 October 1854.

44. *Parl. Pap., Third Report from the Select Committee on the Army before Sebastopol* (House of Commons, 1854–5 (218) IX. part II), 151–52.

45. NeC 10,443, Newcastle (copy) to Stratford, 23 October 1854; Stanmore, *Herbert*, I, 335–36, quoting Herbert to Newcastle, n.d.

Chapter 10: Autumn Apprehensions and Winter Troubles

1. NeC 10,883, fols. 152–53, and NeC 9,881, Raglan (confidential) to Newcastle, 8 October 1854.

2. NeC 9,881, Raglan (confidential) to Newcastle, 8 October 1854; George Wrottesley, *Life and Correspondence of Field Marshal Sir John Burgoyne*, 2:99–102.

3. RP, P.R.O. 30/22/11E, fols. 1598–1601, Newcastle to Russell, 23 October 1854; NeC 9,785, fols. 103–4, Newcastle to the queen, 23 October 1854; W.O. 6/69, fols. 274–75, Newcastle to Raglan, 25 October 1854.

4. W.O. 6/70, fols. 8–10, Newcastle to Raglan, 13 November 1854; NeC 10,883, fol. 153, Newcastle to Raglan, 23 October 1854; NeC 9,785, Newcastle to Prince Albert, 4 November 1854.

5. NeC 10,425, Newcastle (copy) to Dalhousie, 9 November 1854.

6. NeC 9,976, Newcastle (private) to Raglan, 30 October 1854. Included in this list were six thousand militia jackets and woolen trousers.

7. NeC 9,977 and NeC 10,811, Newcastle (private) to Raglan, 3 November 1854. One of the two steamers was secured quickly and sailed with half the battering train within a few days. The steamer also conveyed five hundred tons of clothing for the army (NeC 10,257, Graham to Newcastle, 10 November 1854).

8. NeC 9,977, Newcastle (private) to Raglan, 3 November 1854.

9. W.O. 59/76, fols. 157–58, Treasury Minute, 20 October 1854.

10. NeC 9,977 and NeC 9,979, Newcastle (private) to Raglan, 3 and 9 November 1854. Newcastle had long been in favor of making Sebastopol the main winter quarters for the Allied armies, a proposition Palmerston readily supported (PP, GC/CL/570, Palmerston [copy] to Clarendon, 7 September 1854).

11. NeC 10,883, fols. 167–68, Raglan to Newcastle, 18 October 1854.

12. Ibid., fols. 168–69, Raglan to Newcastle, 23 October 1854.

13. NeC 9,890, Raglan to Newcastle, 23 October 1854. The duke wrote in answer, "There can be no doubt the army requires repose, and ought to have it, it richly deserves it, and I wish there were an Eden prepared for it. My own idea is that if you were able to winter in the south of the Crimea the climate of the neighbourhood of Simpheropol and the want of provisions would prevent the Russians from molesting you by a winter campaign" (NeC 9,979, Newcastle [private] to Raglan, 9 November 1854).

14. NeC 9,891a, Raglan (private) to Newcastle, 23 October 1854.

15. NeC 9,894, Raglan (private) to Newcastle, 28 October 1854; NeC 10,883, fols. 179–80, Raglan to Newcastle, 3 November 1854; and NeC 9,900, Raglan (private) to Newcastle, 3 November 1854.

16. NeC 10,883, fols. 185–87, Raglan to Newcastle, 8 November 1854; cf. Christopher Hibbert, *The Destruction of Lord Raglan*, 198–232.

17. NeC 9,901, Raglan (private) to Newcastle, 8 November 1854; John Gough Somerset, Lord Calthorpe, *Letters from Head-Quarters*, 1:398–99; H. P. Collins, "The Crimea: The Fateful Weeks," 95. Newcastle told the Roebuck Committee that no conscious decision was made to winter in the Crimea before Sebastopol; the decision simply grew out of the circumstances following the battle of Inkermann (*Parl. Pap., Third Report from the Select Committee on the Army before Sebastopol* (House of Commons, 1854–5 [218] IX. part II, 120).

18. Wrottesley, *Burgoyne*, 2:123, Burgoyne to Colonel Matson, 12 November 1854. Burgoyne severely criticized the French for being overly cautious. They were, he noted, "too much bound by system and ordinary method for our pressing circumstances" (Whitworth Porter, *History of the Corps of Royal Engineers*, 1:434, quoting Burgoyne to Matson, 2 November 1854).

19. *Parl. Pap., Fielder's Letter on report of Commission of Inquiry* (House of Commons, 1856 [2042], 362).

20. A. W. Kinglake, *The Invasion of the Crimea*, 7:103–5; Hibbert, *Raglan*, 251–52; Porter, *Royal Engineers*, 1:436–37.

21. NeC 9,907, Raglan (private) to Newcastle, 13 November 1854.

22. NeC 10,883, fols. 219–20, Raglan to Newcastle, 15 November 1854. The following clothing was lost on the *Prince*: woolen socks, 35,700 pairs; woolen frocks, 53,000; woolen drawers, 17,000; watchcoats, 2,500; blankets, 16,100; rugs, 3,700.

23. NeC 9,920, Raglan (private) to Newcastle, 18 November 1854.

24. NeC 9,918, Raglan (private) to Newcastle, 18 November 1854. General Estcourt's letter is printed in Lord Stanmore, *Sidney Herbert, Lord Herbert of Lea*, 1:280–81.

25. NeC 9,922a, Raglan (private) to Newcastle, 28 November 1854.

26. NeC 9,924 and NeC 9,927a, Raglan (private) to Newcastle, 2 and 8 December 1854.

27. Quoted Hibbert, *Raglan*, 258.

28. *Parl. Pap.*, 1854–5, IX, part II, *Third Report*, 130–32.

29. Cf. Hibbert, *Raglan*, 191–92, referring to General Airey's address before the Board of General Officers, 1856. See also Herbert's letter to Raglan, 5 March 1855, printed in Stanmore, *Herbert*, 1:326–30.

30. NeC 9,903, Raglan (private) to Newcastle, 11 November 1854; NeC 10,883, fol. 207, Raglan to Newcastle, 13 November 1854, forwarding Dr. Hall's letter to Raglan, 11 November 1854.

31. RA B13/219, Newcastle to the queen, 22 December 1854; NeC 10,883, fol. 207, Hall to Raglan, 11 November 1854.

32. NeC 10,883, fol. 222, Newcastle to Raglan, 2 December 1854; NeC 10,825, Newcastle (copy) to Lord Hardinge, 6 December 1854; NeC 9,993, Newcastle (private) to Raglan, 11 December 1854; NeC 10,450, Newcastle (copy) to Benson, 11 December 1854; W.O. 6/70, fols. 65–67, Newcastle to Raglan, 11 December 1854.

33. On 11 November, Prince Albert warned Lord Aberdeen that the government would never be forgiven if Raglan succumbed for lack of support. He suggested several steps that might be taken, including the transfer of militia regiments abroad for garrison duty to release regular regiments for active service in the Crimea and the formation of a foreign legion (*Aber. Corres., 1854–5*, 272–74, Prince Albert to Aberdeen, 11 November 1854). Herbert wrote memoranda recommending an increase in the number of embodied regiments of militia and removing re-

strictions on recruiting parties visiting the embodied regiments (*Parl. Pap.*, 1854–5, IX, part III, Appendix II to *Fourth Report*, 335–38.

34. Cf. C. C. Bayley, *Mercenaries for the Crimea*, 37–38; J. B. Conacher, *The Aberdeen Coalition, 1852–1855*, 509. Newcastle later told the Roebuck Committee that he believed too much reliance had been put on recruiting from the militia (*Parl. Pap.*, 1854–5, IX, part II, *Third Report*, 203).

35. NeC 10,817a, Newcastle (private) to Lord Stratford, 23 November 1854.

36. *Parl. Deb.*, CXXXVI, 135; W.O. 6/70, fols. 18–21 and 35, Newcastle to Raglan, 18 and 23 November 1854; NeC 10,883, fols. 184 and 191, Newcastle to Raglan, 23 and 29 November 1854; NeC 10,819, Newcastle (private) to Sir William Reid, 25 November 1854; and NeC 9,785, Newcastle to the queen, 22 November 1854.

37. Sir James Graham noted that British army requisitions for transport were postponed to meet the French request (Conacher, *Aberdeen Coalition*, 507, n. 2, citing Graham to Newcastle and Palmerston, 14 and 18 November 1854). On 22 November Newcastle told the queen that he had been in concert all day with Graham, Hardinge, Herbert, and all the naval and military departments endeavoring to expedite the transport not only of men but ammunition, warm clothing and huts (NeC 9,785, Newcastle to the queen, 22 November 1854).

38. W.O. 6/77, fols. 200–204, Mundy to Wood and Lord Wodehouse, 18 November 1854; W.O. 6/70, fols. 21–22, Newcastle to Raglan, 18 November 1854; NeC 10,463, Newcastle (copy) to Lord Stratford, 18 November 1854. The first vessel containing huts sailed from England on 3 December 1854.

39. *Parl. Pap.*, 1854–5, IX, part II, *Third Report*, 125. The War Office requested the Ordnance to place orders for many other items following the confirmation of the loss of supplies in the storm of 14 November. Unfortunately, many of these items, particularly the boots, proved to be of poor quality (*Parl. Deb.*, CXXXVI, 54, Newcastle's speech, 12 December 1854.

40. NeC 9,989, Newcastle (private) to Raglan, 2 December 1854; W.O. 6/70, fols. 62–64, Newcastle to Raglan, 8 December 1854.

41. *Parl. Pap.*, 1854–5, IX, part II, *Third Report*, 130; W.O. 6/70, fols. 57–58, Newcastle to Raglan, 6 December 1854; Michael Robbins, "The Balaklava Railway," 29–32.

42. W.O. 6/70, fols. 68–71, Newcastle to Raglan, 12 December 1854; W.O. 6/68, fols. 25–27, Roberts to Trevelyan, 15 December 1854.

43. W.O. 6/78, fols. 161–62, Mundy to Wood, 28 November 1854; W.O. 58/93, fols. 274–75, Trevelyan to Filder, 28 November 1854; NeC 10,822, Newcastle (copy) to Sir William Monsell, 29 November 1854. Raglan thought the plan to establish depots at Malta an excellent one (NeC 9,938, Raglan (private) to Newcastle, 18 December 1854).

44. NeC 10,825, Newcastle (copy) to Hardinge, 6 December 1854; NeC 9,993, Newcastle (private) to Raglan, 11 December 1854.

45. NeC 9,984, Newcastle (private) to Raglan, 18 November 1854.

46. NeC 9,992, Newcastle (private) to Raglan, 8 December 1854.

Chapter 11: The Government Divided and Besieged

1. RA G17/89, Prince Albert memorandum, 7 October 1854. From late September on, Russell's correspondence with Clarendon and Graham revealed the depths of his feelings, particularly toward Lord Aberdeen. Russell also felt the sharp criticism of some of his Whig followers who believed that he, as leader of the House of Commons, was not obtaining for them their just due. See, for example, his memorandum of 18 October 1854, which he probably did not circulate (RP, P.R.O. 30/22/11F, fols. 1567–75).

2. Aber., Add. MS. 43068, fols. 179–84 and 187–88, Russell to Aberdeen, 17 and 18 November 1854.

3. PP, GC/CL/582, Palmerston's note of 2 December 1854 on back of Clarendon to Palmerston, 30 November 1854; RA G20/78, Prince Albert memorandum, 4 December 1854; RA G20/87, Aberdeen to the queen, 7 December 1854.

4. RA G20/17, Prince Albert memorandum 27 November 1854.

5. RP P.R.O. 30/22/11F, fols. 1723–24, Aberdeen to Russell, 21 November 1854.

6. Aber., Add. MS. 43068, fols. 198–205, Russell to Aberdeen, 28 November 1854. Russell cited the incident concerning the transfer of the 97th Regiment from Corfu to the Crimea which he had suggested in October but which was not done until late November. Newcastle had wanted to complete

the transfer at the time Russell suggested it, but was stymied from doing so by the Foreign Office.

7. RP, P.R.O. 30/22/11F, fols. 1781–3, Aberdeen to Russell, 30 November 1854.

8. Aber., Add. MS. 43068, fols. 221–22, Russell to Aberdeen, 3 December 1854; RA G20/17, Prince Albert memorandum, 27 November 1854.

9. George Douglas, Duke of Argyll, *Autobiography and Memoirs of George Douglas, Eighth Duke of Argyll*, ed. the Dowager-Duchess of Argyll, 1:508–10; Aber., Add. MS. 43198, fols. 213–16, Sir Charles Wood memorandum, 6 December 1854.

10. Sir Herbert Maxwell, *The Life and Letters of George William Frederick, Fourth Earl of Clarendon*, 9:53–54.

11. RA G20/87 and 101, Aberdeen to the queen, 7 December 1854, and Prince Albert memorandum 9 December 1854.

12. RP, P.R.O. 30/22/11F, fols. 209–13, Palmerston to Russell, 3 December 1854; NeC 10,044, Palmerston to Newcastle, 4 December 1854.

13. RP, P.R.O. 30/22/11F, fols. 1910–13, Lansdowne to Russell, 10 December 1854. The Whigs were slow to forgive Newcastle for his harsh and critical evaluation of them. "I do not agree with you in thinking that Palmerston would be a better Secretary of War than Newcastle," Lord Granville wrote to Russell. "The best man connected with the Department appears to be Sydney Herbert. He is by far the best judge of men, is practical, unegotistical and without official nonsense" (Ibid., fols. 1991–94, Granville to Russell, 23 December 1854).

14. Ibid., fols. 1886–95 and 1914–22, Wood to Russell, 7 and 11 December 1854; Aber., Add. MS. 43198, fols. 213–16, Wood memorandum, 6 December 1854.

15. RA G20/134, Aberdeen to the queen, 16 December 1854.

16. *Times*, 13 December 1854.

17. *Parl. Deb.*, CXXXVI, 10–36. This speech followed precisely the plan of action that Derby had outlined to Disraeli for the session (Dis., B/XX/S/128, Derby to Disraeli, 3 December 1854).

18. *Parl. Pap., Third Report from the Select Committee on the Army before Sebastopol* (House of Commons, 1854–5 [218], IX, part II), 189.

19. Henry Reeve, ed., *The Greville Memoirs*, 7:84; Bro., Add. MS. 56567, Broughton Diary, 12 December 1854; *Times*, 13 Decem-

ber 1854. Lord Grey thought that "for feebleness & tiresomeness" Newcastle's speech exceeded anything he had ever heard from a minister (GP, C3/18A, Lord Grey's Journal, 12 December 1854).

20. *Parl. Deb.*, CXXXVI, 36–74.

21. Lord Grey told Sir Charles Wood, "What had obviously caused all the mischief is that Newcastle neglected to form in the first instance some clear & well considered plan for the conduct of the war, to be resolutely & energetically acted upon" (Hick., A4/55/3, Grey to Wood, 15 November 1854).

22. *Parl. Deb.*, CXXXVI, 129–60, partly printed Lord Stanmore, *Sidney Herbert, Lord Herbert of Lea*, 1:239–42.

23. *Parl. Deb.*, CXXXVI, 253.

24. Ibid., 344; C. C. Bayley, *Mercenaries for the Crimea*, 48–51.

25. Cf. Bayley, *Mercenaries*, 51–55; J. B. Conacher, *The Aberdeen Coalition, 1852–1855*, 513–14.

26. *Times*, 30 December 1854. The newspaper storm, Kinglake asserted, "was a fury set loose, though unwittingly, by Ministers failing in loyalty towards their general engaged in the field" (A. W. Kinglake, *The Invasion of the Crimea*, 7:271). Kinglake's assertion that the *Times* launched its attack against Lord Raglan and his staff at the inspiration of the ministers is totally off the mark.

27. *Times*, 19 and 23 December 1854.

28. Ibid., 30 December 1854.

29. *The History of the Times*, Vol. II: *The Tradition Established*, 172–73; Olive Anderson, *A Liberal State at War*, 70–79 and 101–7.

30. Sir Gilbert Frankland Lewis, ed., *Letters of Sir George Cornewall Lewis to Various Friends*, 287–89, Lewis to Head, 29 December 1854.

31. NeC 9,929a and NeC 9,938, Raglan (private) to Newcastle, 13 and 18 December 1854.

32. PP, GC/CL/581, Clarendon to Palmerston, 23 November 1854; RP, P.R.O. 30/22/11F, fols. 1991–94, Granville to Russell, 23 December 1854.

33. NeC 9,995 and NeC 9,996, Newcastle (private) to Raglan, 18 and 22 December 1854.

34. NeC 9,997, Newcastle (private) to Raglan, 25 December 1854.

35. NeC 9,998, Newcastle (private) to Raglan, 29 December 1854.

36. NeC 9,999, Newcastle (private) to Raglan, 1 January 1855.

37. Cf. Kinglake, *Invasion*, 7:254–74. Mar-

tineau essentially accepted Kinglake's argument, but added that the pressure from his colleagues in the cabinet forced Newcastle to launch the attack upon Raglan and his staff (John Martineau, *The Life of Henry Pelham, Fifth Duke of Newcastle, 1811–1864*, 223–24. J. W. Fortescue described Newcastle's action in particularly strong terms: "The whole proceeding was characteristic of the not uncommon type of man who tries to veil weakness and fright under an outburst of spasmodic violence." It was, he continued, "an exhibition of administrative futility and bad taste." The ministers' "attempt to transfer this odium of its miscarriage to Raglan's staff suggests a very mean form of cowardice" (*A History of the British Army*, 13:161–62).

38. Sidney Herbert explained this to Raglan in a letter of 5 March 1855 (printed Stanmore, *Herbert*, 1:326–30). In this letter Herbert told Raglan that "in your answers to Newcastle's despatches you have fallen into error in thinking that he adopted the stories told, or brought them as accusations against you. He, as I conceive, recited what had been told him, wishing to have from you the explanation or contradictions."

39. Kinglake, *Invasion*, 7:254–74.
40. NeC 9,940a, Raglan (private) to Newcastle, 23 December 1854; Stanmore, *Herbert*, 1:282, Estcourt to Herbert, 22 December 1854.
41. PP, GC/NE/97, Palmerston (copy) to Newcastle, 4 January 1855.
42. RP, P.R.O. 30/22/11F, fols. 2026–31, Russell (draft) memorandum, 30 December 1854. On 1 January, Russell commenced a letter of resignation in which he complained of the failure of the government to take his advice regarding the more vigorous prosecution of the war. His advice was not taken for fear of casting an imputation of incompetence upon Newcastle. The unfinished letter was never sent to Aberdeen (cf. Conacher, *Aberdeen Coalition*, 522–23).
43. RP, P.R.O. 30/22/12A, fols. 34–41, Herbert to Russell, 3 January 1855. Herbert elaborated his views on the Crimean situation for the cabinet in another long memorandum of 9 January (printed Stanmore, *Herbert*, 1:318–25).
44. RP, P.R.O. 30/22/11F, fols. 1809–10, Argyll memorandum, n.d.; and P.R.O. 30/22/12A, fols. 50–69, memoranda by Sir George Grey, Sir Charles Wood, and Lord Clarendon, 8 and 12 January 1855; NeC

10,861, Molesworth memorandum, n.d.; Her., Gladstone to Herbert, 14 January 1855, printed Stanmore, *Herbert*, 1:313–14.
45. PP, GC/NE/74, Newcastle to Palmerston, 9 January 1855.
46. NeC 10,001, Newcastle (private) to Raglan, 8 January 1855. Kinglake called this letter "a clandestine fling at the 'Times'" (*Invasion*, 7:272).
47. W.O. 6/70, fols. 136–43, Newcastle to Raglan, 6 January 1855. Although the draft of the dispatch is dated 6 January, it was not sent until after Newcastle received the cabinet's sanction at the meeting of 11 January (RA G22/21, Aberdeen to the queen, 11 January 1855).
48. Arthur C. Benson and Viscount Esher, eds., *Letters of Queen Victoria*, 3:86, the queen to Newcastle, 12 January 1855.
49. Stanmore, *Herbert*, 1:303–6, quoting Herbert to Newcastle, 8 January 1855.
50. NeC 10,857, fols. 1–4; NeC 10,858, fols. 1–3; and NeC 10,859, fols. 1–2, copies of minutes for meetings at War Department, 3, 10, and 20 January 1855. RA E5/13, Aberdeen to the queen, 20 January 1855.
51. NeC 9,699, Prince Albert memorandum, n.d.
52. NeC 10,823, Newcastle (copy) to Paulet, 1 January 1855; W.O. 6/70, fols. 112–33, Newcastle (private) to Paulet, 5 January 1855.
53. W.O. 58/45, fols. 421–22, Roberts to Admiralty, 9 January 1855; W.O. 58/93, fol. 366, Roberts to Filder, 18 January 1855: NeC 10,589, "Memorandum of Arrangements Made in December 1854 and January 1855 for Supply of Hay to the Crimea."
54. John Sweetman, "Military Transport in the Crimean War, 1854–1856," 84; W.O. 43/973, part I, fols. 6–10, McMurdo memorandum, 7 January 1855; W.O. 6/78, fols. 167, Newcastle to Herbert, 19 January 1855; W.O. 6/70, fols. 168–69, Newcastle to Raglan, 20 January 1855; NeC 9,786, fols. 29–31, Newcastle (copy) to Prince Albert, 12 January 1855. It was not until 24 February that the Transport Corps received official sanction in the form of an authorization to McMurdo to raise the establishment.
55. RA G22/7, Newcastle to Prince Albert, 10 January 1855; NeC 9,700, Prince Albert to Newcastle, 11 January 1855.
56. NeC 10,002 and NeC 9,786, fols. 33–35, Newcastle to Raglan, 12 and 20 January 1855.
57. NeC 9,955a; NeC 9,965; and NeC

9,958, Raglan to Newcastle, 13, 18, and 29 January 1855.

58. NeC 9,960a, Raglan to Newcastle, 20 January 1855.

59. W.O. 1/371, fols. 219–91, Raglan to Newcastle, 30 January 1855.

60. NeC 10,006, Newcastle (private) to Raglan, 22 January 1855.

61. NeC 9,963, Raglan (private) to Newcastle, 27 January 1855. Raglan referred the pertinent parts of Newcastle's dispatch of 12 January to the appropriate departments for consideration and comment. Even before the return of the departmental reports, Raglan told Newcastle, "I shall be able clearly to show that no blame rests on the military departs" (ibid.). He took no further action on the government's request for a thorough inquiry into the operation of the departments. Copies of departmental reports were forwarded after Newcastle had left office (W.O. 1/371, fols. 311–20 and 363–69, Airey's reply; 410–13, Estcourt's reply; 389–94, Dr. Hall's reply; and 295–307, Filder's reply).

62. Kinglake, *Invasion*, 7:273.

63. NeC 10,007, Newcastle (private) to Raglan, 26 January 1855. Newcastle had informed Aberdeen, but none of the others in the cabinet, of his intention to resign even before the parliamentary session began and Roebuck gave notice of his motion (*Aber. Corres., 1854–5*, Appendix 378–79, Arthur Gordon's journal entry of 22 January 1855).

64. NeC 9,970, Raglan (private) to Newcastle, 10 February 1855.

65. RA A84/30, Prince Albert memorandum 25 January 1855, printed Benson and Esher, eds., *Letters of Queen Victoria*, 3:91–93; Aber., Add. MS. 43069, fol. 294, Palmerston to Aberdeen, 24 January 1855; RP, P.R.O. 30/22/12A, fols. 108–10, Palmerston to Russell, 24 January 1855.

66. RA A84/34, Prince Albert memorandum, 25 January 1855; John Morley, *The Life of William Ewart Gladstone*, 1:522, Gladstone memorandum, 9 March 1855. Russell expected Sir George Grey, Sir Charles Wood, and Lord Granville to follow him in resigning from the cabinet; when they remained in office, he complained to Grey that none of his old Whig colleagues had tried to get him to withdraw his resignation (G. P. Gooch, ed., *The Later Correspondence of Lord John Russell, 1840–1878*, 2:182, Russell to Sir George Grey, 9 February 1855).

67. *Times*, 20 and 23 January 1855.

68. *Parl. Deb.*, CXXXVI, 960–74.

69. Glad., Add. MS. 44745, fols. 31–32, Gladstone memorandum, 9 March 1855.

70. *Parl. Deb.*, CXXXVI, 982–1002, printed Stanmore, *Herbert*, 1:247–50.

71. Quoted Morley, *Gladstone*, 1:524–25.

72. *Aber. Corres., 1855–60*, 8–9, Arthur Gordon's Journal, 30 January 1855. In the majority there were 200 Conservatives, 2 Peelites, and 83 Liberals; in the minority there were 100 Liberals, 34 Peelites and 14 Conservatives.

73. NeC 10,008, Newcastle (private) to Raglan, 29 January 1855.

74. *Parl. Deb.*, CXXXVI, 1094–1105.

75. Osbert Wyndham Hewett, *Strawberry Fair*, 111.

76. *Parl. Deb.*, CXXXVI, 1238–54.

77. *Times*, 2 February 1855. Lord Derby, who spoke immediately after Newcastle, satirically praised the duke's excellent "Picture of an Interior—the Cabinet *peint par soimeme*." He confessed that between the two noble colleagues (Newcastle and Russell), he believed that the duke "has considerably the best of the argument" (*Parl. Deb.*, CXXXVI, 1257). Chichester Fortescue, one of Russell's few defenders, described the duke's speech as "too whining, & defending himself agst. charges never made" (Osbert Wyndham Hewett, ed., *Mr. Fortescue: A Selection from the Diaries from 1851 to 1862 of Chichester Fortescue, Lord Carlingford, K.P.*, 80).

78. Bro., Add. MS. 47230, fols. 82–85, MSS. account of the Resignation of the Aberdeen Administration; Add. MS. 56567, fols. 69–70, Broughton Diary.

79. GP, G3/18A, Lord Grey's Journal.

80. RA, G23/77, Phipps memorandum, 3 February 1855.

81. RA, E5/25, Ellice to Col. Charles Grey, 24 January 1855.

Chapter 12: Political Isolation

1. Sir George Douglas and Sir George Dalhousie Ramsay, eds., *The Panmure Papers*, 2:483.

2. Ibid., 1:53–54, "Memorandum of Measures Taken to Establish a Better Order of Things in the Crimea," 12 February 1855. Early in May, Palmerston strongly urged Panmure to replace Smith, Filder, Airey, and Estcourt, the "knot of Incapables, who in the

last eight months have been the direct cause of the disability and death of thousands of our brave men," with intelligent, competent men. Panmure, however, resisted the prime minister's requests, using General Simpson's favorable review of Airey and Estcourt and the improved reports from the Crimea as justification (Pal., Add. MS. 48579, fols. 12 and 15, Palmerston to Panmure, 1 and 8 May 1855; and PP., GC/PA/101, Panmure to Palmerston, 1 May 1855).

3. Cf. Olive Anderson, *A Liberal State at War*, 65–68.

4. *Times*, 25 April 1855.

5. Ibid., 26 April 1855.

6. NeC 12,244 and NeC 12,245, Elizabeth Herbert to Newcastle, 29 April 1855, and Newcastle (copy) to Elizabeth Herbert, 1 May 1855.

7. *Aber. Corres., 1855–6*, 67, Clarendon to Aberdeen, 27 May 1855. An important commentary on the political events of 1855 and 1856 is provided by John Vincent, "The Parliamentary Dimension of the Crimean War," 37–49.

8. Ibid., 82–83, Gladstone to Aberdeen, 28 June 1855; Her., Gladstone to Herbert, 2 July 1855; NeC 12,443, Aberdeen to Newcastle, 25 June 1855.

9. *Parl. Pap.*, *Fifth Report from the Select Committee on the Army before Sebastopol* (House of Commons, 1854–5 (218) IX. part III), 365–87.

10. NeC 10,884a, Newcastle's Crimean Journal, part 1:6–7.

11. Ibid., 23. Aberdeen informed Sir James Graham about Canning's appointment: "In many respects the appointment is good, and I trust he will do well. Newcastle is very angry, and with reason, in consequence of what passed between Wood and him on the subject last year. The most extraordinary part of the story is, that Vernon Smith, in answer to the strong recommendation of the Chairs, told them he had consulted me, Palmerston, and Lansdowne; and that we had assured him Newcastle had positively refused to go. Now, I never had the advantage of any kind of conversation with the said Mr. Vernon Smith in my life!" (*Aber. Corres., 1855–60*, 84–85, Aberdeen to Graham, 29 June 1855). In light of the Sepoy Mutiny of 1857 and the severe problems that Canning would face, perhaps Newcastle was fortunate for a change in not being named governor-general of India.

12. NeC 10,884a, Newcastle's Crimean Journal, part 1:42.

13. Ibid., 59; Clar., dep. c. 42, fols. 67–70, Newcastle to Clarendon, 23 July 1855. Newcastle noted to Clarendon that his official distrust of Dr. Cumming was greatly reinforced by personal acquaintance: "With such a man at the head of so vast an Establishment you may any day be liable to another disaster."

14. NeC 10,884a, Newcastle's Crimean Journal, part 1:70–71.

15. Ibid., 76.

16. Ibid., part 2:109–10.

17. Ibid., part 1:79; Clar., dep. c. 42, fols. 73–86, Newcastle to Clarendon, 30 August 1855.

18. Clar., dep. c. 42, fols. 73–86, Newcastle to Clarendon, 30 August 1855.

19. NeC 10,884a, Newcastle's Crimean Journal, part 1:79.

20. Ibid., 96; Clar., dep. c. 42, fols. 73–86, Newcastle to Clarendon, 30 August 1855.

21. Clar., dep. c. 42, fols. 73–86, Newcastle to Clarendon, 30 August 1855.

22. Douglas and Ramsay, eds., *Panmure Papers*, 1:390–91, quoting Prince Albert to Clarendon, 17 September 1855.

23. Ibid., 394 and 396, quoting Palmerston to Panmure, 20 September 1855, and Panmure to Simpson, 22 September 1855; Clar., dep. c. 29, fols. 202–5 and 208–21, Panmure to Clarendon, 13 September and 4 October 1855.

24. Clar., dep. c. 30, fols. 497–98, Granville to Clarendon, 16 September 1855.

25. PP, GC/CL/705, Clarendon to Palmerston, 4 October 1855; Douglas and Ramsay, eds., *Panmure Papers*, 1:427, quoting Clarendon to Panmure, 5 October 1855.

26. Douglas and Ramsay, eds., *Panmure Papers*, 1:393, quoting Prince Albert to Clarendon, 17 September 1855.

27. NeC 10,884a, Newcastle's Crimean Journal, part 2:169.

28. Clar., dep. c. 42, fols. 95–98, Newcastle to Clarendon, 15 September 1855.

29. NeC 10,884a, Newcastle's Crimean Journal, part 2:205–23. Newcastle advocated a Confederacy of Principalities in Circassia under the protection of the great powers. The confederacy would form a buffer on Russia's southwestern frontier (Clar., dep. c. 42, fols. 124–36, Newcastle to Clarendon, 19 December 1855).

30. Henry E. Carlisle, ed., *Selections from*

the *Correspondence of Abraham Hayward*, 1:257, Newcastle to Hayward, 18 November 1855.

31. G-G MSS, Hayward to Newcastle, 9 November 1855; NeC 12,250, Maxwell to Newcastle, 12 July 1855.

32. Aber., Add. MS. 43197, fols. 66–67, Newcastle to Aberdeen, 8 December 1855; Clar., dep. c. 42, fols. 114–18, Newcastle to Clarendon, 14 December 1855.

33. NeC 12,552, Herbert to Newcastle, 11 January 1856; Aber., Add. MS. 43197, fols. 68–69, Newcastle to Aberdeen, 18 April 1856.

34. Osbert Wyndham Hewett, ed., *Mr. Fortescue: A Selection from the Diaries from 1851 to 1862 of Chichester Fortescue, Lord Carlingford, K.P.*, 89–91; Hewett, *Strawberry Fair*, 120.

35. Aber., Add. MS. 43197, fols. 74–77, Newcastle to Aberdeen, 24 Novenber 1856; *Aber. Corres., 1855–60*, 224, Graham to Aberdeen, 23 November 1856; NeC 12,448, Aberdeen to Newcastle, 27 November 1856. Palmerston observed to the queen that Newcastle was "a good man of business, of active habits and likely to make a very efficient Lieutenant" (RA A25/146, Palmerston to the queen, 13 November 1856).

36. *Aber. Corres., 1855–60*, 282–83, and *Supplement to Corres., 1855–62*, 39–40, Aberdeen to Gladstone and Graham, 22 and 24 January 1857.

37. Glad., Add. MS. 44263, fols. 1–9, Gladstone (copy) to Newcastle, 30 January 1857, and Newcastle to Gladstone, 10 February 1857.

38. Ibid., fols. 14–17, Newcastle to Gladstone, 15 February 1857.

39. Ibid., fols. 18–19, Gladstone (copy) to Newcastle, 21 February 1857. Gladstone's objectives and strategy concerning the 1857 budget are discussed by Angus B. Hawkins in "A Forgotten Crisis: Gladstone and the Politics of Finance During the 1850s," 300–312.

40. G-G MSS, Palmerston to Newcastle, 9 March 1857, and Clarendon to Newcastle with copy of the queen to Clarendon, 10 March 1857; RA A26/37, Palmerston to the queen, 6 March 1857.

41. *Aber. Corres., 1855–60*, 288–89, Aberdeen to Gordon, 22 March 1857.

42. G-G MSS, Clarendon to Newcastle, 11 April 1857, and Newcastle (copy) to Clarendon, 12 April 1857; RA B16/21, Clarendon to the queen, 9 March 1857.

43. NeC 11,743, Newcastle (copy) to Gladstone, 24 June 1857. Gladstone's failure to effect his political and financial objectives in 1857 brought him "to a profound personal crisis," which resulted in his temporary withdrawal from active politics and served as the essential background to his "equivocal public life during 1858 and 1859" (Hawkins, "A Forgotten Crisis," 313–16).

44. Glad., Add. MS. 44263, fols. 23–27, Gladstone (copy) to Newcastle, 15 August 1857, quoting *Morning Post*, 14 August 1857.

45. Hewett, *Strawberry Fair*, 131.

46. Ibid., 132. See Goldwin Smith, *Reminiscences*, 162–67, for a discussion of Cooke and the original staff of writers of the *Saturday Review*.

47. *Aber. Corres., Supplement to Corres., 1855–62*, Aberdeen to Graham, 7 October 1857.

48. Hewett, ed., *Mr. Fortescue*, 113; Hewett, *Strawberry Fair*, 131.

49. NeC 12,193, Cooke to Newcastle, 26 November 1857.

50. NeC 12,371, Newcastle (copy) to Hayward, 21 February 1858.

51. Aber., Add. MS. 43197, fols. 80–83, Newcastle to Aberdeen, 21 February 1858.

52. NeC 12,530 and NeC 12,531, Derby to Newcastle, 21 February 1858, and Newcastle (copy) to Derby, 21 February 1858; RA C29/16, the queen (draft) to Derby, 22 February 1858.

53. Hewett, *Strawberry Fair*, 137; NeC 12,372, Newcastle (copy) to Hayward, 3 April 1858; NeC 12,195, Cooke to Newcastle, 17 May 1859.

54. NeC 12,297, Smith to Newcastle, 30 May 1858.

55. *Parl. Deb.*, CL, 1842–1845; and CLI, 384–86, 2100–2103, and 817–21.

56. G-G MSS, Salisbury to Newcastle, 28 May, 4 and 12 June 1858; Newcastle (copies) to Salisbury, 3, 6, and 14 June 1858.

57. G-G MSS, Salisbury to Newcastle, 28 May, 4 and 12 June 1858; Newcastle (copies) to Salisbury, 3, 6, and 14 June 1858. Goldwin Smith was professor of modern history at Oxford at the time of his appointment to the commission. William Charles Lake, formerly of Newman's circle, was a friend and ardent supporter of Gladstone. He was later dean of Durham from 1869 to 1894. Sir John Taylor Coleridge, nephew of Samuel Taylor Coleridge, had just left the Justice of the King's

Bench. The other members of the commission were Nassau William Senior, professor of political economy at Oxford, 1825–1830 and 1847–1852; Edward Miall, an Independent minister of Leicester, founder of *The Nonconformist*, and M.P. for Bradford; and William Rogers, curate of St. Batolph's. See Smith, *Reminiscences*, 116–120, for a discussion on the Education Commission.

58. Cf. Sir Llewellyn Woodward, *The Age of Reform, 1815–1870*, 481; Smith, *Reminiscences*, 116–120; *Parl. Deb.*, CLXIV, 493–506, Newcastle's speech on Report, 8 July 1861.

59. Glad., Add. MS. 44263, fols. 40–47, Newcastle to Gladstone, 25 October 1858.

60. Ibid., fols. 79–82, Newcastle to Gladstone, 22 January 1859.

61. Stra., W W 43/5, Newcastle to Lady Waldegrave, 29 May 1859.

62. RA F38/78, Newcastle to the queen, 1 February 1863; Hewett, *Strawberry Fair*, 141.

63. RA C30/25, Palmerston to the queen, 15 June 1859.

64. PP, GC/NE/76, Newcastle to Palmerston, 15 June 1859.

65. On 1 August 1859 Fortescue noted in his diary that the speaker had driven him to London from Strawberry Hill: "He talked of my chief the Duke & told me a great deal of him, his misfortunes, his mistakes, his vanity, with good intentions" (Hewett, ed., *Mr. Fortescue*, 152).

Chapter 13: Colonial Secretary

1. George Eden Marindin, ed., *Letters of Frederic Lord Blachford*, 227–28, Rogers to his mother, Lady Rogers, 17 June 1860.

2. NeC 10,889, fols. 107–8, Newcastle (private) to Palmerston, 18 January 1860; G-G MSS, Palmerston to Newcastle, 19 January 1860.

3. James A. Gibson, "The Duke of Newcastle and British North American Affairs, 1859–1864," 144.

4. E. E. Morris, *A Memoir of George Higenbotham*, 167.

5. NeC 11,480, newspaper cutting from *Mackenzie's Toronto Weekly Message*, 4 August 1860.

6. NeC 11,439, fols. 4–12, Newcastle to the queen, 24 July 1860; NeC 11,469, news-

paper cutting from the *Newfoundlander*, 30 July 1860.

7. NeC 11,469, newspaper cutting from *The Royal Gazette*, 31 July 1860.

8. NeC 11,439, fols. 39–41, Newcastle to the queen, 7 August 1860.

9. PP, GC/NE/81, Newcastle to Palmerston, 5 September 1860.

10. Ibid.

11. RA Z/467, Palmerston to the queen, 20 September 1860; NeC 12,612, Palmerston to Newcastle, 24 September 1860; NeC 12,744, 12,745, and 12,746, the queen to Newcastle, 4 August, 8 and 20 September 1860.

12. PP, GC/NE/82, Newcastle to Palmerston, 12 September 1860.

13. Ibid.

14. Stra., W W 43/10, Newcastle to Lady Waldegrave, 30 September 1860.

15. PP, GC/NE/83, Newcastle to Palmerston, 30 September 1860; NeC 11,439, fols. 89–99, Newcastle to the queen, 23 September 1860.

16. PP, GC/NE/84, Newcastle to Palmerston, 14 October 1860.

17. Osbert Wyndham Hewett, *Strawberry Fair*, 148; RA Y82/86, King Leopold to the queen, 22 November 1860.

18. NeC 12,747, the queen to Newcastle, 19 November 1860; RA B18/148, Newcastle to the queen, 20 November 1860.

19. NeC 10,890, fols. 94–98, Newcastle to Palmerston, 11 November 1861.

20. *Times*, 20 October 1864.

21. Ibid., Newcastle's speech at the Anniversary Banquet of the Australian Society at Freemason's Tavern, 12 February 1862; Marindin, ed., *Letters of Blachford*, 299–300; Henry Taylor, *Autobiography of Henry Taylor, 1800–1875*, 2:234–35.

22. Cf. Colin C. Eldridge, "The Myth of Mid-Victorian 'Separatism' : The Cession of the Bay Islands and the Ionian Islands in the Early 1860s," 341.

23. Cf. Colin C. Eldridge, "The Colonial Policy of the Fifth Duke of Newcastle, 1859–1864," 68–78, 81–83.

24. Gibson, "Newcastle and British North America," 156.

25. C.O. 48/415, Newcastle Minute on Treasury to C.O., 4 February 1862.

26. Eldridge, "Colonial Policy of Newcastle," 73.

27. Quoted John Martineau, *The Life of Henry Pelham, Fifth Duke of Newcastle, 1811–*

1864, 308, Newcastle to Herbert, 18 November 1859.

28. NeC 11,764, Newcastle (copy) to Gladstone, 15 February 1864.

29. RP, P.R.O. 30/22/25, Russell (copy) to Newcastle, 10 February 1860; NeC 10,889, fols. 117–18, Newcastle (private) to Russell, 11 February 1860.

30. C.O. 34/9, Newcastle to Seymour, 30 March 1860.

31. Prince William of Denmark, a younger brother of Alexandra, the princess of Wales, was the British candidate. He ascended the Greek throne on 30 March 1863 as King George I.

32. PP, GC/NE/92, Newcastle to Palmerston, 9 December 1862.

33. Cf. Eldridge, "Colonial Policy of Newcastle," 160–63.

34. Ibid., 366–67, 383–84.

35. C.O. 267/271, Newcastle Minute, 14 December 1861, on Hill to Newcastle, 14 November 1861.

36. For example, see C.O. 87/79, Newcastle to D' Arcy, 23 March 1864.

37. C.O. 96/56, F.O. to C.O., 7 February 1861; Eldridge, "Colonial Policy of Newcastle," 178–79.

38. C.O. 147/1, Newcastle to Freeman, 16 December 1861.

39. C.O. 471/3, Newcastle to Freeman, 22 August 1862.

40. C.O. 147/5, Newcastle Minute, 2 June 1863, on Freeman to Newcastle, 30 March 1863.

41. C.O. 267/280, Elliot Minute, 16 March 1863, on Blackall to Newcastle, 21 February 1863; C.O. 147/4, Elliot Minute, 12 July 1862, on Freeman to Newcastle, 4 June 1862.

42. C.O. 147/6, Newcastle Minute, 19 February 1864, on Freeman to Newcastle, 9 January 1864; Colin C. Eldridge, "Newcastle and the Ashanti War of 1863–64: A Failure of the Policy of 'Anti-Imperialism,'" 72.

43. See W. E. F. Ward, *A History of the Gold Coast*, for the causes of the Ashanti War of 1863–1864.

44. C.O. 96/62, Newcastle Minute, 20 December 1863, on Pine to Newcastle, 9 November 1863.

45. C.O. 96/61 and C.O. 96/63, C.O. to W.O., 18 December 1863, and Newcastle to Pine, 21 December 1863. Being seriously ill at the time, Newcastle did not write the famous dispatch of 21 December 1863 that ex-

tended conditional authority to Pine to advance on Ashanti territory. The dispatch was written and signed by Sir Frederic Rogers "in the absence and by the authority of the Duke of Newcastle," who was well enough to peruse it a few hours before it was sent (Eldridge, "Newcastle and the Ashanti War," 82).

46. C.O. 96/63, Newcastle to Pine, 21 December 1863.

47. Cf. Eldridge, "Newcastle and the Ashanti War," 84.

48. Quoted J. H. Rose, A. P. Newton, and E. A. Benians, eds., *CHBE*, 2:673. Cf. Eldridge, "Newcastle and the Ashanti War," 88.

Chapter 14: Colonial Nation Building

1. Cf. John W. Cell, *British Colonial Administration in the Mid-Nineteenth Century: The Policy-Making Process*, 81–116; Colin C. Eldridge, *Victorian Imperialism*, 32–43; J. W. Rose, A. P. Newton, and E. A. Benians, eds., *CHBE* 2:677–704.

2. J. M. Ward, *Empire in the Antipodes: The British in Australasia, 1840–1860*, 74.

3. C.O. 201/453, Newcastle to Fitzroy, 18 January 1853; Rose, Newton, and Benians, eds., *CHBE*, 7:285.

4. NeC 9,555, fols. 13–20, Newcastle (private) to Fitzroy, 4 August 1853.

5. Ibid., fols. 93–94, Newcastle (private) to Young, 3 December 1853.

6. C.O. 408/37, Newcastle to Denison, 19 January 1854; *Parl. Deb.*, CXXVII, 56–69, and CXXIX, 23–28.

7. NeC 9,552, fols. 703–4, Newcastle to Hamilton, 13 October 1853.

8. Ibid., fols. 707–14, Hamilton to Newcastle, 3 November 1853.

9. C.O. 193/139, Newcastle Minute, 31 January 1854.

10. NeC 9,554, Newcastle to Cathcart, 14 March 1853.

11. C.O. 423/1, Newcastle to Sir George Bowen, 27 January 1862.

12. NeC 11,039, Denison (private) to Newcastle, 9 April 1860; G-G MSS, C.O. Letter Book, fols. 213–22, Newcastle to Denison, 20 July 1860.

13. *Parl. Deb.*, CLXIII, 168–79.

14. Cf. Colin C. Eldridge, "Responsible Government and 'Patriot Kings' : Newcastle,

the Colonial Office and Sir Alexander Bannerman in Newfoundland," 92.

15. Sir William Denison, *Varities of Vice Regal Life*, 1:497.

16. NeC 10,886, fols. 142–44, Newcastle (private) to Young, 26 May 1862.

17. G-G MSS, C.O. Letter Book, fols. 213–22, Newcastle (private) to Denison, 20 July 1860.

18. NeC 10,887, fols. 21–25 and 50–56, Newcastle (private) to Monck, 29 November 1862, and to Gordon, 1 and 15 November 1862; cf. Rose, Newton, Benians, eds., *CHBE*, 2:689.

19. NeC 10,885, fols. 88–95, Newcastle (private) to Gore Browne, 26 April 1861.

20. Ibid., fols. 36–40, Newcastle (private) to Bannerman, 8 March 1861.

21. C.O. 194/165, Rogers Minute, 19 April 1861, on Bannerman to Newcastle, 14 March 1861, and Newcastle Minute, 25 April 1861.

22. Cf. Eldridge, "Responsible Government and 'Patriot Kings.'"

23. *Parl. Deb.*, CXXVI, 234–58.

24. NeC 9,552, fols. 225–26, Newcastle to Elgin, 29 April 1853.

25. *Parl. Deb.*, CXXXIV, 159–65 and 846–63.

26. Cf. Colin C. Eldridge, "The Colonial Policy of the Fifth Duke of Newcastle, 1859–1864," 313.

27. Rose, Newton, and Benians, eds., *CHBE*, 2:686–88; David Swinfen, *Imperial Control of Colonial Legislation*, 167–83.

28. C.O. 43/152, Newcastle to Head, 13 August 1859; Rose, Newton, and Benians, eds., *CHBE* 6:349–50.

29. W. S. Childs-Pemberton, *Life of Lord Norton, 1814–1905: Statesman and Philanthropist*, 178, quoting Lowe to Adderley, 31 December 1862.

30. Cf. Colin C. Eldridge, "'Forgotten Centenary': The Defence Review of the 1860s," Rose, Newton, and Benians, eds., *CHBE*, 2:827–29; NeC 10,892 and NeC 10,893, Elliot Reports on Military Expenditures in the Colonies, 7 September and 11 November 1859.

31. Eldridge, "Forgotten Centenary," 94–95.

32. C.O. 280/347, Newcastle Minute, 3 June 1860, on Young to Newcastle, 13 March 1860.

33. *Parl. Pap.*, *Report from the Select Com-*

mittee on Colonial Military Expenditure, 1861, House of Commons, XIII (423), 277–302.

34. Ibid.; Rose, Newton, and Benians, eds., *CHBE*, 2:829–32; Eldridge, "Forgotten Centenary," 91–92.

35. Rose, Newton, and Benians, eds., *CHBE*, 2:834.

36. Eldridge, "Forgotten Centenary," 99.

37. G-G MSS, Palmerston to Newcastle, 24 May 1861; Her., Palmerston to Herbert, 3 June 1861; NeC 10,889, fols. 203–4, Newcastle (private) to Palmerston, 25 May 1861.

38. NeC 10,885, fols. 134–44, Newcastle (private) to Head, 5 June 1861.

39. NeC 11,369, Head (private) to Newcastle, 19 July 1861.

40. Pal., Add. MS. 48582, fols. 84–87, Palmerston to Newcastle, 26 August and 1 September 1861.

41. NeC 10,890, fols. 47–54, Newcastle (private) to Palmerston, 3 September 1861.

42. G-G MSS, Palmerston to Newcastle, 7 November 1861.

43. PP, GC/NE/89, Newcastle (private) to Palmerston, 11 November 1861.

44. NeC 10,885, fols. 232–36, Newcastle (private) to Monck, 5 December 1861; NeC 10,886, fols. 6–13, 24–28, and 30–34, Newcastle (private) to Mulgrave, 7 December 1861; to Gordon, 7 and 14 December 1861; and to Monck, 14 December 1861.

45. C.O. 188/137, Gordon to Newcastle, 31 December 1862.

46. NeC 10,886, fols. 178–89, Newcastle (private) to Monck, 26 July 1862.

47. C.O. 42/635, Newcastle to Monck, 21 August 1862.

48. Eldridge, "Colonial Policy of Newcastle," 109.

49. Eldridge, "Forgotten Centenary," 97.

50. NeC 11,074, fols. 116–18, Lewis (printed) to Gore Browne, 26 July 1860.

51. G-G MSS, C.O. Letter Book, fols. 189–91 and 225–27, Newcastle (private) to Browne, 27 June and 27 November 1860.

52. Osbert Wyndham Hewett, ed., *Mr. Fortescue: A Selection from the Diaries from 1851 to 1862 of Chichester Fortescue, Lord Carlingford, K.P.*, 180; *Parl. Deb.*, CLXIII, 168–79.

53. C.O. 209/156, Newcastle to Grey, 5 June 1861; NeC 11,083, Grey (private) to Newcastle, 4 November 1861; *Parl. Deb.*, CLXIV, 1576–1579; Eldridge, "Colonial Policy of Newcastle," 226–27.

54. NeC 11,085, Grey (private) to Newcas-

tle, 9 January 1862; C.O. 209/165, Grey to Newcastle, 30 November 1861.

55. C.O. 209/165, Newcastle Minute, 7 March 1862, on Grey to Newcastle, 30 November 1861.

56. NeC 10,886, fols. 132–38, Newcastle (private) to Grey, 26 May 1862.

57. C.O. 209/169, Newcastle Minute, 4 December 1862, on Grey to Newcastle, 26 August 1862, and Newcastle to Grey, 26 February 1863.

58. NeC 10,887, fols. 92–102, Newcastle (private) to Grey, 26 February 1863.

59. Ibid., fols. 180–85, Newcastle (private) to Grey, 26 June 1863.

60. Ibid., fols. 209–22, Newcastle (private) to Grey, 27 July 1863.

61. C.O. 209/177, Newcastle Minute, 3 September 1863, on W.O. to C.O., 22 August 1863.

62. NeC 10,888, fols. 71–73, Newcastle (private) to Grey, 25 December 1863.

63. C.O. 48/395, Newcastle to Grey, 4 August 1859.

64. C.O. 48/406, Newcastle Minute, 28 January 1860, on Grey to Newcastle, n.d.; Rose, Newton, and Benians, eds., *CHBE*, 8:408.

65. C.O. 48/410 and 405/3, Lincoln to Wodehouse and Scott, 5 December 1861; Rose, Newton, and Benians, eds., *CHBE*, 8:409.

66. NeC 10,886, fols. 168–71, Newcastle to Wodehouse, 4 July 1862; Rose, Newton, and Benians, eds., *CHBE*, 8:409.

67. NeC 11,260, Newcastle (draft) "Remarks on Gladstone's Memorandum on Intercolonial Railway," early 1862.

68. C.O. 217/230, Newcastle to Mulgrave, 6 July 1862. Newcastle sent similar letters to the other governors.

69. Rose, Newton, and Benians, eds., *CHBE*, 6:443.

70. NeC 10,886, fols. 107–12, Newcastle (private) to Monck, 12 April 1862.

71. NeC 11,418 and NeC 11,429, Monck (private) to Newcastle, 16 May and 12 September 1862; NeC 11,171, Gordon (private) to Newcastle, 12 September 1862; Rose, Newton, and Benians, eds., *CHBE*, 6:444–45.

72. Rose, Newton, and Benians, eds., *CHBE*, 6:447.

73. NeC 10,887, fols. 86–88, Newcastle (private) to Monck, 21 February 1863.

74. Cf. Rose, Newton, and Benians, eds.,

CHBE, 6:447–62; J. M. S. Careless, *Canada: A Story of Challenge*, 230–49.

Chapter 15: Final Misfortunes

1. Osbert Wyndham Hewett, *Strawberry Fair*, 168.

2. Ibid., 147; Virginia Surtees, *A Beckford Inheritance: The Lady Lincoln Scandal*, 131.

3. Roger Fulford, ed., *Dearest Child*, 249–50, 252: Hewett, *Strawberry Fair*, 147.

4. Quoted Giles St. Aubyn, *Edward VII: Prince and King*, 155–56.

5. The Earl of Selbourne, *Memorials, Family and Personal, 1766–1865*, 1:256–58.

6. Quoted Surtees, *A Beckford Inheritance*, 132.

7. J. R. Vincent, ed., *Disraeli, Derby and the Conservative Party: The Journals of Lord Stanley, 1849–69*, 165–66.

8. Surtees, *A Beckford Inheritance*, 133.

9. Ibid., 134; Hewett, *Strawberry Fair*, 153.

10. Surtees, *A Beckford Inheritance*, 134.

11. Hewett, *Strawberry Fair*, 153.

12. Vincent, ed., *Disraeli, Derby and the Conservative Party*, 168.

13. Surtees, *A Beckford Inheritance*, 134.

14. John Golby, "A Great Electioneer and His Motives: The Fourth Duke of Newcastle," 218.

15. "The Duke of Newcastle and His Tenantry," *Nottingham Journal*, 19 December 1851. This article was published in pamphlet form under the same title by John Murray (London, 1852).

16. *Aber. Corres., 1855–1860*, 466, Clarendon to Aberdeen, 26 September 1859.

17. George Eden Marindin, ed., *Letters of Frederic Lord Blachford*, 239–42.

18. Goldwin Smith, *Reminiscences*, 191–92.

19. NeC 13,589a-c, Shireoaks Statement for year ending 31 December 1860, included in Charles Wright to Newcastle, 23 March 1861.

20. NeC 13,593 and NeC 13,607a, Wright to Newcastle, 11 December 1861 and 25 August 1862.

21. Quoted Hewett, *Strawberry Fair*, 176. Hope died on 4 December 1862, leaving £300,000 in money to his widow, as well as the life interest in his vast landed estate, after which they were to pass to his daughter (Vincent, ed., *Disraeli, Derby and the Conservative Party*, 399, n. 9).

22. Hewett, *Strawberry Fair*, 168–69.

23. Ibid., 172.

24. RA Y110/25, the queen to King Leopold, 3 December 1863, published G. E. Buckle, *The Letters of Queen Victoria*, 1:130–31.

25. Both Lady Waldegrave and Mrs. Norton urged the duke to seek rest. The beautiful and gifted Caroline Norton, 1808–1877, poetress and formerly Lord Melbourne's mistress, remained the duke's close friend for nearly two decades.

26. NeC 12,461, Manning to Newcastle, 12 February 1864.

27. NeC 12,768, the queen to Newcastle, 3 March 1864.

28. G-G MSS, Palmerston to Newcastle, 2 April 1864.

29. Ibid., Russell to Newcastle, 4 April 1864.

30. RA B20/70 and 71, the queen to Newcastle, 2 April 1864, and Newcastle to the queen, 4 April 1864.

31. NeC 11,064, Cardwell to Sir John Young, 25 May 1864.

32. Vincent, ed., *Disraeli, Derby and the Conservative Party*, 219. The reference to the "odd speech" probably is to Gladstone's speech on 11 May 1864 on the second reading of the borough franchise bill, which was one of his most celebrated speeches. See *Parl. Deb.*, CLXXV, 324, for the most important passage of the speech in which he stated that, with a number of qualifications, "every man who is not presumably incapacitated by some consideration of personal unfitness or of political danger, is morally entitled to come within the pale of the Constitution."

33. RA Y132/6, the queen to King Leopold, 16 June 1864.

34. Quoted Roger Fulford, ed., *Dearest Mama: Letters between Queen Victoria and the Crown Princess of Prussia, 1861–4*, 347–48.

35. *Times*, 13 and 18 August 1864.

36. Foot and Matthew, eds., *The Gladstone Diaries*, 6:309.

37. *The Doncaster, Nottingham and Lincoln Gazette*, 28 October 1864.

CONCLUSION

1. Virginia Surtees, *A Beckford Inheritance: The Lady Lincoln Scandal*, 134.

2. See Giles St. Aubyn, *Edward VII: Prince and King*, 156–59, for details of the affair.

3. Cf. Surtees, *A Beckford Inheritance*, 135–37; Colin C. Eldridge, "The Lincoln Divorce Case: A Study in Victorian Morality," 36.

4. Llewellyn Jewitt and S. C. Hall, *The Stately Homes of England*, 317–26; Roger A. Redfern, *The Dukeries of Nottinghamshire*, 25.

5. *Times*, 4, 19, and 28 October 1937 and 17 February 1938.

6. Ibid., 5 February and 24 August 1938 and 27 October 1944; Redfern, *The Dukeries*, 27.

7. *Times*, 19 October 1864.

Bibliography

A. Manuscript Collections

Aberdeen Papers, British Library
Broughton Papers, British Library
Clarendon Papers, Bodleian Library
Derby Papers, Knowsley (currently in the custody of Lord Blake, Queen's College, Oxford)
Disraeli Papers, Bodleian Library (microfilm copy, British Library of Political and Economic Science)
Ellenborough Papers, Public Record Office, London
Gladstone Papers, British Library
Glynne-Gladstone MSS., St. Deiniol's Library, Hawarden
Goulburn Papers, Surrey Record Office
Graham Papers, Bodleian Library (microfilm copy)
Granville Papers, Public Record Office, London
Grey Papers, Department of Palaeography and Diplomatic, University of Durham
Herbert Papers, Wilton Estate Office
Hickleton Papers, Bodleian Library (microfilm copy)
Newcastle Papers, Manuscripts Department, University of Nottingham
Palmerston Papers, National Register of Archives, London, and British Library
Peel Papers, British Library
Royal Archives, Windsor Castle
Russell Papers, Public Record Office, London
Strachie Papers, Somerset Record Office
Trevelyan Letter Book, University Library, Newcastle-upon-Tyne

B. Public Documents, Public Record Office, London

Colonial Office Files (C.O.)
War Office Files (W.O.)

C. Printed Sources

Aberdeen Correspondence, privately printed by Lord Stanmore, 9 vols., British Library.
Bell, Kenneth, and Merrell, William P., eds. *Select Documents on British Colonial Policy, 1830–1860*. Oxford, 1928.
Hansard's Parliamentary Debates, 3d series.

Parliamentary Papers:
   Correspondence Explanatory of the Measures Adopted by Her Majesty's Government for the Relief of Distress Arising from the Failure of the Potato Crop in Ireland, 1846 [735], 37.
   Memorandum and Explanation of Sir Charles Trevelyan in Regard to the Report of the Board of General Officers, 1857 (117 Sess.), 9.
   Report from the Select Committee on Colonial Military Expenditure, 1861 (423), 13.
   Reports from the Select Committee on the Army before Sebastopol, 1854–1855, 9, parts 1, 2, 3.

D. Reference Sources

Doubleday, H. A., and de Walden, Lord Howard, eds. *The Complete Peerage*. Vol. 9. London, 1936.
Stephen, Sir Leslie, and Lee, Sir Sidney, eds. *Dictionary of National Biography*. Vols. 2, 4, 5. New York, 1917.
Townsend, Peter, ed. *Burke's Peerage*. 151st ed. London, 1970.

E. Biographies, Memoirs, Diaries, and Letters

Argyll, Duke of. *Autobiography and Memoirs of George Douglas, Eighth Duke of Argyll*. Ed. the Dowager-Duchess of Argyll. 2 vols. London, 1906.
Ashley, A. E. M. *The Life and Correspondence of Henry John Temple, Viscount Palmerston*. 2 vols. London, 1879.
Aspinall, A., ed. *Three Early Nineteenth Century Diaries*. London, 1952.
Atkins, John Black. *The Life of Sir William Howard Russell*. 2 vols. London, 1911.
Balfour, Lady Francis Campbell. *The Life of George, Fourth Earl of Aberdeen*. 2 vols. London, 1922.
Bassett, Arthur Tilney, ed. *Gladstone to His Wife*. London, 1936.
Battiscombe, Georgina. *Mrs. Gladstone: The Portrait of a Marriage*. London, 1956.
Bell, H. C. F. *Lord Palmerston*. 2 vols. London, 1936.
Benson, Arthur C., and Esher, Viscount, eds. *Letters of Queen Victoria*. London, 1907.
Brooke, John, and Sorenson, Mary., eds. *The Prime Ministers' Papers: W. E. Gladstone*. Vol. 2: *Autobiographical Memoranda, 1832–45*. London, 1972.
Buckle, G. E., ed. *The Letters of Queen Victoria*. 3 vols. London, 1926–1928.
Carlisle, Henry E., ed. *Selections from the Correspondence of Abraham Hayward*. 2 vols. London, 1886.
Childe-Pemberton, W. S. *Life of Lord Norton, 1814–1905: Statesman and Philanthropist*. London, 1909.
Denison, Sir William. *Varieties of Vice Regal Life*. 2 vols. London, 1870.
Douglas, Sir George, and Ramsay, Sir George Dalhousie, eds. *The Panmure Papers*. 2 vols. London, 1918.
Finer, S. E. *The Life and Times of Sir Edwin Chadwick*. London, 1952.
Fitzmaurice, Lord Edmond. *The Life of Granville George Levenson Gower, Second Earl of Granville*. 2 vols. London, 1905.
Foot, M. R. D., and Matthew, H. C. G., eds. *The Gladstone Diaries*. 6 vols. Oxford, 1968–1978.
Fulford, Roger, ed. *Dearest Child: Letters Between Queen Victoria and the Princess Royal, 1858–61*. London, 1964.

———. *Dearest Mama: Letters Between Queen Victoria and the Crown Princess of Prussia, 1861–4*. London, 1968.

———. *The Prince Consort*. London, 1949.

Gash, Norman. *Mr. Secretary Peel*. Cambridge, Mass., 1961.

———. *Sir Robert Peel*. London, 1972.

Gooch, G. F., ed. *The Later Correspondence of Lord John Russell, 1840–1878*. 2 vols. London, 1925.

Hewett, Osbert Wyndham, ed. *Mr. Fortescue: A Selection from the Diaries from 1851 to 1862 of Chichester Fortescue, Lord Carlingford, K.P.* London, 1958.

———. *Strawberry Fair: A Biography of Frances, Countess Waldegrave, 1821–1879*. London, 1956.

Jones, Wilbur Devereur. *Lord Derby and Victorian Conservatism*. Oxford, 1956.

Lewis, Sir Gilbert Frankland, ed. *Letters of Sir George Cornewall Lewis to Various Friends*. London, 1870.

Magnus, Philip. *Gladstone: A Biography*. London, 1963.

Marindin, George Eden, ed. *Letters of Frederic Lord Blachford*. London, 1896.

Martin, Theodore. *A Life of Lord Lyndhurst*. 2d ed. London, 1884.

Martineau, John. *The Life of Henry Pelham, Fifth Duke of Newcastle, 1811–1864*. London, 1908.

Maxwell, Sir Herbert. *The Life and Letters of George William Frederick, Fourth Earl of Clarendon*. 2 vols. London, 1913.

Moneypenny, W. F., and Buckle, G. E. *The Life of Benjamin Disraeli, Earl of Beaconsfield*. 6 vols. London, 1914. Only vols. 3 and 4 pertain to this period.

Morley, John. *The Life of Gladstone*. 3 vols. New York, 1909. Only vol. 1 covers this period.

Morris, E. E. *A Memoir of George Higenbotham*. London, 1895.

Parker, Charles S. *Life and Letters of Sir James Graham*. 2 vols. London, 1907.

———. *Sir Robert Peel: From His Private Papers*. 3 vols. London, 1899.

Peel, George, ed. *Private Letters of Sir Robert Peel*. London, 1920.

Peel, Sir Robert. *Memoirs*. Ed. Lord Mahon and Edward Cardwell. 2 vols. London, 1857.

Prest, John. *Lord John Russell*. Columbia, S.C., 1972.

Reeve, Henry, ed. *The Greville Memoirs*. 8 vols. London, 1898–1899.

Russell, Lord John. *Recollections and Suggestions, 1813–73*. 2d ed. London, 1876.

Selbourne, The Earl of. *Memorials, Family and Personal, 1766–1865*. 2 vols. New York, 1896.

Smith, Goldwin. *Reminiscences*. Ed. Arnold Haultain. New York, 1910.

Somerset, John Gough, Lord Calthorpe. *Letters from Head-Quarters*. 2 vols. London, 1856.

Southgate, Donald. *The Most English Minister: The Policies and Politics of Palmerston*. London, 1966.

Stanmore, Lord. *The Earl of Aberdeen*. London, 1893.

———. *Sidney Herbert, Lord Herbert of Lea*. 2 vols. London, 1908.

St. Aubyn, Giles. *Edward VII: Prince and King*. New York, 1979.

Taylor, Henry. *Autobiography of Henry Taylor, 1800–1875*. 2 vols. London, 1885.

Temperley, H. W. V. *Life of Canning*. Westport, Conn., 1970.

Vincent, J. R., ed. *Disraeli, Derby and the Conservative Party: The Journals of Lord Stanley, 1849–69*. Hassocks, Sussex, 1978.

Walpole, Sir Spencer. *The Life of Lord John Russell*. 2 vols. London, 1889.

Woodham-Smith, Cecil. *Florence Nightingale, 1820–1910*. London, 1950.

Wrottesley, George. *Life and Correspondence of Field Marshal Sir John Burgoyne*. 2 vols. London, 1873.

F. Monographs and Other Secondary Books

Airelie, Countess of. *With the Guards We Shall Go*. London, 1933.
Anderson, Olive. *A Liberal State at War*. New York, 1967.
Bayley, C. C. *Mercenaries for the Crimea*. Montreal, 1977.
Bodelsen, Carl A. *Studies in Mid-Victorian Imperialism*. Copenhagen, 1924.
Brackenbury, George. *The Campaign in the Crimea*. 2 vols. London, 1856.
Careless, J. M. S. *Canada: A Story of Challenge*. 3d ed. Toronto, 1972.
Cell, John W. *British Colonial Administration in the Mid-Nineteenth Century: The Policy-Making Process*. New Haven, 1970.
Clark, G. Kitson. *Peel and the Conservative Party, 1832–1841*. London, 1929.
Clinton, Henry Pelham (duke of Newcastle). *Thoughts in Times Past Tested by Subsequent Events*. London, 1837.
Conacher, J. B. *The Aberdeen Coalition, 1852–1855*. Cambridge, 1968.
———. *The Peelites and the Party System, 1846–52*. Newton Abbot, 1972.
Deacon, Richard. *The Private Life of Mr. Gladstone*. London, 1965.
De Kiewiet, Cornelius W. *British Colonial Policy and the South African Republics, 1848–1872*. Oxford, 1941.
Eldridge, Colin C. *Victorian Imperialism*. London, 1978.
Fortescue, John W. *A History of the British Army*. Vol. 13: *1852–1870*. London, 1930.
Gallagher, John, and Robinson, Ronald. *Africa and the Victorians: The Official Mind of Imperialism*. London, 1961.
Gash, Norman. *Politics in the Age of Peel*. London, 1953.
———. *Reaction and Reconstruction in English Politics, 1832–52*. Oxford, 1965.
Gibbs, Peter. *Crimean Blunder*. London, 1960.
Gordon, Hampden. *The War Office*. London, 1935.
Hamley, Sir Edward. *The War in the Crimea*. New York, 1890.
Harrop, A. J. *England and the Maori Wars*. London, 1937.
Hibbert, Christopher. *The Destruction of Lord Raglan*. Baltimore, 1963.
The History of the Times. Vol. 2: *The Tradition Established, 1841–84*. London, 1939.
Jewitt, Llewellyn, and Hall, S. C. *The Stately Homes of England*. London, 1877.
Jones, Wilbur Devereux, and Erickson, Arvel B. *The Peelites, 1846–1857*. Columbus, Ohio, 1972.
Kinglake, A. W. *The Invasion of the Crimea*. 6th ed. 9 vols. London, 1877–1879.
Lewis, R. A. *Edwin Chadwick and the Public Health Movement, 1832–1854*. London, 1952.
MacMunn, Sir George. *The Crimea in Perspective*. London, 1935.
McDowell, R. B. *The Irish Administration, 1801–1914*. Toronto, 1964.
Martin, Chester. *Foundations of Canadian Nationhood*. Toronto, 1952.
Martin, Kingsley B. *The Triumph of Lord Palmerston*. New York, 1924.
Morrell, W. P. *British Colonial Policy in the Mid-Victorian Age*. London, 1969.
Morton, William L. *The Critical Years: The Union of British North America, 1857–1873*. Toronto, 1964.
Pearsall, Ronald. *The Worm in the Bud: The World of Victorian Sexuality*. London, 1969.

Porter, Whitworth. *History of the Corps of Royal Engineers*. 2 vols. Chatham, 1951.

Redfern, Roger A. *The Dukeries of Nottinghamshire*. Clapham, North Yorkshire, 1974.

Rose, J. H., Newton, A. P., and Benians, E. A., eds. *Cambridge History of the British Empire*. 9 vols. Cambridge, 1929–1959.

Russell, William H. *The War from the Landing in Gallipoli to the Death of Lord Raglan*. London, 1855.

Schuyler, Robert L. *The Fall of the Old Colonial System: A Study in British Free Trade, 1770–1870*. New York, 1945.

Sinclair, K. *The Origins of the Maori Wars*. London, 1957.

Southgate, Donald. *The Passing of the Whigs, 1832–1886*. London, 1965.

Stewart, Robert. *The Politics of Protection*. Cambridge, 1971.

Surtees, Virginia. *A Beckford Inheritance: The Lady Lincoln Scandal*. Wilton, Salisbury, 1977.

Swinfen, David. *Imperial Control of Colonial Legislation*. Oxford, 1970.

Temperley, H. W. V. *The Foreign Policy of Canning, 1822–1827*. London, 1925.

Vincent, John. *The Formation of the Liberal Party, 1857–1868*. 2d ed. New York, 1976.

Ward, John M. *Colonial Self-Government*. London, 1976.

————. *Empire in the Antipodes: The British in Australasia, 1840–1860*. London, 1966.

Ward, W. E. F. *A History of the Gold Coast*. London, 1948.

Winks, Robin. *Canada and the United States: The Civil War Years*. Baltimore, 1960.

Woodham-Smith, Cecil. *The Great Hunger*. London, 1965.

————. *The Reason Why*. London, 1953.

Wrottesley, George. *The Military Opinions of General Sir John Fox Burgoyne*. London, 1859.

Young, G. M. *Early Victorian England*. 2 vols. London, 1963.

————. *Victorian Essays*. Oxford, 1962.

G. Articles

Aydelotte, W. O. "The House of Commons in the 1840s." *History* 39 (October 1954): 249–62.

————. "Voting Patterns in the British House of Commons in the 1840s." *Comparative Studies in Society and History* 5 (January 1963): 134–63.

Cahill, G. A. "The Protestant Association and the Anti-Maynooth Agitation of 1845." *Catholic Historical Review* 43 (October 1957): 273–308.

Clark, G. Kitson. "The Electorate and the Repeal of the Corn Laws." *Transactions of the Royal Historical Society*, 5th series, 1 (1951): 109–26.

————. "Hunger and Politics in 1842." *Journal of Modern History* 25 (December 1953): 355–74.

————. "Repeal of the Corn Laws and the Politics of the Forties." *Economic History Review*, 2d series, 4 (1951): 1–13.

————. "'Statesmen in Disguise' : Reflections on the History of the Neutrality of the Civil Service." *Historical Journal* 2 (1959): 19–39.

Collins, H. P. "The Crimea: The Fateful Weeks." *Army Quarterly* 71 (1955): 86–96.

Conacher, J. B. "Peel and the Peelites, 1846–1850." *English Historical Review* 73 (July 1958): 431–52.

"Correspondence of Lord Aberdeen, 1850–53." *Edinburgh Review* 158 (October 1883): 547–77.

Eldridge, Colin C. "' Forgotten Centenary' : The Defence Review of the 1860s." *Trivium* 5 (1970): 85–103.

———. "The Lincoln Divorce Case: A Study in Victorian Morality." *Trivium* 11 (1975): 21–39.

———. "The Myth of Mid-Victorian 'Separatism' : The Cession of the Bay Islands and the Ionian Islands in the Early 1860s." *Victorian Studies* 12, no. 3 (March 1969): 331–46.

———. "Newcastle and the Ashanti War of 1863–64: A Failure of the Policy of 'Anti-Imperialism.'" *Renaissance and Modern Studies* 12 (1968): 68–90.

———. "Responsible Government and 'Patriot Kings' : Newcastle, the Colonial Office and Sir Alexander Bannerman in Newfoundland." *Trivium* 10 (1975): 85–100.

Fisher, D. R. "Peel and the Conservative Party: The Sugar Crisis of 1844 Reconsidered." *Historical Journal* 18, no. 2 (June 1975): 279–302.

Galbraith, John S. "Myths of the Little England Era." *American Historical Review* 67 (1961): 34–48.

Gibson, James A. "The Duke of Newcastle and British North American Affairs, 1859–1864." *Canadian Historical Review* 44 (June 1963): 142–56.

Golby, John. "A Great Electioneer and His Motives: The Fourth Duke of Newcastle." *Historical Journal* 7, no. 2 (1965): 201–18.

Gooch, Brison. "The Crimean War in Selected Documents and Secondary Works Since 1940." *Victorian Studies* 1 (March 1958): 271–79.

Hart, Jenifer. "Sir Charles Trevelyan at the Treasury." *English Historical Review* 75 (January 1960): 92–110.

Hawkins, Angus B. "A Forgotten Crisis: Gladstone and the Politics of Finance During the 1850s." *Victorian Studies* 26 (Spring 1983): 287–320.

Hitsman, J. Mackay. "Winter Troop Movement to Canada, 1862." *Canadian Historical Review* 43 (1962): 127–35.

Laws, M. E. S. "Beatson's Bashi Bozooks." *Army Quarterly* 71 (1955): 80–85.

Munsell, F. Darrell. "Charles Edward Trevelyan and Peelite Irish Famine Policy, 1845–1846." *Societas* 1, no. 4 (Autumn 1971): 299–315.

Nowlan, Keven B. "The Political Background." In *The Great Famine*, ed. Robert Dudley Edwards and T. Desmond Williams, 131–207. New York, 1957.

O' Neill, Thomas P. "Organization and Administration of Relief." In *The Great Famine*, ed. Robert Dudley Edwards and T. Desmond Williams, 207–59. New York, 1957.

Robbins, Michael. "The Balaklava Railway." *Journal of Transport History*, old series, 1 (1953): 28–43.

Stuart, C. H. "The Formation of the Coalition Cabinet of 1852." *Transactions of the Royal Historical Society*, 5th series, 4 (1954): 45–68.

Sweetman, John. "Military Transport in the Crimean War, 1854–1856." *English Historical Review* 88 (January 1973): 81–91.

Vincent, John. "The Parliamentary Dimension of the Crimean War." *Transactions of the Royal Historical Society*, 5th series, 31 (1981): 37–49.

H. Unpublished Ph.D. Dissertations

Eldridge, Colin C. "The Colonial Policy of the Fifth Duke of Newcastle, 1859–1864." University of Nottingham, 1966.

Munsell, F. Darrell. "Peelite Opinions and Political Activities, 1846–1859." University of Kansas, 1967.

I. Newspapers

Morning Chronicle
New York Herald
Nottingham Journal
The Doncaster, Nottingham, and Lincoln Gazette
Times (London)

Index